"THE GREAT SAGA OF THE 'SILENT SERVICE,'

the most elite of the Navy, and the most dangerous.
Heroes surge through these pages!"

NORFOLK VIRGINIAN-PILOT

"SUPERB! . . .

Thrilling stories of hazards and heroisms!"

ARMED FORCES

"THE DRAMA AND TENSE EXCITEMENT

behind the sinking of more than five million tons of
enemy shipping in World War II!"

LEATHERNECK

"THE 'SILENT SERVICE,'

operating under a cloak of secrecy during the war, tells
its thrilling story freely and in great detail in this
important official history!"

WASHINGTON STAR

PIG BOATS
THE STORY OF THE FIGHTING
SUBMARINERS OF WORLD WAR II

A Note on the Abridgment

PIGBOATS, The True Story of the Fighting Submariners of World War II, *is the author's own abridgment of a book he wrote for the United States Naval Institute. This book was titled* UNITED STATES SUBMARINE OPERATIONS IN WORLD WAR II *and contained much matter of a technical nature.*

To make an exciting and interesting book for the general reader, the author removed the more technical material, leaving clear and intact the dramatic, personal stories of the men of the U. S. Submarine Service and their heroic deeds.

PIGBOATS *is a book for every American to read!*

PIG BOATS

THE TRUE STORY OF THE FIGHTING SUBMARINERS OF WORLD WAR II

(Originally published under the title
**UNITED STATES SUBMARINE OPERATIONS
IN WORLD WAR II**)

Authorized abridgment

by Theodore Roscoe

Written for
The Bureau of Naval Personnel
from records prepared by
**Rear Admiral R. G. Voge, USN
Captain W. J. Holmes, USN (RETD.)
Commander W. H. Hazzard, USN
Lieut. Comdr. D. S. Graham, USN
Lieut. H. J. Kuehn, USNR**
and from submarine patrols reports
and data from the
United States Strategic Bombing Survey

Illustrated by Lieut. Comdr. Fred Freeman, USNR

BANTAM BOOKS
TORONTO · NEW YORK · LONDON
®

DEDICATION

... to the valiant submariners of the United States Navy who lost their lives in World War Two ...

PIGBOATS: THE TRUE STORY OF THE
FIGHTING SUBMARINERS OF WORLD WAR II
Originally published under the title
UNITED STATES SUBMARINE OPERATIONS IN WORLD WAR II
*A Bantam Book / published by arrangement with
The United States Naval Institute.*

PRINTING HISTORY

U.S. Naval Institute edition published December 1949

2nd printing ..... January 1950	4th printing .... March 1954
3rd printing ...... March 1950	5th printing ...... August 1956

Bantam edition published December 1958

2nd printing ... December 1958	4th printing ...... August 1959
3rd printing ..... January 1959	5th printing ..... June 1960
6th printing ...... October 1967	

Acknowledgment is gratefully made for permission to reprint the following selections: Part I, page 1, verse by Robert Haven Schauffler from "Divers," Dodd, Mead and Company; Part III, page 189, verse by Ridgley Torrence from "Hesperides," copyright 1925 by The Macmillan Company; Addenda, page 445, verse by Leslie Nelson Jennings from "Lost Harbor," Third Book of Modern Verse, Houghton-Mifflin Company.

PRINTED IN THE UNITED STATES OF AMERICA

Contents

☆ ☆ ☆

Foreword

Future students and historians of our naval war in the Pacific will inevitably conclude that the Japanese commander of the carrier task force which wrought so much damage at Pearl Harbor on 7 December 1941 missed a golden opportunity in restricting his attack to one day's operations, and in the very limited choice of his objectives. The capital ships he sank or severely damaged could not have operated effectively in the far western Pacific for many, many months, whereas our submarines began unsupported operations in Japanese home waters immediately after the commencement of the war. How effective were those submarine operations against his Fleet and against his vitally important shipping is dramatically told in the following pages.

That the Japanese Naval High Command failed to evaluate at their true worth the potentialities of our submarines is incredible. Up to the shattering blow at Pearl Harbor the Japanese had accurate and up-to-the-minute intelligence of the situation at Pearl Harbor. They knew of our dependence on the dockyard, on the fuel supplies and on the Submarine Base, all of which were objectives of the first importance. They knew that they had taken out practically all our Air on 7 December. They knew that all our fuel storage was above ground and very vulnerable. Also known to them was our great dependence on the dockyard facilities, the destruction of which would have thrown us back on the West Coast for many months and possibly years. Finally, they were aware of our submarine establishment and they must have known that only that branch of the Service could operate effectively *at once* in the critical waters between Japan and the Netherlands East Indies.

Fortunately for the United States, our great Submarine Base in Hawaii with its supplies and facilities and our submarines were undamaged. When I assumed command of the Pacific Fleet on 31 December 1941 our submarines were already operating against the enemy, the only units of the Fleet that could come to grips with the Japanese for months to come.

It was to the Submarine Force that I looked to carry the load until our great industrial activity could produce the weapons we so sorely needed to carry the war to the enemy. It is to the everlasting honor and glory of our submarine personnel that they never failed us in our days of great peril. The world will now learn from the following pages how well they did their work in spite of real hardships and heavy losses.

C. W. Nimitz

Introduction

In a democracy such as ours National Defense policies are set by the general public. The Secretary of Defense, the Secretaries of the Army, the Navy, and tne Air Force, the Joint Chiefs of Staff may make their recommendations, but it is the public, acting through its representatives, that makes the final decisions. The people elect their representatives to Congress, and Congress appropriates the money for military expenditures. In so doing, the elected representatives follow the will of their constituents. This may not be strictly true in time of war when military expenditures are hidden in a cloak of secrecy, but in time of peace the budget is a matter of public domain, and an unpopular or little-understood weapon is apt to be paid scant heed by the lawmakers. As a consequence, with the world in its present stage of political unrest, and with the various world powers girding for, or to avoid, another conflict, it is incumbent upon the layman, as well as the militarist, to have a clear understanding of the capabilities and limitations of each weapon in the National Defense arsenal.

If public opinion is to decide the issue, that opinion must be based on fact rather than fiction. Neither publicity nor propaganda must be permitted to sway the Nation into placing undue emphasis on any one weapon at the expense of others of relative importance. Hitler made that fatal mistake and thereby lost a war and a world empire. Yet even a superficial study of the history of World War I would have pointed out to him the road to success. Germany, on February 1, 1917, declared unrestricted submarine warfare. By April of that year British ship losses had reached such proportions that Admiral Jellicoe, First Sea Lord of the Admiralty, declared, "They will win unless we stop these losses and stop them soon." The record was available that all might read, but Hitler chose to follow his intuition rather than the lessons of history. Naval protagonists were given but little voice in matters of high policy. The democracies of the world may well pray that their future enemies will have such a bigoted viewpoint. It is common knowledge how perilously close the German submarines came to winning the Battle of the Atlantic in World War II. Yet Germany started that war with but 76 submarines in commission. Think what the ultimate outcome would have been had Hitler had 500 submarines available at the outset, a force that would not have been out of proportion to the size of his army and his air force.

The mistakes that a dictator makes through bigotry can be duplicated in a democracy through ignorance or misunderstanding on the part of the populace. The public cannot properly evaluate a weapon about which it knows nothing, and no authoritative and comprehensive account of the work of U.S. submarines in World War II has heretofore been published. The Submarine Service has too long been content to let the record speak for itself. A record buried deep in the classified files of the Department of the Navy speaks only in a whisper, and then only to the archivist or researcher. It is the purpose of this volume to bring that record to public view.

The book had its beginning in July 1945. At that time the Submarine Service found itself, like Alexander, with no more worlds to conquer, or, more accurately, no more Japanese ships to sink. The last big submarine offensive—the penetration of the Sea of Japan—had been successfully completed in June. Japanese shipping had been driven from the seas. Submarines were going to every extreme to stir up a little excitement and at the same time harass the enemy. One submarine put a landing party ashore to blow up a Japanese railroad bridge and followed that exploit by bombarding several coastal towns with rocket and machine-gun fire. Another submarine, patrolling off the coast of southern China, sighted two Japanese destroyers at anchor in a harbor, and brazenly patrolled on the surface in broad daylight in full view of the enemy, trying to entice him to come out and fight. The bulk of the submarines were engaged in lifeguard missions for the B-29 raids on Japan. In short, submarine operations were in the doldrums.

It was then that Vice Admiral C. A. Lockwood, Jr., Commander Submarine Force, Pacific Fleet, on board his flagship, USS HOLLAND, at Guam, sent for his Operations Officer. From his two and one-half years of association with the Admiral the Operations Officer had learned to expect almost any type of order, but this time it was something radically different: "You've been handling operations long enough to know the score. Pack up your duffle, thumb a ride to Pearl Harbor and then sit down and write the submarine history."

Admiral Lockwood, one of God's true noblemen, was not one to surround himself with "yes" men. If any member of his staff disagreed with his decisions he expected that staff officer to tell him so, and why. The reaction in this case was immediate: "Admiral, I have never written a book. I don't know how to write a book. I don't want to write a book." As is usual in such cases, three stars prevailed over four stripes, and a few days later I was on board a plane en route to Pearl Harbor.

It was my original intention to limit the scope of the work to the operations of the Submarine Force, Pacific Fleet. However, it soon became evident that such a limitation was not feasible. There were three U.S. Submarine Forces in existence during World War II, and although each force constituted a separate entity, their operations were so coordinated and interrelated that it was impossible to treat independently any one force and still present a complete picture. A call for assistance was sent out to the other force commanders, and Commander W. H. Hazzard and Lieutenant Commander Donald S. Graham were assigned to record the deeds of Submarines, Southwest Pacific and Submarines, Atlantic Fleet, respectively.

In December 1945, Captain W. J. Holmes, USN (Ret.), was assigned to SubPac to assist with the enterprise. A few months later, upon my detachment, he took charge of the entire project. Captain Holmes was preeminently qualified for the task assigned. Until his retirement for physical disability in 1935 he had been a submarine officer of outstanding ability. In 1941 he was recalled to active duty with Naval Intelligence at Pearl Harbor and his duties there gave him an intimate knowledge of the daily doings of all the submarines throughout the war. In addition, during the years of his retirement, and while serving as a professor of engineering at the University of Hawaii, he attained considerable renown as a writer of submarine fiction under the pen name of Alec Hudson. Since mid-1943 Vice Admiral Lockwood had tried, without avail, to have Holmes assigned to him to write the submarine history while that history was in the making. Fleet Admiral Nimitz, knowing the value of Holmes' services to the Intelligence organization, refused to release him until some months after the cessation of hostilities.

Under Holmes' direction the compilation was completed and sent on to Washington in the fall of 1946—some ten pounds, more or less, of typewritten manuscript. Almost simultaneous with its arrival in Washington the office of Coordinator of Submarine Warfare was created in the Navy Department. Prior to that time there had been no central agency in Washington charged with submarine affairs, and the new office of Coordinator had neither the personnel nor the funds available to undertake the publication of the history. In addition, the manner in which the manuscript had been prepared precluded its issue to the public in its original form. The original outline called for covering the subject matter from the point of view of the strategy or tactics involved. This resulted in a lack of continuity and considerable repetition.

The manuscript thereupon proceeded to gather dust on the shelves of the Navy Department while its advocates searched for a sponsor, or, in theatrical parlance, an "angel" who would finance the show. The "angel" was eventually found in the person of Rear Admiral T. L. Sprague, Chief of Naval Personnel. Admiral Sprague detailed the project to Captain J. M. Will, veteran submariner and just the officer to blow the dust off such a manuscript.

Captain Will, in his capacity as Director of Training was, among many other things, in charge of the preparation of textbooks and training manuals for naval personnel. He wished to develop a textbook to point up the operational lessons of World War II to future submarines, and the submarine history appeared to be the answer to the problem. He assigned Mr. Theodore Roscoe, then under contract to the Bureau of Naval Personnel, to the project of rewriting the text, with the duel objective of having it serve as an account to the layman in addition to its prime purpose as a textbook for submarine personnel. Mr. Roscoe, a writer of established reputation and unquestioned ability, little knew what he was letting himself in for when he accepted the assignment. The deeper he delved into the subject the deeper he became engrossed, and the project which was originally scheduled to take but a few months extended over eighteen. It must be emphatically pointed out that while the combine of Holmes, Hazzard, Graham, and Voge compiled the record upon which this history is based, the text as herein presented is entirely the work of Theodore Roscoe.

The text had to include enough technical data to satisfy the needs of the future submariner, but not too much to bore the layman. It was my pleasure and privilege to assist the writer in the final stages of editing this volume—my job was to check his writings for errors of fact, or phraseology, both nautical and subnautical. The job was a sinecure. The few errors that I did detect could readily be traced to source material. On the other hand, during the course of his work the writer had become such an ardent admirer of the submariners' work in the war that my hardest task was in getting him to tone down some of his panegyrics. Then, too, there was the weather to contend with. Those unfamiliar with the climate of our national capital will find it difficult to understand the occupational hazards of creative writing in midsummer Washington. The sun, with no thought of protocol, beats down on mighty and commoner alike, but the seats of the mighty are all located in air-conditioned offices. Not so were Roscoe's and Voge's, and the sultry air resembled nothing so much as a hot towel in a barber shop. That, in a small measure, accounts for some of the delay in getting this volume to press.

It is human nature to learn more from our mistakes than from our successes, and for that reason, although a few toes may be stepped on, this book presents a candid picture of submarine operations as they were and not always as we might have wished them to be. Thus the full story of the submarine torpedo has been included. It contains a lesson too valuable to be buried in the archives. It should be required reading for every officer in the Navy.

Richard G. Voge
REAR ADMIRAL, USN

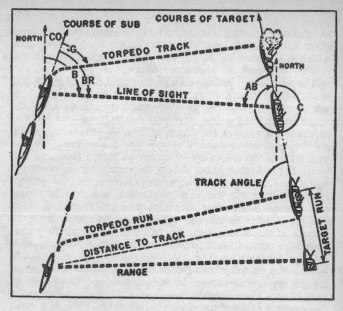

TORPEDO FIRING TERMINOLOGY

Ab—Angle on the Bow
B—True Target Bearing
Br—Relative Target Bearing

C—Target Course
Co—Own Course
G—Gyro Angle

Gyro angle. The angle between the fore-and-aft axis of own ship and final track of torpedo, measured clockwise from own ship bow.

Own course. The angle between the North-South line and the fore-and-aft axis of own ship, measured clockwise from North to own ship bow.

Target course. The angle between the North-South line and the fore-and-aft axis of target, measured clockwise from North to target bow.

Angle on the bow. The angle between the fore-and-aft axis of target and the line of sight (LOS), measured from target bow to starboard or port.

Relative target bearing. The angle between the fore-and-aft axis of own ship and the line of sight, measured clockwise from own ship bow.

True target bearing. The angle between the North-South line and the line of sight, measured clockwise from the North.

Track angle. The angle between the fore-and-aft axis of the target and the torpedo track, measured from target bow to starboard or port.

Range. The distance in yards from periscope to target.

Torpedo run. The distance in yards which the torpedo travels from tube to target.

Target run. The distance in yards traveled by target during time of torpedo run.

Distance to track. The distance, in yards, from the submarine to the target track, measured along a line perpendicular to the target track.

PART ONE

Submarines to War

(December 1941)

Stumbling we grope and stifle here below
In the gross garb of this too cumbering flesh,
And draw such hard-won breaths as may be drawn,
Until, perchance with pearls, we rise and go
To doff our diver's mail and taste the fresh,
The generous winds of the eternal dawn.
R. H. SCHAUFFLER

Chapter 1

Holocaust at Pearl Harbor

☆   ☆   ☆

Two-ocean War

The Japanese strike in the Pacific immediately involved the United States in a two-ocean war.

To many Americans it seemed as if the Japanese had run amuck. Those who took a global view of the situation realized the Pacific strike was shrewdly calculated.

In December 1941, England was holding on by little more than the skin of a bulldog's teeth. The Axis partners held Western Europe prisoner in Hitler's Fortress Europa. Rommel's army was on its way to Cairo. London was a city of bleeding ruins, the Royal Navy was striving desperately to retain control of the Atlantic, and Nazi shipyards were launching U-boats by the squadron.

In Russia, German invasion forces hurled thunderbolts at the gates of Moscow. Allied experts gave the Russians until Christmas. The expected Nazi conquest of the USSR would remove a potential enemy from Japan's back door and release thousands of Japanese troops from Manchuria for use against Chinese and American forces.

The major portion of the U.S. Navy's strength was gathered in the Atlantic—eight battleships, four aircraft carriers, 13 cruisers, some 90 destroyers and 60 submarines. In the Pacific, the U.S. Navy could muster about 100 surface warships, and expect support from some 50 British and Netherlands naval vessels. Against these the Imperial Navy could pit about 170 warships. There were 51 American submarines in the Pacific and a few British and Dutch submersibles. The Japanese considered these inconsequential. In December 1941, they themselves had 63 ocean-going sub-

2

marines in commission, and their shipyards were spawning schools of "baby" submersibles for use in coastal defense.

The American industrial potential was a matter to be considered. But against this factor stood German and Japanese labor, already operating in high gear on a totalitarian basis. Such raw material disparity as existed, the Japanese intended to balance by seizure of the immense oil and rubber resources of the East Indies, and capture of the world's supply of quinine. With everything to gain, Tojo and Yamamoto struck.

Four days after the Pearl Harbor raid, Germany and Italy, in accordance with their Axis pact, declared war on the United States. The squeeze-play was on.

Washington strategists, however, had long foreseen the possibility of a two-ocean war with the Axis nations, and had determined on a concentration of effort to defeat Nazi Germany while the Japanese offensive was contained. This strategic plan recognized Germany as the most formidable Axis power and the Atlantic threat as the one more immediately menacing the security of the United States. Defeat of Japan was considered inevitable once the Nazis were beaten. This meant winning the Battle of the Atlantic while American naval forces in the Pacific went on the defensive.

It was realized that shipping would be the weakest link in the chain drive of a Japanese seaborne offensive. On December 1, 1941, Japanese merchant shipping was estimated as approximating 6,000,000 tons of ocean-going, steel ships (vessels over 500 tons). No nation on the globe was more dependent upon ocean shipping than Dai Nippon. Neither in foodstuffs for civilian consumption nor in raw materials for industry were the home islands self-sufficient. Nearly all of the basic raw materials for the munitions industry alone had to be brought in by water, and the Imperial Navy, merchant marine, and air force operated literally on seas of imported oil.

The Japanese merchant fleet was divided into separate Army, Navy and civilian pools. Allocated some 4,000,000 tons at the word "Go!", the military obtained the bulk of available merchantmen, and civilian shipping was expected to carry on with about 1,900,000 tons.

Aware of the Japanese War Machine's dependence on shipping, the U.S. Navy's strategists had planned to block the enemy's sea lanes with strong units of the Pacific Fleet. United States submarines were expected to play a stalwart part in the Pacific defense. But the stunning strike at Pearl Harbor, which resulted in the complete immobilization of the battleship force, and the overwhelming Japanese onslaught on the Philippines and Malaya deranged American-Pacific strategy. The surface fleet, which had been counted on to defend the Central Pacific, was "out of it" and would remain so for a long time. In the Philippines, Admiral Hart's small surface force could not hope to cope with the mighty armadas storming down from Japan. Months would pass before adequate air, land and naval reinforcements could reach the Central and Southwest Pacific fronts. But one naval arm remained unimpaired by the Pearl Harbor smash. That arm was the United States Navy's Submarine Service.

On the eve of the war's outbreak, the U.S. Navy's submarine strength was 111 in commission and 73 building. Of the 51 submarines on duty (or available for duty) in the Pacific, 29 were attached to the Asiatic Fleet based at Manila, and 22 operated with the Pacific Fleet based at Pearl Harbor.

To United States submarines, then—those 51 submersibles on duty or available for duty in the Pacific—fell the major portion of the improvised defense.

At best, this was a large order for 51 submersibles! And it was soon apparent that circumstances were far was "best." The fighting directive was issued by the Chief of Naval Operations the afternoon of December 7:

EXECUTE UNRESTRICTED AIR AND SUBMARINE WARFARE AGAINST JAPAN

Underwater Attack (December 7th)

Contrary to popular opinion, the first angry shot at Pearl Harbor was fired at, and not by, the attacking intruder.

At 0342 on the morning of December 7, 1941, the USS CONDOR, a minesweeper, nearly collided with a small submarine traveling at periscope depth not far from the Pearl Harbor entrance buoys. This was in a defensive sea area, and a moment later the startled minesweeper's blinker was flashing a message to the destroyer (DD) WARD.

SIGHTED SUBMERGED SUBMARINE ON WESTERLY COURSE . . .
SPEED NINE KNOTS

A DD of the Inshore Patrol, WARD immediately began a search for the unidentified submarine. But a hasty probe failed to locate the trespasser. This invited the conclusion that the minesweeper's lookout had been mistaken concerning the unidentified sub.

Meanwhile, CONDOR proceeded to the harbor entrance where the channel was protected by an antitorpedo net.

Some thirty minutes later, the USS ANTARES with a 500-ton steel barge in tow was standing in. At 0630, ANTARES' lookout sighted what appeared to be a small submarine about 1,500 yards off her starboard quarter. Her bridge blinkered this information to WARD, and at 0640 WARD sighted the submarine which seemed to be trailing ANTARES into Pearl Harbor.

WARD'S captain sounded General Quarters and sent the destroyer steaming for the submarine at top speed. Beating the DD to the gun, a Navy PBY, returning from long-range patrol, circled the area and dropped two smoke pots to mark the submarine's location.

At 0645, range approximately 100 yards, WARD opened point-blank fire. Her first shot missed, but her second punctured the submarine's conning tower (and in all probability its occupant) just below the waterline.

Immediately the injured boat heeled over and sank. Charging forward, the destroyer thrashed the swirling water with depth bombs.

At 0653, WARD sent the following radio message to the Commandant, Fourteenth Naval District:

WE HAVE ATTACKED FIRED UPON AND DROPPED DEPTH CHARGES UPON SUBMARINE OPERATING IN DEFENSIVE SEA AREA

Received by the Bishop's Point radio station, this message was at once relayed to the Officer in Charge, Net and Boom Defenses, Inshore Patrol; the Communications Officer, Fourteenth Naval District; and the ComFourteen Duty Officer. At 0712 the ComFourteen Chief of Staff was notified, and the Duty Officer of the Commander-in-Chief, Pacific Fleet, at 0715. The relief ready duty destroyer MONAGHAN was dispatched to join forces with WARD. But no alert was sounded.

Apparently previous cries of "Wolf!" had deadened the impact of any submarine alarm. Taking their orders from Washington, the military and naval guardians of Pearl Harbor had been somewhat misled by dispatches received on November 7th. At that date Admiral Husband E. Kimmel, Commander-in-Chief of the United States Fleet with Headquarters at Pearl Harbor, had been advised, "Japan is expected to make an aggressive move within the next few days." But reference was made to "an amphibious expedition against either the Philippines, Thai or Kra Peninsula, or possibly Borneo." At the same time, Lieutenant General Walter C. Short of the Hawaiian Department received official warning that a hostile Japanese move was "possible at any moment."

However, he was ordered to take defense measures in a manner that would not "alarm the civilian population or disclose the intent." Thereupon General Short alerted his department against sabotage and placed Hawaii under a condition of "limited preparedness."

It is not within the province of this volume to criticize American defense measures, or lack of them, which permitted a large Japanese carrier force to attain striking distance of the Hawaiian Islands and launch a devastating surprise attack. Of concern to students of submarining, however, is the build-up to the surprise assault and the part played therein by strategically employed submarines.

Admiral Yamamoto, Commander-in-Chief of the Combined Japanese Fleet, had formulated the Pearl Harbor attack plan the preceding January. As early as July, Japanese submarines were reported in Hawaiian waters, apparently keeping the approaches to Pearl Harbor under surveillance.

Yamamoto completed his planning by mid-September. There was increasing evidence of Japanese submarine activity off Hawaii in November.

On November 22 Yamamoto's striking force assembled in the Kuriles, and on the 26th it set out on a circuitous North Pacific course for the target islands. On December 6 the Japanese commanders received the fateful code-phrase:

CLIMB MOUNT NITAKA

Early morning, December 7, the carriers were in range, some 200 miles north of Oahu. And a squadron of Japanese submarines (Sixth Fleet Submarine Force) was in position off the entrance to Pearl Harbor. With this squadron were five midget or "baby" submarines. It was one of these babies which WARD had sunk at dawn.

Meanwhile, a midget submarine slipped undetected into the open harbor entrance, and eased into the inner harbor early that Sunday morning. This pocket-size submarine's casual junket around Pearl Harbor is a feat every submariner will recognize as remarkable. Its presence unsuspected, the underwater footpad was hugging the bottom off Ford Island when the air attack began. While the harbor was being bombed, this submarine launched both of its torpedoes. The first passed between the seaplane tender CURTISS and the cruiser RALEIGH, and exploded on the Ford Island shore. The other burrowed into the mud not far from the old timber-covered target ship UTAH. Promptly sunk by CURTISS for its pains, the midget in question constituted the enemy's second submarine loss.

One small submersible, soon to be a needle under a haystack of shattered American warships, might seem of little account. But this sinking of an enemy submarine in the heart of Pearl Harbor emphatically underlines that most important faculty of the undersea boat—its ability to penetrate naval defenses, conduct an unobserved approach and deliver a surprise attack.

Another Japanese midget submarine lost its bearings and crawled up on a reef near Bellows Field southeast of Kaneohe Bay. There, the day following the raid, it was captured intact. Also captured intact was the Japanese commanding officer, Sub Lieutenant Sakamaki, who swam ashore and surrendered, preferring Hawaii to *hara-kiri.* Sakamaki dolefully informed his interrogators that he had failed in his mission. His mission, of course, had not been to become America's first Japanese P.O.W.

The captured midget submarine bore the designation "I-18," obviously relating it to a Japanese I-class ocean-going submarine which must have served as its "mother." Found on a chart recovered from the midget were notations, "IZ16," "I-20," "—22," "I-18," "I-24," spotted in the entrance channel between Hammer Point and Hospital Point. The implications were clear. At least five Japanese "mother" submarines had been lurking in the waters off Pearl Harbor.

The mother submarine carried her dwarf offspring on the main deck abaft the conning tower where it was fastened to the pressure hull by heavy clamps. Tied to its mother's apron strings by a 200-mile cruising radius, the baby had to be "piggy-backed" close to its objective before launching.

The Japanese midget submarine captured at Bellows Field was approximately 79 feet long, with a 6-foot beam, electrically powered, and capable of a maximum speed of 24 knots and a cruising speed of 4 to 6 knots.

The little craft was equipped with a gyro compass, a magnetic compass, radio (made in the U.S.A.) and underwater sound gear. It was armed with two 18-inch torpedoes, and a demolition charge capable of converting the midget itself into a giant torpedo.

While the midgets at Pearl Harbor were generally regarded as minor novelties, the mothering I-boats in the waters off Oahu constituted a major menace to the assailed Pacific Fleet. The I-boats were submarines of the long-range reconnaissance type. The typical I-16 class had a surface displacement of 2,180 tons, and was 348 feet in length, with a 30-foot beam. With a total horsepower of 9,000, the boats attained a surface speed of around 22 knots. Eight 21-inch tubes gave them a firepower equal to that of all but the newest American submarines.

For a number of days these big submarines had been off Oahu in company with their midget brood. But midget-tending and scouting for Yamamoto's carrier force were only part of this squadron's mission. Its chief mission, revealed in a captured copy of the Japanese plan of operation, was concisely stated as follows:

"Will observe and attack American fleet in Hawaii area. Will make a surprise attack on the channel leading into Pearl Harbor and attempt to close it. If the enemy moves out to fight he will be pursued and attacked."

From the above and foregoing detail, an interesting highlight emerges.

The war in the Pacific began as a contest between surface forces and submarines.

In this preliminary foray the eluded and deluded surface forces remained at a disadvantage. That they were American and the submarines were Japanese was a factor awaiting speedy revision.

Submarines, Pacific Fleet

The Pearl Harbor Submarine Base was home for the 22 submarines which, under the command of Rear Admiral Thomas Withers, operated with the Pacific Fleet. The base contained machine shops, a torpedo plant, supply stores, major repair installations, an escape training tank and other training devices, berthing facilities for submarines and tenders, and housing facilities for 2,400 men and 98 officers. The Pacific Fleet submariners were proud of their Pearl Harbor base. Perhaps it was fortunate that, on the morning of December 7, not many of the submarines were home.

On that fateful Sunday of December 1941, the submarines of the Pacific Fleet were widely dispersed. Of the 22 which comprised the force, 16 were modern fleet-type submarines, and six were S-boats of older vintage. These last, being shorter of wind and leg than the moderns, were at that date on the American Pacific coast, several undergoing repair, and others employed in training exercises at San Diego. The fleet-type submarines (the layman may recognize them as being named after fish) were, in the main, on duty in the Central Pacific.

At the hour when the Japanese struck, the submarines ARGONAUT and TROUT were already conducting defensive patrols near Midway Island. TAMBOR and TRITON were patrolling off Wake. THRESHER was en route to Pearl Harbor after a 43-day training patrol in the Midway vicinity. POLLACK, POMPANO and PLUNGER were en route from San Francisco to Pearl Harbor. TUNA and NAUTILUS were being overhauled at Mare Island Navy Yard. Not far from Pearl Harbor, GUDGEON was conducting aircraft-submarine training exercises at Lahaina, Maui.

Five submarines, all in various stages of overhaul, were at the Pearl Harbor Submarine Base.

The Air Strike

At 0750 the first wave of Japanese planes struck Kaneohe Naval Air Station on the eastern side of Oahu. Through

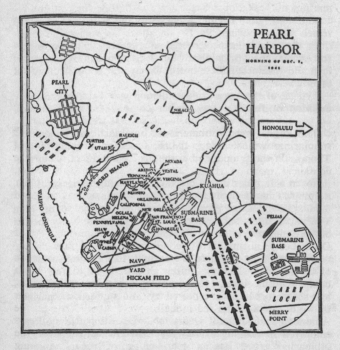

clouds banked over the Koolau Range the bombers stormed on westward to attack Pearl Harbor. Hickam Field, the Naval Air Station at Ford Island, and the Marine Corps station at Ewa were marked as primary targets. Following this assault on the airfields, the planes roared in from two directions to strike Battleship Row.

Seven battleships (BB's) were moored in Battleship Row and BB PENNSYLVANIA was sitting helpless in drydock. These eight composed the battleship force of the United States Pacific Fleet. Nine cruisers, 28 destroyers, tenders, minesweepers, supply ships, auxiliaries—a total of 86 naval vessels—crowded the harbor.

The five submarines at Pearl Harbor Submarine Base were the CACHALOT, CUTTLEFISH, DOLPHIN, NARWHAL and TAUTOG—with the submarine tender PELLIAS. Situated on the south side of the harbor, the Submarine Base was a box seat flanking the bombing-run of the planes which came hurricaning over Hickam Field on their way to Ford Island.

Like many of the fleet units caught at Pearl, the five submarines of Task Force Seven were in harbor for rest and reconditioning after strenuous exercises and patrols. Few naval vessels are as vulnerable to air attack as surfaced submarines, and a submarine tethered to a pier by charging cables and water lines is helpless. Yet the submariners caught at their Pearl Harbor base were to give a good account of themselves.

Typical of their precarious situation was TAUTOG'S. Sunday morning of the 7th, few of her complement were aboard. Of her submarine sailors on hand, several were readying for church, others were thinking about breakfast, and undoubtedly someone was listening to "Music for Your Morning Mood." It was almost time for the routine sounding of Colors at 0800.

When a familiar drone of planes invaded the peaceful sky, it sounded like a flight returning to Hickam.

Husky explosions growled in echo across the south. Men looked up surprised. "Say, this is what this Navy needs! Sunday morning practice! Realistic stuff!"

So thought a number of submarine officers at first glimpse of the oncoming bombers. To several, like Lieutenant W. B. (Barney) Sieglaff, duty officer aboard TAUTOG, this touch made a fitting climax for weeks of extensive drill. Then a low-flying torpedo plane roared by, and stunned submariners stared in shock at the red fireball.

Alarm bell! General Quarters! "Man all battle stations!" Sieglaff mustered a gun crew as TAUTOG'S sailors boiled out on deck. Weapons had to be broken out of lockers; ammunition passed up from below. The submariners manned TAUTOG'S 3-incher. Aboard the submarine NARWHAL, a gun crew opened fire as a Jap torpedo plane came hurtling over Merry Point. TAUTOG'S gunners blazed at the plane. The plane burst into flames and crashed in the channel. The two submarines shared credit with the DD for this first kill. Another flight of torpedo planes came racing in. On TAUTOG'S deck a machine gun chattered.

A Browning .50-cal. machine gun was strictly improvisation in the face of this tornado. But it proved the best thing at hand. TAUTOG'S deck gun was frozen, unable to elevate after days of submergence during that long trial patrol. While gunner's mates worked desperately over the malfunctioning 3-incher, Torpedoman Pasqual Mignon manned the machine gun and opened up on the Jap planes.

A low-flying "V" of torpedo planes was storming up the track for Battleship Row. Two destroyers which had been covering the zone immediately beyond the Submarine Base simultaneously ceased fire. In that few seconds' interval, Torpedoman's Mate Mignon got in his shot. Observers of the action saw the fiery whip of bullets lash out from TAUTOG'S deck and lick across the Jap plane's fuselage. A binding flash —then, streaming a plume of smoke, the plane nose-dived into the channel.

This was the first Japanese warrior destroyed, single-handed, by a U. S. submarine in World War II.

Ordeal by fire

Battleship Row was hard hit. Stabbed by four torpedoes, OKLAHOMA rolled over. WEST VIRGINIA, battered and aflame, wedged neighboring TENNESSEE in a fiery grip against the concrete quay. Torpedoed, CALIFORNIA settled in a lake of blazing oil. MARYLAND was blasted. NEVADA was struck. On the north side of Ford Island, old UTAH, mistaken for an aircraft carrier, capsized and sank under a bombing. A freak mischance sent a bomb down one of ARIZONA'S stacks. In this one horrendous blast, 1,100 officers and men were slain.

At Ten Ten Dock, the cruiser HELENA and minelayer OGLALA were wounded by a torpedo blast. OGLALA capsized. CURTISS and RALEIGH were disabled. The destroyer SHAW was almost torn to pieces. Destroyers CASSIN and DOWNES were scorched in drydock as though in a furnace. CALIFORNIA, already injured, was speared. Although damaged, NEVADA managed to escape her moorings and start for the harbor entrance.

A few Army fighter planes rising to meet the attackers were quickly eliminated. So were several unarmed Flying Fortresses which blundered into the melee. Naval planes from the aircraft carrier ENTERPRISE, which was at that time 200 miles off Oahu, ran into Jap dive bombers and indiscriminate anti-aircraft fire, and 11 were shot down. Some 18 enemy planes also perished in that morning's inferno, and the submariners

could look back with pride on their contribution to the attacker's casualty list.

The last Japanese plane was reported over the harbor
about noon. Littered with burning hulls and calcined wreckage, its piers and quays strewn with scrap iron, Pearl Harbor
was a weltering Aceldama. Nineteen warships had been sunk,
gutted, or savagely mangled. Shore installations on Ford Island were reduced to shambles. Over 3,000 Navy and Marine
Corps officers and men had been killed.

To the submariners, this reduction of the U.S. Navy's great
Central Pacific base came as a staggering initiation to modern
warfare.

Pearl Harbor Aftermath

At the Pearl Harbor Submarine Base the crews reassembled,
and technicians worked at top speed to ready the boats for
departure. By evening of the 7th, several of the submarines
were fueled and ready to go.

But a number of days would pass before one of these
submarines would venture out on war patrol, and the submariners welcomed the opportunity to complete the overhauling of their boats. It was a fortunate feature of the Pearl
Harbor onslaught that the Submarine Base escaped a bomb
hit.

Although prepared with meticulous care and masterfully
executed by the pilots, the Japanese attack-pattern neglected
this vital detail. Bombs and torpedoes were specifically
marked for expenditure on the battleships in the Row and
the carriers thought to be moored off Ford Island. Submarines and submarine repair facilities were presumed to be
minor targets. It was a presumption the Japanese High Command would eventually regret.

Under the driving leadership of Rear Admiral Thomas
Withers, submarines of the Pacific Fleet operating out of
Pearl Harbor would presently launch an undersea offensive
that would more than return the bread so ruthlessly cast
upon the waters by the Japanese militarists. And the war was
but a few days old when the Pearl Harbor submariners arranged for the Imperial Navy a meaningful epitaph.

The midget submarine sunk by CURTISS was raised from
the mud and found to be wrecked beyond useful examination. At the Submarine Base a new pier was under construction. Fill-in material was needed. The battered little boat—a
coffin for its two-man crew—was cemented into the founda-
tions of the Submarine Base pier.

Chapter 2

Central Pacific Front

☆ ☆ ☆

Japanese Myopia

In their all-out surprise smash at Pearl Harbor, the Japanese evidently hoped to copy their successful Port Arthur performance which opened the Russo-Japanese War of 1904. Intention was to deal the U.S. Pacific Fleet a blow that would paralyze American sea power for months to come. Gaining the initiative, the forces of Dai Nippon would gather the Southwest Pacific into the embrace of the "Greater East Asia Co-Prosperity Sphere" and fortify this territory before the U.S. Navy could strike back.

The master minds in Tokyo assumed that American naval forces would then concentrate for a strike at the Japanese homeland. Yamamoto intended to meet this attack with minefields, dive bombers and a superior concentration of naval power. Lured into Empire waters, this United States fleet, far from its home base, would be destroyed. Thus victory would be assured the Japanese.

In their over-all war plan the Imperial strategists overlooked the U.S. submarine fleet, even as the five submarines at Pearl Harbor were blandly ignored. For several generations Japan's Shinto-inspired militarists had been plotting Pacific conquest. During World War I, Premier Shigenobu Okuma had said in the face of the Allies, *In the middle of the Twentieth Century Japan will meet Europe on the plains of Asia and wrest from her the mastery of the world.* Abrupt substitution of the Pacific Ocean for the plains of Asia may have muddled Japanese planning. But even in the 1930's, when fleet-type submarines were replacing the older S-boats, Japanese Foreign Minister Baron Kijuro Shidehara declared,

13

"The number of submarines possessed by the United States is of no concern to the Japanese inasmuch as Japan can never be attacked by American submarines."

The baron's view appears to have been shared by the Imperial Navy's leaders, who failed to see that an island is a body of land completely surrounded by a submarine's favorite element. Their underestimation of the submarine is a strategic error difficult to comprehend. In World War I Japan's naval observers had seen the U-boat blockade bring England to the verge of defeat. Again in 1940 the undersea fleet of Nazi Admiral Doenitz all but sank the United Kingdom. The similarity of Japan's insular position to that of the British Isles is apparent on any map. Certainly the U.S. Navy was aware of the analogy.

However, the Japanese may have judged American undersea power by the U.S. submarine fleet which existed in 1939 when World War II exploded in Europe. On September 8, 1939, when President Roosevelt declared a limited national emergency, there were only 55 U.S. submarines in active commission. But the Nazi conquests in Europe and the spread of U-boat warfare in the Atlantic set a pace for American submarine building. Work was accelerated on submarines then building in the yards, and an energetic construction program was implemented by emergency appropriations voted by Congress.

But the milk was spilled in the War Plans Section of the Imperial High Command before even the first shot was fired. American submarines were considered secondary targets.

Fleet-type Submarines and S-boats

To understand submarine operations, however, the layman should have at least a bowing acquaintance with submersibles.

At the time of the Pacific War's outbreak the U.S. Navy's submarines were of two general classes—the long-range, fleet-type submarines (bearing the name of fish), and the older shorter-range S-boats which were numerically designated.

While not of one homogenous type, the modern fleet submarines had one common feature. Able to remain at sea for approximately 75 days, they could cover some 10,000 or more miles at normal cruising speeds without refueling.

The PIKE and PERCH classes, constructed between 1935 and 1936, had a displacement of some 1,320 tons. In length 300 feet, beam 25 feet, they were capable of a surface speed of 20 knots, submerged speed of 10 knots, and had a 12,000-mile cruising radius. PIKE-class submarines were equipped

with an all-electric drive. Whereas the Diesels had formerly
been connected directly to the propellers, those installed in
the PIKE class drove generators whose power was converted
into electricity which in turn drove motors connected to the
propeller drive shaft.

Eight torpedo tubes, a 3-inch deck gun and a machine
gun gave greater firepower to SALMON and SARGO-class submarines built in 1938 and 1939. Displacement of these boats
was 1,450 tons. This class was succeeded in 1940 by the
TAMBORS which were 308 feet in length, with 27-foot beam,
and a displacement of 1,475 tons. TAMBOR was driven by
four Diesels, totaling 6,400 H.P., at a surface speed of 21
knots. A 3-inch deck gun and two machine guns armed her
against attack. Ten torpedo tubes carried this class to the
fore in striking power.

Newest of the fleet-type submarines, the GATO class, built
in 1941, was to remain standard for eventual wartime construction. Including GREENLING and GROUPER, this class
embodied the best features of the previously built long-range
submarines—all-welded construction, all-electric drive, oceanic cruising range, ten torpedo tubes. Minor refinements
would be made after war experience, but there were no basic
changes in the design of these boats which had a displacement of 1,500 tons; length, 307 feet; beam, 27 feet; horsepower, 6,400; and surface speed, 20 knots. This was the
submarine produced by American builders throughout World
War II.

The older S-class submarines, constructed primarily for
defense purposes in the decade following World War I, were
not designed to cruise the vast expanses of ocean which had
to be covered by Pacific patrols. The early S-boats, modeled
after the S-1, were capable of only limited cruising and
comparatively brief submergence. Stowage space, at a premium on any submarine, was restricted to absolute necessi-
ties, and quarters were cramped beyond comfort. Even in the
later S-boats, lack of air-conditioning made the atmosphere
mephitic and the heat overpowering during prolonged submergence in tropic waters. In this regard, the S-boat more
than lived up to the nickname "pig boat." But for all its deficiencies, the S-boat was to demonstrate hardy sea-keeping
qualities that made "pig boat" a shining *nom de guerre*.

Last of the S-boats, the S-42 type was 225 feet in length
with a 21-foot beam and a surface displacement of 906 tons.
Two Diesel engines produced 1,200 H.P. to drive the boats
at a maximum speed of 14½ knots. Electric motors of 1,500
H.P. gave them a maximum submerged speed of 11 knots.
Structurally, S-48 was similar to the larger V-boats—divided

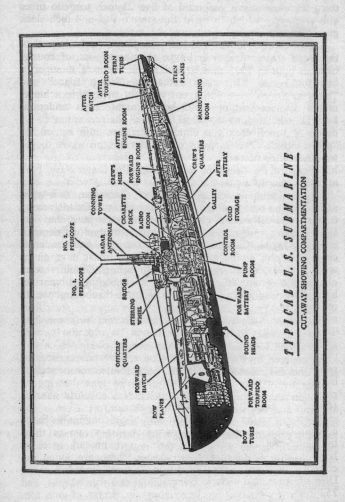

TYPICAL U.S. SUBMARINE

CUT-AWAY SHOWING COMPARTMENTATION

Labels: BOW TUBES, BOW PLANES, FORWARD TORPEDO ROOM, FORWARD HATCH, SOUND HEADS, OFFICERS' QUARTERS, STEERING WHEEL, BRIDGE, NO. 1. PERISCOPE, NO. 2. PERISCOPE, RADAR ANTENNAE, CONNING TOWER, CIGARETTE DECK, RADIO ROOM, CREW'S MESS, FORWARD ENGINE ROOM, AFTER ENGINE ROOM, AFTER HATCH, AFTER TORPEDO ROOM, STERN TUBES, STERN PLANES, MANEUVERING ROOM, CREW'S QUARTERS, AFTER BATTERY, GALLEY, COLD STORAGE, CONTROL ROOM, PUMP ROOM, FORWARD BATTERY into six watertight compartments with double hull construction amidships and single hull construction at bow and stern. Her armament consisted of five 21-inch torpedo tubes (four at the bow and one at the stern) and a 4-inch deck gun. Her complement numbered 44 men.

Longer legged, longer winded, with firepower heavier than the S-boats, the modern fleet-type submarine was, of course, better equipped for combat and in all respects a superior "weapon." Its "habitability"—that is, "living space" and "breathing space"—was the last word in submarine achievement. Its sea-keeping—and, one might say, underseakeeping—qualities were second to none. The maximum diving depth of this fleet-type submarine was, and still is, labeled "secret." But it could go down under the sea to a depth well below 200 feet (greater depths will be reported in this history), and it could remain submerged as long as any rival at that time operating.

Like all submarines of the period, American fleet-types and S-types were engine-driven on the surface and driven by motors when submerged. The layman will note that the Diesel engine's dependence on fuel and the motor's dependence on battery "juice" limit the surface and undersea cruising ranges of all submarines. Engines must have air as well as fuel. As the batteries which ran the motors were charged by generators run by the engines, the submarines had to surface after a number of hours' submergence in order to charge the batteries. (Thus, to conserve their batteries, submarines ran on the surface as much as possible. The submerged runs were made when stalking the enemy, avoiding detection, or evading counter-attack.)

Ton for ton, the modern submarine is without question the most compact and complicated man-of-war ever conceived by man's inventive mind. Reference to the plan drawing on page 16 will give the reader an idea of the World War II (fleet-type GATO class) submarine's interior.

As shown in the drawing, the submarine contains as many compartments and cubicles as a fighting ship two or three times its size. Tucked into a space approximately twice as large as the average six-room house, there are living accommodations for a crew of 80 or 90 men, a control room, Diesel engines and electric motors, fuel and water tanks, and 252 battery cells, each cell weighing in excess of one ton. There are air compressors and high-pressure air banks for blowing tanks and charging torpedo air flasks. There are torpedo rooms fore and aft, 10 torpedo tubes, stowage space for 24 torpedoes. Crammed into the remaining nooks and crannies are refrigerated and dry stores, stills for manufacturing fresh water, air-conditioning and air-purifying equipment, ice machines, shower baths, main ballast tanks to give "positive buoyancy" when cruising on the surface and "neutral buoyancy" when running submerged, variable ballast tanks for adjusting trim, electrical equipment for operating bow and stern planes, and wells for the periscopes. Lazaret, chain locker, ammunition magazines, galley. Navigational instruments, fire control instruments, radio and radar and sonar gear. Some of this paraphernalia is indicated in the illustration. Only a complicated blueprint could show the multiplicity of valves, gages, meters and operating levers which are the sensitive organs of this undersea vessel; the maze of oil, air and water lines that are its veins and capillaries; the electric cables that are its nervous system. All this within a watertight hull capable of withstanding tremendous pressures deep under the sea! One may believe the submariner who asserts that his is the most complex war engine of all.

Command Organization

At the outbreak of the war, submarines of the U.S. Navy were divided among the three existing fleets—Atlantic, Pacific and Asiatic. Each submarine group had its own administrative command: Submarines, Atlantic Fleet, with headquarters at New London, Connecticut; Submarines, Scouting Force, Pacific Fleet, with headquarters at the Submarine Base, Pearl Harbor; Submarines, Asiatic Fleet, with headquarters on board the submarine tender CANOPUS in Manila Bay.

Shortly after the Pearl Harbor attack, it was determined that the submarines of the Pacific Fleet would operate directly under CinCPac rather than under Commander Scouting Force. Commander Submarines, Scouting Force, Pacific Fleet, then became Commander Submarines, Pacific Fleet (ComSubPac). Less than a year later the title was again changed to Commander Submarine Force, Pacific Fleet. Commander Submarines, Asiatic Fleet, eventually became Commander Submarines, Southwest Pacific (ComSubSoWesPac). When all naval forces operating in the Southwest Pacific were designed as the Seventh Fleet he received the alternate title of Commander Submarines, Seventh Fleet.

Each of the three submarine force administrative commands functioned as a separate entity under its own fleet commander, and there were no official ties that bound them together. All of the cooperation, coordination, and standardization of doctrine among the three forces was effected by mutual consent of the force commanders rather than by high command edict. Commander Submarines, Atlantic (Com-SubLant) controlled all submarines operating in the Atlantic and in European waters. He also had operational control over Panama-based submarines patrolling the Pacific approaches of the Panama Canal.

The boundary line between the areas patrolled by Submarines, Pacific Fleet, and Submarines, Asiatic Fleet, at the start of the war was subject to revision as the conflict widened. The boundary finally stabilized at a line drawn along the parallel of 20° north from the coast of China to a point a few miles east of the easternmost point of the Philippine Archipelago, thence directly south to the equator, and then eastward along the equator. While this was the established line, temporary exchanges of areas were made from time to time to meet the needs of any particular operation or tactical situation. Normally, those waters to the north and east of the line were patrolled by Pacific Fleet submarines, those to the south and west by SubSoWesPac.

New-construction submarines, after being fitted out and trained by ComSubLant, reported for duty and became units of SubPac upon passing through the Panama Canal. In accordance with a plan developed some months after the war's outbreak, ComSubPac operated under a directive from the Chief of Naval Operations to keep SubSoWesPac up to a fixed numerical strength. Whenever a submarine was lost in the Southwest Pacific or became due for an overhaul in the States, ComSubPac would furnish a submarine from his command to serve as a replacement.

To decentralize the administrative organization and relieve the force commander of unnecessary details, submarines are organized into divisions and squadrons. The normal division consists of six submarines, and two divisions form a squadron. Each squadron is either assigned its own tender or is assigned to a submarine base. In either case the functions of the tender and the base are the same—to supply office space and quarters for the squadron and division commanders and their staffs, to billet repair personnel and relief crews, to undertake all submarine repairs, short of complete overhauls. Everything from the replacement of a damaged propeller to the adjustment of a cranky sextant, the supplying of all necessary food, fuel, clothing, spare parts, munitions, medical stores—the care of all the material needs of the submarines and physical needs of the submariners—these are the tasks accomplished by submarine tender or submarine base.

In peacetime the squadron and division commanders exercise a considerable degree of operational control over their boats. During the war they served in a wholly administrative capacity. The force commanders controlled all combat operations, and in so doing, they dealt directly with the submarine captains—there were no intervening command echelons. A submarine returning from patrol in enemy waters was assigned to a squadron commander for refit. (Not necessarily his own squadron commander, as the refit workload had to be equalized.) The submarine was also assigned to one of the division commanders of that squadron for training. A relief crew from the squadron would take over the submarine while the regular crew was ashore. After a period of rest and recreation, the regulars would return on board. One day would then be spent in testing machinery and equipment, and in making a trim dive. Four days would be devoted to refresher training at sea under the division commander. Two days would be spent loading stores, food, fuel, and torpedoes, and in getting ready for sea. Finally on the "readiness-for-sea day," the submarine would pass to the direct command of the force commander, who would issue the operation order to the submarine's captain and send the submarine on her way.

Unless unusual repair work or special training was required, the period of refit and training covered three weeks. With the patrol then lasting anywhere from 45 to 60 days, the normal patrol cycle was 75 days. Standard procedure was to send the submarine from the Pacific to a navy yard on the West Coast for complete overhaul after five patrols had been made. During these overhaul periods, the crews were granted leave in the States.

Internal Submarine Organization

The submarine's crew is an organization of specialists. Brain rather than brawn is the selection criterion. There are many "sergeants" but few "privates"—non-rated men constitute less than 20% of the entire complement. Each officer and man must be a specialist in his own job, but he must know his shipmate's job as well. Before an officer or man can be designated as "qualified in submarines" he must pass a rigid written and oral examination on all machinery, piping and equipment throughout the boat. The electrician's mate must know how to fire the torpedo tubes, the torpedoman's mate how to charge batteries. There are no spare parts in a submarine's crew—each member is a cog in the wheel, and each cog must do its job to perfection if the organization is to function smoothly, efficiently, and above all, safely.

From a numerical standpoint, motor machinist's mates, electrician's mates and torpedoman's mates predominate in the crew. These three groups approximate half of the enlisted personnel. Next come radiomen and operators of the submarine's electronic gear. Three quartermasters or signalmen, two ship's cooks, two steward's mates, one pharmacist's mate, one gunner's mate, one yeoman and a number of firemen and seamen complete the complement. The senior chief petty officer on board, usually a chief torpedoman's mate, is designated the "Chief of the Boat."

The senior officer on board is, of course, the submarine's captain. ("Old Man" to the crew, he was, at the outbreak of World War II, a lieutenant commander whose age was probably 34 or 35). He is followed in seniority by the executive officer who also serves as navigator. Aside from these two —captain and exec—seniority does not enter the picture. The submarine captain assigns officers to the various ship's duties in accordance with their experience and capabilities. There are the chief engineer, torpedo and gunnery officer, communications officer and commissary officer. (When radar equipment was installed during World War II there was sometimes a radar officer.) The officers may be, and frequently are, assigned more than one of the above-listed duties.

In the pre-war days the complement of a fleet-type submarine consisted of five officers and 54 enlisted men. As newly developed fire control, radar, radio and sound equipment was added to the submarines, and as war experience dictated the need for more personnel, the complement grew. At war's end it approximated eight officers and 75 enlisted men.

For purposes of watch-standing, the submarine crew is divided into three sections. All hands, the captain excepted, stand watches "one in three" with four hours on duty and eight hours off. The work of the captain, in the words of the well-known sideshow pitch, "is goin' on all the time." He must be constantly on the alert and always on call. Each section is organized to man all necessary stations for diving, surfacing, and surfaced or submerged cruising. With the exception of routine cleaning and minor repair jobs, little work is done on a submarine at sea, and sections off watch occupy their time with eating, reading, acey deucey, and sleeping.

Torpedo or gun attacks are, of course, all-hands evolutions. When contact with the enemy is made, the captain takes over the periscope and conducts the approach and attack. Breathing over his shoulder is the exec. It is his job to check the captain's observations and estimates, and to assist with the adroit mental gymnastics required for a submarine approach. Other officers serve as diving officer, torpedo data computer operator, and plotting officer. One officer is usually assigned to each torpedo room.

The stranger on board a submarine on war patrol might have difficulty distinguishing between captain and seaman. Both eat the same food and wear similar garb. Submarines and submarining do not provide space for the protocol of rank. Each member of the crew, from cook to captain, stands on his own two feet as an important individual.

Warfare Unrestricted

The unrestricted warfare directive issued by the Chief of Naval Operations on December 7 was startling. It meant "total war" on the sea—a war in which a fishing boat or freighter was to be considered a target as legitimate as an enemy battleship.

Indiscriminate war on merchant shipping had never been advocated by American naval authorities. Veteran submariners recalled America's abhorrence for the unrestricted German campaigns of 1917-1918 when the U-boat was denounced as the "stiletto of the seas."

Neither by training nor indoctrination was the U.S. Submarine Force readied for unrestricted warfare.

Among the official publications allowed to each submarine was a small volume entitled: "INSTRUCTIONS FOR THE NAVY OF THE UNITED STATES GOVERNING MARITIME AND AERIAL WARFARE." Such paragraphs as the following were impressed on the memory of every submarine commanding officer:

"*In their action with regard to merchant ships, submarines must conform to the rules of International Law to which surface vessels are subject.*

"*In particular, except in the case of persistent refusal to stop on being duly summoned, or of active resistance to visit or search, a warship, whether surface vessel or submarine, may not sink or render incapable of navigation a merchant vessel without having first placed passengers, crew and ship's papers in a place of safety.*"

On the opening day of World War II, the Nazi U-boat which sank the ATHENIA torpedoed these legal niceties. And the Mikado's military leaders, for all their reverence for the Code Bushido, had long shown little respect for rules of "civilized" warfare. But it was not reprisal so much as military imperative that caused Washington to reverse its opinion on the already abrogated naval laws.

Webster defines a merchant vessel as "a ship employed in commerce." There were to be no merchant ships in the Pacific for the duration of the war. Armed or not, merchantmen were in effect combatant ships. "Transports," "freighters," "tankers" were hollow titles for auxiliaries of war, and it was the realistic duty of the submarine forces to reduce these ships to hulls as hollow as their titles. Converted by a directive into commerce raiders, American submarines in the Pacific went to war to sink everything that floated under a Japanese flag.

Action at Midway and Wake

Timed with the attack on Pearl Harbor, surprise blows were landed by the enemy on America's outpost islands—Midway—Wake—Guam. At Midway and Wake, American submarines had their opening encounter with Japanese surface forces.

The defenders had been alerted by the first radio alarm from Hawaii which came that morning at 0630, Midway time. Throughout the day Marines stood tensely at their battle stations. When night extinguished the brief twilight, the defenders were still waiting in suspense.

The little harbor was blacked out, but a bright tropic moon whitewashed the beach and revealed shore installations in stark silhouette. For Japanese naval gunners Midway was a beautiful target.

The first projectiles fell in the lagoon at 2130, shattering the silence with the sudden violence of rocks dropped on a mirror. Lookouts in the communication tower spotted the flash of turret guns far to the southwest.

Another salvo flashed. Blasts rocked the beach.

A third salvo struck the Midway hangar, starting a furious conflagration.

The Marines now saw the answer to the ease with which the distant warships got on target. A Japanese destroyer and what appeared to be a light cruiser (CL) were closing in at top speed, and spotting for the warships on the horizon.

Salvos from the distant warships smashed the Marine command post and exploded near the burning hangar. The Marines lashed the enemy warships with heavy machine-gun fire, and the shore guns hit both targets. But the set-up favored the heavier naval guns. And Midway's defenders were steeled for an all-out bombardment, when the destroyer and the cruiser veered away and retired as suddenly as they had charged. As abruptly, the ships on the horizon ceased fire and executed a high-speed withdrawal.

Many strategists have put a big question mark behind the withdrawal of the first Japanese striking force from Midway's waters. While Midway was not on Yamamoto's agenda for early conquest, it seems possible that U.S. submarine action may have interfered with the December 7th bombardment.

Submarines TROUT and ARGONAUT were conducting defensive patrols in the Midway area on that momentous date. Both submarines were on the surface that Sunday evening. Both sighted ominous flashes on the horizon.

TROUT (Lieutenant Commander F. W. Fenno) had received news of the Pearl Harbor bombing that morning. Then had come a radio dispatch ordering her to locate ARGONAUT. All day she had tried to contact the big submarine which was patrolling south of her. But ARGONAUT, in accordance with training routine, had submerged for the day, and TROUT could only wait for sundown when the big V-boat would come to the surface.

Now, sighting the gun flares against the evening sky, Fenno drove his submarine at top speed to the north of Midway, hoping to intercept the enemy in that direction. Meantime, ARGONAUT, cruising off Sand Island, had picked up word of the Pearl Harbor raid when she surfaced just after sunset. Not long after that she sighted the Japanese force shelling Midway. This was it! ARGONAUT's captain, Lieutenant Commander S. G. Barchet, ordered the submarine under, and began an approach on the enemy vessels.

TROUT, north of Midway, was unable to close with the warships. But ARGONAUT's submerged approach brought her within attack range. Before diving, however, she had been sighted in the brilliant moonlight, and one enemy warship rushed to search the area. With a cruiser or large destroyer probing for the submarine with echo-ranging gear, Barchet gave the order to rig for depth charges, and ARGONAUT, in the parlance of the submariners, "went deep." The first days of the war were trial-and-error ones for American submarine captains and crews, who had not yet fired a torpedo in anger and were unacquainted with the devices of the enemy. So ARGONAUT's brush with the foe at Midway resulted in no material damage to either side. But the Midway bombardment was broken off while the hunt for the submarine began. Here at the outset of the war was an example of the submersible's ability to divert surface forces and disrupt an enemy attack.

Unfortunately, submarine action at Wake Island, while

more aggressive than that at Midway, was unable to fend
the enemy's blow.

Flanked by the Japanese Mandates—the Marshalls and
the Caroline Islands—Wake was decidedly vulnerable. And
the island's defenses, despite belated reinforcement, were
weaker than Midway's. Originally designated a bird sanctuary by the U.S. Government, and later employed as a Pacific
way-station by Pan-American Airways, Wake was not armed
until early in 1941. To any determined Japanese assault, the
defenders could offer only back-to-the-wall resistance. The
war-makers in Tokyo had determined to seize Wake Island.

About 0700, December 8 (Wake time), the Wake garrison
received word of the Pearl Harbor attack. Mid-morning,
Wake was struck by enemy bombers.

Two days of aerial pounding preceded the arrival of a
Jap task force consisting of three light cruisers, six destroyers, two transports and two scouting submarines. Before this
overpowering force the island was to fall after 16 days of
sacrificial resistance by its handful of Marines.

U.S. submarines Tambor and Triton were on practice
war patrols off Wake when the Japanese struck.

Tambor (Lieutenant Commander J. W. Murphy) was
some 40 miles northeast of Wake when word of the Pearl
Harbor strike came in by radio. On the night of December
8-9, Tambor's bridge watch could see fires bursting out on
Wake Island, and during the ensuing onslaught the watch
had periscope views of air raids and a glimpse of the attacking warships. Tambor was unable to close the range and attack the Jap naval force.

Patrolling south of Wake, Triton found herself in position to intercept the enemy naval force. Just before midnight
on December 10, Triton was on the surface finishing a
battery charge. Suddenly two bright flashes lit the horizon,
and the officer of the deck made out a Jap man-of-war silhouetted against the illuminated sky. A large destroyer or
light cruiser, it appeared to be heading toward the submarine. Triton had been ordered not to attack unless attacked,
so her skipper, Lieutenant Commander W. A. Lent, gave
the command to go deep, and the submarine submerged to
start evasive tactics.

The crew rigged for depth charges, and there was a harrowing wait while the sound operator at the listening gear
reported a rush of high-speed screws, indicating the enemy
was on the hunt. Nerves tightened as the warship's propellers
could be heard closing in, fading off, returning. As the
hunter closed in once more, Lent decided to attack the

hunter. At 0317, after more than three hours of lethal hide-and-seek, he maneuvered TRITON into position, and fired four after-tubes at the stubborn enemy.

Fifty-eight seconds after the first torpedo was fired, a blunt explosion was heard. The muffled blast sent vibrations through the submarine, and there seemed little doubt that the enemy was hit. The chase was over. TRITON was credited with damaging one Japanese warship. This was the first torpedo attack made by a Pacific Fleet submarine in World War II.

Thus U.S. submarines began unrestricted warfare in the Pacific by exchanging blows with the Imperial Japanese Navy. But the war was soon to expand at four-engine speed into an epic conflict of attrition.

Pearl Harbor Postscript

Guam, practically defenseless and within easy striking distance of Saipan, was captured by the Japanese early in the morning of December 10th.

"So sorry," said a Japanese naval captain to Ensign Leona Jackson of the U.S. Navy Nurse Corps. "Sorry to tell you all your fleet sunk. No more."

Braggadocio. The Japanese High Command knew better. Yamamoto and his staff had obtained a fairly accurate estimate of the damage done to the United States Pacific Fleet, and Jap announcements of its total destruction were so much propaganda.

Yet the Imperial Navy's leaders did miscalculate. They failed in their estimation of the speed with which the United States Navy could make a comeback.

Immediately after the strike at Pearl Harbor, Yamamoto's carrier force made a high-speed withdrawal to the northwest. About three hours later, Japanese Imperial Headquarters, with a sense for the anti-climactical, issued a rescript from Tokyo declaring war on the United States and Great Britain. The embattled U.S. Navy, with no time for diplomatic formalities, was already in action.

At the Pearl Harbor Submarine Base preparations were rushed for a counter-attack on the enemy. Follow-up raids were expected, and the harbor defenses were hair-triggered. THRESHER, approaching Hawaii, ran into some of these keyed-up defenses.

THRESHER was about 60 miles off Barber's Point, the southwest corner of Oahu, when she received the alarm which was broadcast on the morning of the Japanese strike.

PEARL HARBOR ATTACKED . . . THIS IS NO DRILL

The submarine was at that time under escort of the destroyer LITCHFIELD. Lieutenant Commander W. L. Anderson, THRESHER'S captain, intending to submerge until nightfall, released the destroyer to join a surface task force scouting for the Jap attackers. The DD raced off. Then, just as THRESHER was going under, she picked up a radio dispatch cautioning her not to release her escort. The submarine promptly sent a radio message to the destroyer, arranging for a rendezvous at the diving point. Two hours later, at the rendezvous position, Anderson ran up the periscope. A destroyer—an old "four piper"—was on the spot. But this DD was not the LITCHFIELD, as THRESHER discovered when her conning tower broke water.

Gunfire blazed from the destroyer. Anderson took THRESHER deep, and did not attempt to approach Pearl Harbor until the morning of December 8th.

In accordance with orders received some hours before, the submarine surfaced at 0600, off the harbor entrance. Again she was attacked by friendly forces—this time by bombing planes. Driven under by this slashing attack, THRESHER remained submerged until the destroyer THORNTON came steaming out to escort her home.

Fortunately, GUDGEON, entering Pearl Harbor the following day, was unmolested. One by one the other submarines arrived—POLLACK, POMPANO and PLUNGER from San Francisco, and later that month, TAMBOR, recalled from Wake, and TROUT and ARGONAUT from Midway, and finally TRITON. One by one they slid in from the sea, and their crews stared in shock at the harbor's devastation, and boats and crews were readied to go out again and fight the war.

First to leave were GUDGEON and PLUNGER, heading out on December 11th. With but 24 hours' lay-over, GUDGEON, captained by Lieutenant Commander E. W. Grenfell, set a course for Japan to conduct a pioneer patrol in Empire waters off the Bungo Suido—the strait between Shikoku and Honshu. She was provisioned for a 51-day patrol (some three-fourths of which would be spent in the long haul, going and coming). Like Columbus, Grenfell and the submarine skippers who followed him to make those first patrols in Japan's home waters were setting out for the Unknown. They were not faced with "going over the edge," perhaps. But ahead of them lay the mystery of the enemy's home defenses—a dark mystery of minefields, anti-submarine patrols, air screens. Defenses to be tested and penetrated. Dangerous ventures to try the steel of American submarines and submariners.

PLUNGER (Lieutenant Commander D. C. White) headed for the Kii Suido—the passage between Shikoku and Kyushu. When only a few miles out of Pearl Harbor, she was forced to return to base for repairs to a leaky after-battery hatch. Three days later she made a fresh start. Heading once more for Japan, PLUNGER carried the first radar set into battle—the SD aircraft warning installation.

On December 13, POLLACK (Lieutenant Commander S. P. Moseley) left Pearl Harbor to strike out for the Tokyo Bay area—waters lying at the very mouth of the Japanese dragon. The submariners could count on those waters being closely guarded. Would the dragon jaws snap on the invading submersible? Would she run into tongues of flame, or be caught by teeth of steel? POLLACK would soon find out.

On the 18th, POMPANO, captained by Lieutenant Commander L. S. Parks, went pioneering in another direction. Her voyage of discovery was to take her southwest to the Marshall Islands where she was to investigate the Japanese defenses in that area—defenses no less mysterious and baleful than those which guarded the Empire waters off the home coasts of Japan.

To the Marshalls in POMPANO'S wake went DOLPHIN (Lieutenant Commander G. B. Rainer), departing Pearl Harbor on Christmas Eve.

TAUTOG (Lieutenant Commander J. H. Willingham) presently followed DOLPHIN, bent on another perilous exploratory mission.

So the Pacific Fleet submarines were under way. The New Year would see these pioneers from Pearl Harbor torpedoing the Japanese High Command's high hope that the Imperial Navy could handily cope with American undersea power.

But the enemy had yet to ride the crest of triumph before descending into the trough of defeat. Before the U.S. submarine forces could counter-attack effectively, the invader's tidal-wave offensive swamped the Philippines. Caught in the storm that broke around Manila were the submarines of the United States Asiatic Fleet.

Chapter 3

Philippines Invasion

☆ ☆ ☆

Situation SoWesPac

With Pearl Harbor shattered, Midway dented, Guam captured and Wake's fall a certainty, the Japanese were satisfied that America's mid-Pacific outposts were canceled for the opening phase of the war, if not permanently. The Yamamoto-Tojo war plan now called for an amphibious offensive against the Philippine Islands, Indonesia, and the Netherlands East Indies.

For months the U.S. authorities had anticipated a Japanese drive for the oil-rich Netherlands East Indies. Such a drive would mean head-on collision with British and American forces based at Singapore and Manila on the flanks of Java and Sumatra.

Extension of Philippine fortifications had long been prohibited by treaty with Japan. Attempting last-minute defense measures, the War Department in 1941 began a program of reinforcement. General Douglas MacArthur was appointed Commander of U.S. Army Forces in the Far East. Fortifications were rushed at Corregidor, guarding the entrance to Manila Bay, and at Mariveles Bay, sheltered by Bataan Peninsula, while the U.S. Navy labored to strengthen its facilities at Cavite. The inadequacy of these efforts was to prove nearly as shocking as the unpreparedness at Pearl Harbor.

Headquartered in the Marsman Building in Manila, Admiral Thomas C. Hart had taken all possible emergency steps to prepare his naval forces for the expected blow. His fleet consisted of the cruisers HOUSTON, MARBLEHEAD and BOISE, 13 over-age destroyers, a flotilla of small gunboats and auxiliary vessels, a squadron of 30 slow, cumbersome PBY's, six PT-boats and the previously mentioned 29 submarines with their tenders HOLLAND, OTUS and CANOPUS and the submarine rescue vessel PIGEON.

Admiral Hart was fully aware that his fleet would face appalling odds were it isolated in combat with the naval forces of Japan. The Japanese had ten battleships for action against the three American cruisers. Three Japanese heavy or light cruisers were available for battle against each over-age Asiatic Fleet destroyer. For good measure the Imperial Navy of Nippon boasted nine aircraft carriers, 113 destroyers, 63 submarines and hundreds of aircraft waiting to strike from near-by bases. It was obvious that when war eventuated, the Asiatic Fleet could do little more than fight a delaying action in an attempt to hold the Philippines until the Pacific Fleet arrived from Pearl Harbor.

Meantime Admiral Hart counted on support from Dutch and British allies—in particular the British with their base at Singapore backed up by Britain's most powerful battleship, HMS PRINCE OF WALES, and the battle cruiser HMS REPULSE. It was realized, however, that a three-pronged Japanese attack, stabbing at Malaya, the Philippines and the East Indies simultaneously, could pin the British and Royal Netherlands naval squadrons in their own waters. For shock troops to slow the drive he suspected was imminent, Admiral Hart was relying on his fleet's strongest element—the submarine forces.

On November 27 Admiral Hart received from the Chief of Naval Operations the following message:

THIS DISPATCH IS TO BE CONSIDERED A WAR WARNING. . . . AN AGRESSIVE MOVE BY JAPAN IS EXPECTED WITHIN THE NEXT FEW DAYS. THE NUMBER AND EQUIPMENT OF JAPANESE TROOPS AND THE ORGANIZATION OF NAVAL TASK FORCES INDICATE AN AMPHIBIOUS EXPEDITION EITHER AGAINST THE PHILIPPINES, THAI OR KRA PENINSULA, OR POSSIBLY BORNEO. EXECUTE AN APPROPRIATE DEFENSIVE DEPLOYMENT

Admiral Hart readied his sea forces and ordered the PBY's of Patwing Ten to fly extensive patrols.

On December 8 the Japanese landed on beachheads 400 miles north of Singapore, and the invasion of Malaya was begun.

Simultaneously (about 0300, December 8) news of the Pearl Harbor raid reached Manila. The storm had broken.

Submarines Asiatic

The Asiatic Fleet Submarine Force comprised the following roster:

SUBMARINE DIVISION 21 (COMMANDER S. S. MURRAY)

SALMON, Lieutenant Commander Eugene B. McKinney
SEAL, Lieutenant Commander Kenneth C. Hurd
SKIPJACK, Lieutenant Commander Charles L. Freeman
SARGO, Lieutenant Commander Tyrrell D. Jacobs
SAURY, Lieutenant Commander John L Burnside
SPEARFISH, Lieutenant Roland F. Pryce

SUBMARINE DIVISION 22 (COMMANDER J. A. CONNOLLY)

SNAPPER, Lieutenant Commander Hamilton L. Stone
STINGRAY, Lieutenant Commander Raymond S. Lamb
STURGEON, Lieutenant Commander William L. Wright
SCULPIN, Lieutenant Commander Lucius H. Chappell
SAILFISH, Lieutenant Commander Morton C. Mumma
SWORDFISH, Lieutenant Commander Chester C. Smith

SUBMARINE DIVISION 201 (COMMANDER R. B. VANZANT)

S-36, Lieutenant John R. McKnight, Jr.
S-37, Lieutenant James C. Dempsey
S-38, Lieutenant Wreford G. Chapple
S-39, Lieutenant James W. Coe
S-40, Lieutenant Nicholas Lucker, Jr.
S-41, Lieutenant Commander George M. Holley

SUBMARINE DIVISION 202 (COMMANDER W. M. PERCIFIELD)

SEADRAGON, Lieutenant Commander William E. Ferrall
SEALION, Lieutenant Commander Richard G. Voge
SEARAVEN, Lieutenant Commander Theodore G. Aylward
SEAWOLF, Lieutenant Commander Frederick B. Warder

SUBMARINE DIVISION 203 (COMMANDER E. H. BRYANT)

PERCH, Lieutenant Commander David A. Hurt
PICKEREL, Lieutenant Commander Barton E. Bacon
PORPOISE, Lieutenant Commander Joseph A. Callaghan
PIKE, Lieutenant Commander William A. New
SHARK, Lieutenant Commander Louis Shane, Jr.
TARPON, Lieutenant Commander Lewis Wallace
PERMIT, Lieutenant Commander Adrian M. Hurst

TENDERS

HOLLAND, Captain Joseph W. Gregory
CANOPUS, Commander Earl L. Sackett
OTUS, Commander Joel Newsom
PIGEON (rescue vessel), Lieutenant Commander Richard E. Hawes

Among the first submarines to leave Manila Bay on war patrol were SCULPIN and SEAWOLF, ordered to escort a convoy made up of the aircraft tender LANGLEY, the tanker PECOS, and the destroyer tender BLACK HAWK, heading south. Skippered by Lieutenant Commanders F. B. Warder and Lucius Chappell, the WOLF and SCULPIN stood out with darkened convoy that night.

On December 9 the eight "reserve" submarines were sent out on patrol. S-40 went out to Verde Island Passage. S-41 was assigned the approaches to Looc Bay, Tablas Island. SHARK was stationed in Santa Cruz Harbor, Marinduque Island. TARPON was positioned in Masbate Harbor, PERMIT and PERCH were assigned areas off the west coast of Luzon. SAILFISH and STINGRAY were started for the Lingayen Gulf area.

Beyond this defense ring of patrol areas which embraced Luzon, still other submarines were rushed to cover the enemy's possible roads of advance. SEARAVEN went north to

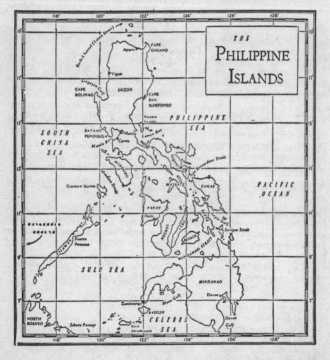

patrol off Formosa Strait. SKIPJACK headed eastward toward the Pelews where the enemy base at Palau flanked Mindanao. SNAPPER was sent out to relieve PIKE in the Hainan Gulf area.

Meantime, the Japanese assault on the Philippines had begun. Jap aircraft were bombing and strafing the outlying Philippine bases. Coordinated sea-air attacks slashed at Mindanao Island, the enemy bombers concentrating on the Navy's PBY base at Davao. Against a horde of fighters, bombers and dive bombers, the Navy's 30 seaplanes rose like a covey of eagles winging up to fight clouds of predatory hawks and condors. Perhaps the hopelessness of their situation is best described in a message which is said to have been radioed back to his base by the pilot of a PBY:

HAVE SIGHTED ENEMY PLANES . . . PLEASE NOTIFY NEXT OF KIN

While the Japs struck the Philippine fringe, the expected attack on Manila, Corregidor and Cavite was delayed. The reason, somewhat obscure, seems in part attributable to bad weather over Formosa which grounded the Japanese air forces in the north for a number of hours. But rather than disrupting the Japanese schedule, this postponement served to disarm the U.S. Army Air Force on Luzon. Around noon of December 8, Army planes which had been out on early war patrol came in to refuel. On Clark and Iba Fields they were parked wing to wing when the bombers from Formosa finally arrived. Dive bombers and strafers blasted landing strips, hangars and planes out of existence. By midnight of December 8 the Philippine Islands were practically without air cover.

This was grim news for the Asiatic Fleet. It was particularly dismaying to the submarine forces which had been hopefully relying on land-based aircraft to keep enemy bombers out of tropic skies which looked down on some of the clearest coastal waters in the world. Now the submariners knew they must advance into the narrow Philippine straits and the glassy shallows of Lingayen Gulf with little more protection against aircraft than that afforded by risky emergency dives or suicidal surface fighting with Browning machine guns.

Grim news—but it was of small import compared with the appalling word which came to them from Pearl Harbor.

THE PACIFIC FLEET HAS BEEN IMMOBILIZED

On December 10, the Japanese onslaught struck Manila.

The Strike at Manila

The attack lacked the shock of surprise that had stunned Pearl Harbor. The war was in its third day, and air-raid sirens and ack-ack greeted the invader. The Japanese air armada came sailing down the sky as though each echelon were in a groove. The attack was characterized by the leisurely manner in which the two bomb groups circled the city in perfect V-formation, unperturbed by anti-aircraft fire and undeterred by the few planes which rose to meet them. Against the blue of broad daylight they might have been performing for an air show. They were casual about it. They took their time. The few American fighter planes were scattered and shot down. One Japanse "V" proceeded to Nichols Field to add a neutralizing bombing to previous devastation. The other proceeded to bomb the shipping in Manila Harbor. The two "V's" then converged over Cavite to blast the Navy Yard.

Strategically dispersed, the Asiatic Fleet cruisers were not in the Manila area. HOUSTON had been dispatched to Iloilo. BOISE was at Cebu. MARBLEHEAD had gone to Tarakan, Borneo, with four destroyers. For defense, the Navy Yard depended on recently installed anti-aircraft batteries.

The Japanese bombers had the afternoon at their disposal. Cavite, under their bomb-sights, was virtually helpless. Anti-aircraft batteries—nine 3-inch guns—barked in a desperation of futility. With a maximum range of 15,000 feet, they might as well have sent up a barrage of popcorn against the Japanese planes.

In the sky above the naval base the bombing planes moved back and forth at a sauntering pace. Sticks of bombs, seemingly slow, drifted down with murderous accuracy. Oil tanks began to explode, sending up mountainous eruptions of smoke. Machine shops, docks and storehouses burst and crumbled. Within half an hour Cavite was a molten furnace. A third formation of Japanese bombers came down from the north to join in the carnival of destruction.

From a window at Headquarters in the Marsman Building overlooking Manila Bay, Admiral Hart had a dramatic view of the bombing. He noted the unhurried, methodical progress of the bombers.

"If they were not completely satisfied with their aim," he told reporters, "they held their bombs and kept making runs until they were satisfied."

Tons of bombs crashed into the harbor, and Cavite Navy Yard was reduced to a fire-swept limbo.

Here again—as at Pearl Harbor—the Japanese bombers concentrated on obvious targets and overlooked the American submarines. As the attack began, the submarines left their mooring places at buoys and alongside tenders, and evacuated the danger area at four-engine speed, submerging as soon as they cleared the harbor's breakwater.

All but one of the Asiatic Fleet submarines escaped into

Manila Bay's deeper waters. The submarine unable to escape was one of the two undergoing overhaul at Cavite. There, tied up at Machina Wharf, was SEADRAGON. Alongside lay SEALION. Outboard of SEALION was the minesweeper BITTERN. Not far distant in the harbor were the submarine rescue vessel PIGEON and the minesweeper QUAIL.

PIGEON (Lieutenant R. E. Hawes) was standing by with a crippled rudder in need of repair. Since receiving word of the Pearl Harbor raid, she had maintained a steaming watch and was on the alert for air attack. QUAIL and BITTERN were also in for repairs. Squeezed in against the wharf by the vessels lying outboard, the two submarines were in a tight spot when the Jap bombers struck during the noon hour. The first stick of bombs landed some 150 yards astern of SEALION.

Loss of Sealion

When the air-raid alarm split the quiet with its banshee wail, SEALION's captain, Lieutenant Commander R. G. Voge, her executive officer, Lieutenant Albert Raborn, and a number of her men were on the submarine's bridge. All hands went below except Voge, Raborn and three gunners, who remained topside to man the machine gun.

The planes droned overhead, and the bombs came laddering down. The blasting shook Machina Wharf. Noting that anti-aircraft fire was unable to touch the high-altitude bombers, Voge ordered the submarine's bridge cleared. A few minutes later, the planes made another bombing run, and two bombs struck SEALION almost simultaneously.

One struck the after end of the conning-tower fairwater. The explosion wrecked the main induction, the battery ventilation and the after conning-tower bulkhead, and completely demolished the machine-gun mount which had just been vacated. Bomb fragments ripped through SEALION's pressure hull, wounding three men in the control room. Another fragment of this bomb penetrated the conning tower of SEADRAGON near by, instantly killing Ensign Samuel H. Hunter of SEADRAGON's crew—the first submarine fatality of the war.

An instant later, the second bomb smashed through SEALION's main ballast tank and pressure hull, and exploded in the maneuvering space in the after end of the engine room. Four men who had been working in that compartment were killed.

The after engine-room flooded immediately, and SEALION settled by the stern. In the after torpedo-room and forward engine-room, water surged in through holes ripped in the bulkheads. As the submarine settled, the living crew escaped through the hatches which were still above water. With a list to starboard, SEALION sank by the stern and finally came to rest on the bottom with about half of her main deck submerged.

The bomb which burst in SEALION's after engine-room could not have hit a more vital spot. Had overhaul facilities been available, however, she might have been repaired. But the bombing which wrecked SEALION also obliterated the Cavite Navy Yard. With nearest overhaul facilities at Pearl Harbor, 5,000 miles away, SEALION's case was hopeless. To prevent her from falling into enemy hands, ComSubsAsiatic ordered her destroyed. Three depth charges were rigged in her compartments, and on Christmas Day, 1941, the charges were exploded. So went down SEALION, the first U.S. submarine lost in World War II.

Escape of Seadragon

Although scarred by the blasting which wrecked SEALION and the crimson tempest which swept Machina Wharf, SEADRAGON managed to get away. Defying inferno, the rescue vessel PIGEON moved in and passed a towing line to the threatened submarine. Men from SEALION clambered on SEADRAGON's deck. Slowly she was jockeyed away from the wharf, towed from her berth to a position where she could back out into the channel.

Once she reached the channel, SEADRAGON was able to continue under her own power. Leaking and lamed, she retained her sea legs, and her skillful crew worked her out into the Bay. That night she was once more taken under PIGEON's valiant wing, and Lieutenant Hawes and his technicians contrived a repair job described by observers as miraculous.

SEADRAGON was in need of more than a miracle—she needed a careful overhaul. Undoubtedly in peacetime she could not have passed her "physical." But this was war. Her leaks plugged, her pressure hull patched, the SEADRAGON went out on war patrol to become a legend off the Indo-China coast and a thorn in the side of such propagandists as Tokyo Rose.

Philippine Twilight

At Cavite the devastation was absolute. The yard was in black ruins, and the charred shops and wrecked piers could only be abandoned. Over 1,000 people were killed in the Cavite bombing, and 400 died later in the hospital. Yet, with the exception of SEALION and SEADRAGON, the submarines in the Bay remained unscathed. Submarine tenders HOLLAND and

OTUS remained on duty to support the submarine forces through the hardest phase of the war. And CANOPUS remained with her submariners to go down in history as the indomitable "Old Lady," supporting not only the hard-driven boats but the embattled defenders who fought to the last at Bataan.

By the morning of December 11, the submariners of the Asiatic Fleet realized they were going to war against unimaginable odds. While the Japanese bombers had been bearing down on Manila Bay, another Japanese air armada was winging over the Gulf of Siam. Shortly before noon of the 10th, this second air armada sighted HMS REPULSE and HMS PRINCE OF WALES off the Malay coast. The news reached the Philippines while the raid was on at Manila. PRINCE OF WALES and REPULSE had been sunk!

The Japanese invasion was roaring down from the north like a typhoon. And *the Allies were without a single capital ship in the Far East*!

Without air cover, without battleship support, its Cavite base burned behind it, the Asiatic Fleet was left to fight off the Philippines invasion "like a man with bare fists fighting a killer with a tommy-gun." The description was Admiral Hart's.

Assigned to the front line were the Manila-based submarines.

Submarines into Battle

The Manila submarines went out in the dark like cats, walking softly to go far.

Submarine commanding officers had been advised to use extraordinary caution and feel the enemy out on their first patrol, for it was realized this would be the most perilous encounter of all. The enemy was an unknown adversary—a foe whose power was recognized, but whose methods and equipment had been developed in secrecy and whose fighting techniques had yet to be discerned. Japanese electronic devices were a mystery. What was their destroyer strength? Had they acquired secret weapons from Germany? Answer to these and similar questions could only be obtained by exploratory probing—a process that demanded steel nerve and the utmost care on the part of the explorer. The Asiatic Fleet submariner were not disposed to underestimate the enemy.

Original plan was to limit the first patrols to about three weeks to enable the collection of first-hand information on enemy tactics at an early date. By analysis of such data the enemy's measure could be taken and the submarine forces could devise counter-strategy accordingly.

This policy could not be carried out, however, and the submarines had to enter the conflict "b'guess and b'God," individually learning of the enemy from close-contact experience and fragments of information dispatched from other boats. Weeks would pass before a definite assessment of Japanese matériel and tactics could be made. Meanwhile, the enemy's naval strength and attack patterns in the Philippines had to be discovered by periscope. Allied air reconnaissance was practically nil from the start of the war.

It was evident from the first that the Philippines capital could not long hold out. The submariners who cruised from Manila in these opening days of the war took with them uncertainty and apprehension—uncertainty as to how, where or when they could again be supplied and serviced—apprehension of an enemy of unknown capabilities.

But these were men schooled to face uncertainties and apprehensions. Pick of a service wherein many are called, but few are chosen, they had been indoctrinated in emergency and inoculated against defeatism. From bridge to galley all hands were aware that they faced an unprecedented ordeal. Over the ship radio came the dispatches from HQ, the somber news bulletins and broadcasts from Don Bell at Manila.

The enemy was bombing Hong Kong and Singapore. Jap amphibious troops were landing near Vigan. Immense invasion forces were approaching the Philippines.

"Where is the United States Fleet?" jeered Tokyo Rose, introduced by a jiujitsu rendition of *It's Three o'clock in the Morning.* "I'll tell you where it is, boys. It's lying at the bottom of Pearl Harbor."

The Asiatic Fleet submariners knew better. They knew that S-boats and fleet submarines of their own force were entering action.

One of the veteran Manila boats had already featured in a memorable chapter of submarine history. When she headed out for her first war patrol, her officers and men may have been thinking of that other time she was rigged for a dive— May 23, 1939.

She was making a test dive off Portsmouth, N.H. Then instead of leveling off, she kept on going. Water in the engine room. Down by the stern. Mechanical failure in the operating gear of the main-engine air induction valve. The submarine hit bottom at 240 feet.

Few men had ever survived such a disaster, but miraculously 33 were saved. The sunken boat was located by the submarine SCULPIN, and a salvage rescue ship raced to the scene. Divers attached a McCann diving bell to the forward escape-hatch. Four times the bell was raised to the surface. So ended the tragic dive of the USS SQUALUS.

She was raised by Navy salvage engineers three months later and hauled into Portsmouth Navy Yard. Completely overhauled and refitted, she was recommissioned for active service as the USS SAILFISH.

But submariners remembered. A shadow lingered over this boat—a shadow undispelled by the wonder of her resurrection. Among the men she was known as the SQUAILFISH.

SAILFISH joined the SubsAsiatic Force with Lieutenant Commander Morton C. Mumma as her captain and Lieutenant Hiram Cassedy as her exec.

While the Japs were bombing Manila, she set out to put an end to any lingering superstitions. During a short 9-day trial patrol she made contact with an enemy convoy and burrowed in to fire four torpedoes at the troopships. Mumma reported a hit.

The hit could not be confirmed, and subsequent reports do not credit SAILFISH with either damaging or sinking this enemy. Possibly the torpedoes were prematures. The captain, who had exorcised the shades, transferred to the PT-boats. Under Lieutenant Commander Richard Voge, who was given her command, and later under Lieutenant Commander R. E. M. Ward, SAILFISH was to win the name of one of the great fighting submarines of the war.

SEAWOLF, another of the great, encountered her first enemy off the northeastern coast of Luzon, not far from Aparri. On the morning of December 14, about 0900, she sighted a Japanese destroyer, portside to, bearing three one zero relative.

Sea conditions prevented an attack on the DD. But the following morning Warder fired a spread of torpedoes at what looked like a big Jap seaplane tender. Explosions sounded like hits. But positive proof of a sinking could not be established, and Warder did not even claim damage.

SARGO (Lieutenant Commander Tyrrell D. Jacobs) sighted a convoy. Jacobs maneuvered the submarine into this herd of Nipponese ships, and fired five torpedoes. Each torpedo missed its mark. Baneful luck seemed to follow the submarine. On this, her first patrol, she made a total of eight day-submerged attacks—fired thirteen torpedoes with zero results and zero in the hearts of her crew. His patrol report was soon to feature in one of the war's more startling disclosures.

Meantime, another aggressive anti-*maru* campaign was begun by Chester Smith and crew of SWORDFISH, patrolling in the South China Sea. Smith launched four attacks. Fired nine torpedoes. Reported two sinkings. But the hits could not be confirmed.

December 15 (16 in her locality) was another day. This time SWORDFISH got her big one. She trapped her target off the coast of Hainan Island, made a submerged approach, and Smith fired three torpedoes. An undoubted hit roared in the sound gear, followed by the clash, crackle and static of breaking-up noises. Shrouded in smoke and fire, the large freighter was seen going down by the stern. This vessel was identified as the 8,663-ton ATSUTUSAN MARU. And SWORDFISH (Chester Smith and crew) won credit for the first confirmed sinking of a Japanese ship by a U.S. submarine.

These maiden war patrols of SAILFISH, SEAWOLF, SARGO and SWORDFISH were more or less typical of those accomplished by the other SubsAsiatic boats. One consistent adversity plagued all the submarines that entered combat during this desperate period. Like a dark thread in a pattern, it is woven through the record of the hard-pressed SubsAsiatic Force. Discernible in the patrol reports of SAILFISH, SEAWOLF, SARGO and SWORDFISH, it is apparent in the summarized experiences of the following submarines:

S-38 (Lieutenant W. G. Chapple) sighted a transport on December 12th. Directing a night-surface attack, Chapple fired one torpedo at the target. It sounded like a hit, but the damage could not be confirmed and the torpedo may have prematured.

S-39 (Lieutenant Coe) sighted a 5,000-ton AK on December 13th. Coe sent his S-boat boring in, and fired four torpedoes at the unsuspecting merchantman. He reported a solid hit. Damage or sinking could not be subsequently verified.

PICKEREL (Lieutenant Commander Bacon) sighted a Jap patrol craft on December 19th. Bacon fired a total of five torpedoes at this vicious little vessel—for a total of five zeroes.

Manned by crack crews under ace skippers, SPEARFISH, STURGEON, SEARAVEN, SNAPPER, PERMIT, SKIPJACK, PERCH and TARPON waylaid Jap freighters and warships, and fired torpedoes that should have hit each bull's-eye. The score? Zero.

The dark thread woven through the record delineates the didoes of a defective torpedo.

Action in Lingayen Gulf

In Lingayen Gulf, where the Japanese made their main landing, the submarines were balked at every turn. The experience proved the more bitter in that the landing at this point had been long expected. In anticipation of the enemy's move, S-36 (Lieutenant J. R. McKnight) had been dispatched to guard the area early in December. Defective radio gear forced the S-boat to abandon the patrol.

Meantime, STINGRAY (Lieutenant Commander R. S. Lamb) was shifted up to Lingayen to keep the Gulf under surveillance. She arrived in time to find the Gulf aswarm with Japanese transports. Her report, radioed on December 21, was the first indication that the invader had reached Lingayen Gulf. It was also an indication of the absence of Allied air reconnaissance. Had aircraft been on hand to observe the enemy's advance on the Gulf, a strong group of submarines could have been mustered to intercept the invasion forces.

As it was, four more submarines were rushed to Lingayen's waters in answer to STINGRAY's report. These were S-36 (Lieutenant W. G. Chapple), S-40 (Lieutenant Nicholas Lucker, Jr.), SAURY (Lieutenant Commander J. L. Burnside), and SALMON (Lieutenant Commander E. B. McKinney). Here, for the first time in the war, submarines had an opportunity to disrupt a full-scale enemy landing. The counterstrike failed for a number of reasons.

First, the move was belated. Then, the invading force was legion, and could gang up on the scattered defenders in such fashion that the contest would be all but suicidal. Finally, shallow Lingayen Gulf did not lend itself to submarine defense. The Japanese exploited the obvious marine advantage with an invasion fleet composed of small vessels which could barge around in four or five fathoms of water. In the background were heavy units of Vice Admiral Kondo's Second Fleet which was supporting the Philippines invasion. Inject into the equation an undependable torpedo, and the plight of the submarines is evident.

Only two of the five at Lingayen traded hard blows with the enemy, and but one of the five managed to penetrate the Gulf. One of the hard blows was struck by SALMON late in the evening of December 22, when, patrolling the approaches to the Gulf, she engaged in a scrimmage with the enemy in the backfield.

The scrimmage began when SALMON's lookouts spotted a ship off in the gloom. In the thickening twilight the vessel was not at once recognized as a Japanese destroyer, and by the time SALMON made identification, the warship was up ahead and turning toward the submarine. Simultaneously a companion destroyer hove into view.

McKinney kept SALMON on course while the destroyers advanced slowly, boxing her in. For perhaps half an hour this game went on, the DD's and the submarine withholding fire while the dusk darkened and the atmosphere was like a drawn breath. Certainly the Japs by this time had recognized the American conning tower.

"I confess I felt a lot like diving," McKinney said later. "But I was curious, too. We stayed on the surface and the DD's came on. I guess the Jap skippers were just as inexperienced and puzzled as I was."

Sooner or later this prickly armistice was bound to burst —the surface was not big enough for a submarine and two enemy destroyers. And SALMON's bridge personnel were feeling the strain when McKinney decided to end the byplay.

The criss-crossing warships had come too close for comfort, and the range was too good for further delay. One of the destroyers was crossing SALMON's stern. McKinney gave the order to fire two torpedoes.

The DD saw them coming, and veered aside. The torpedoes missed. The "party" was over now. The destroyers came charging, one behind the other, to ram and blast the submarine.

McKinney clung to the bridge. If he took SALMON down (a suggestion made by several of his officers) she would be in for a depth-charge lambasting. With two "fish" remaining in the stern tubes, he could get in a solid shot at the rampaging "cans."

The leading destroyer was charging head-on. Plumes of spray made flying wings under her bow, and her smoke streamed back flat. McKinney gave the order "Fire—!" The torpedo sped on its way.

In the last of the gloaming the destroyer saw the deadly wake, and started a swing to starboard. McKinney and his bridge personnel saw a geyser spout high where the torpedo must have struck the DD directly under her bridge.

The second torpedo was on its way, heading straight for the No. 2 destroyer which had swung to port. McKinney "pulled the plug" at this moment, and Sound reported echoes of demolition.

Three days later, having avoided a hunting party of patrol boats, corvettes and destroyers, SALMON was on the track of an enemy transport. McKinney directed a night-surface attack, and fired four torpedoes at the silhouetted AP. Unluckily none hit.

The waters off Lingayen Gulf were boiling when SALMON finally quit the area. But crew and captain were satisfied they had done a good week's work. In firing at the oncoming lead destroyer, McKinney launched one of the first "down-the-throat" shots on record—a torpedo aimed squarely at the nose of a vessel and calculated to strike her if she veers either way.

The sinking of a Japanese destroyer during the Lingayen invasion could not subsequently be corroborated.

While SALMON was not credited with a kill, her captain and crew were credited for a display of what it takes to run a fighting submersible—guts.

Meanwhile, SAURY attacked a Jap destroyer on the evening of December 22nd. The torpedo failed to strike, and SAURY went under to evade a depth charging.

Three of the other submarines at Lingayen had indifferent luck. But S-38 got in where they were, and her battle inside the Gulf remains one of the outstanding submarine forays of the war.

S-38 vs. All the Odds

On the evening of December 21, S-38 received radio orders to proceed into Lingayen Gulf. Early the following morning, she entered that baleful body of water, crossing the seaward end of the reef that extends north from Cape Bolinao. By taking his submarine across the reef in this fashion, S-38's skipper, Lieutenant Wreford (Moon) Chapple, probably out-flanked the destroyer patrol that was barring the entrance of the other submarines.

In the dark before dawn the S-boat submerged. By 0615 it was light enough for a periscope survey of the situation, and the scope was quickly focused on a clutter of Japanese transports. The transports were guarded by circling destroyers and several large motor launches laden with depth charges. Chapple immediately began approach maneuvers, and, undetected, S-38 gained firing position.

Chapple fired four torpedoes at four selected targets. Aimed at a 3,000-ton transport, the first torpedo missed. The second torpedo missed. The third torpedo missed. The fourth torpedo missed. S-38 was experiencing the plague which ruined the bravest efforts of the war-going submarine forces. Unbeknown to Chapple and crew, the Mark 10 torpedo carried by the S-boats was running four feet deeper than set. And each of the four torpedoes just fired had passed impotently under its intended target.

Chapple presumed he had misjudged the draft of the Jap vessels, estimated as 12 feet. His next torpedo was set for a depth of nine feet. The S-boat, of course, had only four tubes, and Chapple had ordered her deep under for a reload after the firing of her opening salvo.

All chance for a surprise attack went glimmering with the four misses. Sighting the torpedo wakes, enemy lookouts raised the alarm. As the S-boat's crew rushed reload operations, a Jap destroyer raced over on the hunt and dropped three fairly close depth charges. The other escorts began a search for the intruding submarine, the DD's probing with supersonic. For three-quarters of an hour, the S-boat dodged and veered this way and that, evading her furious pursuers. She managed to elude them in this game of tag, and at 0758 Chapple had her once more at periscope depth, stalking an anchored transport—a "sitting duck."

Moving in on this unsuspecting target, Chapple fired two torpedoes at close range. Thirty seconds later there was a boat-rocking explosion, and three minutes after that, Jap destroyers were blasting the tide around the S-boat, attempting to gouge her out of the water.

Rigged for depth charges, the submarine went deep—that is, as deep as a submersible could go in those turbulent shallows. For the next hour and a half, S-38 burrowed in one direction and then another, striving to escape the "pinging" destroyers which were determined to track her down. While thus maneuvering to evade, she sideswiped a submerged ledge and threatened to broach. Chapple ordered the auxiliary tanks flooded, and the submarine groped her way along the bottom, bumping as she coasted.

Presently she ran into a mud bank. Chapple stopped all machinery except the motor generator on the lighting circuits. Men took off their shoes and conversed in whispers. The S-boat "played possum," listening. Sometimes the depth charges sounded distant and sometimes they sounded close aboard as the destroyers continued a frantic hunt. The DD's were persistent, and S-38 could do nothing but sit it out.

Moon Chapple started a cribbage game in the control room, but no player could honestly say he was interested. In other quarters of the submarine the men began to think about the S-boat's lack of air conditioning. Nobody talked much or moved about—at their stations the men remained silent, conserving oxygen. Time dragged. One hour. Two hours. Small boats passed overhead at regular intervals. Some large vessel fouled the clearing lines and bent the submarine's forward stub mast. Was her number up? Another tense wait in perspiration and inertia.

Moisture condensed on the bulkheads and began to drip as the air thickened, becoming mephitic. It was as though the submarine herself were sweating in the stifling heat. Soda lime was sprinkled to absorb the carbon dioxide.

Sound reported high-speed screws coming back again.

Chapple ordered the sound man to stow his phones. What couldn't be cured had to be endured, and it was easier to endure it without hearing it.

The "pinging" continued for most of the day, but died out after sundown. The deck was greased with sweat, the heat becoming unendurable and the air unbreathable when Chapple finally decided it was dark enough to surface. Exhausted men blew her ballast as her skipper backed her out of the mud. The port propeller was damaged, but S-38 got clear, and at 2100 was proceeding submerged toward the west side of the Gulf. There were 11 inches of mercury pressure in the boat when Chapple finally ordered her to the surface. After 12 hours of submergence, all hands were wilting, and it was high time for fresh air and a battery charge.

At 2300 the boat was on the surface, going ahead on one engine and charging batteries with the other.

Her conning tower had not been long in the fresh air when S-38 was sighted by a patrolling destroyer, and once more she had to go under. The boat had been aired somewhat, but her weary crewmen could have used more relief, and now they were in for another ordeal.

So, S-38 received another "going over," laconic enough in her patrol report, but extensively punishing in reality. Again she managed to evade. Finally she reached a position a mile off the beach where she was anchored in 18 fathoms of water. At dawn Chapple ordered a stationary dive to the bottom, and the submarine remained there throughout that day, giving the crew a chance to rest. At sunset the S-boat surfaced and remained at anchor, charging batteries. She was forced under once by a patrol boat, and it was not until 0500 on December 24 that the battery charge was completed and the air tanks were filled.

With night fading in the east, Chapple started S-38 on a tour of the Gulf. Cautious periscope exposures were made now and then, and a distant destroyer was finally sighted. Then six transports trudged into view, heading south. Chapple was maneuvering to close the range when a thunderclap explosion—probably an aircraft bomb—blasted the water not far from the submarine. Both control room depth gages were put temporarily out of commission. Chapple took her down to 90 feet and headed north, evading by silent running.

From noon until sunset, patrol boats hounded her. At 2230 on that Christmas Eve she ran aground a second time. The jolt gave her a shaking up, but the crew brought her clear, and Chapple ordered her to the surface off Hundred Islands.

No sooner had the water drained from the superstructure

with the boat riding high, than there was an explosion in the after battery! Chapple had given the order to ventilate the hull outboard and the battery into the engine room.

Apparently someone started the blowers too soon, before the air had time to circulate and freshen the gaseous atmosphere in the battery room. A spark from the thrown blower-switch may have caused the blast. Chapple rushed below. Thick smoke was surging from the compartment, and fire flickered in its gloomed interior.

Two men had been painfully burned by the explosion, and Chief Machinist's Mate Harbin had suffered a broken spine. The captain and a young electrician's mate carried out the injured Chief.

Two or three of the battery cells were found to be cracked, and the electricians worked at top speed to cut the damaged cells out of the circuit. Daylight of December 25 was graying the east before the mangled battery room was cleaned up. There was one relieving note—a radio dispatch ordering the S-boat to leave the Gulf. Then it was discovered that the engine-room hatch, which had been opened, could not be tightly closed because of deteriorated gaskets. While the men struggled to dog down the hatch, the lookouts sighted a destroyer squadron bearing down. Just in time the hatch was secured.

S-38 got deep enough to evade, but thanks to her damaged and noisy propeller, she was presently picked up by a patrol boat that drove her to the bottom. Then for a third time, she ran aground! The submarine was jammed on a mud bank with her bow angled up 50 feet higher than her stern. But the crewmen kept the pumps going, and finally she worked free. Only to slide down the mud bank to a depth of 350 feet—one hundred and fifty feet deeper than her tested depth. The ballast tank compressed enough to cause the battery decks to buckle up, but they expanded as she surfaced. Then, in coming to periscope depth, the submarine broached.

Every Japanese lookout in the harbor must have seen this spectacle, and the S-38 crew expected the Japs to attack with the enthusiasm of harpooners who have sighted a spouting whale. In desperation, Chapple held the submarine on the surface. She was on the reef north of Bolinao, and nothing was in sight. Then two destroyers appeared about 12 miles distant on the other side of the reef. Chapple sent her down under once more, hoping to evade detection. While the submarine was creeping forward she struck an underwater obstruction.

The jolt smashed the outer glass of several gages, splintered the paint on bulkheads, shook the boat from stem to stern. But to offset this last blow, there was one Christmas gift. Chapple sent S-38 to the surface, determined to run for it, and the two destroyers turned out to be one auxiliary vessel which failed to sight the sub.

Hours later, S-38 worked her way out of Lingayen, and headed for Manila. Only Spartan courage, surpassing skill and a relenting smile from Lady Luck brought her through. Depth bombs, groundings, underwater collision, a broaching, mechanical maladjustments and an internal explosion had been defeated by all hands and a boat remarkable for stamina.

Official records credit S-38 with sinking the second Japanese ship on the American undersea score—HAYO MARU, freighter, 5,445 tons—the transport torpedoed at its anchorage inside the Gulf.

Guarding the approaches to Vigan, north of Lingayen Gulf, the submarine SEAL (Lieutenant Commander Hurd) torpedoed and sank the third and last Japanese ship destroyed by American submarine fire in December 1941. This vessel, sunk on the 23rd, was HAYATAKA MARU, a small 850-ton freighter.

The transport downed by S-38 was the only ship sunk by the Asiatic Fleet submarines dispatched to intercept the Japanese invasion forces at Lingayen. One transport out of an armada which numbered more than 80 ships does not stand as impressive on the record. What stands as impressive is the performance of the crews who manned such boats as S-38, and the fact that, outnumbered scores to one, and handicapped by a defective weapon, the submarines that met the enemy in the Philippines survived at all.

Strategic Withdrawal

December 25th Manila was declared an open city. The Philippine capital was militarily indefensible. General MacArthur had already begun his withdrawal toward the Bataan Peninsula where he hoped his troops could maintain a stand until the arrival of reinforcements. Rear Admiral Francis W. Rockwell had gone to Corregidor to establish a naval headquarters. And to prevent a wholesale slaughter of the Manila populace, the remaining American military and naval forces were ordered to evacuate.

Loss of Manila was a severe blow to the submarine command. It compelled the abandonment of practically all S-boat spares and many Mark 14 torpedoes—an extremely serious deprivation to a force already worried about replacements.

Before leaving Manila, the SubsAsiatic Command Staff was divided into two groups. It was decided that the S-boats and some of the fleet submarines should use the facilities of the Dutch Submarine Base at Soerabaja in the Netherlands East Indies.

Meantime, the tender HOLLAND had been ordered to proceed to Darwin, Australia. As head of the administrative part of the divided staff. Captain James Fife, Jr., was to establish headquarters in Darwin.

Admiral Hart left Manila by submarine, traveling to Java on SHARK (Lieutenant Commander Shane.)

On December 31, the last submarine left Manila Bay. She was SWORDFISH, heading for Soerabaja with Captain John Wilkes and his operational staff.

Among a few remaining units were the submarine rescue vessel PIGEON and the submarine tender CANOPUS.

General Homma marched into Manila the day after New Year's, and the Imperial Japanese Navy forged an iron ring around the Philippine Islands.

It remained for American submarines to lead the counteroffensive that smashed that ring.

Chapter 4

Undersea Lanes to Victory

Strategic Imperative

On New Year's Day, 1942, representatives of 26 Allied countries convened in Washington. There, in the White House, they signed the document which founded the United Nations. But there were grave expressions among the signers. This two-ocean war against the Axis was going to be a long war. A horde of U-boats was cutting the Anglo-American lifeline in the Atlantic. In the Pacific a small fleet of American submarines was the mainstay of the Allied naval defense.

The U-boats must be defeated. American submarines must hold the Pacific defense line until reinforcements arrived. On these two imperatives hinged the outcome of the two-ocean war.

Pacific Defense Line

Following the Pearl Harbor debacle, President Roosevelt appointed Admiral Ernest J. King Commander-in-Chief of the U.S. Fleet with Headquarters in Washington, D.C. Vice Admiral Royal E. Ingersoll replaced Admiral King as Commander-in-Chief of the Atlantic Fleet and Admiral Hart remained in command of the Asiatic Fleet. And Admiral Chester W. Nimitz, making a secret flight from Washington to Pearl Harbor in civvies, on the last day of December 1941 became Commander-in-Chief of the Pacific Fleet.

Navy men noted that both Admiral King and Admiral Nimitz were, like Admiral Hart, veterans of the undersea

49

service. Thus, of the four top-ranking admirals of the Navy, three were prominent submarine officers.

No naval officer in submarines was better qualified to wear the dolphins than Fleet Admiral Chester W. Nimitz. It was a submariner's submariner who took hold at Pearl Harbor on that black New Year's Eve of 1941.

Before he left Washington for Pearl Harbor Admiral Nimitz realized he was facing an unparalleled defense problem.

Months would pass before the Pacific Fleet could be strongly reinforced. With its surface arm broken and its air arm badly wounded, it could only retreat before the Japanese juggernaut.

Retreat how far? The Japanese must not be permitted to break through the Central Pacific or the island chains flanking Australia. Nor could they be allowed to gain a foothold in the Aleutians. A line drawn from Dutch Harbor to Midway, to Samoa, to New Caledonia, to Australia marked the frontier to be held by American and Allied forces.

Submarine Strategy

This is an axiom of warfare: Where concealment is equally available to both sides, it favors the inferior force.

The Philippines invasion supplied naval strategists with a notable demonstration of the axiom. It gave American submarines a narrow margin which enabled them to operate in enemy-infested seas and carry out their primary mission—the destruction of Japanese shipping.

The Imperial Navy did not lose a single major unit during the Philippines invasion. But as the Japanese moved down on the Malay Barrier they began to lose merchant ships here and there. And with the advent of the New Year, ships started going down off the coasts of Japan. American submarines were beginning the war of attrition.

Preview of Victory

The submarine forces in the Pacific "got in there" and fought. The Manila boats diverted the enemy's naval vanguard and impeded the drive on the Netherlands East Indies. Pearl Harbor submarines joined battle in the Central Pacific, patrolled the line extending from Australia to the Aleutians, drove over to the East China Sea and cut the shipping lanes to Japan.

With mid-Pacific bases lost—with Asiatic bases lost—with air cover lost—the Pacific Fleet immobilized—supplies cut off—spare parts lost—Manila torpedoes captured—with all these disadvantages, the submariners entered the conflict and kept on going.

They kept on going, despite the fact that the enemy had the initiative. The fact that the S-boats were old and the enemy destroyers new—that Japanese bombs were known to contain an explosive charge greater than any at that time developed by the Allies. Loss of forward bases, fleet support, repair facilities, stores—these never imperilled the submarines as did torpedo failure. *For almost two years American submarines went into action handicapped by a defective torpedo!*

In spite of this and all other handicaps, the submariners led the United States offensive. They aided in the defense of Midway and battled the foe in the Aleutians. They helped to parry the enemy's thrust at Guadalcanal. They blockaded the ports of the Jap home Empire. Laid mines. Reconnoitered for air strikes. Rescued refugees. Served as lifeguards. Struck the Imperial Navy some of the hardest blows it ever received. Swept the merchant fleets of the Rising Sun from the Central and Southwest Pacific. Penetrated the Sea of Japan. And finally halted at the beachheads of Kyushu, Shikoku, Hokkaido and Honshu.

Above all, the U.S. submarines accomplished the No. 1 mission of submarining. They sank ships!

In the Addenda the reader will find the score sheet of those sinkings—indelible testimony to the ruthless efficiency and superb valor of the U.S. Submarine Force. Composed of no more than 1.6% of the Navy's personnel, this incomparable service arm accounted for 73% of Japanese ship losses from all causes during the first two years of the Pacific War. The final score, verified by post-war inquest, credits U.S. submarines with sinking 54.7% of the Japanese merchantmen and 29% of the Japanese naval vessels sunk in World War II.

The figures sum up the record. The following chapters detail the manner of its making.

PART TWO

The Fighting Defense

(1942)

Though I Be Wounded, I Am Not Slain!
I'll Lie Me Down To Bleed Awhile,
And Then I'll Rise and Fight Again!
EARLY ENGLISH BALLAD

Chapter 5

Pioneers Pacific

 ☆ ☆ ☆

Oceanic Job

With patrol areas extending from the Aleutians southward to the Solomons, New Guinea, and the Dutch East Indies, and from Midway westward to the coast of China and Indo-China, the American submariners in the Pacific had a whale of a job on their hands. One square mile of land (640 acres) is a sizable piece of real estate. A square mile of ocean is even larger, for the nautical mile is longer than the statute mile. A million square miles adds up to a lot of acreage by land or sea. With these figures in mind, one can appreciate the task detailed to the Pacific and Asiatic Fleet submarines—the task of driving Japanese shipping from some 8,000,000 square miles (over 5,000,000,000 acres) of ocean. Evenly divided among the 50 starting submarines, this oceanic sphere would have yielded 10,000,000 acres apiece!

Of course, the Pacific vastness was not apportioned in such fashion. In general, the patrolling Pacific Fleet (Pearl Harbor) submarines restricted their operations to particular areas assigned, covering waters where enemy ship traffic was anticipated. The Asiatic Fleet (Manila) submarines were detailed to strategic sectors of a fluid front that constantly shifted with the advance of the Japanese offensive.

With but 50 submarines to do the job (and experience soon revealed that not more than one-third of these could be maintained on patrol station simultaneously—the other two-thirds being either en route to or from the area, or undergoing refit or overhaul) the submarine effort had to be spread exceedingly thin. Throughout the greater part of 1942 the problem of area coverage remained an equation in which pressures had to be balanced against probable results.

Pioneer Tactics (Day-periscope Attack)

The first three submarines to go out on war patrol from Pearl Harbor—GUDGEON, PLUNGER and POLLACK—were pioneers in a number of respects. They were the first Pacific Fleet submarines to make the long and hazardous 3,400-mile voyage from Oahu to Japan. As such, they were the first American submarines to invade Empire waters. And they were first in other militant ways and means.

PLUNGER, patrolling the Kii Suido Area with the first radar set carried into action, was first to test the air defenses of the Japanese homeland. POLLACK, in the Tokyo Bay Area, sank the No. 1 Japanese merchantman on the Pacific Fleet Submarine Force list. GUDGEON scored a first that was original in the annals of the U.S. Navy—by sinking the first enemy warship in history to go down from the fire of a United States submarine.

PLUNGER had an adventurous maiden patrol. While she tested Japan's air defenses with her novel radar equipment, she underwent the first depth-charging sustained by a Pacific Fleet submarine.

Absorbing this punishment, PLUNGER's pioneers learned a number of things about the enemy's anti-submarine tactics. Such warcraft as assailed PLUNGER repeatedly demonstrated a facility for locating submerged submarines by means of sonar. The Japanese were to lag behind in wartime development of electronics, but at the war's beginning their sonar devices were good. Good enough, at any rate, to worry PLUNGER.

The depth charges which thundered around PLUNGER amounted to something like 2½ tons of explosive. The depth charge was the favorite anti-submarine weapon of the Japanese, and the Imperial Navy was later known to feature a king-size model weighing close to 1,000 pounds. The charges dropped on PLUNGER, however, were probably the standard Type 2, Model 2—350-pounders which had an explosive charge of about 230 pounds. Japanese fleet destroyers carried 30 depth charges of this type.

Two weeks later PLUNGER's submariners demonstrated that they could deal it out as well. Sighting a Japanese freighter, Lieutenant Commander David C. White sent his crew to battle stations and directed a day-periscope attack. Early battle reports were as brief as these Pacific pioneers were stoic, and the official account of PLUNGER'S action is as bare of drama as a recital in arithmetic.

Between the lines, however, a reader can visualize half-naked men racing through the submarine's interior as the alarm sends them to battle stations. The approach party in a huddle over the plotting table in the control room. Hands working the wheel that opens the outer doors to the bow tubes. Torpedomen tense at their stations. The sound man crouched at his gear. Engineers at their posts in the forward and aft engine rooms. Electricians at the controls. The glistening metal shaft of the periscope gliding up and down in its well in answer to sharp orders from the captain. Up periscope! Down periscope! Up periscope! The commanding officer pressing his forehead to the sponge-rubber eyepiece for another look at the nearing target. Rotating the pillar with his arms draped over the training handles. Steady! Stand by to fire one! Now—! Action, suspense, lightning decision, and reflex action high-geared into a teamwork that made of submarine and submariners a unified precision machine.

Apparently White's direction of the approach was conventional as to method, ending in a demonstration of the normal daytime periscope attack. The day-periscope attack —as distinguished from the deep submerged attack in which fire control depended solely on sound apparatus, and the night-surface, or night-periscope attack—remained the fundamental method of torpedo attack throughout the early part of the war. Contrary to pre-war expectations, sound attacks conducted from deep submergence soon proved to be of minor importance. There had been little training for the night-periscope attack, which was always limited by visibility conditions. And the night-surface attack, conducted from the submarine's bridge, did not come into its own until 1943 when fire control was considerably advanced by radar.

Before the war, the day-periscope attack had been featured as the chief battle tactic to be mastered by combat submarines. This proved fortunate, for the problems presented by the periscope attack were fundamental to the torpedo fire control problem. With good instruments for the conduct of the periscope attack, only minor adaptations remained necessary to meet new developments. As designed and devised by U.S. submariners and technicians, American torpedo fire control instruments and methods were second to none.

Primitive submarines of the HOLLAND type had to be maneuvered into position so that their bow tubes aimed directly at the target and the torpedo was fired point-blank—in effect, the submarine served as a gun which was trained on target for the firing of a projectile. Improvement of the gyroscopic steering apparatus permitted the setting of gyro angles which determined the torpedo's course. According to the gyro angle which was set, the torpedo could be made to run dead ahead, or veer off on a tangent.

Detection and sighting of the target depended on the lookout's eye and on short-range "listening gear" until sonar entered the picture as both an anti-submarine device and a device employed in torpedo fire control. Submarines were ordered to run deep between periscope exposures to escape air observation. Firing by sound from deep submergence was encouraged. While it reduced the chances of a hit by about one-half, an attack made without any periscope exposure also greatly reduced the possibility of detection.

The torpedo data computer (T.D.C.) now made its appearance. This device continuously computed the hitting gyro angle, and either transmitted it to the torpedo room or automatically set the angle on the torpedo. Installation of this robot computer ended the necessity of maneuvering a submarine into position on a predetermined course in order to launch torpedoes on a selected track with a selected gyro angle. Thus last-minute submarine maneuvers were practically eliminated once a favorable firing position had been obtained. The torpedo was angled to suit the condition of fire.

Although new fire control devices were to be developed, the standard doctrine for making a submerged daylight periscope attack, as practiced by the Pacific pioneers, was to undergo little change throughout the remainder of the war. When a submarine established contact with enemy smoke or masts on the horizon, the first problem was to determine the target's direction by a few observations in the change in true bearing. When this was done, the submarine came to the "normal approach course," closing the target's track on a course at right angles to the true bearing.

During the approach the submarine endeavored to draw within 1,000 yards of the target's track, at a range equal to about 7½ minutes of the target's run and within two minutes since the last zigzag. From such a position (and barring unforeseen eventualities), the submarine's attack was assured. The approach phase was now ended, and the submarine commenced maneuvers to gain the best possible firing position.

The ideal firing position would place the submarine on a course for the optimum track angle (a little more than 90°) with small or zero gyro angles and a firing range of about 1,000 yards. This ideal, however, was not an imperative. As the war progressed and sufficient data became available for statistical analysis of torpedo shots, several surprising facts were disclosed. For example, it was found that shots fired at 3,000 yards scored about as often as those fired at 1,000.

The tendency for percentage hits to hold up with increased range proves difficult to explain. Theoretically, an increase in range should mean a decrease in hits, but actually a falling off in percentage hits at close range is revealed by the statistics. It can only be assumed that control errors mount rapidly with the heightening of emergency as range is reduced, and that the incidental errors are caused by the rapid rate of change of bearing incident to close ranges.

In any event, on January 18, 1942, PLUNGER was operating in the realm of actuality, not theory. And Lieutenant Commander White, at the periscope, was observing the course, speed, range and size of a Jap cargo ship (AK). His estimate of her size, recorded as 7,200 tons, was on the heavy side—a common error in the guesswork of those days. But his other figures were right "on the beam." Appropriate data were fed into the T.D.C. Gyro angles were set automatically. PLUNGER was maneuvered into the best possible firing position. And two torpedoes were fired for two hits.

Down at sea went EIZAN MARU, 4,700 tons. "X" marked the spot at lat. 33-30 N., long. 135 E. Score one for PLUNGER.

Of more significance than this successful day-periscope attack was PLUNGER's pioneer work with radar. Making no contacts on her SD aircraft warning installation, PLUNGER substantiated supposition that the Japanese had not set up extensive air patrols over the Empire.

PLUNGER's pioneers turned to Pearl Harbor after 52 days with the assurance of explorers who have accomplished a voyage of discovery. Successful patrol!

Pioneer Tactics (*Night-periscope and Night-surface Attack*)

Another adventurous pioneer patrol was POLLACK's, skippered by Lieutenant Commander Stanley P. Moseley. POLLACK was cruising off the south coast of Honshu on New Year's Eve.

Lookout sighted a small Japanese destroyer bustling across the dark seascape, and Moseley sent his men to battle stations. As POLLACK slid under the waves, she began the first night-periscope attack made by a SubPac submarine.

POLLACK's pioneers encountered a difficulty which troubled many submarines early in the war. The periscope then in use was inadequate for night operations. Only on clear, bright moonlight nights was the instrument wholly effective. Even so the periscope in use at the outbreak of World War II was a scientific marvel in comparison with the myopic World War I model. Automatically raised and lowered in its well, the modern scope could be elevated to a height which afforded vision to a submerged submarine operating at a "keel depth" of over 50 feet. The best in optical science had gone into the lens system, employing devices which absorbed excess light and greatly clarified the image. On some of the large submarines three periscopes had been installed. But night vision remained dim.

Directing POLLACK's attack on the DD off the Honshu coast, Lieutenant Commander Moseley found it impossible to distinguish enough of the target's features to make an accurate estimation of course or range. As the destroyer blurred off in the night, Moseley fired two torpedoes, hoping for a hit. Both missed, and the opportunity was gone. Moseley resolved to avoid the tactic thereafter unless conditions were extremely favorable.

POLLACK scored off Tokyo Bay on January 7, sinking DAI I UNKAI MARU, a small freighter. Moseley got in with a daytime periscope approach.

Then, on the night of the 9th, POLLACK scored with a night-surface attack. As was the case with most of the submarines of this period, POLLACK was not equipped with radar. A surface attack required the utmost in competence and daring. Moseley and his crew had what it took.

American submarines had not been adequately prepared for night warfare—nor had such preparation been possible. Due to the hazards inherent in night exercises, and the difficulties involved in simulating a submarine attack, pre-war training in night-surface tactics had been superficial. For night firing on the surface, experienced submarine officers recommended that the periscope angle computed for a straight bow shot be set as a gyro angle on the torpedoes, and the order to fire be given as the point of aim passed the jackstaff.

These or similar methods were employed by Moseley on that night of January 9 when POLLACK made contact with a merchantman off Inubo Saki, Honshu. Target was picked up at 0050. In spite of the fact that DAI I UNKAI MARU had been torpedoed in this vicinity two nights before, the Jap steamer was burning dimmed running lights. Evidently this freighter's captain did not believe lightning could strike twice in the same place. Moseley undertook to prove the old rule by an exception.

At 0130, after a 40-minute surface approach, Moseley fired two torpedoes from the bow tubes—and missed! Whether the failure lay in faulty torpedoes or faulty fire control, the records fail to indicate. If faults there were, Moseley managed to correct them. Swinging POLLACK around, he brought her stern tubes to bear. Two more torpedoes rushed at the target, and one hit the target squarely. TEIAN MARU, 5,387 tons, went down by the stern.

Later that same night Moseley ordered a submerged attack on a DD which came foaming out on the prowl. Again he was presented with a difficult night-periscope problem. He fired one torpedo at the destroyer—missed—and then removed POLLACK from the neighborhood.

That concluded the drama in his submarine's first patrol. But she had experienced enough. Having sunk two ships totalling some 11,000 tons, with the possible addition of a 4,000-tonner, POLLACK returned to home base, after 39 days, with all torpedoes expended. Successful patrol!

Gudgeon vs. I-173

First of the Pacific Fleet submarines to leave Pearl Harbor for a foray into Japan's home waters, GUDGEON patrolled the Bungo Suido area in comparative peace and quiet. This was not the fault of her skipper, Lieutenant Commander Elton W. Grenfell. Doughty as they make 'em, Grenfell (known to the force as "Jumping Joe") was looking for action. And he kept GUDGEON on her toes, so to speak, and ready for the gong. But, predictions to the contrary, ship traffic was almost conspicious by its absence from the western entrance to the sea of Japan. For GUDGEON the gong rang only twice in the Bungo Suido area, and both rounds were to prove disappointment. On January 4, contact was made with a cargo ship. Grenfell directed a day-submerged attack on this AK, and fired two torpedoes for two misses. On the 10th of January another freighter was sighted. Directing a night-surface attack, Grenfell maneuvered GUDGEON into position and fired three shots at this likely target. Two torpedoes appeared to hit. A sinking was cheerfully reported but it could not be confirmed by the investigation made later. Things were like that with submarines and ships that passed in the night.

As were her companion pioneers in those early days, GUDGEON was hampered by lack of radar, by night-periscope difficulties, by inadequate fire control apparatus, and by torpedo trouble. Her operations were also inhibited by headquarters instructions which read: *"When within radius of enemy patrol planes (about 500 miles) it will generally be advisable to remain submerged during daylight, proceeding on the surface during dark."*

GUDGEON's instructions were in keeping with that prewar doctrine which overestimated the aircraft as a submarine foe. In anticipation of heavy losses, submarine skippers were ordered to proceed with "extreme caution." Headquarters believed that the only hope of inflicting serious damage on the enemy lay in the use of such tactics as firing by sound from deep submergence, and avoiding surface exposure as much as possible. GUDGEON's submariners were indoctrinated accordingly. But peacetime doctrine and authoritative tactical concept were soon to undergo speedy revisions, and GUDGEON's practical experiences played a part in the changes made.

Commander Submarines, Pacific Fleet, was to comment on GUDGEON's patrol report:

It is noted that the GUDGEON spent a total of 51 days from base to base, of which only 12 were submerged on station. Eight days prior to the arrival on station, and seven days after departure from station or a total of 15 days, GUDGEON submerged during daylight. This represents a terrific overhead in time, a great part of which should have been spent on station. It is realized GUDGEON did not have radar for plane detection, but it is considered that with efficient lookouts more surface cruising could have been done prior to and after departure from station. The GUDGEON reports only two aircraft having been sighted, and these in the operating area.

Here is an indication of the rapidity with which tactical concepts can shed peacetime theory for wartime practice. Within a period of 51 days, ComSubPac was able to criticize adversely a patrol carried out in conformance with original operational instructions.

However, the sharpest of lookouts and the best of electronic devices cannot produce ships in areas where they are absent. After days of unproductive search GUDGEON was forced to head homeward with an empty bag and a large supply of unused torpedoes.

Then, on January 25, when GUDGEON was about 600 miles off Midway, events took another turn.

On January 26—time: 2320—GUDGEON received a message from ComSubPac. When last located, one of three enemy submarines was on a track which had her heading for GUDGEON's immediate vicinity.

Grenfell and his officers eagerly studied the chart. True enough, if the enemy sub continued on her present course, she would all but collide with GUDGEON the following morning. Here was the opportunity begged for by every submarine skipper—a chance to bag an enemy warship! Grenfell decided to maintain a submerged patrol and attempt to nail the Jap submarine from ambush.

Submarine warfare against submarines is warfare in a medium of fast action. The duelists are more or less evenly matched and each is acquainted with the methods and capacities of submarining. The submersible is the only naval craft which can pursue an enemy submarine beneath the sea, and a deadly underwater contest can develop after contact. Results of such combat are most difficult to ascertain. But when the submarine attacked is on the surface, and the attacker is the one submerged, the target may be watched by periscope and the outcome discerned. Such was the case with GUDGEON and the Japanese submarine which came junketing over the horizon on the morning of January 27th.

At 0859 GUDGEON's sound man detected the enemy's screw. Periscope contact followed immediately. At the scope, GUDGEON's exec, Lieutenant H. B. Lyon, could hardly believe the luck. As though without a care in the world, the big I-boat was excursioning along in the morning sunshine, cutting the surface at a speed of around 15 knots, her prow pointed for Japan.

Men raced to battle stations as Captain Grenfell took over the periscope to direct GUDGEON's approach. Praying that the enemy's sonar man might be slightly deaf, he set GUDGEON on the enemy's track. Course, speed and other factors were rushed through the T.D.C. Down periscope! Up periscope! Grenfell, too, could hardly credit his vision as he watched the Japanese submarine grow on the periscope scale —saw the Jap officers standing on the bridge—brown faces in a cluster—men around the conning tower, sunning.

Time: 0908. Fire one! Fire two! Fire three! Streaking the surface with a frothy ribbon, the first torpedo ran straight for the mark as GUDGEON's periscope went down. Sound heard the roar of a violent explosion, and a tremor went through the American submarine. A moment later there was another detonation. Then silence in the listening gear—only the sound of GUDGEON's motors running.

Grenfell kept her under, thinking of other Jap subs in the area. And two could play at this game. But when he raised the periscope after a cautious interval for a look-see, it was no-see.

But it was not until GUDGEON reached Pearl Harbor that the crew of Grenfell's boat shook hands all around—the first U.S. submariners in history to score the first confirmed sink-

ing of an enemy warship. Grenfell had reported only damage, but ComSubPac had the word. A trio of Japanese submarines reported off Midway had been traced there from the
American Pacific coast. Radio had traced two of the trio all
the way home, but the third I-boat had evaporated somewhere
around lat. 28-24, N., long. 178-35 E.—where GUDGEON
fired those three torpedoes. Subsequently identified by post-
war investigation, GUDGEON's victim proved to be I-173, a
Japanese cruiser submarine, 1,785 tons.

A Fleet Headquarters release packed into the following
paragraph the story of those pioneer submarines who blazed
that perilous Pearl Harbor-Japan trail.

*THEY CAME BACK TO THEIR BASE—GRINNING,
TRIUMPHANT, TACITURN. MOST OF THEM HADN'T
SEEN THE LIGHT OF DAY FOR WEEKS. THEY HAD
CARRIED THE WAR RIGHT TO THE ENEMY'S FRONT
DOORSTEP, TORPEDOED HIS SHIPS, SOMETIMES AL-
MOST IN VIEW OF LOOKOUTS AT HIS PRINCIPAL
HOME PORTS, AND SUSTAINED THE WORST DEPTH
CHARGE ATTACKS HE COULD LAUNCH.*
*THEY WERE THE SUBMARINES OF THE PACIFIC
FLEET.*

Chapter 6

Pioneers SOWESPAC

☆   ☆   ☆

Soerabaja

"The true speed of war," said Mahan, "is not headlong precipitancy, but the unremitting energy which wastes no time." Captain John Wilkes improved on this aphorism. Combining "headlong precipitancy" with "unremitting energy," he wasted no time whatever in transferring SubsAsiatic headquarters from Manila, P.I., to Soerabaja, N.E.I.

HOLLAND and OTUS had already gone. CANOPUS was at Corregidor. Cavite was wiped out, and the 28 submarines of the Asiatic Fleet had been ordered to the Malay Barrier. Captain Wilkes boarded SWORDFISH with his operational staff and headed for Soerabaja.

Captain Wilkes, in tourist parlance, traveled light. The staff carried just three essential items: the pay accounts for the force—one typewriter (treated like a mascot)—and one radio receiver. Which might lead one to remark that the true speed of war does not depend on nine carbon copies of everything.

SWORDFISH made a fine taxi—no better skipper in the service than Chester Smith—and the Java base was reached on January 7th. There, disembarking amidst an excited chatter of Dutch, *bêche-de-mer* and Javanese, Captain Wilkes' staff must have experienced several misgivings. From the first it was apparent that the Malay Barrier might be a language barrier. Submarines cannot be dispatched and repaired by sign language. The stout Dutch colonial with his *reis taffle* and his Bols, as hospitable as he was rotund, could speak only broken English. The average American submarine officer could speak no Dutch at all. Dutch submarine parts, like Dutch adjectives, were not designed for American use.

Under ordinary circumstances Soerabaja would have been an excellent submarine base. The harbor embraced a sheltered overhaul basin, ample docking space, some of which was roofed over, a floating drydock, and fine machine shops with modern equipment. But in January 1942 the circumstances were far from ordinary. Dutch submarines, in from war patrol, were booked for repairs. Overhaul facilities were taxed to the breaking point by the inrush of Allied naval vessels.

By the time Captain Wilkes reached Soerabaja the U.S. subs were crowded in like so many SS SARDINES. Spare parts could not be had. Docking space was at a premium. Dutch technicians and native mechanics were baffled by American machinery. As though to cork the bottleneck, the Navy Yard did not work on weekends (*Ja, Mynheer,* the situation is serious, but here everything must go by custom).

Admiral Hart had already established Fleet Headquarters in a house on the outskirts of Soerabaja, and there Captain Wilkes installed his staff, his payroll and his typewriter. ComSubsAsiatic was in business.

Fleet submarines came back from the front, some needing little more than fuel and supplies, some with lamed engines and burnt-out gear, their hulls dimpled by the blasts of depth bombs. Tired S-boats limped in, foul from lack of air conditioning, a few with jammed bow planes, out-of-kilter periscopes, malfunctioning motors, leaking bulkheads. All needed careful inspection. And the captains and crews who crawled up out of the innards of these subs and stood blinking and staring in the sunshine (not all of them grinning and triumphant)—these captains and crews needed rest.

But at Soerabaja, with the Japs booming down, there was little rest for the weary. Java was too close to the front line. Bearded, unwashed, as famished and slow-footed as refugees, the American submariners were hustled to the mountain town of Malang where there was a rest camp operated by the Dutch Submarine Force. Thrown open to the Americans, this camp offered splendid facilities for recuperation—if the submariner had the time.

The captains and crews of the SubsAsiatic Force did not have the time. Officers and men had to remain aboard the submarines to oversee repairs and handle work details. Lacking spare parts, engineers had to manufacture them out of this and that and thin air. Electricians contrived jobs that rivalled the inventive works of Edison and Marconi. Torpedomen, motor macs, all hands up to the cook pitched in. At best the crews obtained no more than three days at the Malang rest camp.

At SubsAsiatic Headquarters the typewriter went like a machine gun and the radio in the garage was hot. Staff heard that the Japs had landed on the coast of Sarawak in northwest Borneo and captured Tarakan on January 11, gaining possession of some of the richest oil wells in the world. Strong units of the Imperial Navy were operating in the Celebes Sea, and fresh invasion forces were gathering for a drive at Kendari on the southeast peninsula of Celebes, ominously close to Bali and eastern Java. Soerabaja was growing warm.

Fortunately, close liaison could be maintained with Admiral Hart, although CinCAF spent a good part of his time at Batavia where Dutch Admiral Helfrich was headquartered. Less fortunately, the degree of operational control to be exercised by ComSubsAsiatic was not clearly defined and the extent of Captain Wilkes' command was more or less ambiguous. CinCAF, in command of the American-British-Dutch-Australian (ABDA) fleet, issued directives that were so specific as to permit little interpretation or flexibility in the execution of the tasks assigned. Thus, submarines were ordered to static positions in defense of points where enemy landings were expected. Perhaps convinced they could have been used to better advantage if aggressively employed to cut enemy supply lines, ComSubsAsiatic was, nevertheless, without authority to alter their disposition.

Inexperience in the strategic and tactical aspects of submarine warfare was partly responsible for the ineffectiveness of the Asiatic submarines in this period. Again, the pre-war concept of the submarine as a fleet adjunct served to restrict operations. Finally, the Allied Fleet Commander was faced with a desperate crisis which impelled him to muster all available forces for a showdown battle with the enemy. With Allied naval forces driven back everywhere, and Dutch Admiral Helfrich pounding the table and demanding a stand, Admiral Hart groped for every warship available and issued the directive ordering the submarines to defend the Malay Barrier.

With Supreme Allied Commander General Wavell setting up Soerabaja headquarters in the house occupied by Admiral Hart and Captain Wilkes, the ABDA command became a fairly compact body. But its forces, only skeletal to begin with, were rapidly shrinking. Battered by the Japanese sea-air drive, the surface squadrons of ABDAFLOAT retreated and dwindled. Only the submarines escaped this piecemeal destruction. The few PBY's and Allied planes which constituted

ABDAIR were far short of the number needed to provide coverage for Soerabaja.

On February 3 the first enemy aircraft roared over, and bombs crashed into the harbor. The attack on Soerabaja had begun.

Australia and Down Under

Darwin, Australia (population 600), was not the best submarine base in the Pacific. Selected because it seemed a sheltered harbor, it was within coverage of Allied fighter strips on the northern coast of Australia, and at the war's beginning it was the focal point for water-borne supply ships routed through Torres Strait. But Captain James Fife had hardly entered the port with his administrative staff aboard SEAWOLF before he recognized the deficiencies.

As a base for submarine tenders (HOLLAND was already there) the harbor was vulnerable. Rail connections with Brisbane and Perth were nonexistent. Air protection was inadequate. And the waters off Darwin were vulnerable—another feature calculated to make the base unsatisfactory. Boarding HOLLAND with his staff, Captain Fife was not too favorably impressed with Port Darwin.

The submariners found Darwin a ghost town—Main Street deserted, stores boarded up, stray dogs slinking along the curbstones. Red dust smoked up under the blazing sun and the local thermometer bubbled at 110 degrees. Most of the townspeople had headed for the interior. Word that the Japs had bombed Rabaul in New Britain and Tulagi and Kieta in the Solomons had sent the populace packing.

But Captain Fife and his staff pitched in. HOLLAND was ready to take on the submarines. The plan called for two-thirds of the SubsAsiatic Force to base at Soerabaja, the remaining third at Darwin, the submarines to rotate between these bases. Darwin wasn't Utopia, but there was a war going on.

Having delivered the SubsAsiatic administrative staff, SEAWOLF loaded anti-aircraft and machine-gun ammunition—cargo for Corregidor. Taking on this freight, she was one of the pioneers to prove the submarine's versatility as fighting ship, passenger carrier, scout, merchant raider, rescue vessel, freighter and whatever else was demanded of her on or under the sea.

While the WOLF was loading at Darwin, USS TARPON hobbled in, looking as though she had been on a cruise in Hades. Her skipper, Lieutenant Commander Wallace, reported that he had been forced by a low battery to surface in a typhoon. TARPON had nearly foundered when a monster wave climbed over the open conning-tower hatch, flooding the control room and short-circuiting the radio and the motors. The repair forces at Darwin had a job to do.

Not long after TARPON's arrival, SCULPIN (Lieutenant Commander Lucius H. Chappell) came rolling in. Chappell delivered an interesting battle report.

SCULPIN had been patrolling Lamon Bay. Proceeding from there to Darwin, she had been running submerged during daytime and making what distance she could on the surface at night. On the night of January 10, somewhere around lat. 10-05 N., long. 123-55 E., she had encountered a couple of Japs.

SCULPIN surfaced that evening at 1840. At 2304 the officer of the deck called Chappell to the bridge and reported sighting a darkened ship, bearing 195°T, at a range of 2,000 yards.

Chappell peered through the darkness. "I can't see a damned thing! Are you sure there's something off there?"

The officer of the deck was sure. This was in the days before much was known about the protection of night vision. Blue lights were still in use aboard darkened ships, and red glasses were unheard of. Chappell was unable to discern the target, and SCULPIN's approach depended almost entirely on the 20-20 vision of the bridge lookout.

Target range was a matter of estimation. With the simple pelorus it was difficult to take accurate bearings. But a ship was out there, and about one minute after this first vessel was sighted, the O.O.D. picked up a second, bearing 165°T.

SCULPIN eased around to course 290°, closing the range on the first target. The target's speed was estimated at 12 knots, and the course at 290°. It was impossible to get much out of the torpedo data computer. Periscope angle was estimated by rule of thumb, and a 30° right gyro angle was set on two torpedoes. The range closed to 1,000 yards.

Chappell gave the order to fire as the target's bow passed the jackstaff. Two torpedoes were launched from the bow tubes in a longitudinal spread (one directly behind the other) with a four-second firing interval. Silence grew oppressive as the seconds ticked off and there were no torpedo detonations.

Chappell ordered 45° right gyro angle on a second pair of forward torpedoes, and fired again. These torpedoes were hardly out of the tubes when the explosion came—55 seconds after the initial salvo, and just three minutes after the target was sighted.

Chappell now maneuvered SCULPIN to attack the second

ship with stern tubes. At 2307 the vessel which had been hit opened fire with a pompom or a battery of small guns. Chappell cleared the submarine's bridge and gave the order to take her down. Breaking-up noises roared into the sound gear as SCULPIN's diving officer "pulled the plug."

Tracking the second ship by sound proved difficult, and SCULPIN was unable to obtain an attack position. A few depth charges were dropped, but the counter-attack was not pressed home. With the targets fading away, the submarine remained submerged and continued on her course for Port Darwin.

North of the Malay Barrier

When Japanese invasion forces appeared off Tarakan on January 10, three submarines—S-37, S-41 and SPEARFISH—were ordered to intercept the enemy landing. The three submarines arrived too late to inflict damage.

On January 11, Japanese forces landed at Menado and Kema, Northeast Celebes, and according to report they were assembling an invasion fleet at Kema. Again ComSubsAsiatic was directed to dispatch three submarines to intercept the invaders.

A striking force of destroyers, with the cruiser MARBLE-HEAD in support was withdrawn when the submarines PIKE and PERMIT, scouting ahead, reported no large enemy concentration at the northeast Celebes port.

As it turned out, the surface force was withdrawn too soon. Scouting off Kema a few days later, SWORDFISH discovered the harbor alive with Japanese shipping which had arrived at a later date than had been expected. The dispatching of SWORDFISH to Kema resulted in the penetration of that enemy harbor—another feat of submarine pioneering.

Prowling off Kema on January 24, SWORDFISH observed two freighters anchored in the roadstead north of the port. Lieutenant Commander Chester Smith quickly sized up the situation.

To get at one of the freighters, the submarine would have to go through the lower part of narrow Lembeh Strait—a squeeze the enemy could easily have defended with channel barriers. But no boom defenses were in evidence. The target was waiting.

The exactions demanded by submarine service are plainly manifest—submariners and submarine welded into a unit—brain-power, machine-power and fire-power incorporated by the brand of leadership exhibited by pioneering Chester Smith. Given such leadership (and good equipment) submarines are not dominated by the factor of luck. This uncomfortable indeterminable (referred to by submariners as the "Jesus Factor"—in polite company, the "Jay Factor") is present, of course, in every operation. Napoleon put much confidence in generals he considered lucky. But it might be remarked that Napoleon ended up on Elba, and the Jay Factor may be manipulated and frequently controlled by those who make few errors in judgment and can confidently act on their own decisions with appropriate know-how and skill.

So SWORDFISH went forward at Kema, proceeding northward and making periscope observations every 20 or 30 minutes, and running at 90-foot depth between exposures. Smith was not depending on any Jay Factor to save him from detection by enemy patrols.

Entering the channel, the submarine hugged the Lembeh shore. The day was bright with tropic noon, the water brassy in hot sunlight. Jap ships lay down-channel in view of SWORDFISH's periscope. Smith directed a wary approach.

Accurate determination of the channel's current (a factor to be estimated in torpedo fire on an anchored target) was impossible. For this reason Smith decided to fire two torpedoes at each target. Anchored in the roadstead, the ships were "sitting ducks," and four shots ought to get them.

Streaking the channel's surface with wakes of froth, the torpedoes rushed at the No. 1 target. Smith swung SWORDFISH toward the second ship. About two minutes after the first salvo, he heard the rumbling explosion. Two torpedoes raced toward the second target—straight bow shots at a range of 3,600 yards. A moment later came another detonation.

Smith took SWORDFISH down to 180 feet and headed her out of the channel for open water. Small-boat propellers were heard, and angry depth charges blew holes in the tide well astern. These anti-submarine measures were futile in the face of a *fait accompli*. For SWORDFISH was already safe on her way, leaving behind her the remains of MYOKEN MARU—4,000 tons of Japanese invasion shipping—on the bottom.

Two days later, SWORDFISH attacked an enemy destroyer (day-submerged approach), firing two torpedoes with zero results. The following day she attacked and missed a shot at a freighter. Valentine's Day she tackled still another freighter, and Smith fired two torpedoes for a hit. And on February 19, Smith reported the sinking of an oil tanker. While the sinkings of these last two vessels could not be corroborated, the *maru* torpedoed at Kema went down without any doubt. For this daring foray, SWORDFISH was credited with a successful patrol. Lieutenant Commander Chester Smith was awarded the Navy Cross, *"for especially meritorious conduct as commander of a submarine operating in the Southwest Pacific."*

Another pioneering SubsAsiatic skipper who struck hard uppercuts at the oncoming enemy was Lieutenant Commander William L. Wright, captain of STURGEON. Affectionately known throughout the Service as "Bull"—a sobriquet which paid tribute to his talents as a raconteur—Wright could make history as well as recount it.

After the Japanese seizures of Tarakan and Kema, American and Dutch submarines were stationed in the Straits of Makassar. Dutch air patrols had reported a large enemy convoy moving southward down the strait, apparently heading for the oil port of Balikpapan. Here, again, three U.S. submarines—PORPOISE, PICKEREL and STURGEON—were dispatched to intercept the invasion forces. Stationed in the strait between North Watcher and Mangkalihat, PORPOISE and PICKEREL scouted the forward line, while STURGEON played the backfield in reserve.

On January 22 the forward submarines reported the Japanese convoy steaming south in full array. An umbrella of planes, screening the convoy train, had made daylight attack most hazardous. Now dusk was dimming the seascape when STURGEON received the word from PORPOISE and PICKEREL. Almost simultaneously her sound gear picked up the murmur of ship's screws. Excited, the sound man reported the vessel was probably a carrier or a cruiser.

Wright rushed the men to battle stations, and the submarine squared away for a surface attack. Multiple ship screws droned in Sound's ear, and what looked like a 10,-000-tonner came down through the gloom. STURGEON's crew waited in tightening tension. Target bearing, speed, range went into the T.D.C. Gyro angles were set on the torpedoes.

Four torpedoes raced from the tubes. Two hits roared in the sound gear. Wright "pulled the plug."

Although post-war inquest failed to identify a Japanese carrier or cruiser sunk at lat. 01 N., long. 199 E., and Wright reported STURGEON's target as "unknown," a ship was undoubtedly hit and damaged, and STURGEON was entitled to that classic characterization dispatched by Wright in his memorable radio report:

STURGEON NO LONGER VIRGIN

Pioneer Tactics (The Sound Attack)

By pre-war definition, a sound attack was one delivered

from deep submergence, the approach officer depending solely on "sound information" that is, sonar "pinging" to obtain target range, or hydrophone-type "Pistening" which "hears" the target ship. Pre-war tacticians had composed a body of doctrine to guide submariners making such an attack. And peacetime target practice had invited confidence in the submarine's ability to hit with "sound shots." Combat experience soon proved these pre-war concepts faulty. Concerning them, a submarine captain was to write, *"They should forever stand as monuments to the dangers inherent in reaching sweeping conclusions, as regards tactics, from target practices conducted under artificial conditions."*

The quoted criticism was substantiated by statistical analyses made by the Submarine Operations Research Group (SORG) during and after the war. This body, organized in Washington and later installed with an IBM machine at Pearl Harbor, analyzed 4,873 submarine attacks, and listed only 31 of these as conducted by sound.

In the 31 sound attacks listed by SORG, seven credited sinkings are included. But positive identification of the vessels sunk could not be made.

Results of the sound attack made by STURGEON on January 26, 1942, were never conclusively determined.

On February 24, SEAL (Lieutenant Commander K. C. Hurd) was patrolling submerged north of Lombok. At 0800 Sound heard pinging, and shortly thereafter smoke was sighted.

SEAL came to a normal approach course, and about an hour later a convoy of four cargo vessels escorted by three destroyers was sighted. Hurd gave the order to go deep, and then speeded up in an effort to close the track. Ten minutes later he ordered SEAL to periscope depth. The range was now 5,800 yards, angle on the bow 50° port, and speed 13 knots. Hurd selected the biggest ship as SEAL's target, and went to 110 feet to attack by sound.

Dismayingly enough, Sound lost the target on the high-speed run in. Therefore, at 0940, when T.D.C. generated gyro angles were approaching zero, SEAL slowed to pick up the target once more. Contact was successfully made, but the bearing, compared with the generated bearing, indicated that the target had zigged to the left.

Four minutes later, with T.D.C. matching continuous bearings from Sound, Hurd fired four torpedoes. Some of the crew reported hearing two explosions, but Hurd was not satisfied that hits had been scored—not until an hour later, when he ordered SEAL to periscope depth and no sign of the target could be seen. But if victim there was, she was erased from Japanese records as well as the surface of the sea. Because the vessel's loss could not be verified. SEAL was not officially credited with a sinking. But her sound attack is noteworthy as one conducted exactly in accordance with the accepted pre-war doctrine.

As combat experience was gained, and the danger of being detected by air screens or supersonic screens was more realistically evaluated, the "doctrine of sound approach" became extinct. By the late summer of 1942, a submarine commander who conducted his patrol in conformance with the doctrine expounded at the war's beginning would undoubtedly have been relieved of command.

Pioneer Tactics (Night-periscope Attack)

As the war advanced into 1942, a number of night-periscope attacks were attempted in the Philippine and Dutch East India areas.

STURGEON made some of these night attacks. And Wright, arriving at conclusions which differed from those reached by POLLACK'S Captain Moseley, became enthusiastic over the tactic. He wrote:

"I don't know whether or not everyone fully appreciated the possibilities and advantages of periscope approaches in moonlight. I believe that, in most cases, it is the ideal condition, if a few principles are followed:

"1. *Get a good estimate of the target course before submerging.* . . .

"2. *Use periscope freely and feed bearings to TDC constantly.* . . .

"3. *Close to a good firing range. You can generally choose your position far better than in a daylight approach.*

"4. *Fire straight shots. Then a range error makes no difference.*

"A great many of my pre-war ideas as to night visibility have been knocked into a cocked hat by experience. For instance, the idea that the sector toward the moon is always the sector of best visibility. This is very often not at all so. Generally speaking, the sector of best visibility is that sector where there is the greatest contrast between color of sky and water, that is, where the horizon is most definitely defined. More often than not, the sectors bordering the path of the moon are the sectors of poorest visibility.

"Also, I am convinced that, except on a very dark night, a

surface attack on almost any target will be detected before a decent firing range can be reached. On an escorted target, it will almost certainly be detected."

Perhaps STURGEON's periscopes were better than those of POLLACK. As to the chance of being detected in a night-surface attack, Wright's estimate was probably at that time justified. Night camouflage was as yet undeveloped, and submarine visibility was a moot question.

The first identified ship to be sunk in a night-submerged attack was torpedoed by SEADRAGON on February 2, 1942. Therein lies not only a study in tactics, but a saga concerning camouflage.

The matter of protective coloration may have had considerable influence on SEADRAGON's skipper, Lieutenant Commander W. E. Ferrall, when it came to a choice of tactics. On her first three war patrols, dated between early January and late July 1942, SEADRAGON made 19 attacks. Of these only two were night surface. The remainder, with the exception of the submerged attack on the night of February 2, were day submerged. Apparently SEADRAGON was all for keeping under the surface, day or night. Tactics can hinge on such matters as camouflage, and when it came to paint, SEADRAGON had a problem.

The problem had its beginnings on that morning when she was lying alongside ill-fated SEALION in the harbor at Cavite. The blasts which wrecked the LION scorched the DRAGON's hull and blistered the paint on her superstructure.

She was spotted like a leopard when she reached her station off the coast of Luzon. Some members of her crew considered her conspicuous. If a leopard cannot change its spots, one may remark that the feat is equally difficult for a dragon dodging about in hostile seas. Ferrall might well have ordered his diving officer, "Take her down, and keep her down!"

SEADRAGON attacked the invasion shipping which swarmed down on Luzon. Her adventures resembled those of the other SubsAsiatic boats battling the Japanese tidal wave. She harassed the convoys. She eluded depth bombs and patrols. She stalked and evaded. She prowled along the surface, and belly-crawled in the bottom mud, and generally behaved like any normal submersible in action.

In her January attacks she fired 15 torpedoes for one hit— a single out of that batch!

Luck relented, however, on the morn of February 2nd. A bright tropic moon gilded the water. The submarine, on the hunt off the western Luzon coast, sighted five ships on the sharp horizon.

Contact was made at 0416. Japanese transports—five of them in column!—carrying troops and equipment to reinforce General Homma. Ferrall decided to bore in for a periscope attack. SEADRAGON went to periscope depth, and the approach was begun.

Ferrall put the submarine on the convoy's track and chose his target—the fourth ship in the column. The approach lasted a little over an hour. At 0522 SEADRAGON was in firing position and two torpedoes were launched. The torpedo run was 500 yards.

Two hits were observed—geysers spouting high. Eight minutes later Ferrall sent one torpedo racing at the fifth ship in column. The torpedo missed.

At 0653 the transport which had been torpedoed was still afloat, and Ferrall attempted to deliver a *coup de grâce*, firing one torpedo at a range of 800 yards, depth-setting eight feet. Another miss!

Daylight on the water, it was time for SEADRAGON to leave the vicinity. As SEADRAGON left the scene, TAMAGAWA MARU was going under—a 6,441-ton APK that never reached the Philippines.

Radar and improved submarine camouflage would popularize the night-surface approach, but the night approach and attack made at periscope depth were by no means to be discounted.

Submarine Camouflage (Dragon in Pirate Costume)

The subject of submarine camouflage was of more than passing interest to the pioneers. Many a wardroom discussion waxed hot on the topic of war paint.

An unrelieved black had been considered the best color for defeating aircraft observation of a submerged submarine. With pre-war doctrine emphasizing aircraft evasion, U.S. submarines entered World War II painted black. Hence the nickname, "Black-bottom Boats," for these submersibles. But argument raged. Should a submarine be painted the color of Charon's Ferry in a latitude where the sun blazed like a spotlight? Wouldn't a stove-black conning tower be silhouetted in moonlight? How about coffee color for muddy tides? Blue, like the Britishers used in the Mediterranean? Or slate gray? While captains argued, their crews joining in as art critics, all were in agreement on one point. No combat submarine should be Baker red.

But SEADRAGON was. Or so they said. In the South China Sea her blistered paint peeled off like sunburn. Presently her hull was a beautiful rusty crimson. And so Tokyo Rose began to wail that the U.S. Navy had sent a fleet of "red submarines" to terrorize Asian waters. These Red Pirates (as Rose called them) would be properly exterminated for their nefarious forays. Listening to these short-wave tirades from Tokyo, Navy monitors were mystified. But the crew of SEADRAGON wasn't. They were only too aware of the source of Rose's story. And SEADRAGON, patrolling the Indo-China coast, continued to cherish submergence, shy as any lady dreading public exposure in red underwear.

The costume is not recommended for the publicity-shy submersible. Thanks to her unabashed personnel, SEADRAGON survived the experience and sank three merchantmen on her third patrol. But she was never a pirate fleet. She was just one fleet submarine. If the story is true, she was the only bright red submarine in the history of naval warfare.

Chapter 7

Battle for the Malay Barrier

☆   ☆   ☆

Submarine vs. Destroyer

The first enemy destroyer to be sunk by a U.S. submarine was torpedoed on February 8, 1942, by S-37. For an S-boat this was a doubly notable performance.

For she was, as her designation indicates, one of that veteranly vintage launched in the decade following World War I. This was not to say such boats were entirely superannuated. However their rivets were apt to weep a little if a depth charge came too close, or the oceanic pressure was too great. Lacking the latest fire control apparatus and gear, they were not the equal of fleet submarines. And in selecting a destroyer for a target, S-37's skipper, Lieutenant James Charles Dempsey, took his risks.

Destroyers, it goes without saying, were the "born enemy" of submarines. A Japanese destroyer, bearing down on the attack with a bone in her teeth and her sonar pinging as she bore, was as dangerous a foe as a submersible would wish to meet.

Characterized as deadly, the destroyer was also considered a secondary target over which transports, troopships, oil tankers and other surface vessels were given high priority. The duty of the submarine was to get in under the destroyer screen and attack the convoy.

Hard hitting and hard to hit, the DD was considered a savage to be attacked only when encountered alone, or when convoy targets could not otherwise be reached.

77

The DD, however, could be downed. One had been sunk by a Dutch submarine the day after Christmas, and now on the 8th of February an S-boat was squaring away for an American performance.

S-37 had been patrolling off Makassar City. After the Japanese landings in the Celebes, six submarines had been stationed in Makassar Strait and three had been stationed off Ambon, south of Molucca Passage. STURGEON had disputed the enemy's advance to Balikpapan, but the Japanese sea-air drive had relentlessly smashed forward. Whereupon the undersea force in the Strait of Makassar had been withdrawn with the exception of S-37 left behind on guard.

Off Makassar City Dempsey's submarine kept a periscope watch on the harbor. On the February evening in question, her exec, Lieutenant W. H. Hazzard, was at the periscope. Twilight was graying into dusk when the scope spied a pigstick on the horizon—a minuscule splinter about the size of an exclamation point on the skyline. It developed into the mast of a Jap destroyer that came roaring forward in the gloaming at bat-out-of-hell speed.

The DD was heading for Makassar City at a pace too fast to be overhauled. Hazzard decided it was a high-speed scout —a deduction in which Captain Dempsey concurred. The destroyer was hardly abeam before four more came nosing over the horizon in a slow-moving column barely visible in the last of the evening light. Then, as the submariners watched in fascination, a dark caravan of larger ships formed in the far-off gloom. These silhouettes were too blurred and distant for periscope identification. But there could be no doubt that S-37 was standing in the road in front of an invasion convoy.

Someone may think of a Model-T Ford caught in a maze of switchtracks in a night-gloomed terminal yard with a host of trains coming in from five directions. So it may have sounded—like scores of clashing wheels and crackling switches—in the S-boats saturated listening gear. And so it may have looked to the S-boat's periscope watchers, with signal lights beginning to twinkle here and there in the darkness and black shades looming left and right. Somewhere over the horizon a pale searchlight fanned across the sky. That was probably a cruiser. The S-boat began to move. With traffic closing in, it was time to get off the Main Line.

The clock had been at 1947 when the submarine sighted the destroyer column. Now that the night was thickening, Dempsey ordered the S-boat to the surface, and started on the trail at top speed. He was unable to run around the destroyer column for an attack on the larger ships beyond, and resenting this interference, he decided to attack the destroyers.

The opportunity vs. risk equation was solved by determination to seize the former. Attack on an escort when a convoy could not be reached was in accordance with doctrine. Night-surface attack gave the submarine advantage of high speed. And Dempsey probably preferred the risk of gunfire to that incurred by a creeping submerged approach which might mean sonar detection followed by counter-attack.

So S-37 ran in for a night-surface attack. Dempsey fired one torpedo at each of the destroyers in column. Fire control depended largely on the night vision of Lieutenant Hazzard, who was operating the dummy pelorus on the bridge. The ingenious lieutenant had fitted the brass rim of this device with an embossment of brads for finger-reading in the dark. Crude though it was, it "put the finger" on one of the DD's. The third destroyer in the column was hit.

The blast buckled the vessel in the middle, heaving the amidships section a good 20 feet above the bow and stern. Evidently the torpedo exploded in the fire room, as a cloud of soot burst from the destroyer's stack in a gust of orange light. Wrapped in a shroud of flame and smoke, the destroyer started down.

S-37 went under at safe distance and burrowed deep to evade. The DD's hunted, but could not find her. They next heard of her three nights later when she attacked another destroyer in the Strait of Makassar.

She missed that one. But an S-boat could hardly be expected to sink every destroyer in the Pacific, although it would seem that S-37 tried. She ended her 18-day third patrol with a record of five straight attacks on destroyers. The one that went down off Makassar City was the Imperial Navy's NATSUSHIO.

Loss of S-36 (Submarine Aground)

One of the major hazards which imperiled American submarines in the East Indies area was grounding. Among the archipelagoes lie some of the world's more treacherous waterways. Dutch charts were good, but not all of the American subs were provided with them.

The first of four U.S. submarines lost from grounding during the war was S-36. On her second patrol, having completed a successful attack on a small transport moored in Calapan Harbor, Mindoro, in the Philippines, she was proceeding to Soerabaja, Java. Just before dawn on the morning of January 20, she ran hard aground on Taka Bakang Reef in Makassar Strait.

Currents in this area are strong and hard to predict. S-36 had traveled at least 100 miles since last she had been able to fix her position. When the blow came, she was standing south at standard speed in the tropic night. Taka Bakang, awash at low water, could not be seen. A sudden violent jolt —a grinding snarl—propellers churning futile froth—S-36 was stranded.

Her forward battery, flooded, appeared to be generating chlorine gas. All efforts to move the boat proved unavailing. And the alarming situation impelled the submarine's commander, Lieutenant J. R. McKnight, Jr., to send out a plain language message that S-36 was aground and sinking.

When ComSubsAsiatic at Soerabaja finally received the message a PBY was sent to survey the stranded submarine's situation. By the time the plane arrived, McKnight was confident that with assistance he could salvage his submarine. The plane raced to Makassar City to request aid from the Dutch authorities. A Dutch launch was dispatched the following morning.

The launch took off two officers and 28 men, the remainder of the submarine's crew staying aboard in the hope S-36 could be hauled clear. But conditions steadily worsened. When the Dutch ship, SS SIBEROTE, arrived that afternoon, McKnight decided to abandon. S-36 was rigged for flooding, and the submariners transferred to the SIBEROTE which took them to Makassar City.

All hands reached Soerabaja on February 25.

Escape of USS Tarpon

TARPON (Lieutenant Commander Wallace) ran aground at 12 knots in Boling Strait on the night of February 22. Crew lightened ship by blowing water ballast and reserve oil, shifting lube oil aft, lowering anchors and jettisoning 3-inch ammo. TARPON refused to budge. Three "fish" were jettisoned. No go. Wallace tried kedging, with an anchor outboard and the crew working a winch. The reef held TARPON fast.

With daylight coming and Japs in the offing, the crew rigged for demolition. Then a Dutch missionary was brought aboard from nearby Adunara Island. He informed the stranded submarines that Jap aircraft were in the area. By way of better news he assured TARPON's sailors there would be a high tide from 1600 to 1800.

These tidings, good and bad, prompted the submariners to stick by their guns. Three engines were backed, and the crew heaved in on the anchor windlass, and TARPON was finally moved. Aided by Providence and the flooding tide, the crew got her off at 1600—a pioneer exploit which showed the Force that submariners capable of surviving hell and high water could also live through hell and low.

Tjilatjap

With the Japanese ashore in Borneo, Celebes and the Moluccas, their forces swarming into Balikpapan, and Ambon, the hot breath of invasion began to scorch Java.

Defense of the Netherlands East Indies with a skeleton force had been a forlorn hope at best. On February 4, the Japanese struck Admiral Hart's ABDA Fleet a blow that all but broke the back of the skeleton. Caught without air cover in Madoera Strait, the Allied squadron was nearly slaughtered. U.S. cruisers MARBLEHEAD and HOUSTON took a murderous blasting. Meantime, Soerabaja crumbled under a cyclonic bombing raid. Hart's maimed and battered ships headed for Tjilatjap on the southern coast of Java.

Lying at the head of a long, narrow, river entrance, Tjilatjap (pronounced "Chilachap") had already been selected as a reserve base to be used in the event that Soerabaja became untenable. On February 4, tenders HOLLAND and OTUS were dispatched to Tjilatjap from Darwin, Australia.

Tjilatjap was by no means secure. The submarine tenders found a grim harbor—MARBLEHEAD battle-scarred and fire-blackened in the floating drydock; HOUSTON's crew burying her dead; submarines coming in from patrol, haggard and hungry for supplies; every hour bringing word that the enemy was drawing nearer. The catastrophic situation was made apparent by the fact that the cruiser HOUSTON, even with her after turret destroyed, was the strongest warship remaining to the ABDA Fleet. MARBLEHEAD, her wounds patched, was sent to Trincomalee, Ceylon, under escort of the submarine tender OTUS. An unusual assignment for a submarine tender, but no other escort could be spared.

Whittled down to the bone, Admiral Hart's skeletal fleet was disposed to defend Java. Operations at Soerabaja were coming to a standstill. Submarines were ordered to clear the restricted overhaul basin and submerge in the outer harbor during air raids. One Dutch submarine, tardy in complying with the order, was bombed and sunk inside the basin. Daylight refits could no longer be accomplished, and the Subs-Asiatic boats were ordered to Tjilatjap.

OTUS gone, only HOLLAND remained to serve the Subs-Asiatic Force—a single tender for all the submarines in the Southwest Pacific Area. The one small drydock at Tjilatjap was given over to destroyers. The tender force rolled up its sleeves, and somehow the boats were refitted as they came in from patrol. Among those which made port at Tjilatjap were SAILFISH, SALMON, SEAL, SNAPPER, and STINGRAY.

On February 14 came the word that Admiral Thomas C. Hart had been relieved of command of the ABDA Fleet—the command going to Dutch Admiral Helfrich. For the American admiral it had been a heartbreaking battle. He had sent his forces out to fight a delaying action, knowing that retreat and defeat were inevitable—that victory would be won by other forces later.

On February 18 Japanese invasion forces landed on the island of Bali. The following night an ABDA surface force fought a savage battle in Badoeng Strait with the enemy's invasion convoy. In the melee the Dutch destroyer PIET HIEN was sunk, the cruiser TROMP seriously damaged, and the cruiser JAVA wounded. Two Japanese destroyers were badly battered—small consolation. The blows struck the little Allied fleet were all but paralyzing at a moment when every ship was needed.

It was now realized that Tjilatjap could not long be held. The channel entering Tjilatjap was a snare. Entry at night was navigationally unsafe, and one sunken ship could block the entrance and trap the vessels in the harbor. These dangers, plus a total lack of air protection, resulted in the dispatch of HOLLAND (February 20) to Exmouth Gulf.

On February 26 the last effort at refitting submarines at Soerabaja was concluded when S-37 precipitately departed for patrol. Admiral Wilkes and the remaining members of the staff set out over the mountains by automobile. There was still some hope of holding on at Tjilatjap. Help was on the way.

To Java were coming two Allied aircraft tenders—USS LANGLEY and HMS SEAWITCH. Between them they carried 59 fighter planes with munitions, pilots and ground personnel. But LANGLEY was destined never to arrive. About 100 miles off Tjilatjap, she was sighted by a Japanese scouting plane. Summoned to the target, nine enemy bombers roared over. Somehow the vessel remained afloat. But she was too badly damaged to make port. The command was given to abandon. LANGLEY was sunk by shellfire from the destroyer WHIPPLE—a tragic ending for the old "Covered Wagon," the U.S. Navy's first aircraft carrier.

Two days later HMS SEAWITCH arrived at Tjilatjap unharmed. But the reinforcements she brought were too little
and too late.

Pioneer Special Missions

The French term for it in World War I was *"mission
extraordinaire."* An air pilot was detailed the job of dropping
a secret agent behind enemy lines—a soldier disguised as
a peasant was sent out to carry a message across Belgium—
a navy crew was dispatched to do a little gun-running or
blow up a harbor obstruction.

The submariner's designation for it in World War II was
"Special Mission."

Submarine special missions may be divided into the following general types: reconnaissance, supply, evacuation or
rescue, transportation of coast watchers and intelligence
agents, lifeguarding, mining. Miscellaneous tasks included
weather reporting, minefield detection, anti-picket boat
sweeps, shore bombardment, support of commando raids,
and serving as marker beacons for surface ships. A submarine in accomplishing a special mission might perform
more than one of these enumerated tasks.

Few special missions were more dramatic than those accomplished in the war's opening weeks. Every mission demanded iron nerve from all hands, and all the imagination
and initiative the commanding officer could muster.

The first submarine to perform a special mission in the
Southwest Pacific was SEAWOLF. She loaded anti-aircraft ammunition at Darwin, Australia, and departed on January 16
for Corregidor. If her skipper, Lieutenant Commander
Warder, was uneasy sitting on top of 37 tons of .50-caliber
ammunition, he did not wear the fact on his sleeve. But he
must have entertained a few anxious doubts. Crammed "to
the gills" with such cargo, SEAWOLF, under a depth-charging,
might blow up like a giant grenade. The crew was indisposed
to worry. As one of them stoically expressed it, "If they hit
us, they'll just blow us a little higher, that's all."

Traveling submerged by day and on the surface at night,
SEAWOLF pursued a cautious and steady course. One night
she spied a Japanese task force—three or four cruisers, a
squadron of destroyers, seven transports. Here was the sort
of situation which made special missions unattractive to
submariners—a whole gallery of targets, and not a chance
to shoot. The mission was primary, and SEAWOLF perforce
continued on her way. But when the Jap ships were under

the horizon, Warder brought his submarine to the surface and radioed a detailed description of the enemy force to the Submarine Command.

The Japanese had fastened a blockade on the Philippines, but Warder took the WOLF through without detection, and a PT-boat escorted her in through the minefields to Corregidor.

On leaving, SEAWOLF took out with her 25 Army and Navy aviators, a load of submarine spare parts and 16 torpedoes for delivery to Soerabaja.

Trout Goes to Rainbow's End

The second U.S. submarine to pioneer a special mission was TROUT (Lieutenant Commander F. W. Fenno). Of the Pacific Fleet Force, she enters this SubsAsiatic chapter by way of orders dispatching her to Corregidor with 3,500 rounds of desperately needed anti-aircraft ammunition. Return trip, she was to carry what was undoubtedly the most valuable ballast ever loaded into a submarine. Certainly TROUT's was a mission extraordinary.

Having glimpsed the Jap strike at Midway, she was home at the Pearl Harbor Submarine Base, where technicians were reducing her superstructure's silhouette, when she received the orders which rushed her to the Philippines. TROUT was standing out to sea on the morning of January 12th.

First stop, Midway, where she replenished her fuel supply ("topped off," in seagoing vernacular). Then she headed on a great circle course north of Wake and Marcus, following a route calculated to take her through Balintang Channel above Luzon. Running south through enemy-patrolled waters west of Luzon, she was off Corregidor on February 3rd. Japanese bombers were hammering the Rock, so TROUT remained submerged until nightfall when a patrol boat came out to guide her in through the minefields.

Jap planes were winging across the sky and fiery tracers were soaring up from PT-boats in Manila Bay as the submarine groped her way into the lagoon and tied up at South Dock. Immediately the submariners pitched in to unload the precious ammunition.

Grapefruit, cigarettes, canned food and news were also passed out to Corregidor's hungry defenders. Ammunition ashore, there were six 3,000-pound torpedoes to be lugged aboard and stowed below. All this under the compulsion of making haste slowly, while the gunfire over on Bataan fluttered like summer lightning and any moment a shower of bombs might fall from the night sky. By 0300 every man aboard TROUT was ready to "hit the sack."

Such jobs as the foregoing were soon to be commonplace undertakings for submarines on special mission assignments. But TROUT's mission did assume a peculiar distinction. En route to Corregidor, Fenno felt that his submarine could use more ballast.

"Our weight conditions had been figured out on paper," he remarked afterwards. "We were supposed to have had a leeway of about five thousand pounds. This, as we approached Corregidor, seemed hardly enough. Consequently, with our arrival report, we requested twenty-five tons of ballast, preferably sandbags so that we could move them around as necessary to effect a trim."

Reporting in person to Admiral Rockwell at Corregidor Naval Headquarters, TROUT's captain learned that sandbags were not to be had on the embattled Rock. But wait—

In the bank vaults at Manila there had been a large gold store. This bullion, along with a fortune in silver, currency and securities, had been spirited to Corregidor for safekeeping. If TROUT could use bars of gold for ballast—

TROUT could, and did! Two tons of gold bars. And 18 tons of silver pesos, plus stacks of negotiable securities and bags of vital State Department documents and U.S. Mail. Throughout the night of February 4, in a dark scene lit by the gunfire on Bataan, gleaming yellow bars and clinking sacks of silver were stowed in the submarine's holds. Freighted with this treasure, TROUT submerged off Corregidor at dawn, and the following evening she went out through the minefields and stood seaward like a submersible National Bank.

Her orders called for a brief war patrol in the East China Sea area, and Fenno headed her northward on the hunt for enemy shipping. Five days out of Corregidor, with a Japanese freighter in view, he directed a submerged attack and pitched three torpedoes at the target. Two explosions sent the AK under. Post-war inquest identified the vessel as CHUWA MARU, 2,718 tons.

Homeward bound, off the Bonin Islands TROUT sighted a small Jap patrol craft. Three torpedoes were fired, one struck the mark, and the 200-ton PC was blown from the Pacific's surface.

The remainder of the voyage was uneventful. Reaching Pearl Harbor, TROUT's fabulous ballast was unloaded for transshipment to the States. On a mission which lasted 57 days, she had been to Rainbow's End, picked up the jackpot, made a home-run through enemy-infested waters and sunk two Jap vessels along the way.

Rescue in the Java Sea

S-38's crew were unaware that they were about to set a pace. Life-saving duty as a submarine assignment was in the future. S-38 was on war patrol.

Nor were her submariners aware that a great sea battle was in the making. The world outside the pressure hull is remote to those in a submersible. Particularly so when the "pressure" outside the hull dictates precautionary radio silence and submergence during daylight. Information then comes in brief radio fragments at night, and the day's war picture can only be surmised.

On the night of February 28, nearing the end of her patrol, S-38 was on the surface, homeward bound. The Diesels were drumming a good sound, and the old S-boat was going like a horse to its stable. Then—

A call from the lookout. Captain on the bridge with focussed glasses. A dark blur on the water off the starboard bow—a low, flat, unidentifiable silhouette that might be drifting wreckage, a mat of seaweed or a huddle of sampans.

Wreckage, Munson decided. But he couldn't take chances. Ordering out the gun crew, he held the submarine at top speed, veering over for a look-see.

As the submarine neared the blurred mass, a voice cried out of the darkness, "My God, they're not finished with us yet!"

Astounded at hearing English, Munson answered the cry with a hail. "Who are you?"

A weird chorus of muffled voices rose in the dark. Someone shouted, "We're men of His Majesty's Ship ELECTRA!"

S-38 hove to. The sea seemed alive with struggling men. Men clinging to life rafts, floating timbers, clutched together in a sprawl of debris. It was necessary to launch a boat to get them aboard. They were sighted around 0400, and dawn was tinting the sky when the last man was picked up.

Plucked as from a common grave, they crowded the submarine—fifty-four of them. They were oil smeared, lacerated, sick, half-drowned, burnt from fire and sea salt and thirst. Tottering anatomies, they had to be carried down the hatch. Seventeen were badly wounded. One of them was dying. They were the men of HMS ELECTRA, sunk by Japanese destroyers in the Battle of the Java Sea.

The men of the S-38 took them in, fed them, tended their wounds, and carried them to safety—the first of many open-sea rescues to be accomplished by submarines. By way of an encore, S-37 (Lieutenant J. C. Dempsey) in the same area rescued two American sailors, survivors of the cruiser DE RUYTER, and supplied a boatload of the Dutch cruiser's men with five days' provisions.

Retreat to Australia

The human flotsam picked up by S-38 and S-37 was residue of the Battle of the Java Sea—a bloody carnage that ended the Allied grip on Indonesia.

A statue with feet of clay, Singapore had fallen on February 15. Three days later, Jap invasion forces seized Bali. Java and Sumatra were caught in a vise.

Committed by Dutch Admiral Helfrich to a do-or-die showdown, the remnant ABDA fleet steamed out on February 27 to meet an oncoming Japanese naval armada. Outweighed and out-gunned, the Allied ships waded into an inferno of Jap shells and torpedoes. One after another the Dutch, British and American ships were either knocked out of action or sunk.

Last to go down was U.S. cruiser HOUSTON, riddled, afire, sunk with over half her crew.

So ended the Battle of the Java Sea, and with it the Malay Barrier was lost. The battle was hardly over before Japanese troops occupied beachheads west of Soerabaja. The following morning (March 1) the ABDA Fleet was dissolved. Admiral Glassford ordered the remaining American ships to proceed to Australia.

That same day, the submarine SEAL (Lieutenant Commander Hurd) attacked and possibly damaged a Japanese light cruiser in Lombok Strait. In the waters off Bali, SEAWOLF attacked a destroyer, a transport and two other ships, probably hitting them for damage. In the waters off Java, S-38 reported a torpedo hit on a YUBARI-class cruiser, but this, too, could not be confirmed.

Confirmable, however, is the fact that while the Japanese conquered the Netherlands East Indies, they had yet to conquer the surrounding seas. The ABDA surface fleet was gone. But the submarines remained.

They remained to slash the Japanese communication lines. To penetrate the enemy-held harbors. To litter the beaches with water-logged supplies and wrecked ships. To strew the sea bottom with the hulks of sunken merchantmen and the bones of Imperial naval vessels.

Chapter 8

Thunder Down Under

☆ ☆ ☆

*Skirmish in the Mandates
(Pioneer Reconnaissance)*

The war was only a few days old when the first submarine reconnaissance missions were ordered. On December 18, 1941, POMPANO (Lieutenant Commander L. S. "Lew" Parks) left Pearl Harbor to patrol off the Marshall Islands. *"Primary mission: To sink Jap ships, and secondary to find out what the Nips have at various bases."* Four days later her orders were changed, and reconnaissance was made her primary mission.

Pre-war planning and training had included submarine reconnaissance. A pamphlet, "Current Submarine Doctrine," issued in January 1942 after its pre-war preparation stated:

Submarines are capable of performing three types of reconnaissance missions:
(a) *Visual reconnaissance through periscope,*
(b) *Photographic reconnaissance through periscope,*
(c) *Reconnaissance by landing party.*

All three types were to be conducted by submarines during the war. A fourth type—minefield reconnaissance—was eventually developed.

The early reconnaissance missions, conducted by Pearl Harbor submarines, were simple in comparison to those that came later. Simple, and beset with all manner of complexities. The operations were exploratory. Techniques were new and untried. The operator, delving into mystery, reconnoitered into the Unknown where the Unexpected may lie.

In particular the islands which had been under Japanese mandate were question marks. Heavily fortified, concealing supply bases and airfields, the Mandates—the Marianas, Marshalls and Carolines—had been cloaked in secrecy for two decades. It was the submarine's business to spy out military installations, harbor defenses and beachheads for possible landings.

Normally, aerial photography for intelligence purposes was far superior to periscope photography. However, the presence of aircraft performing photographic reconnaissance over enemy islands has one drawback—it alerts the enemy. The submarine may reconnoiter without being detected. Too, there was one type of information impossible for planes to obtain—aircraft were unable to check the accuracy and orientation of charts. And charts became vitally important when amphibious landings were contemplated. Obviously accurate charts could mean all the difference between landing or shipwreck.

POMPANO, ordered out on the first submarine-reconnaissance mission, was slated to visit Wake, Ujelang, Ponape, Rongelap and an insignificant atoll named Bikini. Before departing on the mission, her skipper, Lew Parks, visited the Emergency and Repair Shop at the Pearl Harbor Submarine Base, in search of an adapter to hold a camera.

It was suggested that the fitting of an adapter was an exacting business that would consume long hours. Parks did not have the hours. But he did have a knowledge of photography. Taking the matter in his own hands, he himself made tests to find the periscope's focal point, and succeeded in installing a small camera on the scope. POMPANO thereby became a pioneer in submarine periscope photography as well as the first frontiersman on reconnaissance.

Facing an extremely hazardous venture, she was almost eliminated when but two days out. The eliminators in this case were not Japanese, but American—dive bombers from the aircraft carrier ENTERPRISE. Trouble began at 0700 on December 20 when a PBY patrol bomber spotted the submarine and rushed over to lay an egg on POMPANO. Fortunately the egg hatched some distance away. But worse was to come. Racing off to the blue horizon, the PBY informed the aircraft carrier of POMPANO's position. Three enterprising flyers from ENTERPRISE arrived overhead at 1400, and three bombs were dropped—one—two—three—on the submarine. The second bomb was close enough to loosen rivets in her mid-section and loosen the mid-sections of her disconcerted crew. They escaped by the proverbial hair, but for the remainder of the cruise POMPANO trailed fuel oil from a leaky tank.

Nevertheless, she visited the islands on her itinerary, and Parks recorded what there was to see. One of the things to be seen was the Jap flag flying over the Pan-Am Airways Administration Building at Wake. A few Japanese ships were sighted. POMPANO launched four shots at a minelaying destroyer—two torpedoes were prematures and two missed the target—and her crew experienced the metallic taste of a depth-bombing.

It was dangerous work, prowling into island waters that might be mined or otherwise set with traps. Running up the scope for a look-see. Peering into coves and harbors where anti-submarine patrols might be lying in ambush. In spite of Jap patrols and leaking oil, POMPANO accomplished the reconnaissance mission.

Shortly after POMPANO left Pearl, DOLPHIN (Lieutenant Commander G. B. Rainer) departed on similar scouting detail. TAUTOG (Lieutenant Commander J. H. "Joe" Willingham, Jr.) soon followed DOLPHIN.

DOLPHIN and TAUTOG concentrated on the mysterious Marshalls. TAUTOG got back to Pearl Harbor little the worse for wear from a rugged depth-charging. DOLPHIN got back. Bearded, famished and as full of adventure stories as a pirate novel, each submariner climbed out into the sunshine and headed for the Royal Hawaiian. The captains turned in their reconnaissance reports. Admiral Withers directed three more submarines to investigate the Japanese Mandates.

On February 1, 1942, Rear Admiral Halsey's carrier task force made the Navy's first retaliatory strike on enemy territory, attacking the Marshall Islands. Late in February the same force pounded the enemy on Marcus.

While these punitive raids failed to interrupt the Japanese offensive in the Southwest Pacific, they did serve early notice on the enemy that the U.S. Navy remained to be dealt with. They also heartened the home front in that darkest period of the war.

The Australian Front

For the United States forces in the Southwest Pacific, the month of March 1942 came in like a lion and went out like a lion. Japanese troops swarmed into the Malay States and walked across the Netherlands East Indies. An iron clamp tightened around the American forces in the Philippines. With the exception of Bataan and Corregidor, the Japanese were now in virtual control of a vast segment of the Orient extending from the conquered shores of China to Timor below the Banda Sea and from the Kurile Islands in the far north to Wake, the Marshalls, the Gilberts, and Rabaul in the Bismarck Archipelago. In a little over three months, the enemy had completed the first phase of the strategic war plan devised by Imperial General Headquarters.

The second phase of this plan called for stabilization of the conquered territory and construction of strong defenses for the island outposts of its Pacific perimeter. A third phase was in a process of incubation on the planning table. This phase concerned the expansion of the Japanese front—conquest of the Solomon Islands and New Guinea, a thrust into the New Hebrides and possible invasion of Australia. Anticipating Axis victory in Europe, a stalemate in the Pacific and eventual Allied peace-feelers, Tokyo was jubilant. Already the riches of the Co-Prosperity Sphere had begun to flow toward Japan. The Sons of Heaven were coming into their own. *Banzai!*

There was no elated cheering in the Allied camp. Rather there was stern determination to hold on until reinforcements arrived. At all cost, an enemy drive at Australia must be beaten back. He must not be allowed to consolidate his gains, and he must be deprived of the raw materials he was gathering for shipment to Japan. But there was no Allied air force on hand to raid his lines. The ABDA Fleet was gone. To block the enemy's advance, to stop his ships in their business of loot-carrying there were only the submarines. In the Southwest Pacific there were all too few of these—a halfdozen or so remaining to the British and Dutch, and the small SubsAsiatic Force now based in Australia.

Leaving Tjilatjap on February 20, HOLLAND had headed for Exmouth Gulf in company with the old destroyer tender BLACK HAWK, escorted by STINGRAY and STURGEON. But Exmouth Gulf, western Australia, was unsuitable for a submarine base. The port was swept by bitter windstorms, and heavy swells rolled in from the sea, making anchorages difficult and unhandy. HOLLAND was therefore ordered to take aboard a load of passengers (refugees from Java) and move south to Fremantle. Near the southwest corner of the continent, Fremantle had the look of a hospitable base.

Loaded with food and submarine spares, two supply ships from the States were already in the harbor. To "Ma" HOLLAND these were a most welcome sight. At the war's start she had been carrying a full supply of food, munitions and spares—enough to last her normal complement of 12 submarines a good six months. However, in Darwin and Tjilatjap she had serviced any submarine that came alongside. She had doled out her stores sparingly, and many submarines had been forced to leave on patrol with short provisions. Boats that would normally take aboard 1,600 pounds of meat received as little as 600 pounds at Darwin and Tjilatjap. Nevertheless "Ma" HOLLAND'S supplies had run low, and she reached Fremantle in a condition approximating Mother Hubbard's.

Now her cupboards were once more filled, and Captain Pendleton and his tender force could dispense to the submarines adequate rations as well as service. Work went forward to establish in Fremantle the first American submarine base in Australia. Twelve miles up the Swan River from the Port of Fremantle, the city of Perth opened its doors and its heart to the submariners. Machine shops, a rail head and recreational facilities were at last available. Repair work could go on a 24-hour shift, Sundays included. All hands heaved a sigh of relief and shook hands with the realistic Aussies.

A few days after HOLLAND'S arrival, Captain Wilkes and the remainder of his Operational Staff reached Fremantle. They had come down from Java aboard SPEARFISH, STURGEON, SARGO and SEADRAGON. And Fremantle began to look like Old Home Week to the submariners when OTUS put in, after her long excursion to Ceylon with MARBLEHEAD.

Shortly after OTUS made port, HOLLAND steamed for Albany, West Australia, 300 miles farther south. As she was the only fully equipped submarine tender in the Southwest Pacific, the force commanders were taking no chances with her security. Albany made a good backfield base.

At Fremantle the force at last found sanctuary. Here, in reasonable security, the tenders could devote all their time and effort to caring for the submarines—the submarines still fighting north of the Barrier, delaying the enemy's advance, and winning time. Time for Nimitz, Spruance, Halsey and MacArthur to mount a counter-offensive. Time for reinforcements to come. There could be no further retreat. Australia was the end of that line.

But some of the SubsAsiatic boats were a long time reaching Australia, and some were destined never to make port. March was a dark month on the submarine calendar—a month in which the force lost two fleet-type submarines.

Loss of Shark

After transporting Admiral Hart and his staff from Manila to Soerabaja on her first patrol, SHARK (Lieutenant Commander Lewis Shane, Jr.) had entered the thick of the fighting. Late in January '42 she patrolled Molucca Passage. Then her patrol area was extended to include Banka Passage.

On February 2 she reported to Soerabaja that she had been depth-charged off Tifore Island, and had missed on a torpedo attack. Five days later she reported an empty cargo ship heading northeast. Thereafter no messages were received from SHARK.

She was told on February 8 to proceed to Makassar Strait via the north coast of Celebes. A later message from Soerabaja asked her for information. SHARK made no reply. On March 7, 1942, she was reported as presumed lost.

Post-war examination of Japanese records reveals a depth-charge attack on a submarine east of Menado, northern Celebes, on February 11th. If SHARK was lost through enemy action, this depth-charging seems responsible. She had been ordered to that vicinity. But the exact date of her loss and the specific cause remain beyond mortal determination. She went out. She was in the fight. She did not come back. If destroyed by depth charges, she was the first U.S. submarine to be sunk by enemy surface craft in the Pacific.

Loss of Perch

Tragic, although many of her crew survived, was the loss of PERCH. On her first patrol, conducted west of the Philippines, she attacked and possibly sank a 5,000-ton Jap freighter. In February she was ordered into the Java Sea. There Lieutenant Commander David A. Hurt and crew waded into the savage Java Sea Battle.

While making a surface attack on the night of February 25, PERCH was struck in the conning-tower fairwater by a shell. The explosion ruptured the antenna trunk, the standard compass flooded, and minor damage was sustained. Three nights later, in the vortex of the Java Sea Battle, PERCH got a message directing all submarines to disregard assigned areas and attack the invading convoy at the landing point.

On the night of March 1, she was on the surface, steaming on a westerly course approximately twelve miles northwest of Soerabaja, when she sighted two Jap destroyers. Hurt ordered a dive. It was a bright moonlight night with good periscope vision, and one of the destroyers was seen maneuvering itself into a position suitable for a stern-tube attack. But when the range was down to 600 yards, the destroyer suddenly changed course, presenting a zero angle on the bow and coming in at high speed. Hurt ordered 180 feet, thinking he had 200 feet of water under him.

PERCH had reached 100 feet, when the destroyer came over and dropped a string of depth charges. The submarine hit bottom at 147 feet with the motors still turning over. No damage resulted from this depth-charging or from the accidental bottoming. But the destroyer returned.

On the DD's second run, four depth charges were dropped. PERCH was punished by this barrage. Maximum damage and shock was in the motor room and engine room. All motor-field relays tripped and were reset. Power was lost on one shaft. Ninety percent of the engine-room gages were broken. The hull ventilation supply-stop valve was frozen closed. The high-pressure air bank in the after battery started a bad leak. Number Five main-ballast vents were frozen closed. The engine air-induction inboard-stops were jammed closed. Both batteries showed a full ground. In the after battery the hull was compressed for about 6 feet by 1 foot, to a depth of 2½ inches. The crew's toilet bowl was broken to fragments.

The third string of charges came while PERCH was nestled in the mud with motors stopped. Maximum damage and shock hit amidships. In the control room the hull exhaust-duct section flooded, soaking the fire-control panel. The battery exhaust valve apparently opened and reseated. Several depth gages were broken. The conning tower was compressed to a depth of 2 inches over an area about 3 feet by 1 foot. Number Two periscope was frozen. Number One periscope would raise, but required four men to turn it. The engine-room hatch, conning-tower hatch and conning-tower door gaskets, were crimped so that they leaked steadily. The air-conditioning water-supply flange cracked at the weld and leaked copiously.

Shortly thereafter the crew freed PERCH from the mud, and Hurt commenced evasion tactics. In about two hours PERCH managed to shake the destroyers. It was discovered later that loss of air and oil had convinced the enemy that the submarine had been demolished, and the Japs had discontinued the attack accordingly. However, their depth charges had been set shallow and detonated above. Reason: Japanese depth charges were designed for a limited number of settings and would not detonate if they bottomed before making their set depth. Therefore, when dropped on a submarine on the bottom, the charges had to be set shallow. For her part, PERCH could only lie on the bottom and take it. Stuck in the mud, she was unable to attempt evasion. Most submariners concede that it is psychologically harder to take a severe depth-charging when lying helplessly on the bottom than it is when maneuvering to evade. In this, PERCH's crew concurred.

At 0300 PERCH surfaced. All the antenna insulators were found broken. A bushel of depth-charge fragments was picked up on deck. Both periscope windows were broken and both periscopes were flooded. The blinker light was flattened as though by a giant fist. Number One main engine ran away on starting. Number Four main-engine camshaft was broken. Number Two main engine was put on battery charge. Number Three main engine was put on propulsion. Lieutenant Commander Hurt headed PERCH for the position of the Japanese landing. The submarine had been down, but she was far from "out" as she drove back in to the attack.

About an hour later, with dawn two hours away, a pair of enemy destroyers hove in sight. PERCH made for the bottom. Hurt figured she had a better chance on the bottom. To run submerged in the condition PERCH was in, the noisy trim pumps had to be operated, but on the bottom all machinery could be stopped, and the submarine could lie quietly. Unfortunately, she had been sighted, and the Jap destroyers were on top of her with a vengeance.

The first string of charges dealt her no additional damage. She was on the bottom in 200 feet of water. But the second attack was murderous. One underwater blast after another shook the submarine. The air-conditioning circulating-water-supply flange leaked quarts as the flange studs elongated under successive shocks. The same casualty caused bad leaks on the suction and discharge lines of the high-pressure air-compressor circulating water system. Number One main-ballast vent was damaged—or the tank was cracked—for it proved impossible to blow the tank. Air could be heard passing up alongside the hull when blowing, but the tanks would not hold air.

There were leaks in the engine circulating water line and in various high-pressure air lines. Toilet bowls in the maneuvering room and after battery were shattered. The antenna trunk leaked. PERCH was badly injured, hemorrhaging internally when a third string of five charges was laid directly overhead from stern to bow. The bow planes, on a 20° rise, were rigged in by force of the explosions, a violence that burned up the bow-plane rigging panel. The JK soundhead went out of commission. Torpedoes No. 1 and No. 2 made hot runs in the tube.

Another depth-charge barrage came down. As explosion followed explosion, the support studs on the bow-plane tilting motor elongated and the shim dropped out. Bow planes had to be operated by hand from then on. The officers' toilet bowl was shattered and thrust out into the passageway. PERCH shook as though in the grip of an earthquake.

The final run of three charges proved the most severe of all. This came at about 0830 on the morning of March 2nd. At one blast, the depth gage suddenly changed from 200 to 228 feet. For an area of some 6 feet by 2½ feet the hull in one of the officers' staterooms was dished in at least 1½ inches. A cell cracked in the after battery (19 cells had previously cracked in the forward battery). All the electric alarm system and telephone circuits went dead, their cables being cut when instruments were flung off the bulkheads. Air banks No. 1 and No. 2 were emptied by leaks. After this savage attack the Jap destroyers steamed away, confident of a kill.

But there was life in the old boat yet. And PERCH's submariners were not dead. But the specter of slow suffocation appeared. Its grisly countenance was determinedly ignored. The men went about their jobs. David Hurt spoke a quiet word here and another there. "We've got to conserve air, so we won't try to get off the bottom until tonight."

During the day, damage to one of the main motors was isolated, returning power to both shafts. Bilges were kept pumped down to avoid the grounding of electrical machinery. Forward and after trim and No. 2 auxiliary were pumped dry. Efficiently the men went about their jobs, sweating it out as best they might.

At 2100, PERCH surfaced after about an hour's struggle. The main vents would not hold air, and emergency vents had to be closed. The barometer in the boat was broken and no one knew what the pressure was. There was a 240-volt ground on both batteries. By going ahead and astern at maximum power on both shafts, the submarine was finally broken from the mud. Somehow she reached the upper night and breathable air.

After successively trying all engines, the reprieved submariners finally got one on the line, and PERCH was under way, making 5 knots. Hull leaks proved so bad on the surface that both trim and drain pumps were required at full capacity to keep bilges from flooding.

Hurt decided they would have to make a trim dive before sunrise. About 0400, before daybreak of March 3, he ordered a running dive. In spite of every effort to make the ship light, and catch a trim by flooding in, she was found logily heavy on the dive. Before the descent could be checked, the injured submarine went down to 60 feet. Conning-tower and engine-room hatches failed to seat and leaked dangerously. The diving officer started blowing as soon as they were under. By the time they regained the surface, water in the engine-room bilges was up to the generators. After surfacing it was possible to expose only the forward half of the deck. Her stern under water, PERCH chugged ahead like a wounded whale.

The crew discovered that the conning-tower hatch was badly twisted, and there was an opening three-eighths of an inch wide that could not be closed. Handicapped by darkened ship, they tried to adjust the dogs on the hatch. While they were busy on the hatch the officer of the deck reported three Japanese destroyers in sight.

The nearest Jap opened fire. For PERCH the situation was hopeless. None of her tubes could be fired. Her deck gun was out of commission. It was obvious that she could not dive.

No use standing by to be massacred. Captain Hurt decided to abandon ship, and ordered the submarine scuttled. All the men got into the water safely. From a distance they watched PERCH start for the bottom, the sea pouring into her open conning-tower hatch. A moment later she was gone.

Then the weary submariners watched the Japs close in. All were picked up by the enemy destroyermen. Taken to the questioning camp at Ofuna, Japan, the men of PERCH were ruthlessly grilled, then hustled off to the Ashio mines. There, nine of their number were to perish as prisoners of war. Fifty-three, including Lieutenant Commander Hurt, survived imprisonment.

Seawolf at Christmas Island

She had moved into those waters south of Java after patrol in the vicinity of Bali. And there she was to be the last submarine to oppose an enemy landing at an invasion point in the Java area. Her opposition at Christmas Island was the sort that will live in history as an undersea warfare classic.

Already her captain, Freddie Warder, was becoming known in submarine circles as an "artist of submarining." A native of Grafton, West Virginia, he had been in submarines since 1928, and in the war since the first bomb dropped on Manila Bay.

Shortly before SEAWOLF's visit to Christmas she picked up a radio message from SALMON giving the position and approximate bearing and speed of a large enemy convoy moving in SEAWOLF's general direction.

SEAWOLF intercepted the invasion force, and there was a battle royal in which torpedo explosions and the watery smash of depth bombs echoed to Tokyo. While official records based on post-war inquest fail to credit SEAWOLF with a sinking at this time, there seems no doubt that enemy ships were damaged. Some torpedoes may have missed and others, erratic as they were, prematured. But a number were heard to run straight and hot, and in the volley of blasts several ships were probably holed.

Protests to the contrary by Radio Tokyo certainly pointed to American submarine successes in the Malay Barrier area. One had only to put reverse English on the propaganda.

"Our fleet has again shown its superiority over the Allied submarines!" (Tokyo Rose speaking.) *"In a recent landing on the island of Bali our forces ran into a nest of them. Not one enemy submarine was able to accomplish a successful attack. It will not be long before we have eliminated the last Allied submarine from Pacific waters."*

Listening in on this bedtime story, SEAWOLF'S crew was unimpressed. Far from eliminated, they were on their way to Christmas Island, a British flyspeck off the southwest coast of Java, to do some eliminating. The island, valuable for its phosphate mines, was a logical enemy objective. Orders directed SEAWOLF to patrol the area and then proceed to Australia.

SEAWOLF arrived off the island in due time. Due time was early morning on the last day of March. Warder moved up cautiously, wary of possible Allied batteries. To shore gunners fighting for their lives, all submarines tend to look alike. But periscope inspection could detect no life on the island. Warder studied the chart. The island's only dock facilities were an inlet called Flying Fish Cove. Obviously the enemy had not yet arrived.

He discussed the matter with his officers. "We could go in there tonight and blow up that dock. But some natives might be killed on the waterfront."

Reported in a book about the SEAWOLF by her Chief Radioman, Joseph Melvin Eckberg, Warder's comment, as quoted, tells a whole volume about "Fearless Freddie" Warder. A humane man who, in the teeth of hell and high water, could find time to think about the natives on a picayune island, time to see them as fellow humans experiencing life on a common star, and, as such, deserving of consideration. But Warder walked on a star unknown to the officers of conquest coming down from Tokyo. Already their forces, on a rampage of exploitation, were pillaging Java. And on the night of March 31, their invasion ships were sighted on the way to Christmas Island.

The contact report came by radio. Warder immediately started defensive patrolling. April 1, at 0730, the enemy hove in sight—four cruisers in column, lined up as though contemplating a shore bombardment.

Light cruisers—two turrets forward, one aft—typical Jap bow—raked stern—pagoda-style fire control tower—plane catapults—the column grew in the periscope scale. Upping and downing the scope, Warder maneuvered the WOLF forward to intercept. He chose a target and described her over the intercom.

"Cruiser NATORI class. Angle on the bow, five starboard. Range 3,000. Seems to be making medium speed."

A moment later, "This ship is patrolling. Planes are still on deck. Range 2,300. Left full rudder. Ahead two-thirds. Come to course three four zero."

Then, "I can see a command pennant. There's an admiral aboard this baby. Down periscope! Forward room, make ready the bow tubes!"

The tubes were made ready. Sound, feeding information to the skipper, reported the target bearing as three five two. She was getting close. "Open the outer doors! Up periscope! Here she comes! Down periscope! Stand by to fire. Fire one!" A whispery cough as the torpedo sprinted on its way. "Fire two!"

Third and fourth shots were fired for good measure. At the periscope Warder saw one hit—a spout of water—jets of steam—Jap officers and men racing about in pandemonium. The cruiser kept on coming.

It was time to go deep. Warder dived down the conning-tower ladder to the control room; the conning tower was sealed off; the WOLF, rigged for depth charges, began evasion tactics.

Explosions slammed somewhere to starboard. Then *slam! slam! slam!* Timed at 15-second intervals they came closer. The submarine vibrated and heaved. SLAM! Locker doors flew open, and flakes of paint and cork scattered across the control room. The men clutched at hand-holds, swaying, grimacing. The explosions faded off to starboard. Then *slam! slam!* they began somewhere to port.

SEAWOLF was not eliminated by that first barrage off Christmas Island. Nor by the follow-up depth-chargings which continued throughout that day. Warder maneuvered the submarine to a position some 15 miles offshore, and waited for nightfall. A brilliant moon held the WOLF at bay until about 0200. After moondown, Warder started in toward Flying Fish Cove.

At 0400, when the submarine was about 11 miles offshore, a cruiser was sighted. SEAWOLF took a dive. The warship was moving slowly—no hurry. At daybreak she was off the port beam. Warder ran up the periscope for a look.

"I'll be damned!" he gripped the training handles, "this

cruiser is like the one we hit yesterday! They've got a dog-gone command pennant flying. Did we shift that admiral around, or are they trying to trick us?"

Warder peered again. The morning light was trying to fool him? The cruiser with the command pennant was plainly there. He began a submerged approach.

On yesterday's target he had expended four torpedoes. With the supply running low, he could afford only three on this CL. The firing began at 0513. A few seconds later there was a jarring explosion. The WOLF went under to listen. Breaking-up noises rattled, clashed, crackled and popped in the sound gear. There was a final crunching roar—then silence. Warder upped the periscope. Where the cruiser had been he could see no cruiser. A broom might have swept her away.

The time was 0517. At 0522 Sound heard high-speed screws. Two DD's came into the scene, and SEAWOLF departed therefrom. She departed in the direction of Flying Fish Cove.

As the morning advanced, the little inlet became busy with Jap ships. Loitering offshore, SEAWOLF watched them. Business was leisurely until about noon when some angry-looking destroyers came out on patrol. Sound could hear them "pinging." They were followed by a cruiser which launched a patrol plane. At the periscope Warder made out a herd of transports getting up steam. It looked as if the convoy was preparing to come out and the Imperial Navy was setting up a big anti-submarine screen.

As Warder watched these preparations, the cruiser which had launched the plane nosed over in SEAWOLF's direction, zigzagging. Warder eyed her in fascination. Had he seen that pennant somewhere before? Well, the bunting might be imaginary, or the Japs might be April fooling, but this was certainly another CL. Lining up as a perfect target!

Warder rushed the crew to battle stations, bore in for the attack, and fired two. An explosion was heard as the submarine dove for cover, but there was no time for periscope observation of the damage. And there wasn't much cover.

Infuriated by the persistent submarine activity the destroyers raced up and down, dropping depth-charges, trying to locate the submersible.

SEAWOLF went under and stayed under, sweating it out. Time dragged. The air conditioning had to be turned off, and the humidity thickened to an almost visible fog. Men and machines began to drip. A reek of perspiration, warm oil, and battery gases coagulated in muggy heat. The refrigerator had to be switched off and the drinking water became as warm as weak tea. The toilet tanks could not be emptied as betraying air bubbles would have traveled to the surface. Gasping for air, the men sprawled in their bunks or moved slowly through tiring little tasks. Chief Pharmacist's Mate Frank Loaiza passed out saline tablets. Some of the men became nauseated.

In this sewer-like atmosphere minds went sluggish and voices were reduced to a squeaky whisper. Warder moved here and there with a forced, "How you doing?" no better off than any of them. They had to take it. The Jap hunters were up there, and they were down here, all in the same boat, enduring.

They endured. But finally the lights went dim, and they had to surface to charge the batteries. If they didn't get up there before the batteries died, they, themselves, would go out with the lights. Warder gave the order, and they climbed.

But they did not reach fresh air. Not yet. The periscope found a destroyer on the surface, waiting for them in the dusk, listening.

"Take her down," Warder ordered. And they started the descent.

Then the depth gage jumped—the deck slid in the wrong direction—they were broaching!

Warder shouted, "Flood negative!" and there was a tumult of escaping air as water flooded into the negative tank. SEAWOLF's conning tower broke the surface, showering spray.

"All ahead, emergency! Bow planes, stern planes, hard dive!"

Motors shocked to action, and the WOLF went down, plunging. The dive had to be checked by blowing negative and, "All back, emergency!" A swirl of froth and bubbles eddied to the surface, and the enemy was overhead directly.

The first depth charge sounded like World's End. Thrown from their footing, the men collided with bulkheads and caromed off greasy wheels and slippery gear. Glass splintered and there was a sound of groaning metal. But the submarine held together.

The WOLF found deeper water. Again the men waited at their stations, wilting in the suffocating murk. They learned they had broached because an order had been misinterpreted and too much water had been blown from the bow buoyancy tank. That wouldn't happen again.

It was after midnight when three blares on the diving alarm announced Warder's order to surface. Without misadventure she climbed—cool night air poured in—all clear. Warder headed for Australia. The Battle of Christmas Island was over.

The following night, SEAWOLF received a radio message from the High Command:

A WONDERFUL CRUISE . . . CONGRATULATIONS

Captain Warder posted a copy on the bulletin board, amending the message with a note.

"To all hands: I want to take this opportunity to express my deepest thanks for your ability and your conduct, and above all, your devotion to duty. It is my firm hope that I will be with you all when we put out to sea on the next patrol. Respectfully, F. B. Warder."

Japanese records do not admit loss of a light cruiser at Christmas Island, and a sinking is not down on the official record, although a cruiser may be down under the waters off Christmas. Certainly something happened there on April First. The Admiral's pennant may have been a trick, but SEAWOLF and Freddie Warder were not fooling.

Retreat from the Philippines (Good-bye to a Great Lady)

The Ides of March boded ill for the defenders of Bataan and Corregidor. Ordered to delay the conquest of the Philippines, American and Filipino troops—60,000 against Tojo's legions—turned the defense into an Asian Verdun.

Jap propaganda to the contrary, the U.S. Navy was also there. The Naval Defense Battalion on Bataan, Lieutenant Bulkeley's PT-boaters and the sailors at Corregidor put up a fight that will long remain a synonym for human valiance and endurance. And in the vortex of this battle, unpublicized at the time, were the submariners who ran the blockade— the special missioners who carried food, medicine, munitions to the besieged troops and took out the evacuees—the men who made a battleship of a tender. The Army could not have achieved its four-month Bataan stand without the Navy at Corregidor, and Corregidor could not have been held without the support of the submariners.

Early in March, General MacArthur, Rear Admiral Rockwell and their staffs made their dash to the southern Philippines and away. On the 31st of that month, SEADRAGON received orders to go to Cebu and ferry rations from there to starving Corregidor. Ferrall and his boys were at Cebu on April 3. Thirty-four tons of food waited delivery to Corregidor's last standers.

The Jap vise was closing on Corregidor when SEADRAGON got there on the 6th. Working at aching speed, the subma-

riners had only time to unload seven tons of cargo before
ordered away from the dock. She stood by off Corregidor
for 48 hours, after which time Ferrall was informed that
further unloading was not feasible. With a passenger list
which included 30 communication officers, 18 enlisted men
and an Army colonel, she headed south for Fremantle.

SNAPPER (Lieutenant Commander H. L. Stone) arrived
off Corregidor on April 9. She had come up from Cebu with
46 tons of food. Stone and his crew were able to deliver
about 20 tons of food to the rescue vessel PIGEON. The submarine then went up to the Rock to take aboard seven naval
officers and 20 enlisted men. With these evacuees she was
ordered to shove off for Fremantle.

In the meantime, SEARAVEN had left Fremantle on April 2
with 1,500 rounds of 3-inch anti-aircraft ammunition for
Corregidor. On April 11, she was ordered to attempt the
rescue of 33 Australian Army personnel on Timor just north
of Keopang. This proved to be a ticklish operation that
might have failed but for the cold-steel nerve of skipper
Hiram Cassedy and crew.

SEARAVEN arrived off Timor in good time, and Cassedy
maneuvered her into alcove at the entrance of a large lagoon.
Shallow water prevented the submarine's entry into the lagoon, but there was nothing to prevent the submariners
from going ashore—except the Japs. Cassedy had no way
of knowing their whereabouts—and little means of ascer-
taining the whereabouts of the Australians marooned in the
vicinity. He had been briefed on recognition signals and
warned of a possible trap. The only way to rescue the Aussies, if any, was to risk the trap.

Two successive night attempts to communicate with the
unseen Australians failed. Finally Ensign George C. Cook
volunteered to take a small boat in to the beach. Rough surf
forced the boat to stand off, and young Cook dived in and
swam through the breakers.

A campfire had been seen in the bush, and Cook, believing
the Australians were at hand, walked boldly forward. In
the laconic wording of SEARAVEN's report:

> He noted about 12 men standing around. When within
> about twenty-five yards of the campfire he turned his
> flashlight upon himself and shouted, at which all hands
> near the fire scattered. He searched the surrounding area
> for about an hour and then reported he was unable to
> make contact.

Cook's one-hour search of the jungle in which a dozen
men had disappeared (or were they phantoms?) is one of
those individualistic dramas that men write home about—or

do when they aren't submariners in a silent service. Struggling and splashing through the swampy jungle-fringe, the ensign flashed his light on vines that looped down like giant pythons and grotesque mats of foliage in which anything might have crouched in ambush. Strange birds flew up screaming in the night. Floundering in mud, he stumbled over something—probably a crocodile.

Cook returned empty-handed from this nightmare limber-lost, wondering if his imagination had played him tricks. Later that night SEARAVEN made radio contact with Headquarters and learned that the Australians were camped on the other side of the lagoon. Cook's scalp must have prickled a little. Of what origin were those shades he had seen around the campfire?

The following night, Cassedy surfaced the submarine, and the indomitable Ensign Cook once more went in with the small boat. Again heavy surf held the boat offshore. So Cook swam in to the beach. And this time he found the Australians.

Suffering from malaria, tropical fever, ulcers and battle wounds, the Australians came out of the bush as figures from a grave. A haggard lieutenant reported that Jap scouts were close by in the jungle. Quick getaway was imperative, but getting the wounded men out to the submarine proved a Herculean task. The small boat capsized in the surf. Cook swam through the surf with one badly wounded Australian on his back, and another submariner—whose name also was Cook—went through the surf with a wounded man. Before the Japs got to the scene, 33 Australians were saved.

For the Aussies and Searaveners the adventure was not yet over. On the run back home to Fremantle a serious fire broke out in the maneuvering room. Smoke choked the after quarters of the submarine. Power went out, and SEARAVEN was immobilized for a number of hours while Cassedy and crew fought to bring the blaze under control. But when SEARAVEN was eventually towed into port, the rescued Australians were convalescing, and the submariners had written another saga for the Silent Service.

SPEARFISH (Lieutenant Commander J. C. Dempsey) was the last submarine to visit crumbling Corregidor. On May 3 she evacuated 12 Army and Navy officers, 11 Army nurses, a Navy nurse and a civilian woman. Up to that date, ladies were uncommon submarine passengers, but these, who had remained in bomb-hammered Corregidor, were uncommon ladies.

And then there was *the* Old Lady—herself, a submariner

who remained in the Philippines to the very last. Her story
—part and parcel of any chronicle on submarining—deserves
a chapter to itself.

She was the submarine tender CANOPUS—a product of
1919, originally built for the merchant service. The Navy
acquired her from the Grace Line in 1921, and converted
her into a tender of "pig boats." Supplied with forges, machine shops, oil tanks and other vitals necessary for her
trade, she had been mothering her submarine broods for
some 20 years when the war broke around her at Manila.

The night before General Homma marched in, she moved
down to Mariveles Bay to tend the Asiatic Fleet submarines
which had been driven from Manila and Cavite. On December 29 Jap aviators spied her, hit her with an armor-piercing
bomb. Her skipper, Commander E. L. Sackett, and her crew
put out the fires and kept her afloat. This was a job on an
old vessel like CANOPUS, but her people were artisans, technicians and mechanics whose specialty was damage control
and repair.

On January 1, 1942, when the Asiatic submarines were
ordered to Java, CANOPUS found herself left behind. Lamed
as she was, she would have made a floating bull's-eye for
enemy planes. A dash for Soerabaja was out of the question.
Her crew hoped she might be able to limp down there later,
but an air attack in early January settled the matter. Striking the tender's old-fashioned smokestack, a fragmentation
bomb clawed her upper decks to ruin and left her listing
and battered with 15 casualties.

"The tough old girl was not ready for her grave yet," Captain Sackett recounted in a biographic article. *"But if she
were to continue in a career of usefulness, it seemed best to
make the Japs think the last salvo of bombs had done the
trick. . . . The next morning, when 'Photo Joe' in his scouting plane came over, his pictures showed what looked like
an abandoned hulk . . . from which wisps of smoke floated
up for two or three days. What he did not know was that
the smoke came from oily rags in strategically placed smudge
pots, and that every night the 'abandoned hulk' hummed
with activity, forging new weapons for the beleaguered forces
of Bataan."*

Unable to sail, she was nevertheless able to operate. Sackett and crew kept her going in high gear. About 100 of the
tender-men took up lodgings in a capacious storage tunnel
which the Army had dug in a cliff flanking the bay. Bunks,
a dressing station and a radio were installed in the tunnel.
Old CANOPUS, listing in the shallows, was turned into a

general machine shop, smithy and manufactory, working on a 24-hour shift to aid and succor the defenders of Bataan and Corregidor.

One of her first jobs was to turn her own 40-foot motor launches into armored craft for the harrying of Jap beachheads. The shipfitters on CANOPUS cut up boiler plate to make gun shields and body armor for the three launches which comprised a tiny task force that won fame as "Uncle Sam's Mickey Mouse Battle Fleet."

To CANOPUS, then, came guns in need of repair, radios in want of gadgets, Marine gear requiring some gizmo, watches that failed to keep time. Word hurried around that the tender was staffed with blacksmiths, tinkers and plumbers capable of anything. What was more, her refrigerators were working and she was chock full of ice cream and ham sandwiches. Want some dungarees? They got 'em on that submarine tender. You broke a finger? They'll fix it for you aboard CANOPUS.

"Nearly every evening, Army officers and nurses who were able to snatch a few hours leave from their duties, gathered on board the CANOPUS," wrote Captain Sackett. *"To enjoy a real shower bath, cold drinking water, well-cooked meals served on white linen with civilized tableware, and greatest luxury of all, real butter, seemed almost too much for them to believe."*

So, sitting in the bay like a stranded river-steamer, all Hades exploding around her and the next bomb liable to blast her into the Hereafter, CANOPUS became a king-pin in the last ditch Philippine defense. Her engineers, who had repaired the Diesels of fleet submarines, now worked on the firing mechanisms of Army pistols. Her undersea technicians built a spare part for an Army plane. Her cooks served hot victuals to Leathernecks and cold drinks to Filipino Scouts. To her radiomen came runners with messages for dispatch. Wounded and dying troopers were cared for by her pharmacist's mates. Her storekeepers distributed skivvies to anyone in need. One of her artisans built for an Army dentist an upper plate. One hundred and thirty of her sailors joined the Naval Defense Battalion to fight ashore.

"Occasionally, our submarines, which were prowling the sea lanes looking for Jap ships to sink, would pay us a visit while en route from patrol stations back to their new southern bases. Other submarines also made special visits when required, bringing in vital medical supplies or ammunition of any kind which happened to be urgently needed. Nearly all of these submarines took out passengers when they left— high political personages, Army and Navy officers, and

*specially trained enlisted men who were badly needed to
carry on the war elsewhere. Greatest comfort of all to those
left behind were the letters these submarines carried to their
loved ones at home."*

The men on the tender could receive no mail, but they
could write to their families in the States and tell the world
they were holding the fort. Through burning February and
blasted March, CANOPUS stuck it out at her bomb-thrashed
anchorage. Hospital, machine shop, P.X., communications
center, supply store, U.S.O.—she was all things to all forces
fighting on Bataan and the Rock. They called her the "Old
Lady," and like her famous namesake in fiction, she "showed
her medals." Her submarine technicians labored like giants
with the craft of jewelers, and her forges were turning out
mechanical gems when the Japs guns were right on top of
Mariveles.

On April 8 the end came.

*"All hope of holding Bataan was gone, leaving us with
the grim duty of destroying everything that might be of value
to the Nipponese. . . . Around the shores of Mariveles Bay,
Navy men blew up the Dewey floating drydock, which had
served the Asiatic Fleet for so many years, and scuttled the
ships which had no part to play in defending Corregidor.
The CANOPUS seemed reluctant to go, but her crew could still
take pride in the fact that the Japs had been unable to knock
her out—she was still able to back out under her own power
to deep water. There she was laid to her final rest by the
hands of the sailors she had served so faithfully."*

She was gone, but the human part of her—her people—
remained. They joined the naval forces for the last-stand
fight at Corregidor. The tender's versatile launches were
turned over to Mine Force sailors to serve as miniature minesweepers. Machinists, engineers, every hand of the CANOPUS
crew who was physically able, supported the Marines manning Corregidor's beach defenses. There was no such thing
as sinking the spirit of the "Old Lady."

During the remainder of April and the first days of May,
the Japs sledge-hammered the Rock with countless tons of
air bombs and monster shells.

*"Flesh and blood could not endure the merciless pounding
indefinitely, nor could the concrete and steel of the forts
stand forever. One by one, pill boxes and gun emplacements were knocked out, leaving little to resist when the
yellow horde should finally pour from boats in the final assault. . . . Two nights before that landing, a submarine
slipped through the screen of Jap destroyers clustered
around the entrance to Manila Bay, and the last group of*

passengers raced out the new channel to meet their rescue ship. . . . What a wonderful relief was the sight of that low black hull looming through the darkness, waiting exactly at her station!"

That submarine was SPEARFISH—there on the spot to pick up this group of Navy and Army nurses and officers who were the last of Corregidor's defenders to be reprieved. Here again was proof of the submersible's ability to operate unsupported in waters under enemy control. With Japanese warships on every hand, SPEARFISH got in and got out, accomplishing one of the war's most perilous rescue missions.

Among those on Corregidor when the Japs arrived were men of the submarine tender CANOPUS—the "old Lady" who was named after a star of the first magnitude, and who more than lived up to her name.

Corregidor fell on May 6, and the Philippine Islands were lost to the Japanese.

MacArthur said he would be back. But the submariners never left the Philippines.

Chapter 9

Stand Tide

Weather Report

Spring 1942. Stormy weather for the Allies—a winter of defeats, reluctant to loosen its grip on the battle fronts of the United Nations. In the Pacific the Japanese offensive rolled on, its spearheads thrusting toward Australia, stabbing into New Guinea and the Bismarck Archipelago. To observers in Washington and London there seemed no break, no slowing of the titanic forces unleashed by Tokyo, no hint of change in the war's weather.

But there were hints of change that spring. Nothing that showed up in banner headlines. No abrupt stoppage of storm and flood. But a faint jolting somewhere out there in the Pacific—or, rather, under it.

It may be that the submarine force commanders were the first to be aware of the break—the undersea phenomena that invited hopeful prophecy. On the surface April and May were bad months for the Allies. Under the surface there was a U.S. submarine rally.

Perhaps it had its source in the fact that by the end of March 1942 the pattern of undersea warfare in the Pacific had begun to clarify. Nearly all of the Central Pacific areas had been covered except those north of Tokyo and in the Sea of Japan. In the Southwest Pacific the enemy's supply lines had been discerned and marked for submarine attention. That was the strategic summary.

On the tactical side, battle tactics had been tested and altered where found wanting. Jap methods had been evaluated and Jap stratagems countered. The enemy destroyer no longer enjoyed its former reputation as the submarine's Nemesis.

109

Most important, the submarines, themselves, had met the fitness test of action, and come through. They'd been able to take it and survive. A program designed to give each crew two weeks' rest and recuperation between patrols was showing excellent results. Morale was on the rebound from initial shock and discouragement. A tendency at war's outbreak to underestimate the enemy can result in consternation at early losses, and consequent overestimation of the opponent's prowess. Now the enemy's character was more realistically appraised. The submarine forces had taken his full measure and found him neither from Lilliput nor Brobdingnag. He was ruthless, clever, skillful, well-trained, courageous. A tigerish foe. But prone to errors of judgment, to weaknesses and miscalculations, and as vulnerable to a bullet as any man.

In short, the submarine forces were acquiring experience and self-confidence. These had their reflection in the patrol reports of April and May.

An air strike at Japan was on the Navy's planning board. Weather conditions, of vital import in such an undertaking, demand study. Into Japanese waters went THRESHER, under Lieutenant Commander W. L. Anderson, to play aerographer and forecaster.

THRESHER'S weather reports timed a storm over Tokyo for April. On the 18th, HORNET, supported by ENTERPRISE, was 700 miles off Japan. Led by Lieutenant Colonel "Jimmie" Doolittle, sixteen Army B-25's took off from HORNET'S flight deck, and the thunderbolt hit Dai Nippon in the heart. Jap submarines had pried into Hawaiian waters, scouting for an air strike. On similar mission, Pearl Harbor submarines scouted off Tokyo Bay.

Pioneer Tactics ("Down-the-throat" Shot)

SKIPJACK went into battle in May under Lieutenant Commander J. W. (Red) Coe.

The ability to analyze a difficult station and improvise emergency measures to offset the difficulties is an invaluable asset to the submariner. Coe could act and think, too (or think and act, too)—a faculty nicely demonstrated during SKIPJACK'S May 1942 patrol.

In pre-war practice it was usually conceded that if a submarine making a torpedo approach were caught at close range dead ahead of the target, the appropriate tactic was to go deep and pray.

War experience, however, was to prove that such a situation was by no means fatal for the sub. On the contrary, if the submarine gained a position in which she could exploit small gyro angles at a firing range of 1,500 yards or less, the chances of hitting were nearly as good as the chances presented by attacks which provided broader track angles.

A torpedo shot fired at close range at the enemy advancing head-on was labeled a "down-the-throat" shot. While this shot was seldom, if ever, deliberately chosen in preference to the more conventional, many commanding officers learned to use it with telling effect. If able to maneuver the submarine into a dead-ahead position, they would head straight for the target. Then, if the target zigged to right or left, a normal attack position was set up. If the target did not zig, and the range closed to 1,500 yards or less, a down-the-throat shot had an excellent chance of punching the ship on the prow.

The first successful down-the-throat shot on official record was fired early in SKIPJACK's third patrol. Date: May 6, 1942. Locale: off Indo-China, near Camranh Bay.

Target sighted at 0300, about seven miles distant with a 90° angle on the bow. A luminous moon was astern of the submarine, and Coe did not want to risk a night-surface approach. Putting all four engines on propulsion, he made a high-speed run to get ahead of the target—a position he hoped to gain by daybreak. Traveling at a good 16.5 knots, SKIP-JACK handily outdistanced the Jap freighter. But in the resulting maneuvers Coe discovered he had overrun the position for straight bow shots.

Overestimation of the target's size may have caused the error in Coe's calculations. Silhouettes in moonlight are often deceptive, and the vessel he had sized up as a 6,000-tonner proved to be a small cargoman of some 2,500 tons. The submariners, deluded by a trick of perspective, bored in for the attack with a speed that took SKIPJACK to a point only 300 yards from the track.

Here was a situation that demanded instantaneous adjustment. According to current theory, Coe should have gone deep and prayed. He did neither.

While the target swelled in size on the periscope scale, Coe's mind raced through some fast analysis. She's coming at 11 knots. The torpedoes must have time to arm. Sufficient range for arming means a new set-up. Take it or leave it? We'll take it.

In order to fire with a range that permitted arming, he had to accept a 20° track with a 50° gyro angle. Abandoning the Mark VI angle-solver for the Torpedo Data Computer, Coe became a convert to the T.D.C. from there on out. The robot came through with the set-up in jig time, and three

torpedoes were fired accordingly. One struck home with a
geysering smash. And under by the head went a ship later
identified as KANAN MARU—the first of many to succumb
to the lethal down-the-throat shot.

Torpedoes for Taiyo Maru

Coe directed eight day-submerged attacks on shipping off
the Indo-China coast. SKIPJACK sank three ships. Undoubtedly her score would have been higher, given a square-
shooting torpedo.

Having consistently sabotaged the efforts of the pioneer sub-
mariners, this Mark 14 torpedo nearly undid the work of
Lieutenant Commander "Pilley" Lent and the men in
GRENADIER.

Lent took her out on her second patrol to hunt in the
East China Sea southwest of Kyushu. At 1852, late in the
afternoon of May 8, she encountered a convoy of six freighters
and a large passenger ship which Lent correctly identified
as the 14,457-ton TAIYO MARU. No escorts were sighted, although their presence in the vicinity was assumed. The assumption proved correct, as events were to disclose.

Ignoring the other ships present, Lent concentrated on the
big passenger liner. At 1931 he fired the first of four torpedoes in a salvo from the bow tubes, 105° starboard track,
range 1,500 yards. The first and last torpedoes were set for a
depth of 24 feet, and the second and third for 28 feet. Time
of explosion indicated that the first and fourth torpedoes
hit, and the other two missed, although the spread indicated
that they should have hit.

Trailed down the home stretch by Sound, the torpedoes had
apparently run straight and hot. Lent concluded that something had gone wrong with the magnetic exploders. These
finicky devices could be "duds" for a variety of reasons, and
Lent determined to make a note of it for the attention of
ComSubPac.

Perhaps he made these notes while GRENADIER had her
"going over." Two minutes after firing, she was burrowing
deep and changing course when a stick of bombs exploded
overhead. A few minutes later, fast screws were heard, and
the ash-cans started coming down. Thirty-six depth charges
roared in the deeps around her. Lent brought her undamaged through the barrage, although several blasts were
close.

Nerves may have received another jarring after Lieutenant
Commander Lent, mistrusting the Mark 14's exploder, reported his suspicions to Submarine Headquarters. Coming on

the heels of other reports protesting the behavior of the Mark 14, Lent's comments sparked prompt reaction. Evidence of torpedo malfunction was summed up for review. Unfortunately the conclusions drawn by the analysts were as wide of the mark as the torpedoes. Rejecting evidence which indicated a bug in the machinery, ComSubPac ordered the depth-settings maintained as before (five feet greater than maximum depth of the target).

The big passenger liner was the only ship sunk by GRENADIER on that patrol. In fact, the liner was to be the only vessel officially credited to her record. A few months later, GRENADIER herself was sunk.

But in sinking the 14,457-ton TAIYO MARU, Lent's submarine dealt a crippling blow to the masters of the Co-Prosperity Sphere. The liner had been en route to the East Indies with a group of Jap scientists, economists and industrial experts bent on expediting exploitation of the conquered territory. Most of these experts went down with the torpedoed liner.

*"Sugar Boats"** to Brisbane*

Following the enemy seizure of the Netherlands East Indies, the war moved front and center into the Solomons-Bismarck area.

Such expansion was, in fact, a military imperative. For if conquerors are to capitalize on territorial gains outer bases must be established to defend the captured areas. In turn, outposts must be set up to secure the defense bases. This imperative is particularly pressing on the conqueror of insular territories wherein one island lies within striking distance of another. To protect Java, for example, it was necessary to seize and establish strongholds on all neighboring islands. But the Celebes group could be secured from attack only by seizure of bases in New Guinea. The New Guinea bases could be held only by securing the Bismarck Archipelago. And Rabaul in the Bismarck Archipelago could be secured only by seizure of bases in the Solomon Islands. Next step: Australia.

The Jap militarists, therefore, were in the position of the liar who must devise one falsehood after another to support an original untruth. The analogous business of conquest—the strategic need for continued expansion—has embarrassed conquerors throughout history.

Nevertheless, the military necessity remained. So long as

---

* "Sugar" is the code name for the letter "S" in "S-boats."

the American-Australian lifeline operated, Australia would be a standing threat to Japan's hold on the East Indies. And in the early spring of 1942, a Japanese drive on Australia seemed far from absurd.

The continent was looking invasion squarely in the teeth, and it was evident that Australia's defense was up to the U.S. Navy. It was equally apparent that the only U.S. naval units immediately available for that defense were those which could be mustered by the submarine forces.

The only subs on hand were those of the now defunct Asiatic Fleet. And they were needed to harry the enemy's ship-lanes in the Philippines and Indonesia seas. So Submarine Division 53—an old S-boat division—was rushed from Balboa, Panama, to Brisbane, Australia. A voyage that turned the submariners concerned into nautical Melvilles and Magellans.

Led by Captain Christie aboard the new submarine tender GRIFFIN, the S-boats set out for Australia in early March. They were S-42 (Lieutenant O. G. Kirk); S-43 (Lieutenant E. R. Hannon); S-44 (Lieutenant J. R. Moore); S-45 (Lieutenant I. C. Eddy); S-46 (Lieutenant R. C. Lynch); and S-47 (Lieutenant J. W. Davis).

The old World War I "sugar boat" had not been designed for a 12,000-mile run—or a 6,000-mile run, for that matter. Now, called upon to hike from Panama to Australia, with but one fueling stop en route—Bora Bora in the Society Islands—the S-boaters must have experienced some private qualms. Time for worry, however, was one of the things the SubDiv 53 submariners did not have. Among other items lacking were air-conditioning systems for the submarines, and the well-known comforts of home. As for the operating condition of the S-boats, "bugs" were anticipated. In this regard, the crews were by no means disappointed. But they got there on April 15 after 42 days at sea without a major breakdown.

Awaiting the Panama boats at Brisbane was battle-scarred S-38. At intervals in the next three weeks, other S-boats from Fremantle came migrating across the Great Australian Bight to join the Brisbane Task Force. Under the command of Captain Christie, the S-boats of the former Asiatic Fleet and the Panama "sugar boats" were welded together into Task Force Forty-two.

The "sugar boaters" went out from Brisbane, and they met more enemies than one. They battled weather, humidity, fatigue, mechanical difficulties and a large assortment of attendant mental hazards. On early patrols anywhere north of 15° south, the submarines were forced to run submerged

all day, surfacing only at night. Temperatures averaged 95°
F., and humidity averaged over 85% in S-boats running submerged. Throughout the day the submariners were in a
soak of sweat, and often enough at night when engine trouble
or failing electrical gear kept them working overtime. A
three-week patrol in equatorial water was enough to wilt the
most stalwart crew.

Battles Above and Below

Ju Island, located between New Guinea and Halmahera, is
not prominent on the map. But it was as unforgettable as
Manhattan to five U.S. Army aviators whose plane made a
crash landing in its jungles early in May. The flyers got off a
call for help, and waited. Presently a periscope peered up at
the beach, and there was PORPOISE on hand to rescue the
Crusoes. Picking up the aviators, she took them to Darwin—
all part of the submariners' work.

Meantime, another submarine was going into action—one
whose name was to be engraved in gleaming chirography
across the broad Pacific. The name: SILVERSIDES. The engrav-
ers: Creed Burlingame and crew.

Burlingame had come up through the conning tower of an
S-boat—the old S-30—and he knew the ups and downs of
submarining. The war was not three months old when, at
Mare Island, he assumed command of SILVERSIDES, newest of
the Pacific Fleet's new-construction submarines.

Sleek, streamlined and modern to the last fitting, she was
a magnificent engine of war. And her launching boded ill for
the Japanese, although her trial run had not been entirely successful. During a quick dive her stern planes had jammed. As
she went down and kept on going, Burlingame "blew everything," but the water wasn't there to save her, and she
slammed her nose into the bottom. A sailor with nautical
superstitions might have wished her a more auspicious beginning.

On their way out to Hawaii they almost lost their radioman
striker, Sam Remington. New man in submarines (he had
joined the Navy but a year before), Remington was standing
lookout on the bridge when the order came, "Take her down!"
Remington heard the yell as his companion lookouts raced
for the hatch. But he had tied the leather thongs of his binoculars to the "A" frame, and now, hasty-fingered, he was
unable to untie the knot.

Diving across the "cigarette deck," he plunged through the
wheelhouse for the conning-tower hatch. He found the hatch
sealed. SILVERSIDES was going down.

"Halloo!" Remington shouted in the bridge telephone. "I'm up here! Man topside!"

No answer on the phone. And it looked like a long swim to nowhere when the submarine suddenly lurched upward and the deck rose clear. Remington's yell had been heard. No one aboard SILVERSIDES was going to loiter on her bridge after that.

Late in April she was assigned to her first patrol in an area off the coast of Japan. Burlingame told all hands they were shoving off for the real thing, and they headed out of Pearl Harbor into tumbling seas.

Rough voyage to Midway gave the crew authentic sea legs. And then on May 10, about 0800, with high seas combing the superstructure, a hail was raised by the lookout.

"Two masts! Four points on the starboard bow! Crossing!"

Burlingame was topside on the double. Binocular inspection revealed the target as a Japanese trawler, maybe 300 tons.

"Patrol boat! We'll sink her with gunfire!"

SILVERSIDES' gunners had to fight to keep their feet on the pitching deck, and the first shots went wild. The sight-setter, struck by a wall of swooping water, went acrobating to the forward engine-room hatch. The shell-passers struggled, fell, hung on. Burlingame drove to closer range, and the gun crew found the target with a succession of hits. Fire burst from the trawler, but she refused to sink. Machine-gun bullets whipped across the submarine's deck. Second loader, Mike Harbin, TM3, fell with a bullet in his temple.

Retaliating, the submarine gunners pumped shells into the Jap trawler. Riddled, spouting flames, the sampan remained afloat like so much burning cork. As the target was wrecked beyond repair, Burlingame broke off the engagement. The gun crew was close to exhaustion, and the loss of a man had made the action painfully costly.

Submariners, usually fatalists, expect to meet death when their number comes up. But they seldom conceive of death as an individual matter. All in the same boat, they think of themselves as "all going out together," and Harbin's solitary loss was a shock to the crew. The torpedoman's body was commended to the deep at sunset. Harbin's mates in the after torpedo room served as pallbearers. Burlingame read the service. Afterwards he addressed the crew at general quarters. "The first fish we fire will have Harbin's name on it."

The torpedo with Harbin's name on it was fired at a Japanese submarine on the afternoon of May 13th. The enemy's conning tower was sighted across an expanse of rough water, and Burlingame directed a surface approach. The torpedo raced on its way and an explosion was heard. The enemy's periscope disappeared. SILVERSIDES cheered a sinking.

While the sinking of this submarine was never confirmed, there was no doubt about the destruction of a 4,000-ton Japanese merchantman in the same area on May 17th. In itself unremarkable, this torpedoing was attended by the sort of incident that spices the conversation of undersea mariners.

On the day in question SILVERSIDES was cruising submerged in a locale that seemed to have been taken over by half the sampans of Nippon. Normally, a ship-hunting submarine would avoid such a raffish fishing fleet. But the area promised bigger game, and Burlingame remained on the lookout, raising his periscope cautiously in white-capped water that made its "feather" less detectable.

Each time he upped the periscope there seemed to be another sampan in view. Then he spied a medium-sized cargo vessel advancing into the scene. Alerting the crew, he headed SILVERSIDES for the target.

A couple of patrol vessels were easily dodged, and SILVERSIDES was making a businesslike approach when Burlingame was suddenly aware of a peculiar noise in the conning tower. Something rustling against the superstructure? Weeds slapping the hull?

"Up periscope!" Burlingame barked at his executive officer. "What the devil is that?"

SILVERSIDES' exec, Lieutenant Commander Roy M. Davenport, didn't know.

Then walking the periscope, the skipper halted abruptly. Pointing aft, the periscope was focused on a great, flapping, winglike appendage which was trailing from the submarine's stern. Weaving and dripping—a weird marine creature with a blur of red in its heart, and a tail of bobbling tentacles—it might have been some species of octopus or fantastic ray.

Burlingame glared in a dismay.

"Down periscope! Take her down!" he roared. "We've tangled into a fishnet! We're dragging a blank-blank Japanese flag!"

Marked by flags held aloft on tall bamboo poles, the native Japanese fishnet was usually visible from a distance. This one, snaring SILVERSIDES, had escaped attention as the submariners concentrated on the target. But the submarine's collision with the net did not escape the attention of the Jap fishermen. Burlingame caught a periscope glimpse of a sampan heading over to warn a patrol boat. With the latter less than a quarter of a mile away, he sent SILVERSIDES deep, hoping to dislodge the trailing net.

Another freighter was contacted on the same course as

the first. Patrol boats were in the van of these merchantmen, and it was a locale where anything might happen. Undeterred, Burlingame sent SILVERSIDES boring in, fishnet and all.

He hit the first AK with two torpedoes out of three. The explosions roared in the sound gear and merged in a blast that shook the submarine. Periscope view showed the ship burst open at the stern, a tower of flame and smoke erupting from her mid-section.

"Munitions ship!" Burlingame cheered to his crew. "Let's get her sister!"

Two shots appeared to hit this second vessel—an 8,000 tonner—and another violent blast was heard. This second sinking was never verified. The submarine was not afforded the leisure for a periscope check. Patrol boats were closing in, and it was time to quit the vicinity.

When SILVERSIDES surfaced that night, strands of fishnet were found snagged in the topside gear—some cordage and a glass ball and a splintered bamboo pole topped by a tassel. The Rising Sun was gone. But, as Lieutenant Commander Davenport remarked, SILVERSIDES was probably the only American submarine to make an approach while flying the Japanese flag.

Submarine Command Areas

In the Southwest Pacific the war was spreading like a forest fire. Submarines were not only called upon to defend an expanding front, but were faced with the problem of covering the conquered territory behind that front—an oceanic "hinterland" that broadened by many acres as the enemy advanced. Strictly speaking, there is no "front line" for the Submarine Force. It plays the entire field. This field had expanded to such an extent by the spring of 1942 that adequate area coverage was out of the question.

To begin with, there were far too few submarines. Loss of SEALION, S-36, S-26, SHARK and PERCH was felt in every theater. Replacements had arrived—SILVERSIDES and other new-construction submarines had reached Pearl, and the Panama S-boats were at Brisbane. Staunch as were these and later reinforcements, months would pass before the pressure was relieved and there were sufficient submarines to patrol the vast network of sea lanes open to enemy ship traffic.

The chart shows the Submarine Command Areas—Central Pacific, South Pacific and Southwest Pacific—as established for coverage by the Pacific Fleet (SubPac) Force based at Pearl Harbor, Task Force Forty-two (Brisbane), and Southwest Pacific (SoWesPac) Force based at Fremantle.

As indicated, the Pacific Fleet Force patrolled the Mandates, the sea lanes to and around Japan in the waters off Formosa, the Nansei Shoto and the Bonins, the East China and Yellow Sea, and the waters of Japan's home islands.

The task force at Brisbane—a port destined to serve as a submarine operating base until March 1945—was devoted primarily to assignments on the Solomons-Bismarck front.

To the submarines based at Fremantle fell the task of patrolling the long road back to the Philippines—the intricate waterways of the Malay Barrier, the Arafura Sea, the Flores Sea, the Banda Sea, the Java and Celebes Seas, the Sulu Sea,

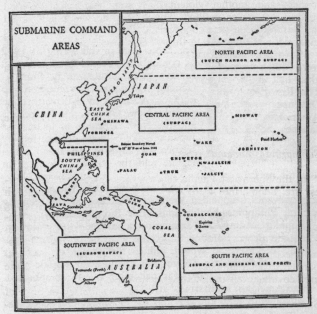

the South China Sea as far north as Hainan and as deep as the Gulf of Siam. Had all the U.S. submarines in the Pacific been concentrated in this one area that spring, there would scarcely have been enough of them to patrol the maze of traffic routes linking the ports of the Southwest Pacific.

No, the Pacific was not teeming with U.S. submarines in May 1942. Yet Japanese ships were going to the bottom, and the economists in Tokyo were already beginning to worry about rice, oil, nickel, tin and other imports required by the voracious War Machine.

Chapter 10

The Battle of Midway

☆ ☆ ☆

Coral Sea Overture

For some time in the spring of 1942 a contentious debate had engaged Japan's grand strategists in Imperial General Headquarters. Question: to outflank Australia by a drive through eastern New Guinea, the Solomons and the New Hebrides, or to buttress Japan's Wake-Gilberts defense line by seizure of Midway in the Central Pacific and the western Aleutians in the far north?

There was much to be said on both sides. The South Pacific adventure appealed to those who favored the securing of the Philippines-Netherlands East Indies territory.

Popular Admiral Yamamoto sponsored the Midway-Aleutians drive. For one thing, the securing of Japan's mid-Pacific defense line would reduce the threat of such air raids as Doolittle's on Tokyo. For another, the logistic problem in the South Pacific was becoming overly complicated. Those American submarines! Ai!

Meanwhile, time and tide refused to wait for Japan's grand strategists. A strong American naval force was assembling in the New Hebrides where bases had been established at Efate and Espiritu Santo. On hand was the task force built around the aircraft carrier LEXINGTON, commanded by Rear Admiral Aubrey W. Fitch, plus Rear Admiral Frank J. Fletcher's task force—with the carrier YORKTOWN.

An attempted raid on Rabaul in the Bismarcks and the blistering attacks on the Japanese bases in New Guinea forced the Jap hand in the South Pacific. Early in April, Japanese shock troops landed on beachheads in the upper Solomons, and established a seaplane base on Tulagi Island

120

in the eastern end of the group. Simultaneously a drive was mounted with Port Moresby in southeast New Guinea as its objective. A Japanese naval force steamed around the eastern end of the Solomons to attack the Allied surface forces in the Coral Sea.

The Japs were stopped in the resulting Battle of the Coral Sea—the first great sea-air engagement of the Pacific. In this oceanic maelstrom, the U.S. Navy lost destroyer SIMS, naval tanker NEOSHO and the 33,000-ton aircraft carrier LEXINGTON—a staggering blow compared with Japanese loss of the small carrier SHOHO. But the Jap thrust at Port Moresby was blocked.

To salvage face—restore to the Japanese countenance the lineaments of implacable conqueror—Imperial Headquarters turned to Admiral Yamamoto. At Admiral Yamamoto's disposal were more than 100 warships, including 11 battleships and four aircraft carriers. The U.S. Navy had lost LEXINGTON. The carrier YORKTOWN (as seen through Japanese spectacles) was severely crippled. Aircraft carriers HORNET and ENTERPRISE had raced to the South Pacific where they had arrived too late to join the Coral Sea Battle. When last accounted for (by Japanese Intelligence) SARATOGA was on the American West Coast undergoing repairs. Thus (according to Japanese deduction) there were no U.S. aircraft carriers in the Central Pacific. Now was the time to seize Midway.

Submarine Support of Fleet Operations

Prior to May 1942, U.S. Submarines (with the exception of those on special mission) had operated as free agents on combat patrols in which the primary mission was the sinking of enemy shipping, merchant and naval.

This sort of offensive patrolling was to continue throughout the war. But as the conflict went on, a gradually increasing percentage of submarine effort was diverted to the support of fleet operations. In each major carrier strike, and in the amphibious operations that were developed, submarines had their part to play. Concentration along the enemy's trade routes and supply lines fell into the category of normal patrolling. On such patrols the submarine generally operated as a "lone wolf," or, when the tactic was adopted, as the member of a pack. But in scouting, running interference and guarding the backfield, submarines team-working with the Fleet made a cardinal contribution to the Navy's battle record.

With the Battle of Midway on the horizon, the SubPac

Force was called upon *en masse* to support fleet operations. At Midway the Pearl Harbor Force converged to operate as a fleet arm—the first instance in the Pacific war wherein submarines were so employed.

Early in May, Admiral Withers had been ordered to the States to command the Navy Yard, Portsmouth, N.H., where he was to supervise the submarine building program. To Admiral Withers all submariners were indebted for the fine recuperation program which included the leasing of Honolulu's Royal Hawaiian Hotel for a rest camp de luxe. The first of such camps, it inaugurated a broad project which was to prove worth its weight in wildcats when it came to physical reconditioning and morale-maintenance in the undersea service. All hands wished the Admiral a heartfelt

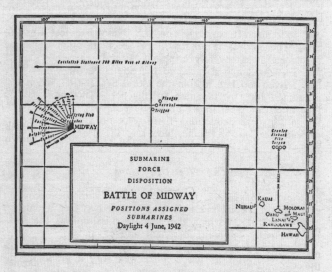

SUBMARINE

FORCE

DISPOSITION

BATTLE OF MIDWAY

*POSITIONS ASSIGNED
SUBMARINES*
Daylight 4 June, 1942

Godspeed. He was relieved by Rear Admiral Robert H. English, who had been serving as Commander Submarine Squadron Four and Commander Submarine Base, Pearl Harbor.

As ComSubPac, Admiral English stepped into the task of directing the Pacific Fleet submarines in the Midway engagement.

Of the 29 submarines which comprised SubPac, only four were to remain out of the Midway battle. THRESHER and ARGONAUT were undergoing overhaul. TRITON, returning from patrol in the East China Sea, was too low on fuel and torpedoes to participate in the battle. SILVERSIDES was ordered to maintain her patrolling off Japan.

Among the 25 submarines available for the Midway engagement, six had never made a war patrol. Eight were just in from patrol and needed repair. Six others were out on patrol when the Midway crisis developed, and they would have to stretch their legs to reach the battle area in time.

Previously designated as Task Force 7, the available Pacific Fleet submarines were now divided by ComSubPac into three task groups.

Task Group 7.1 formed the Midway patrol group.

West of Midway the submarines of Task Group 7.1 were to converge and patrol on stations that were located like the points of an opening fan. A fan that was intended to screen the face of Midway from the oncoming Japanese hurricane.

The second task group—Task Group 7.2—was composed of three submarines.

These three submarines were to cover an area to the east and a little north of Midway, on a scouting line about halfway between Midway Island and Oahu.

The third group—Task Force 7.3—covered a position some 300 miles north of Oahu. The group was composed of four submarines.

Accordingly, on the morning of June 4, the three task groups and their submarine units were in position as shown in the diagram. (See page 122.)

By the morning of June 3, all task group submarines were on station. That night the word was flashed to the three task groups and to the six submarines heading for Midway— *"Enemy planes attack Dutch Harbor."*

So an Aleutian thrust was underway. The Midway "haymaker" could not be far off.

Its direction previously detected by Intelligence, the haymaker was a "telegraphed" punch. Yamamoto's presence in the Midway theater was revealed to the waiting submarines shortly after they heard the word about Dutch Harbor.

The Battle

One of the war's decisive engagements, Midway developed as an air battle. But submarines on both sides dealt deadly torpedoes, and throughout the combat their influence was as a strong undercurrent on the battle's tide.

In over-all tactical command at Pearl Harbor Headquarters, Admiral Nimitz had dispatched the ENTERPRISE-HORNET force to the Midway area on May 28. This force was commanded by Admiral Raymond A. Spruance. It was followed by YORKTOWN and her escorts. The two carrier forces rendezvoused on June 2, and, under command of Admiral Fletcher, steamed to a position north of Midway.

On Midway Island a handful of Army B-26 bombers and B-17's had been mustered. On station were 27 Marine Corps dive bombers and 27 fighters (under command of Lieutenant Colonel Ira L. Kimes), six Navy torpedo planes, and some old Catalinas.

The land-based air and the carrier forces enumerated, plus the submarines of Task Group 7.1 and Task Group 7.2, comprised the bulk of Midway's defense. Rushing from San Diego was the aircraft carrier SARATOGA, but she did not arrive in time.

Converging on Midway in three groups, the Japanese armada advanced. Approaching Midway from the northwest was the Striking Force which would spearhead the attack. This force was composed of destroyers, cruisers and two battleships supporting the four aircraft carriers, AKAGI, KAGA, HIRYU and SORYU—all veterans of the Pearl Harbor assault. A Main Body composed of seven battleships, cruisers and destroyers, led by Yamamoto himself, aboard the battleship YAMATO, was to approach from the west and stand off Midway until the island had been softened up by the Striking Force. After the island had been softened up by the Striking Force and presumably been reduced by the Main Body, the Occupation Force was to move in. This force was accompanied by two battleships, several cruisers and a number of destroyers. Japanese submarines scouted ahead of the armada with orders to take a line west of Pearl Harbor and intercept any American forces sent to Midway's defense.

The defense forces got there ahead of the Jap submarines.

At sunrise, June 4th, the U.S. submarine task groups were in their assigned positions.

For the submariners the show began at 0700. At that hour USS CUTTLEFISH sent out a radio report that she had contacted an enemy tanker bearing 260°, six hundred miles from Midway. ComSubPac ordered her to trail. But the approach of daylight and enemy combatant ships forced CUTTLEFISH to dive. Running submerged, she was unable to regain contact.

Meantime, the island's PBY search patrol, which had been flying the cloudy fringe of the weather-front some 150 miles northwest of Midway, sighted the Japanese Striking Force. Jap bombers were in the air. This news was flashed to Midway. Every plane on the island took off with orders to intercept the enemy planes. Fifteen Flying Forts, already aloft, were directed to bomb the Japanese carriers.

Simultaneously, all submarines in the Midway defensive patrol, with the exception of CUTTLEFISH, CACHALOT and FLYINGFISH, were ordered to attack the Jap carriers.

TAMBOR, TROUT, GRAYLING, NAUTILUS, GROUPER, DOLPHIN, GATO, GUDGEON and GRENADIER pointed their bows toward the enemy, and headed for him at best speed. The planes, of course, were first in action, and they collided full-gun with the Jap air squadrons buzzing toward Midway.

Numbering nearly 100 dive bombers and torpedo planes, escorted by about 50 Zero fighters, the Jap raiders swept in. U.S. Marine pilots fought with unparalleled valor, but their planes were no match for the faster Zeros. Before the Japs retired, 15 Marine planes were lost and seven were forced down, damaged.

Far at sea the American B-26's and Navy torpedo planes were diving on the Japanese carriers. Swarms of Zeros rose to defend the Jap flat-tops. Yamamoto's armada came through practically unscathed, while Midway had received a blasting and its land-based air force had been severely pummeled. But the best-laid plans of mice and Yamamotos gang aft a-gley.

About the time the land-based American planes were beaten back, Jap air scouts sighted the ENTERPRISE-HORNET-YORKTOWN threat on the horizon. This news reached the Japanese Striking Force around 0900. The Jap carrier group promptly veered northeastward to meet the American. Jap bombers which had been loading for a Midway strike were ordered to change their bomb-loads for torpedoes. Ensued a stupendous series of strikes and counter-strikes—a battle that turned the ocean off Midway into a seascape of Inferno. Japanese carrier forces and American carrier forces were hammered, pounded, slugged, battered and thrashed. Air squadrons battled across the blue, fighting through tempests of anti-aircraft fire. Planes fell from the sky like molten meteors. Great smokes rose from the ocean—the volcanic eruptions of burning and exploding ships.

Jap carriers KAGA, AKAGI, and SORYU were transformed into floating furnaces—incinerators of the dead and dying. U.S. carrier YORKTOWN, bombed, afire, stabbed by Jap torpedo planes, was abandoned. But U. S. carriers ENTERPRISE and HORNET remained in action, and by mid-afternoon Yamamoto, with but one carrier left, decided to call it a day.

Dramatic climax of the battle was witnessed by Ensign George H. Gay, sole survivor of HORNET Torpedo Squadron 8. Shot down in the midst of the Jap carrier force, Gay clung to a rubber life raft—a man adrift in maelstrom. He saw the burning carriers—KAGA, AKAGI and SORYU. Saw the fourth carrier, HIRYU, retreat with her escorts to the northeast. Saw the remaining Japanese ships drift off like so much litter on the tide. The mid-afternoon sun scorched a seascape strewn with wreckage, mats of oil, black flotsam. The carrier, SORYU, came drifting near, flame-scorched and smoking like a great iron stove. Men were swarming like ants on her forecastle and a clutter of small boats were hugged up under her bow, apparently working with a towing hawser. She seemed to be moving under her own power, crawling at the pace of a water-buffalo through sludge. Two miles ahead, a pair of cruisers waited to assist.

Then, in this vista of desolation, Ensign Gay saw something else.

Nautilus vs. Soryu

Of the Task Group 7.1 submarines participating in the daytime action of June 4, only three made contact with the enemy.

The first was CUTTLEFISH, contacting a tanker of the Jap Occupation Force. This contact was lost.

The second was GROUPER. As she was diving early in the morning of that day she was sighted and strafed by a Japanese plane. She remained at deep submergence until late in the day, and so was out of the action.

The third submarine to contact the enemy was NAUTILUS. Making her first patrol under Lieutenant Commander William H. Brockman, she was to deal the one decisive blow struck the enemy at Midway by the U.S. Submarine Force.

One of the Navy's three largest submarines, the big V-boat had gone to Mare Island in the autumn of 1941 for an overhaul that amounted to virtual reconstruction. Her old engines were removed and a complete new plant was installed. Her superstructure was streamlined, her air-conditioning apparatus was improved and she was otherwise modernized. Reconditioned, re-engined, and rejuvenated, she reached Pearl Harbor in April 1942—big, fast, and ready to go. All she needed was the same sort of a skipper.

She got that sort in Brockman.

The winning figures began to show on the morning of June 4, at 0755. Patrolling northward of Midway as a unit of Task Group 7.1, NAUTILUS had submerged at 0420. About an hour later a flight of B-17's were seen against the dawn dead ahead. Then at 0710 NAUTILUS had a glimpse of aircraft bombing some target beyond range of the periscope horizon. Brockman changed course to head the submarine full speed toward the action.

At 0755 the periscope picked up ships' masts on the horizon. Simultaneously, a plane skimmed into view and opened fire on the periscope. Bombs tossed up fountains close aboard as Brockman roared the order to go down. Down went NAUTILUS to 100 feet. After a five-minute run submerged, Brockman sent her up again. Raising the periscope, he peered into a picture calculated to do the same to his hair.

Four large Japanese warships swam into the foreground as the periscope revolved. The largest Brockman identified as a battleship of the ISE class (she may have been a HARUNA-class BB or a TONE-class heavy cruiser). The other three Brockman identified as cruisers.

While Brockman was busy with his inventory of this heavyweight quartet, NAUTILUS was spied by a Jap plane. Having determined to attack the battleship, Brockman was beginning the approach when the air bombs came pelting down. At the same time one of the cruisers charged straight for the submarine, and at least two other warships were echo-ranging in an attempt to locate NAUTILUS.

Brockman ordered her to a depth of 90 feet, and the submariners set their teeth as the charges started to explode. At 0810, five depth bombs were dropped. Six more blasted the water a few minutes later, and then a pattern of nine boomed and crashed. Few of the explosions were close. The close ones, however, buffeted the submarine. NAUTILUS was equipped with "deck tubes" from which torpedoes could be fired. These tubes were loaded at the time, and the depth-bomb barrage carried away a retaining pin in one of the tubes, starting the loaded torpedo on a "hot run" in the tube. The noise of the running torpedo must have made a beautiful sound target for Japanese listeners, and the exhaust gases released were trailing the submarine like a marker buoy. Nevertheless, 14 minutes after the first ash-can was dropped, NAUTILUS was again at periscope depth and Brockman was continuing his observations.

"The picture presented on raising the periscope," he wrote afterwards in his report, *"was one never experienced in peacetime practice. Ships were on all sides, moving across the field at high speed and circling away to avoid the submarine's position. A cruiser had passed over us and was now astern. Flag hoists were going up, blinker lights were flashing and the battleship on our port bow was firing her whole starboard broadside at the periscope."*

Certainly peacetime practice had never trained the submariners to face broadsides from an infuriated BB. Nor had it produced a set of rules on what a submarine captain was to do when he found his boat in the middle of an enemy fleet like a champagne bottle in a log-jam.

Actually, Brockman had run up his periscope in the midst of the Japanese Striking Force. And at that hour of the morning, the force had not yet been splintered to pieces by American planes. Vice Admiral Nagumo was proudly flying his flag from AKAGI. KAGA, SORYU and HIRYU paraded in company with the flagship. Battleships HARUNA and KIRISHIMA; heavy cruisers CHIKUMA and TONE; the light cruiser NAGARA and about eleven destroyers—these were the other Jap warships in the picture. Brockman selected a battleship for his target.

Range 4,500. Angle on the bow 80° starboard. Speed 25 knots. T.D.C. and fire control party worked at lightning speed. Brockman gave the order.

"Fire one! Fire two!"

The battleship side-stepped, veering leftward and heading directly away. A salvo from her main battery had almost straddled the submarine. Only one torpedo had raced at the BB—the other had stuck in the tube—and with the range extended to 6,000 yards and a 180° track angle, Brockman ceased fire. The BB's screening vessels had spotted the torpedo wake and were charging in for a kill. Brockman gave the order to go deep. As she slid down to lower levels another ash-can storm broke around her.

But at 0846 she was again at periscope depth with her scope out of water.

Making periscope observation at 0846, Brockman discovered that the battleship and her companions had departed, leaving a destroyer to hunt the submarine. The hunter was evaded, and at 0900 Brockman sighted a Jap aircraft carrier —distance 16,000 yards. Flocks of anti-aircraft shell bursts hovered over the flat-top, indicating she was under bomber attack. Brockman headed NAUTILUS for the carrier.

Before NAUTILUS could close, her periscope was sighted by the rear-guard huntsman. The destroyer (or light cruiser) charged for the submarine at bone-in-teeth velocity. Again NAUTILUS ducked. As she slid down deep, six depth charges exploded close astern.

Brockman held her deep under until the echo-ranging faded out. He managed to combine evasion tactics with approach maneuvers that took the submarine nearer the carrier. 0955. Sound reported all quiet on the NAUTILUS front. But anything was possible on the surface. Brockman ordered the submarine to climb, waited for the periscope to break water, and then walked it around to see the possibilities.

At 1029 ships' masts reappeared on the horizon. The submarine's vertical antenna picked up a message from an American plane reporting damage to a Jap carrier. Great trees of smoke were now towering up on the horizon, spreading gray limbs across the sky. Brockman headed NAUTILUS for the nearest smoke at best speed.

Three-quarters of an hour later the range had not been appreciably reduced, and Brockman decided to increase the speed to two-thirds, whether the batteries could afford it or not. By 1253 NAUTILUS was near enough for close-up identification of the carrier. Carrier was recognized as one of the SORYU class, and her disablement was evident. Smoke rolled up from her decks, and she was blundering along at a speed of two or three knots. However, she was on even keel, no flames were visible and her hull appeared undamaged. Work crews on her forecastle were apparently making preparations to pass a towing hawser. About two miles ahead, a pair of Jap cruisers waited. As NAUTILUS watched, the carrier came to a dead stop. Obviously the hawser was ready for the hitch-up and tow.

During the long approach, the submariners had anxiously studied the silhouette book. As U.S. carriers were known to be in the area, Brockman had to be certain. But now there could be no doubt about the target's identity. Such doubts as there were concerned the other targets—the cruisers.

Lieutenant Thomas Hogan, diving officer aboard NAUTILUS, confided these misgivings later. Hogan remarked, in substance:

"We'd been taking a pretty bad beating that morning. The men weren't used to it. Somebody suggested to Captain Brockman that it might be better to go deep until things looked better topside. 'Hell no!' Brockman said. 'We're going to get a couple of these things.'"

Problem: Attack the cruisers standing by for the tow, and then come back to strike at the stalled carrier; or attack the carrier immediately, and then go after the cruisers.

Not an easy matter to decide. For a strike at the carrier meant that the cruisers, alerted, would come rushing over hell-bent, and NAUTILUS' batteries were getting dangerously low. On the other hand, much battery capacity would be expended in an approach on the cruisers. Swift and powerful, they might evade, and NAUTILUS would be left with a cruiser battle on her hands and no chance to get at the carrier. It was Hobson's choice, either way. Brockman decided to take the bird in hand.

Prowling forward at periscope depth, Nautilus advanced steadily on the carrier.

At 1359, range 2,700 yards, track angle 125° starboard, three torpedoes went speeding on their way. The ribboning wakes were seen to head straight for the target. Three thunderous explosions rocked the aircraft carrier. The men in the submarine took turns looking through the scope. Red flames spouted the length of the carrier, scattering the small boats under her bow. Ant-like figures raced across her decks. They were abandoning!

All this was observed before the cruisers, reversing course, came storming into the foreground. At 1410 Nautilus was again submerged beneath a depth-charge barrage. Brockman took her down to 300 feet, while the charges volleyed and thundered.

About 1800—silence. Brockman ordered the boat to periscope depth for a look around. The cruisers had quit the scene. Only the carrier remained, a drifting smelter-furnace under a mountain of dense black smoke.

Then Brockman—perhaps because he was hungry—gave the scope to the O.O.D. and stepped into the wardroom with his exec for a bite to eat. They were just sitting down when the submarine was shaken by a shocking blast. Who was bombing them now? Racing into the control room, Brockman found the sound man staring in astonishment and the O.O.D. glaring into the scope.

"There's not a thing up there!" the O.O.D. cried. "No ships! Nothing!"

Brockman was reaching for the scope-handles when another underwater blast sent Nautilus rolling. Juggling the scope, the skipper could see no sight of attacking cruisers—or burning carrier. But a dark litter of flotsam and acres of oil carpeted the sea. Underwater, the detonations continued. They came from Soryu's 17,500 tons, exploding as they went to the bottom.

Not until some days afterward did her submariners know that their reported sinking of the carrier had been confirmed. It was confirmed by the survivors of Soryu and by eye-witness Ensign Gay.

End of the Battle

Not long after the Soryu sinking, the bombed-out hulk that was Kaga went down. Akagi, a burning derelict, was sunk by her own destroyer escort that same evening.

In the meantime, the fourth Jap Striking Force carrier,

HIRYU, had come to grief. Escaping northwestward in the afternoon, she had been sighted by scouting planes from YORKTOWN. Soon afterward, dive bombers from HORNET and ENTERPRISE were on location. At nightfall she was burning like a wooden barn, abandoned.

Aboard the battleship YAMATO, Admiral Yamamoto did not enjoy his supper of *suki yaki*. Advised that his four carriers were lost, he immediately canceled his invasion plans and ordered his residual armada to retreat westward. To cover this retirement, he ordered four heavy cruisers from the Occupation Force to move in and shell the Midway Island airstrips—a measure calculated to protect the retreating fleet from attack by American land-based planes. This move was foiled by the U.S. Submarine Force.

At 0215, morning of June 5, TAMBOR (Lieutenant Commander Murphy) about 89 miles off Midway sighted four large ships bearing 270° T, course 050°. Warned that U.S. forces might be operating in this area, Murphy paced the warship formation, holding TAMBOR on a parallel course while he tried to identify the ships.

Night vision being what it was, friend-or-foe identification was not readily made. However, at 0300 TAMBOR sent out a contact report.

The cruisers she had sighted were the CA's SUZUYA, KUMANO, MIKUMA and MOGAMI—a formidable quartet. TAMBOR contacted them on several different courses as they swung toward the north and then veered west. At 0412, visibility had increased and the silhouettes were identifiable as Japanese.

With dawn in the making, TAMBOR was forced to dive. Then, running submerged, she was unable to close for an attack. The next time Murphy elevated the periscope he found only two of the cruisers in sight. One cruiser had a damaged bow. And they were heading away from the dawnlight.

The cruisers were, in fact, retreating. At about the time TAMBOR had sighted them, they had detected TAMBOR. With the submarine on their starboard bow, all four cruisers had executed an emergency turn to the left. On the turn, MOGAMI rammed MIKUMA on the port quarter, full tilt. The collision shattered MOGAMI's bow. Damage was reported by radio, and at 0300 the cruisers had been ordered by Yamamoto to abandon the Midway bombardment operation and retire.

Thereupon SUZUYA and KUMANO had withdrawn at top speed. MOGAMI and MIKUMA, their speeds reduced to 17 knots, were left in the rear. Crippled and leaking oil, MOGAMI was a drag on her companion—a drag that was to prove fatal.

The MOGAMI-MIKUMA collision was tantamount to damage by a torpedo. Marine and Army bombers from Midway came across the wounded cruiser's oil slick the following day. Caught by the planes, MOGAMI was pounded by bombs, and MIKUMA was mortally hit. A crucible of flames, she sank that afternoon.

MOGAMI came within an ace of suffering a like fate. TAMBOR'S contact report had reached Admiral Spruance, who brought HORNET and ENTERPRISE into the chase. MOGAMI absorbed a terrific beating. With one turret smashed, her after mast blown down, her funnel half gone and her decks a fiery shambles, she managed to crawl away after the planes were gone. Somehow she reached Truk.

The Japanese Submarine Force succeeded in striking a final blow. Herculean work by salvage crews had prevented disabled YORKTOWN from capsizing, and the carrier had been headed for Pearl Harbor under escort with the destroyer HAMMANN alongside. Early afternoon, June 6, the Japanese submarine I-168 made swift attack, firing four torpedoes. Two struck YORKTOWN and two hit HAMMANN. The destroyer's depth charges exploded as she sank, killing many of her crew and fatally blasting the damaged carrier. At 0500 the following morning YORKTOWN rolled over and went down.

Yamamoto had long since had enough, and his forces were in full retreat. Four first-line carriers sunk, a heavy cruiser on the bottom, another pounded to scrap, and 4,500 sailors and airmen killed had reduced his Midway drive to an appalling fiasco.

Assessment

Against the Japanese ship losses, the United States was forced to balance the loss of YORKTOWN and HAMMANN. One hundred and fifty U.S. planes were lost (the Japanese lost 258) and 307 Americans lost their lives in action. For Americans the battle had been costly, but the price paid by Japan, in contrast, was stunning. Plus the men and material thrown away in the Midway maelstrom, the Japanese lost the initiative in the Central Pacific. They would never be able to regain it.

Critics of submarine strategy have suggested that the showing made by the 25 U.S. submarines in the battle was somewhat disappointing. Of course, not all 25 were in the battle area. Task Group 7.2 and Task Group 7.3, stationed east of Midway and off Oahu, respectively, were unable to join the battle, as were the six steaming in from distant patrol areas. However, of the 12 in intercepting position west of Midway, only NAUTILUS (and, indirectly, TAMBOR) managed to score.

For several days after the battle's June 4 climax, the submarines near Midway and those coming in from patrol were given a number of contact reports concerning damaged Jap vessels in retreat. In the main these reports, which came from aircraft, were erroneous or misleading. MOGAMI was the only crippled vessel retreating, and although others among the retiring fleet may have been struck, their scars did not amount to serious damage. On the basis of the reports that were made, the pursuing submarines were unable to overtake and come in contact.

On June 9 TROUT fished two Japs from the sea—forlorn survivors of defunct MIKUMA. These were apparently the first Japanese Navy men to be taken prisoner by a U.S. submarine.

The only defensive battle of the Pacific War in which submarines were extensively employed, Midway served to point out lessons which were heeded in later engagements. Lack of search radar for night tracking was seen as a primary reason for submarine frustration at Midway. The SJ radar—the first directional radar used by the undersea force—was installed on most of the submarines within a few months.

Too, it was obvious that if submarines were to use their capabilities to the fullest when participating in fleet actions, some method would have to be devised for designating specific areas in which they could attack freely without fear of sinking friendly ships.

Finally, their deployment in close-in defensive positions in a battle which would be fought out in daylight left submarines few attack opportunities and seriously curtailed their mobility. These factors were noted and taken into account when submarines were thereafter employed to support fleet operations.

For the submariners the Midway Battle was a new experience—more pioneering. Their influence on the battle—remarked as that of an undercurrent—certainly helped to turn the tide.

And with Midway the entire Pacific war-tide was to turn. Japan's offensive had reached its height, and failed to break the American sea wall. Midway, the bastion of Hawaii, would stand. The manifest importance of this naval base is underlined by the fact that, immediately after the battle, FLYING-FISH put in at Midway and received the first submarine refit accomplished there. Six months later, Midway was refitting two submarines at a time, and by the end of the war 12 submarines could simultaneously undergo refitting at Midway. The Midway submarine base went far to solve the SubPac logistic problem by providing a fueling station, 1,100 miles from Pearl on the main line to Japan.

Chapter 11

The Aleutian Maelstrom

"If Japan seizes Alaska she can take New York . . . they won't attack Panama."
General William E. Mitchell

Pioneers Alaska

When Russia offered to sell Alaska to the United States in 1867 the ask-price — $7,200,000 — was considered exorbitant. Eventually negotiated by Secretary of State Seward, the purchase was ridiculed as extravagant folly and Alaska was called "Seward's Ice Box."

Few foresaw the future value of this immense country. As late as 1920 the public mind was picturing Alaska as a yowling wilderness populated by Esquimaux, a few Sourdoughs and Dangerous Dan McGrew. Nome was the end of the world, and the Aleutian Islands seemed as remote as the Pleiades.

The U.S. Navy was somewhat better informed. Its early sailing ships had visited Alaska's icy waters, and at a later date U.S. patrols had chased seal-poachers from the Bering Sea. But by 1920 the Aleutian Chain, a U.S. possession for over sixty years, was still unrecognized as a strategic bastion of the North American Continent.

The Japanese conquest of Manchuria and the increasingly warlike attitude of Tokyo brought home the importance of Alaska and the Aleutian Islands. Late in 1937, in conjunction with a plan for bases at Sitka and Kodiak, Unalaska Island was investigated by the Navy.

Repair facilities installed at Kodiak were to equal those of a submarine tender, and the shops and living quarters erected at this base were designed to accommodate one squadron of S-boats. Dutch Harbor was also set up to provide normal base facilities for a squadron of six S-class submarines. As the war went forward, action eventually centered around Attu and Kiska, and Kodiak's importance as a submarine base diminished. Dutch Harbor became the chief submarine base in the Aleutians.

However, at the beginning of World War II, Dutch Harbor bore a close resemblance to those frosty gold-rush towns featured in wolf-and-dog-team movies. Arriving at this bleak port on January 27, 1942, the submarines S-18 (Lieutenant W. J. Millican) and S-23 (Lieutenant J. R. Pierce) were to be the first to conduct pioneer war patrols in the area.

It was a rugged area for pioneering—a wilderness of gray, blizzard-swept seas studded by islands as inhospitable as rocks. The days were brief and the nights bitter black, deafened by wind-howl and the thunder of surf. Across the archipelago unpredictable storms raged in sudden tantrum. Worse were the fogs which curdled over the reefs like the blinding vapors of ammonia.

Aboard S-23, beginning her first Aleutian patrol on February 7, Lieutenant Pierce and crew slept in their clothing to keep warm. Compartments in the boat were as cold and dank as duck-blinds in a marsh. At the same time there was enough "body-warmth" in the submarine's hull to cause a heavy condensation of atmospheric moisture when the vessel submerged under icy waves. Cold sweat dripped in a constant rain from the bulkheads, wetting everything in the submarine's interior.

And if conditions below decks were as evil as influenza, those encountered on the bridge were as wicked as pneumonia. On their maiden pioneer patrols S-18 and S-23 made no verifiable contact with the enemy. The submariners standing bridge watch saw little more than ice-glaze and reeling water. Much of the time they could see no farther than the bow of the boat. When the islands were not imbedded in wintry fog they were whipped by the polar Williwaws which scourged the area. Even when the weather cleared, which was seldom, the hours of daylight were short and the horizon was engloomed. Snow-capped breakers showered the conning tower with brine that stung like shot salt, and the wind stabbed into a man's lungs like an icicle. In anything like a gale the bridge was almost untenable.

Submarine navigation in this area demanded superior skill. Off Unalaska, Kiska and Attu the water lies in strata of varying density—a phenomenon which made every dive a prob-

lem in unpredictables. Radio reception was eccentric and
sonar sometimes behaved queerly. On her first patrol S-23
encountered a continuous series of barometric lows, at one-
to three-day intervals, accompanied by foul weather, moving
rapidly from west to east. Typical Aleutian weather. Shooting the sun was a feat comparable to shooting a sea lion in
a blizzard—when the sun did appear it loomed in the oceanic
mist as dim and opaque as a cataract-blinded eye.

On the 3rd of April, S-34 (Lieutenant T. L. Wogan) and
S-35 (Lieutenant J. E. Stevens) arrived at Dutch Harbor to
strengthen the undersea defense. These S-boats were soon followed by two more.

The pioneer war patrols of these S-boats were meager in
result. But their mere presence in the area forced the Japanese to delay its penetration. And fighting fog, sleet, high seas,
blizzards and some of the wildest storms in the book, they
won the opening battle against the Aleutian weather—a
victory that made an important contribution to the ultimate
defeat of the Japs in that strategic theater. The stage was set
in June when the Jap drive, timed with the Midway offensive, began.

War on the Northern Front

To fend off the expected Alaska thrust, Admiral Nimitz
dispatched a sizable surface-air force to the endangered area.
Welded into a single task force, its units included five cruisers, 11 destroyers, a large flotilla of smaller warcraft, and
169 planes. Then there were the aforementioned six submarines. Rear Admiral Robert A. Theobald was placed in command of all United States and Canadian forces in the area.

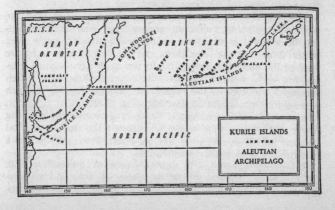

KURILE ISLANDS
AND THE
ALEUTIAN
ARCHIPELAGO

For this diversionary Aleutian drive Admiral Yamamoto had mustered a powerful striking force composed of the aircraft carrier RYUJO, the aircraft carrier HAYATAKA (sometimes called the JUNYO), two heavy cruisers, three destroyers and auxiliaries. The diversion was to be more than a feint, and this striking force moved in advance of two small but sturdy occupation flotillas—one to seize Kiska, the other to seize Adak and Attu. Entrenched in these outer islands, the invaders were to set up bases which would presumably control the Aleutian Chain and serve as springboards for drives at Dutch Harbor, Kodiak and the Alaskan mainland.

The Adak invasion was deleted from the plan, but on June 6 and 7, Attu and Kiska were seized by the Japanese occupation forces.

When the S-boats first entered the Aleutian area, ComSubPac stated that if the North Pacific should become an active war theater, the S-boat force could be bolstered by fleet boats from Pearl Harbor. Dutch Harbor was approximately the same distance from Pearl as from Seattle, and fleet submarines could readily go to Alaskan waters from their Hawaiian base. With the enemy occupying Attu and Kiska, the time had arrived for the fleet boats to step in.

Torpedoes for Invading DD's

Fortunately, reinforcements from Pearl Harbor were already on the way. Into Dutch Harbor on June 28 steamed GROWLER, fresh from Midway. On July 3, TRITON and FINBACK arrived. TRIGGER, GRUNION and GATO came in on the 5th, 9th and 12th, respectively. TUNA arrived a week later, and HALIBUT in mid-August. Thus, by late summer eight modern fleet boats were in Aleutian waters.

The fleet boats began to score almost as soon as they arrived. The first to down an enemy ship was TRITON. She was off Aggatu as of July 3, hunting the invader. Early next morning the fog dissolved long enough to reveal a Japanese destroyer's silhouette fading off in the mist. Lieutenant Commander C. C. Kirkpatrick set TRITON on the trail of this target, and for ten hours the submarine pursued the DD through gusting vapor—Doom in pursuit of a phantom.

Late in the afternoon, Kirkpatrick fired two torpedoes. One struck the destroyer amidships. Through the periscope TRITON's submariners watched the stricken vessel put her port beam under and begin the long roll. As the destroyer gradually capsized, some 100 Japanese sailors and officers in white uniform walked down her starboard side and jumped into the surging water. Then down at sea went the Imperial

Navy's DD NENOHI—1,600 tons, bottom up. The date was July 4th. TRITON celebrated appropriately.

On the day following TRITON'S knockout performance, GROWLER pitched into the Aleutian Battle. This was the submarine's first patrol, and a first patrol for her captain, Lieutenant Commander Howard W. Gilmore. GROWLER and Gilmore—both names were to become immortalized in submarine history.

Ordered to patrol the waters off Kiska, GROWLER was on station early in the morning of July 5th. The dawn was clear and cold, and the watch had a sharp periscope view of Kiska's barren peaks some five miles distant. As the periscope watch maintained a sweeping scrutiny, three Japanese destroyers were detected outside of Kiska Harbor. Gilmore ordered slow speed and silent running, and GROWLER began a direct but cautious approach.

Closer scrutiny revealed the DD's as 1,700-tonners of the AMAGIRI or FUBUKI class. Attaining attack position, Gilmore fired one torpedo at each of the first two destroyers. Two more torpedoes were fired at the third destroyer. A great funnel of smoke was seen billowing up from the destroyer anchorage. The smoke was a funeral shroud for the Imperial Navy's 1,850-ton DD ARARE. Her companion destroyers were towed back to Japan.

Accounting for two Jap destroyers, and dealing damage to several more, the U.S. submarines played a leading part in stalling the Jap drive. Yamamoto was compelled to reinforce his Kiska-Attu supply line by rushing additional naval units to the Aleutians.

Loss of Grunion

A price was to be paid for Alaska's security. There were casualties among the American and Canadian air, surface and ground forces. Native Aleuts died in bombings and scrimmages. And in Aleutian waters the SubPac Force suffered its first submarine casualty.

Reporting for duty in the Pacific War, GRUNION, novice from a new-construction yard, arrived in Pearl Harbor on June 20, 1942. She was given ten days of pre-patrol training, then, on the 30th, she left for the Aleutian front. She was captained by Lieutenant Commander Mannert L. Abele.

On July 10 GRUNION received orders to patrol the waters north of Kiska. Five days later she radioed Dutch Harbor that she had been attacked by an enemy DD. Abele had fired three torpedoes at the destroyer, and all had missed.

On July 28 GRUNION was detailed to guard the exits from

Kiska Harbor. She reported an attack on unidentified enemy ships off Sirius Point that day. Two torpedoes had missed the targets, and she had evaded a depth-charge barrage.

Her last transmission to Dutch Harbor was received on July 30th. She reported a tight anti-submarine screen off Kiska and but ten torpedoes remaining aboard. In reply, Headquarters ordered her to return to Dutch Harbor. GRUNION never returned.

Her fate remains a mystery. She was not contacted or sighted after July 30, and all efforts to locate her proved unavailing. With negative results, planes searched the waters off Kiska, and Headquarters sent out calls. On August 16 GRUNION was reported lost.

Examined after the war, Japanese naval records failed to reveal an anti-submarine attack in the Aleutians during the time in question. Either GRUNION was the victim of an unrecorded attack, or her loss was "operational." She went out. She was in the fight. She did not come back. Her requiem remains in the mourning of the northern winds and the "solemn surge of strange and lonely seas."

Cutting the Japan-Aleutian Supply Line

By late summer the Japanese occupiers of Kiska and Attu were beginning to experience some pangs of malnutrition. Little food could be scavenged on these wind-blighted islands. The natives, themselves, had survived mainly on a thin, raw diet of fish. And now the fishing grounds were under fire, practically all of the provisions for the occupying forces had to be imported from Japan. U.S. submarines were making importations increasingly difficult. Transports had to run into the harbors at dusk, unload under cover of night, and leave before dawn. Late in August, United States forces occupied Adak, and the Japanese supply situation became critical.

In the autumn the submarine forces applied more pressure. This in spite of the fact that GROWLER, TRIGGER, FINBACK and other fleet boats were moved south to patrol stations off Formosa and other Central Pacific areas. The remaining Aleutian patrollers kept the Jap ships on the run. On October 16, S-31 (Lieutenant Commander R. F. Sellars) sank the 2,800-ton cargoman, KEIZAN MARU. This sinking, in the neighborhood of Paramushiru some 500 miles west of Attu, came as a storm warning to the fishermen down through Japan's Kurile Islands.

Throughout the following late autumn and winter months, submarines from Dutch Harbor were to keep the Kurile Island fishermen on tenterhooks. For the S-boats engaged in this operation it was rough going. Lieutenant Commander Vincent A. Sisler, who made one of the later Aleutian-Paramushiru patrols in command of S-28, gave a vivid description of the rigorous submarining involved in these northern waters.

Hull-sweating he described as one of the worst plagues endured by the S-boaters.

There were two ways to combat this. One way was to operate the air-conditioning unit, to evaporate the water and lower the boat temperature, which reduced sweating but forced everyone to wear more clothes. The other way was to rig canvas shields with funnel arrangements to keep the water from dripping on the bunks. But eventually, regardless of the precautions taken, the mattresses, blankets, sheets and everything became soggy, wet and damp. The habitability of S-boats in northern waters was terrible.

Bridge duty was no picnic, either.

It was necessary to lash lookouts, the officer of the deck and the quartermaster to the bridge to keep them from being bashed around by the waves that rolled over the boat. Amazing that all hands didn't have severe colds and pneumonia, but health in general was excellent. The big problem turned out to be teeth. They decayed quickly for lack of calcium. Calcium pills soon became standard issue as did sun lamps. Without them, men soon developed a green, washed-out appearance.

Submarining without regular arctic clothing, calcium pills and sun lamps, the S-boaters who opened the Aleutian campaign would be remembered as rugged pioneers.

Fire and Ice

In the Aleutian Battle there were always two enemies—the Japanese and the weather. Relentless as was the human foe, he was never so dangerous as the inhuman. Wind and tide joined in winter-long conspiracy against the submarines. And in their war with these elemental forces, the S-boaters put up a fight that was almost superhuman. This conflict reached its summit in the battle waged and won by S-35 during the week preceding Christmas 1942.

The struggle began on the afternoon of December 21 when the Aleutian storm-gods unleashed such an offensive as only the North Pacific and Bering Sea could mount against a lonely submarine. It was the sort of weather when whalers stayed in port and landlubbers lay down below. Gigantic seas rolled through the archipelago where the surf burst like gunfire and the wind-whipped waves released a scud as ferocious as shrapnel. The sky was frozen, the horizon obscured as though by a sandstorm, and a spatter of spume, striking a man's naked cheek, burned like liquid fire.

Patrolling in the vicinity of Anchitka Island, S-35 forged her way along the surface through hills of cannonading water and valleys of scalding spray. In this tempest of heaving sea and flying brine the submarine climbed and staggered and drove forward, fighting to keep on course. Late afternoon, the storm worsened. At one-third speed, heavy seas were engulfing the bow and ploughing over the bridge. Water gushed down into the control room, and sometime around 1800 a geysering sea buried the bridge, and the control room was drenched by a cataract.

Topside, the submarine's captain, Lieutenant H. S. Monroe, ordered his men to close the conning-tower hatch. He had hardly given this order when a mountainous sea (time: 1805) charged the conning tower and burst across the bridge in exploding fury. Hurled from his footing, Monroe was flung into the hatch. Agonized by a sprained arm and leg, he made his way to his quarters, leaving the command to his second officer, Lieutenant O. H. Payne.

Monroe had just crawled into his bunk when, at 1830, he was roused by the cry, "Fire in the control room!" Lurching into the control room, the injured captain saw an alarming display of electric arcs and blue flames sputtering out of the main power cables from the forward battery.

Apparently salt water had soaked into the cables, causing a short and igniting the insulation. There was an acetylene-like flare—acrid smoke—the crackle of sparks and hiss of burning rubber. At the same time water was rising in the control-room bilges. Although he was scarcely able to stand, Monroe immediately took charge of the fight to save his ship from this dual peril.

Chief Electrician's Mate E. J. Bergero and others of the crew attacked the flames with fire extinguishers. But no sooner had this fire in the after starboard corner of the control room been extinguished than a similar fire broke out in the forward starboard corner. When this second fire was extinguished, arcing and flames were reported in the forward battery room.

Extinguishers smothered the battery-room fire, but could

do nothing about the choking smoke and fumes of charred cork and burnt rubber. Blinded and coughing, the firefighters retreated aft. The forward battery-breaker and forward power-switch on the main board were pulled to remove the electrical load forward. The forward battery room and torpedo room were abandoned and sealed. Then again, "Fire in the control room!" clamored through the submarine. Two extinguishers were emptied on this new outbreak, but the electrical fire sizzled unabated, and in a pall of asphyxiating smoke the crew was driven back.

The engines were secured and the control room abandoned and sealed. Crowded into the S-boat's after quarters, the ship's company groped through a haze that thickened as smoke contamination and moisture produced large grounds on most of the electrical circuits in the boat. One short circuit after another disabled the electrical equipment. Gyro compass, radio transmitter, electric steering system, engine-order-annunciators and the bow and stern planes were put out of commission. A hole was burned in the top of No. 2 main ballast tank and the lines from No. 1 and No. 5 air banks were burned through. Storming seas above-decks and a choking hell of smoke, chemical fumes and eerie pyrotechnics below—S-35's crew was all but ready to abandon hope.

Submarine warfare is a science, and many of its material and operational problems can be solved by engineers, physicists, strategists and mathematicians. But in submarining, as in all forms of warfare, there is one more important factor that baffles the scales and calipers of the scientist, and even mystifies the psychologist given to dealing with abstractions. That factor is the human factor. In particular, one element of the human factor. The British call it morale. The French know it as élan. Americans have described it as "guts"—that manifestation of grit or fortitude or stubbornness that never says die.

Whatever its composition, this spunky factor has throughout history upset the certainties of mathematics, the laws of probability, the limitations of handicaps, the opposition of long odds. Every war furnishes a dozen examples. Paul Jones in a riddled and disabled hulk tells the world he has just begun to fight. The Schlieffen Plan, devised by Prussia's greatest military scientists, collapses like hollow nonsense under the weight of a single phrase, "They shall not pass!" Time and again refusal to give up has won the day after all but hope has been lost.

Submarine operations in World War II taught many lessons. One lesson learned was that successful submarining depended largely on an attitude that never said die. No ship is lost until commanding officer and crew give up hope. This truism was courageously demonstrated by S-35.

At 1855 a party using smoke-lungs attempted to enter the control room. Not enough oxygen, but a wall of fumes that stifled the men and drove them out. To hell with the fumes. The escape lungs were charged with oxygen, and the men made another try. This time they were able to stay in the compartment long enough to flood the magazines and partially blow No. 3 main ballast tank to increase the submarine's freeboard. They were also able to close the auxiliary induction and completely seal the forward battery.

With her electrical controls burned out, her steering gear disabled, her radio transmitter dead, her interior a Black Hole of Calcutta, a raving storm driving her through midnight, S-35 was in a bad way—few submarines were ever in a worse. Captain Monroe, Lieutenant Payne and the fighters under them refused to despair of it. They held the icy bridge. They fought the below-deck inferno. They met the test of fire and ice, and in the bleak light of morning the crew and their submarine were still there.

Meantime, the boat had been flogged off course. It was necessary to get propulsion on her screws to keep her clear of the deadly beaches of Amchitka. The crew tried to make an air start on the engines, taking a suction through the induction outlets aft. The engines were too cold to start. So the smoke-filled control room was re-entered, and gasping electricians and motor macs made a desperate attempt at starting the motors. These were finally started, and S-35 crawled slowly eastward through the raging storm.

At 0700 a new fire flared up in the control room. As the fire extinguishers had been emptied the night before, the crew could only retreat from the smoke-fogged compartment. Soon the after quarters of the submarine were choked by the stifling smudge. All hands had to clear below deck and go up to the bridge into breathable air.

Lights out—the men groping about with hand lanterns—struggling into bulky arctic clothing—going topside to cling to the bridge and face the polar storm—here was an extremity beyond human endurance. From the frying pan into icy fire, the submariners endured it. Topside they were flayed by a cat-o'-nine-tails wind, and drenched by sheets of frigid water. For an hour and a half they suffered this punishment, hoping that the closure of the conning-tower hatch would smother the fire below.

Then electricians and motor macs entered the control room and the Diesels were started. The cables to the forward battery continued to flash and arc as the battery discharged. But the smoke was to some extent cleared by the running engines, and the crew was able to work below for several hours.

At 1100 all hands were once more forced topside by the suffocating smoke. Again the control room was sealed off. By 1330 it was possible to reopen the control room and go ahead on one engine, taking a suction through the induction outlets aft. Smoke from melted rubber, charred cork and fused metal continued to fog the submarine's interior, and the air became stifling every time the conning-tower hatch was closed—which was each time a heavy sea broke over the bridge. But somehow the engine was kept running, and S-35 kept going through the slow hours of December 22nd. After which, she continued to push ahead through the even slower ones of December 23rd.

At long last, on the day before Christmas, she staggered into Kuluk Bay, Adak Island. There she found the USS GILLIS, and the exhausted submariners were given first aid while emergency repairs were made on the S-boat. S-35 then proceeded to Dutch Harbor, arriving at home base on December 29th.

It was such submariners as these who cut the Japanese transport lines to Attu and Kiska and, before the end of 1942, reduced the invader's supplies to the famishing point.

The term *heroics* has been defined as the accomplishment of the impossible. Certainly that applies to the S-boaters who outfought the Japanese and the weather in the Aleutians.

Chapter 12

Counter-offensive

 ☆ ☆ ☆

Lockwood

Captain John Wilkes, who had held the SubsAsiatic Force together in the long retreat from Manila to Australia, was relieved in May 1942 by Captain Charles A. Lockwood, Jr. Competence and submarining were two words long associated with the name Lockwood.

Now, late in May 1942, he received the stars of rear admiral and the toughest assignment he had ever faced. As ComSubSoWes-Pac and Commander Task Force Fifty-one, he was to take over the war-torn submarines of the Asiatic Force based at Fremantle and Albany. Take over and start an undersea blitz, American version, against the Japanese.

The Southwest Pacific picture was far from encouraging. In spite of the defeat handed Yamamoto at Midway the enemy's South Pacific offensive continued to advance like a slow, dark stain, spreading around New Guinea, enveloping the Bismarck Archipelago, creeping through the Solomons. Although the Midway victory had stopped the Jap thrust at Hawaii, the Australian situation remained critical. Down from Java, down from the Philippines, down from Japan came ship after ship, piling up men and guns in the islands flanking Australia. It would take something more than armchair submarining to blitz these invasion fleets out of the Southwest Pacific. Lockwood, no armchair submariner, walked into the job, swinging.

Headquarters in the Commercial Mutual Life Insurance Building in Perth hit a stride that should have warned Yamamoto (had he been properly advised) to take out some new policies. In every large organization—and the U.S. Navy was swiftly becoming one of the world's largest—there is a necessary amount of paper work and the sort of detail known as tape. There comes a point in administration where carbon copies may clog operations, and detail, becoming red tape, threatens to tangle in the machinery and cause slow-downs. One of Admiral Lockwood's specialties was the cutting of red tape and the elimination of excess paper work.

That the situation needed the Lockwood treatment is evidenced by the following letter which was written before the Admiral's methods were in effect:

Concerning Paper Work

#3s184/L8   S36-1   June 11, 1942
From: The Commanding Officer
To: Supply Officer, Navy Yard, Mare Island
Via: Commander Submarines, Southwest Pacific
Subject: Toilet Paper
Reference:(a) (4608) USS HOLLAND (S184) USS SKIPJACK
                 Req. 7042 of July 30, 1941
            (b) SO NYMI Canceled invoice No. 272836
Enclosure:(A) Sample of canceled invoice.
            (B) Sample of material required.

1. This vessel submitted a requisition for 150 rolls of toilet paper on July 30, 1941, to USS HOLLAND. the material was ordered by HOLLAND to the supply officer, Navy Yard, Mare Island, for delivery to USS SKIPJACK.

2. The supply officer Mare Island on November 26, 1941, canceled Mare Island Invoice No. 272836 with the stamped notation "Canceled. Cannot Identify." This canceled invoice was received by SKIPJACK June 10, 1942.

3. During the eleven and a half months elapsing from the time of ordering the toilet paper to the present date, USS SKIPJACK personnel, despite their best efforts to await delivery of the subject material, have been unable to wait on several occasions, and the situation is now acute, particularly during depth-charge attacks by the "back stabbers."

4. Enclosure (B) is a sample of the desired material provided for the information of the supply officer, Navy Yard, Mare Island. The commanding officer of USS SKIPJACK can not help but wonder what is being used at Mare Island as a substitute for this unidentifiable material once well known to this command.

5. Boat's personnel during this period has become accustomed to the use of ersatz in proportion to the vast

amount of incoming paper work generally nonessential, and in so doing feels that the wish of the Bureau of Ships for the reduction of paper work is being complied with, thus killing two birds with one stone.

6. It is believed by this command that the stamped notation "Cannot Identify" was possibly an error, and that this is simply a case of shortage of strategic war material, USS SKIPJACK probably being low on the priority list.

7. In order to co-operate in the war effort at small local sacrifice USS SKIPJACK desires no further action be taken until the end of the current war, which has created a situation so aptly described as "war is hell."

(Signed) J. W. Coe

Torpedo Test at Albany

One of Admiral Lockwood's first moves was to investigate the Mark 14 torpedo. Ever since SARGO's experience in December 1941, when Lieutenant Commander T. D. Jacobs had fired 13 shots for a string of zero hits, evidence of torpedo malfunction had continued to pile up. During the desperate six months of retreat from the Philippines and the Netherlands East Indies, there had been no time for experimental tests and investigation at Soerabaja, Darwin and other Southwest Pacific bases. That the Mark 14 torpedo was prematuring, failing to explode, and otherwise sabotaging the best efforts of the submariners was apparent in anguished patrol reports and bitter appeals from veteran captains.

Late in the spring, reports from SALMON (McKinney) and SKIPJACK (Coe) joined those written earlier in the war to support SARGO's claim that the Mark 14, along with its other defects, was running deep. Convinced that all this circumstantial evidence meant guilt, Admiral Lockwood promptly arranged to bring the torpedo to trial.

The trial, begun on June 20, 1942, at Albany, Australia, was designed to end all conjecture concerning the torpedo's faulty depth-setting device. A large fishnet was anchored offshore in the quiet waters of Frenchman's Bay. SKIPJACK and Coe were chosen as submarine and skipper to make the test, and Captain James Fife officiated.

A Mark 14 torpedo that had been aboard SKIPJACK was fitted with an exercise head which was filled with calcium chloride solution to simulate in weight a Mark 16 warhead. The torpedo was set for 10-foot depth, and SKIPJACK fired on the surface at the net which was 850 yards distant. The torpedo cut a hole in the net at a depth of 25 feet!

The following day two more torpedoes were fired from SKIPJACK. The first one, set for 10-foot depth, cut the net at 18 feet, having reached that depth at a range of about 700 yards after making its initial deep dive. The second torpedo, set for zero feet, cut the net at a depth of 11 feet. When recovered and examined, this torpedo displayed evidence of having struck the bottom at 60 feet on its initial deep dive.

Admiral Lockwood lost no time in reporting these findings to the Bureau of Ordnance. On the heels of this report, the Bureau of Ordnance received one from Admiral English. The SubPac force commander reported that a Mark 14 exercise torpedo, inadvertently fired at a zero-feet depth-setting, had hit its destroyer target approximately eight feet below the waterline. Information regarding depth performance of all submarine torpedoes, and in particular the Mark 14, was urgently requested. Depth performance for torpedoes set between zero and 10 feet was specifically in question. ComSubPac inquired:

HAVE NET TESTS INDICATED THAT TORPEDOES RUN GREATER THAN FOUR FEET BELOW SET DEPTH

Dispatched on June 24, ComSubPac's message reached BuOrd some 48 hours after the one from Lockwood's Headquarters. Substantiating the report from ComSubSoWesPac, the message from Pearl should have gone far to settle the issue. However, on June 30 the Bureau of Ordnance informed Admiral Lockwood that no reliable conclusions could be reached from the Albany tests because improper torpedo trim conditions had been introduced.

Admiral Lockwood might have shelved the matter at this juncture. But Australia was too near the firing line. Into Fremantle were coming captains like Coe and Warder—war-wearied veterans who had risked their submarines and the lives of all on board, on the caprices of an unreliable torpedo. On July 11 Lockwood informed the Bureau of Ordnance that the tests would be repeated with an exercise-head lengthened to match as nearly as possible the trim and buoyancy characteristics of a Mark 16 warhead. The admiral urged the Bureau to make conclusive tests with its own equipment and inform him of the results by dispatch.

At Albany on July 18 a second depth test was conducted. This time SAURY (Lieutenant Commander L. S. Mewhinney) did the firing. Four Mark 14 torpedoes were fired. The torpedoes were set for 10 feet and fired at a net which was 850 to 900 yards from the firing point.

The first shot was wasted because the net had carried away

during the night. But the remaining three torpedoes all penetrated the net at 21 feet. Here was proof positive, and in a July 20 dispatch the Bureau of Ordnance was informed accordingly. Admiral Lockwood also requested the Bureau to conduct tests using equivalent Mark 16 heads to determine depth performance with zero setting.

Meantime the torpedo problem had come to the attention of Admiral King, Commander-in-Chief, United States Fleet. On July 21 the Commander-in-Chief dispatched a letter to the Chief of the Bureau of Ordnance requesting action. Specifically BuOrd was told to immediately re-check the tactical data for the Mark 14 torpedo fitted with the Mark 15 or Mark 16 warhead. Cominch noted that BuOrd, in conducting additional tests of Mark 14's depth performance, had fired the torpedoes from a torpedo-barge and not from a submarine. Cominch also stated that submarine patrol reports continued to indicate lack of confidence in the Mark 14 and its depth performance, and it was apparent that there were valid reasons for this lack of confidence. In conclusion, Cominch stressed the need for accurate assessment and correct tactical data concerning the torpedo.

On July 29 Admiral English informed his force that torpedoes ran 11 feet deeper than set, and issued orders to set all torpedoes to run about five feet but no more than 10 feet deeper than the target's estimated draft, then to subtract 11 feet to obtain the correct depth-setting.

And on August 1, 1942—almost eight months after the war's outbreak—the Bureau of Ordnance announced that tests conducted at Newport corroborated reports concerning the faulty depth performance of the Mark 14. Fired from the tubes of a submarine near periscope depth, the torpedoes, fitted with Mark 16 warheads, had run 10 feet deeper than set!

Official confirmation! What this meant to the submariners, who had seen their marksmanship consistently betrayed by a defective weapon, may be imagined. Some of the pioneer captains, discouraged by repeated torpedo misses, had come to doubt their own ability. Several had left the Submarine Service. Hundreds of hours had been expended in fruitless approaches, and many thousands of dollars worth of ammunition had gone down the drains. To Jacobs—Bruton—Lent— Bacon — Parks — Coe — McKinney — Wright —Smith Warder — Aylward — Rice — Voge—all of the skippers who fought the battle in the first months of the war, the Mark 14's exposure came as a boon and a relief—one that restored the self-confidence of captains and crews.

Deep-running, however, was not the Mark 14's sole malfunction. The torpedo harbored other defects. Tracked down by consistent inquiry, and finally cornered by the submarine TINOSA (in July 1943—almost a year after the Albany trials), these will be detailed in the chapter devoted to torpedoes. A lot of war would be fought with this erratic "tin fish" in the meantime. But the flaw revealed by the fishnets at Albany was corrected to a degree that greatly benefited fire control. Indicative of Admiral Lockwood's character, nine weeks after he took command at Fremantle the Mark 14's depth-setting deficiency was exposed.

Raiders to Asia

By the summer of 1942, U.S. submarines were conducting attrition campaigns in six regional patrol areas. These may be roughly described as the Empire Patrol, the South China Sea Patrol, the Netherlands East Indies-Philippines Patrol, the New Guinea-Bismarck-Solomons Patrol, the Mandates Patrol, and the Aleutian Patrol.

Thus, while the Pearl Harbor Force had converged for the defense of Midway, Submarines SoWesPac were giving the enemy no respite in Asian waters. Far behind the enemy's Southwest Pacific Lines, SWORDFISH (Chester Smith) roamed the Gulf of Siam. A long haul from Fremantle. Dangerous every mile. But not so dangerous for SWORDFISH as it proved for BURMA MARU, a 4,584-ton freighter torpedoed and sunk by Smith and company off the coast of Thailand on June 12th.

SEAWOLF (Freddie Warder) was at this time off the south-west coast of Luzon where, on June 15, she sank NAMPO MARU, converted gunboat, 1,206 tons.

STINGRAY (Lieutenant Commander R. J. Moore) roamed the waters due east of the Philippines. So did SAIKYO MARU, converted gunboat, 1,292 tons. Meeting occurred at 12-41 N., 136-22 E. Torpedoed June 28, another converted gunboat was subtracted from the Imperial Navy.

Off Lingayen Gulf in the South China Sea was STURGEON under command of "Bull" Wright. Down the track came MONTEVIDEO MARU, a big 7,267-ton transport in the service of Homma and Hirohito. STURGEON sent this liner to the bottom on the first day of July—a loss that added a sizable figure to the enemy's casualty list.

SEADRAGON (Ferrall and crew) shot to pieces a Jap convoy off the Indo-China coast, July 12, 13 and 16th. Down at sea went HIYAMA MARU, SHINYO MARU and HAKODATE MARU one, two, three—a total of 15,636 tons.

And in the meantime, Pearl Harbor submarines had left

Midway to resume their attrition missions. On the last day of June, PLUNGER fired a tricky shot that should have convinced the enemy that nowhere were his defenses wholly secure. The tactic employed by PLUNGER merits description.

Submarine Tactics—The "Up-the-kilt" Shot

Comparable to the down-the-throat shot, which took the target head-on, was the shot which, fired on a 180° track, caught the target from the opposite direction. The shot aimed at a ship's oncoming prow, and the shot aimed at a ship's retiring stern had one advantage in common—in either case, target speed was canceled out of the fire control problem, and the target's course could usually be estimated accurately from the position in which the torpedo attack was delivered.

The shots had a common disadvantage. Were the attack discovered in time, enemy maneuvers to evade were comparatively simple. However, this disadvantage was offset by the fact that a tardy evasive maneuver was worse than none at all, for in zigging or zagging, the target ship presented a broader mark to the torpedo.

An attack from ahead was more likely to be discovered than one from astern. It was also subject to more immediate and efficient counter-measures.

Target maneuvers to avoid were usually successful when the torpedo had to make a long run. To hit, the down-the-throat shot and the shot at a ship's stern had to be fired at relatively close range. In either case the target was narrow, and submarine captains generally preferred the more conventional approaches "on the beam"—attacks which gave the submarine a broader target and normal firing-range.

So the shot at a vessel's stern, like its down-the-throat opposite, was seldom deliberately courted by the submariners. In most cases it was a resort tried when opportunities for a conventional approach had been missed.

However, on June 30, 1942, UNKAI MARU No. 5 went down from a torpedo hit under her taffrail. The shot was fired by PLUNGER, and seems to be the first identifiable sinking of its kind in the Pacific War.

Captained by Lieutenant Commander D. C. (Dave) White, PLUNGER was patrolling in the East China Sea. About midway between Nagasaki and Shanghai, UNKAI MARU No. 5 came steaming along under the Asian moon. PLUNGER sighted the freighter at 0200 and White decided to try a surface approach. He fired the four bow tubes at a range decreasing from 2,500 to 1,500 yards. The four torpedoes were fired on conventional track angles between 90° and 110° port. All missed the target. White ordered the forward tubes reloaded, and sent PLUNGER in pursuit of the Jap freighter which was travelling at an estimated 12-knot speed.

Heavily loaded, PLUNGER could make no better than 14.5 knots, a speed which gave her little latitude for maneuver against the 12-knot ship. The submarine was able to overhaul, however, and close in on the freighter's stern. At a range of 400 yards, White fired one torpedo on a 170° track. The torpedo struck home, the freighter blew up, and five minutes later the *maru's* 3,282 tons were under the surface.

Two days later PLUNGER sank another Jap freighter with a shot in the stern.

Throughout the war there were probably no more than 50 of these attacks essayed—torpedoes fired at close range on track angles between 170° and 180°. Only five or six proved successful, and the method is accordingly recognized as an expedient employed in a forced tactical situation.

Lull Before Storm

While Fremantle submarines were sinking ships from the Gulf of Siam to the Philippine Sea, and PLUNGER was sinking them below Nagasaki, the Aleutian Battle was in full swing and there was a lull in the Central and South Pacific— "lull" meaning there were no major naval engagements in those areas in late June and July 1942. But Pearl Harbor submarines were in there free-lancing, and THRESHER, NARWHAL and SILVERSIDES scored sinkings in this period.

So the war of attrition went on beneath the lull—the lull that presaged a South Pacific storm. Midway had been secured. And before the end of July the Japanese Aleutian thrust had been parried. But in July the enemy landed on Guadalcanal. Jap labor battalions were constructing an airfield at Lunga Plain on the island's north coast. Jap shipping was concentrating in the Bismarcks and gathering in New Guinea. The storm in the Solomons was coming.

The glass was falling, but this time with a difference. Heretofore, Japan's rampaging forces had raised the storm. Now the storm was to be raised by the forces of the United States. Jap bases in the Solomons would seriously threaten Allied bases in Australia, and the Allies decided to strike before the enemy's foothold was established. This time the Americans would take the offensive with a drive on the Solomons.

Strictly speaking, the Solomons Campaign may be referred to as a defensive, or counter-offensive. It was designed to relieve Japanese pressure in Burma, and to stymie the enemy in the South Pacific rather than hurl back a solidified front. It was also designed as a shot in the arm for the United Nations public, engloomed by European reverses. A tough campaign was seen in prospect, for the Marines would be facing seasoned veterans who were thus far undefeated. Infuriated by the Midway fiasco, Yamamoto would order the Imperial Navy to fight to the last gun. Accordingly, U.S. surface and air forces girded for a gruelling contest. And U.S. submarines were read¹ed for rough assignments in what promised to be one of the bloodiest battles of the war.

S-44 vs. Kako

U.S. Marines hit the beachheads of Guadalcanal on the morning of August 7, 1942. Jap Headquarters at Rabaul was taken by surprise. By nightfall 11,000 Marines were ashore on a three-mile front, and 20 hours later they were working on the unfinished Jap airstrip, renamed Henderson Field after the major who died leading a Marine bomber squadron at Midway. Simultaneous landings were made on Tulagi, Gavutu and Florida Islands. Jap torpedo bombers struck at the Florida occupation forces, blasted a transport and torpedoed the destroyer JARVIS. The planes were driven off with sharp losses, and the amphibious unloadings went on. So began the battle for the Solomons.

In the Bismarck Archipelago four Japanese heavy cruisers of the KAKO class, one light cruiser and two or three destroyers were available for counter-action. This force (designated Cruiser Division Six) was ordered into Savo Sound to strike at the Guadalcanal occupation fleet which was lying just east of Lunga Point. The division was underway on August 8, heading for Savo Island which is situated like an outpost in the western entrance of the Sound.

Japanese submarines were already in these waters between Guadalcanal and Florida Island. Warned of their presence, Admiral Noyes had obtained from Admiral Ghormley permission to move the carrier force and its escorts from the Sound. This left the surface forces of Admiral Fletcher and Admiral Turner to hold the waterway soon to become famous as "The Slot."

The advancing Japs were sighted off Bougainville, and again off Savo Island by Army aircraft. Unfortunately the fliers failed to recognize all of the cruisers, mistaking several for DD's. The Japanese made a deceptive reverse toward Rabaul which served to screen their intentions, and then came back at top speed. As a result, the Allied forces in the

Sound were caught off guard, and the consequences were disastrous.

The cruisers CANBERRA, CHICAGO and AUSTRALIA, screened by destroyers PATTERSON and BAGLEY, were patrolling a line between Savo Island and Guadalcanal. Cruisers SAN JUAN and HOBART, with two DD's, patrolled a north-south line between Florida and Guadalcanal. Cruisers ASTORIA, QUINCY and VINCENNES with DD's WILSON and HELM patrolled between Florida and Savo. Two destroyers, BLUE and RALPH TALBOT, were stationed northwest of Savo.

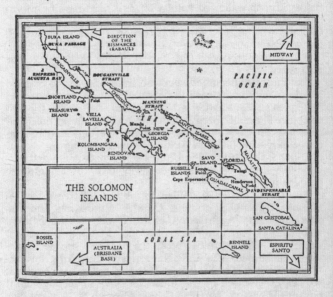

About 0130 on August 9 the enemy column came straight down the track on a line between the TALBOT and BLUE. Although the enemy ships passed within 500 yards of BLUE, the destroyer failed to detect them. The Japanese cruisers continued without interruption down the west side of Savo Island, swung eastward into the Sound, and ran into the destroyers PATTERSON and BAGLEY.

Time 0143. PATTERSON cried the alarm over TBS, and opened fire on the leading cruiser. Return fire smote the destroyer as the cruisers steamed by. BAGLEY was unable to load in time for a shot. Jap seaplanes, launched from the cruisers, illuminated the scene with parachute flares, and the fireworks' glare revealed the Australian CANBERRA and heavy cruiser CHICAGO within range.

Some four hours previous to this, British Rear Admiral V. A. C. Crutchley, commanding the Allied escort groups, had gone with the cruiser AUSTRALIA to hold conference with Admiral Turner who was with the transports east of Lunga Point. Hence CANBERRA and CHICAGO were left to face the Japanese cruiser force, two against five.

Concentrated fire wrecked CANBERRA before her gunners could reach their mounts. Disabled and burning, the Australian cruiser wallowed helplessly until the following morning when her derelict hulk was sunk by U.S. destroyers. CHICAGO was hit by a torpedo. Veering, she raced westward, turned about in confusion and opened fire on PATTERSON. The destroyer returned the fire until her nationality was recognized.

The Japs swept counter-clockwise around Savo, and plunged into head-on contact with the cruisers QUINCY, ASTORIA and VINCENNES. Main batteries blazing, they shelled the trio out of action in a half-dozen minutes. Return fire swept the Japanese flagship CHOKAI, killing 30 men—the only major damage suffered by the Japs in this foray. Steaming on out of the Sound, they brushed into the TALBOT once more and battered the destroyer aside. Then away they rushed into the western night.

The United States-Australian forces had suffered a terrible setback. Three U.S. cruisers, QUINCY, VINCENNES and ASTORIA, and the Australian CANBERRA went to the bottom. About 1,500 American officers and men were killed in action. From the Allied surface forces the Japanese escaped practically unharmed. The U.S. Navy was staggered by this defeat in the Battle of Savo Island. It might stand as the worst setback experienced by the American Navy in action, were it not for the pay-off. Japanese Cruiser Division Six was not permitted to escape scot free.

On the morning of August 10 a lone submarine was patrolling the waters off Kavieng Harbor at the northwestern end of New Ireland. She was an old submarine—an 850-tonner—product of the World War I building program, begun before the Armistice and completed in 1925. Her hull leaked oil. Her engines were tired. Only the ingenuity of an expert tender repair force, and the skill and seamanship of well-trained submariners had kept her going. She was S-44, making her third patrol from Brisbane commanded by Lieutenant Commander J. R. (Dinty) Moore.

On the day after its Savo triumph, Japanese Cruiser Division Six was doubtless still congratulating itself, polishing the brightwork and swabbing down for a victory parade into Kavieng Harbor. Here they were safe home, and not a plane had pursued them. The damage to the flagship was nothing. *"Banzai!"*

So at 0750, on August 10, 1942, the periscope of S-44 sighted two heavy cruisers coming out of the sun at a distance of some 9,000 yards. Two more heavy cruisers hove into view, the ships in column in two sections, line of bearing 45° relative, and angle on the bow 5° starboard. This put S-44 about 800 yards from the enemy track. Moore put the submarine on a course 70° divergent in order to open the distance to the track a trifle and give her a little more sea room for the approach.

Five minutes of maneuvering brought S-44 around to the firing course for an 80° track.

The leading cruisers steamed by. The third cruiser passed. At 0808 the last heavy cruiser was only 700 yards away.

"We were close enough to see the Japs on the bridge using their glasses," Moore recalled afterwards. And that was proximity from an old S-boat's point of view. The enemy cruiser looked bigger than the Pentagon Building and the submarine seemed smaller than a barrel.

Moore fired four torpedoes, zero gyro angle, 80° track. Thirty-five seconds after firing, the first torpedo hit. The explosion thunderclapped in the sound gear as the S-boat went down to 130 feet.

The trailing torpedoes slammed into the warship's hull. "Evidently all her boilers blew up," Moore related. "You could hear hideous noises that sounded like steam hissing through water. These noises were more terrifying to the crew than the actual depth charges that followed. It sounded as if giant chains were being dragged across our hull, as if our own water and air lines were bursting."

The Truk Blockade

Before the Solomons offensive could be effectively launched and the drive on Guadalcanal set in motion, there was one most important Japanese base that had to be blockaded. This was the Japanese naval base at Truk, centered in the eastern Caroline Islands.

In July, while the Brisbane boats of Task Force Forty-two were attacking the enemy in the Bismarck-Solomons area, five fleet submarines from Pearl Harbor were sent to patrol off Truk.

Periscopes maintained a vigilant watch on the road coming down from Guam, and patrollers lay in ambush along the south-bound sea lanes to Rabaul. As September came up on the calendar the submarine blockade of Japan's Central Pacific Gibraltar was in full swing. The guns which thudded on Guadalcanal were echoed by torpedoes off Truk.

By the end of August 1942, when United States forces, turning from the defensive, were girding for the Solomons Campaign, United States submarines had sunk a total of 82 Japanese merchant ships.

The enemy's transportation facilities were showing signs of strain, and the drivers of Japan's War Machine were beginning to worry about the supply lines to such distant outposts as Guadalcanal.

Chapter 13

Guadalcanal Campaign

☆ ☆ ☆

*Diversionary Raid—Nautilus and
Argonaut to Makin*

Submarines NAUTILUS and ARGONAUT,
under Group Commander J. M.
Haines, stood out of Pearl Harbor on
August 8 and headed for the Gilbert
Islands. The Marines had landed on
Guadalcanal the day before, and the
previous evening they had landed on
the decks of ARGONAUT and NAU-
TILUS.

Boarding ARGONAUT, seven officers and 114 men crowded
into the submarine's interior. Six officers and 84 men were
packed into NAUTILUS. These Marines were the pick of the
Corps—Companies A and B of the famous 2nd Raider Battalion, trained and led by hard-hitting Colonel Evans F. Carlson—and they quickly had the submarine situation well
under control.

Their objective in the Gilberts was Makin Island. Mission:
a commando raid. This raid on Makin was primarily planned
to create a diversion—scramble the enemy's plans and make
him re-deploy strong forces which were known to be concentrating for an attack on Guadalcanal. The raiders were to
strike Makin a savage blow, do as much damage as possible,
and gather information on the island.

The run to Makin was accomplished without misadventure.
ARGONAUT, under Lieutenant Commander J. R. Pierce of
Aleutian experience, was making her second patrol after
complete overhaul and modernization at Mare Island. Captain of NAUTILUS was Lieutenant Commander Brockman, and
her ace crew had topped their big exploit at Midway with a
rampage patrol in Empire waters. So the Marines as well as
the submarines were in good hands.

159

Early in the morning of August 16, Makin was sighted. Periscope reconnaissance commenced at daylight. Rendezvous was accomplished at dusk, and plans for the attack were passed to ARGONAUT. The submarines waited offshore while the twilight thickened into darkness. The Marines shouldered into their gear and huddled, tense, as their officers briefed them on the final details. Shortly after midnight NAUTILUS put her rubber boats overside and the first group of raiders disembarked.

By 0421 all Marines were clear of the submarine, and the bridge personnel watched the last boat paddle off in the graying mist. For about an hour the submariners waited, while the gloaming seemed to listen with drawn breath. Then at 0513 word came by voice radio. The Marines were on the beach.

Thirty minutes later a pessimistic and cryptic message was received from Colonel Carlson. *"Everything lousy!"* Four minutes after that the news brightened with, *"Situation expected to be well in hand shortly."* Following this message, there was a blur of static and voice-radio reception deteriorated. Evidently the walkie-talkies had run into trouble. But a few snatches of English got through, and it became apparent that the raiders wanted fire support to neutralize the Ukiangang Point Lake Area where Jap reserves were thought to be.

NAUTILUS promptly opened up with her deck gun, and was on target with the third salvo. She had been firing for a short time when word came through that a merchant ship was sitting in the harbor 8,000 yards from the government pier. Fire was checked at the 24th round, and NAUTILUS maneuvered to fire on this new target.

Both NAUTILUS and ARGONAUT endeavored to remain on the surface throughout the morning. Several times they were forced under by enemy planes.

The submarines surfaced early in the evening, and four boats laden with weary raiders were recovered by 2130. More were due to arrive, and the submariners spent the remainder of the night in a futile search for these.

The 53 Marines who had made it told stories of desperate fighting ashore and the struggle to launch their boats after dark in wild surf. Many boats had capsized. Guns and gear had been lost. Aboard NAUTILUS and ARGONAUT, the Marine doctors and pharmacist's mates had their work cut out for them. One young Marine had eight wounds in his chest. A sergeant walked aboard with a bullet buried deep in his back. "I got a scratch somewhere," he told the surgeon, "and I can't bend forward." The submariners were not going to leave such men behind at Makin, and at daybreak they were still on the surface, searching.

Then several boats were spotted on the beach, the Marines waiting to run the gantlet through the breakers. NAUTILUS closed to within half a mile of the reef, and by 0800 two more boatloads of Carlson's Raiders were aboard. One of the rubber boats was manned by volunteers and sent back to shore with extra weapons, paddles and a line-throwing gun. The volunteers carried a message advising Colonel Carlson that NAUTILUS, if forced by aircraft to submerge, would be back at 1930 and remain offshore indefinitely thereafter. A man from the boat swam in through the surf to deliver this message, and then swam back out to NAUTILUS. But the rubber boat and its complement of volunteers never returned. NAUTILUS was forced to submerge that morning, and apparently the aircraft which drove her under spotted and strafed the boat in the shallows.

Meanwhile, two more boats were recovered by ARGONAUT. She, too, was forced under by enemy planes. As the submarines surfaced later in the morning, they were again driven down by a plane which dropped two random bombs from high altitude. After this attack, the two submarines remained submerged.

At evening they surfaced once more, and Colonel Carlson was contacted ashore. A new rendezvous point was set for two hours later. The submarines maneuvered in, and the remaining five boatloads of Marines battled out through the surf. When the last man was aboard, both submarines set a course for Pearl Harbor. NAUTILUS was home on the 25th. ARGONAUT arrived the following day. It had been a tough assignment, but all hands had played their part, and the mission was highly successful.

The crews of ARGONAUT and NAUTILUS could take pride in their part of this exploit. They carried the Marines to Makin, and they brought them back. They shot up shipping in the harbor. From this pioneer operation they gained invaluable experience which would later aid the planning of full-fledged island invasions. By future submariners, NAUTILUS and ARGONAUT will be remembered as the valiant V-boats which participated in the greatest commando raid carried out in the Pacific during World War II.

Undersea War in the Solomons

After the Battle of Savo Island, the opposing forces had recoiled, then come back to battery, crashing.

Determined to retake lost ground, Japanese Headquarters

dispatched 1,000 crack troops to Guadalcanal. A massive fleet was assembled for a follow-up strike—four transports, four destroyers, a cruiser and an accompanying carrier force built around the large ZUIKAKU and SHOKAKU and the smaller RYUJO. Japanese submarines screened the advance of this armada which was 200 miles north of Guadalcanal by the morning of August 23rd.

Admiral Ghormley had countered by rushing his ENTERPRISE-NORTH CAROLINA-SARATOGA forces to the Eastern Solomons. WASP was in the backfield, and HORNET with her escorts was steaming hell-for-leather down from Pearl Harbor.

Japanese submarines were in the Solomons at this time. Planes from ENTERPRISE sighted a number of them, and bombed them without scoring hits. Their presence in the area was a threat to American convoys and slowed the reinforcement of the Marines holding Henderson Field.

Submarines from Brisbane similarly hampered Japanese efforts to reinforce their Guadalcanal vanguard. Fighting the war of attrition, they damaged enemy merchantmen on the fringe of the Solomons area, patrolled the Rabaul road to Guadalcanal and countered "threat" with menace. Due to the number of hindering factors, results on the American side of the Solomons undersea war were disappointing. Although there was a heavy flow of enemy traffic in the area, most of it traveled at high speed and at night. Until mid-autumn the submarines operating from Brisbane were without surface radar, and only a few arrived with radar during the remainder of the year. Consequently the high-speed, night-going traffic was most difficult to locate and hard to hit.

The running of small destroyer groups and speedy landing craft down the "Slot" to Guadalcanal was more by way of a resort than a stratagem devised by the Japanese. For the Imperial Navy was unwilling to risk large fleet units in the Guadalcanal area. Nevertheless, the resort proved moderately successful. Jap forces came dashing down the "Slot" with such consistent regularity that the Marines dubbed the operation the "Tokyo Express." Land-based American aircraft wrecked the "Express" time and again. But as often it got through under cover of night, and the reinforcements delivered enabled the Imperial troops on the island to make a stubborn stand.

But it was chiefly the Japanese submarine force which held American shipping at bay in this phase of the Guadalcanal campaign. In this period the I-boats scored their greatest strike of the war.

Scouting east of San Cristobal at the end of August, SARATOGA was attacked by submarines and struck by a torpedo which inflicted minor damage. In waters south of SARATOGA'S position, HORNET was barely missed by a submarine torpedo a few days later. Then, on September 14, a large convoy carrying Marines and gasoline set out from Espiritu Santo to reinforce the hard-pressed Guadalcanal garrison. HORNET, WASP and NORTH CAROLINA provided air cover for the convoy.

On the afternoon of the 15th the carrier forces ran into a school of submarines. WASP, NORTH CAROLINA and the destroyer O'BRIEN were all hit by torpedoes within a bracket of ten minutes. A single torpedo blasted an enormous hole in the battleship's hull, the explosion killing five of NORTH CAROLINA'S men. O'BRIEN, badly disabled, sank after she limped back to port. Three torpedoes struck WASP in her magazine and gasoline-storage holds. Nearly 200 men lost their lives in the explosions and fires which resulted. When the ready ammunition began to detonate, tearing out the vessel's vitals, Captain Forrest P. Sherman gave the order to abandon. That night a U.S. destroyer sank the gutted aircraft carrier. Her assailant was the Japanese submarine I-19.

WASP was the second U.S. aircraft carrier to meet destruction at the hands of the Japanese submariners. Credit has been given the Japanese torpedo which at that time contained an explosive charge almost twice as great as that of the American torpedo. The Japanese torpedo also developed greater speed than the American, left less wake, and was generally the superior weapon.

But in the many months of war that followed the WASP torpedoing, the Japanese Submarine Force failed to approach its early successes. On October 26, during the Battle of Santa Cruz Islands, a Jap submarine torpedoed the destroyer PORTER. Disabled, the vessel had to be abandoned and sunk. And on November 13, in the wake of the furious naval battle off Guadalcanal, a spread of Japanese submarine torpedoes struck the damaged American cruiser JUNEAU. The blasting broke the cruiser in two, and she went down immediately— a disaster which took nearly 700 American lives. During the remainder of the war, Japanese submarines were able to sink but two major U.S. naval vessels—the escort carrier LISCOME BAY (November 1943) and the heavy cruiser INDIANAPOLIS (July 1945). Improved anti-submarine defenses, search radar, inferior Japanese submarine strategy—many factors contributed to this phenomenal decline.

Retirement of the Sugar Boats

The old S-boats at Brisbane could not keep the pace. One by one the more battle-worn were sent to the States as fleet-type submarines arrived in Brisbane to replace them. Among the first of these replacements were GRAMPUS, GRAYBACK and GROWLER. Entering the Guadalcanal campaign, they found the South Seas boiling. Throughout the autumn of 1942 replacements continued to come in as the struggle in the Solomons grew hotter. STURGEON, SAILFISH, SAURY, SNAPPER, SEADRAGON, SCULPIN, GROUPER, PLUNGER, GUDGEON, SWORDFISH, TUNA, FLYINGFISH, SARGO, GATO, AMBERJACK and ALBACORE patrolled out of Brisbane that fall. Altogether some 24 fleet-type submarines, about half of them "temporary loans" from Pearl Harbor, comprised the new Brisbane Force.

Most of the retiring S-boats went home to serve as training vessels at submarine and anti-submarine warfare schools.

No force could be more deserving of the Navy's commendation, "Well done!"

Subs to New Guinea and Palau

On October 26 the Japanese were badly mauled in the sea battle off Santa Cruz Islands. Simultaneously Marine and Army forces regained lost ground on Guadalcanal where the Imperial troops met defeat in a carnage that ended all Japanese hopes of winning the island without a major land-sea-air offensive.

The Japanese Army had suffered a painful setback, but Japanese naval forces, despite severe damage to two carriers and a cruiser in the Santa Cruz engagement, remained formidable. And the Santa Cruz victory cost the U.S. Navy a high price—ENTERPRISE damaged by dive bombers—the destroyer PORTER torpedoed—loss of the aircraft carrier HORNET, destroyed by bomb hits and suicide planes. Both sides rushed reserves into the Guadalcanal breach and gathered naval reinforcements for a showdown fight.

After the Java Sea Battle the Japs had seized a large portion of New Guinea. During the spring and summer of 1942 they had pushed the Allies out on the southeast peninsula, and by September they were threatening the Australian-American base at Port Moresby.

To counter this threat, General MacArthur, in supreme command of the Australia-New Guinea Area, planned an autumn drive across the Owen Stanley Mountains to capture the enemy's advance bases at Buna and Gona.

Submarines from Brisbane were assigned the task of stopping enemy naval vessels which were operating off the New Guinea coast near Buna. A number of Japanese destroyers had been sighted offshore at night, and it was believed they were running in reinforcements. Accordingly, the submarines were employed to patrol close-in positions off Buna, Casamata and Vitiaz—Dampier Straits. The directive under which they worked prescribed that the defense of the New Guinea coast was the primary mission and that destruction of enemy shipping was secondary.

Among the submarines participating in the New Guinea operation was ALBACORE, one of the new fleet-types which had arrived in Pearl Harbor in the summer of 1942. From the SubPac command she had been transferred to the Brisbane Force, and in November she was dispatched to the New Guinea front. Patrolling off New Guinea, ALBACORE was to combine the "defense" and "destruction" clauses of the directive by destroying one of the major enemy warships campaigning in those waters.

Into the South Seas the Japanese had rushed all available naval units, including as many light cruisers as the Imperial Navy could spare for duty in that theater. The Imperial Navy's CL's were a motley lot, ranging all the way from AGANO and OYODA, comparable in strength to heavy cruisers, to the training cruiser KASHII, hardly a match for a modern destroyer. Motley though the CL's were, the Japanese placed much faith in these craft, and all of them were pressed into active service, regardless of age or size.

Among the oldest and busiest of the IJN cruiser divisions was CruDiv Eighteen, consisting of TATSUTA and TENRYU. Dating back to 1916, these 3,300-tonners were nonetheless capable of firing guns and dropping modern depth charges, and they performed ably as the major Japanese naval units in the New Guinea campaign. Belying reports that they had been bombed, disabled, blown up and sunk, they continued to ply their trade along the New Guinea coast throughout the autumn of 1942.

Enter ALBACORE. Under Lieutenant Commander R. C. Lake, she had won her combat insignia on the Truk blockade by damaging three ships to make her first patrol a success. Now on her second patrol, she was looking for more action. She found it off the northeast coast of New Guinea.

The date: December 18. Lookout sighted a sizable AP, and Lake directed a day-submerged attack. He fired three shots at this target, and one torpedo hit for probable damage.

After nightfall, ALBACORE attacked a destroyer which came steaming out of the dark. Lake fired a single and the torpedo missed. Then he put the submarine on the track of a larger target which proved to be one of the busybodies of Japanese Cruiser Division Eighteen. Although immediate identification of this rakish silhouette was impossible, ALBACORE's crew realized they were after something big. Tense at the periscope, Lake sent ALBACORE boring in. Two torpedoes were fired. Two hits roared in the sound gear. Down went the light cruiser TENRYU—a link removed from the Jap chain holding New Guinea.

And with this, the first ship officially credited to her record, ALBACORE began an extraordinary career. That it began with the sinking of a CL was presageful. Two months later (February 20, 1943) she sank the Japanese destroyer OSHIO, farther up the New Guinea coast. Having destroyed two warships in South Seas waters, she went on to become a Nemesis to the Imperial Navy. Although she sank but ten ships before her final chapter was written, ALBACORE sent more enemy naval vessels to the bottom than any other U.S. submarine in the war.

Meanwhile, two U.S. submarines were sent from Australia to reconnoitre Palau.

During the first months of the war, the Palau area had been patrolled by Asiatic Fleet submarines with disappointing results. The waters off Palau provided few targets for the hunters.

This apparent lack of game mystified submariners and strategists alike. Before the war's outbreak there had been many indications of the Japs' intent to use this mandated island group as a major base for naval vessels and merchant ships. And information received during the Japanese offensive in the Southwest Pacific confirmed these pre-war indications. Where, then, was the expected ship traffic? Enemy vessels seemed to be coming from and heading for Palau, yet submarines patrolling the area were unable to contact them.

A clue to the mystery was uncovered in October 1942, during the Guadalcanal campaign, when a secret chart was captured from the enemy. The U.S. submarines had been watching the Malakal Passage entrance to the Palau Group. Lying in the southeast barrier, this was the only entrance known to the Allies. The captured chart revealed that Malakal Passage was too shallow for ships of deep draft. Another entrance, Toagel Mlungui Passage, about 17 miles north of Malakal, in the mid-section of the western coral barrier, was the passage employed by the Japanese.

Submarines SEAWOLF and SEAL were ordered to Palau to investigate this "secret door."

Palau Mystery Solved

Seawolf's three-day run to Palau was uneventful. Then, at nightfall on November 11, she raised one of the outer Pelews, and things began to happen. As the submarine moved in cautiously, the watch sighted a fast patrol boat.

Then something faster came over the horizon—a Jap destroyer. A tropical squall wiped out visibility, and the DD was gone before Seawolf could get on her track.

Warder was deploring the weather when two more destroyers were sighted, charging along through the rain. Five minutes later, making a sweep with the periscope, Warder uttered an exclamation—one with a pyrotechnic point.

"There's an aircraft carrier up here! She's as big as a new barn, and those DD's have sucked us out of position! We've got to pour on the coal!"

At four-engine speed, the submarine raced in pursuit of the flat-top. She was still at the carrier's heels on the morning of November 12 when the main motor generator cables went bad. Seawolf radioed the carrier's course and apparent destination to the Allied command, and slowed to make repairs. A few hours later she set a course for Pearl Harbor.

Meantime, Seal (Lieutenant Commander Hurd) had been dispatched from Fremantle to Palau to probe the waters off Toagel Mlungui Passage. Patrolling the area on November 16, Seal sighted a convoy of nine cargo ships escorted by two destroyers.

As the vessels trooped into view, Hurd ordered his submarine to periscope depth and started a submerged approach. Everything clicking in the T.D.C., he maneuvered into attack position and fired two torpedoes at the chosen target—a sizable transport. Explosions thundered as the torpedoes struck home. To the bottom went Boston Maru, 5,477 tons.

Seal herself was nearly sunk in the resulting melee. While maneuvering to evade, she was rammed by one of the ships in the milling convoy. With the overhead roar of an express train speeding across a trestle, the ship skimmed the submarine's conning tower. Both periscopes were damaged and put out of commission. It was a close shave for Hurd and crew. And with depth charges adding insult to injury, it took a fine blend of skill, grit and Jay Factor to save Seal's skin.

But the Palau investigation had been completed.

Submarine Operations (for Appendicitis)

In common with the practitioners of most highly technical and exclusive professions, the Navy's submariners developed a succinct vernacular peculiarly and distinctively their own. There was "can" for battery. "Boiler" for "pig boat." "Ladder chancre" for bruises caused by barking the shins. "Spread," meaning torpedoes fired in series at various angles. "Pulling the plug" for submerging. "Ping jockey" for the operator of sonic "pinging gear." "Brass pounder" for radioman. A variety of names for other technicians of the crew. And the pharmacist's mate was frequently dubbed "Quack."

In the case of Wheeler B. Lipes, PhM1, member of the crew of SEADRAGON, the title was respectfully altered to "Doctor."

Entering the Navy before the war, Lipes had trained as a corpsman in San Diego. Transferred to a service hospital in Philadelphia, he qualified as a lab technician and acquired a special rating as cardiographer. When he reported for duty in submarines he had seen appendectomies performed. But he never, as he admitted afterward, expected to pinch-hit for surgeon and remove a human appendix.

SEADRAGON was patrolling far behind enemy lines in the Southwest Pacific when the crisis arose. The date, September 11, 1942, was one Lipes—and Darrell Dean Rector, Seaman 1—would not soon forget. Someone rushed to Lipes and told him that young Rector had fallen unconscious to the deck. Submariners had passed out before—from heat, fatigue, too thin a diet. But the pharmacist's mate recognized the high temperature and symptomatic pains.

"Appendicitis," he reported to Lieutenant Commander Ferrall. "It may be peritonitis. He'll have to be operated on at once."

SEADRAGON's captain put the question bluntly. "Can you do it?"

"Yes, sir," Lipes stated. "It's his only chance."

Surgical instruments had to be improvised. Lipes fashioned a handle for the scalpel. Bent spoons served as muscular retractors. A tea strainer became an ether mask. The instruments were sterilized in a solution of torpedo alcohol mixed with water and boiled. A searchlight was rigged over the wardroom table.

Rector was carried in and stretched out on the table. Before proceeding with the operation, Lipes roused the patient.

"I've never performed an appendectomy on anybody," he told Rector. "I can do it, but it's a chance. If you don't want me to go ahead—"

The patient whispered, "Let's go."

Pharmacist's Mate Lipes went ahead. As best they could,

the men at the controls held the submarine level, and the motors droned a murmurous monotone. Like a veteran Lipes made the incision, found and removed the appendix, sewed up the incision with catgut. An antiseptic powder made of ground-up sulfa tablets was applied. Bandages were fastened in place. The sponge count came out even. Darrell Rector lived to tell about his operation.

The SEADRAGON appendectomy made news headlines. And the amazed public had hardly digested this remarkable story when a similar operation was performed on board submarine GRAYBACK. Surgeon in this case was Pharmacist's Mate Harry B. Roby. The patient: Torpedoman's Mate W. R. Jones. All hands recovered nicely.

Then came word of an appendectomy performed during Christmas week 1942 on board submarine SILVERSIDES. The patient: a bluejacket named George Platter. The surgeon: Thomas Moore, PhM1. Six days after the operation, the patient was on his feet, standing watch.

The foregoing might lead one to believe that submarine operations in World War II developed into a series of appendectomies. But with the arrival of penicillin, the necessity for emergency appendectomies was largely alleviated.

Statistic: Before the war was over, 11 cases of acute appendicitis were diagnosed and treated by pharmacist's mates aboard U.S. submarines. Pioneering the emergency appendectomy, Wheeler B. Lipes, Harry Roby, and Thomas Moore established a tradition that would inspire every pharmacist's mate and corpsman. Not a single death resulted from appendicitis originating on a submarine in war patrol in World War II. Proof of superlative Navy training and the submariner's intestinal fortitude.

Incidentally, SEADRAGON took time out during this medical period to sink Japanese submarine I-4 off Rabaul. GRAYBACK, too, sank a Japanese I-boat at this season in the same general area. The hapless Japanese submarines did not live to tell about these operations.

Guadalcanal Conclusion

Their exit from the Solomons under fire, the Japs strove desperately throughout January and February 1943 to evacuate their forces from Guadalcanal. As the Jap guns went silent in the jungle, the major threat to Australia evaporated.

A summary of the Guadalcanal campaign must highlight two features. In the five-month struggle for control of Guadalcanal (August-December 1942) United States surface forces suffered drastic casualties. These included the loss of two aircraft carriers, four heavy cruisers, two light cruisers and 14 destroyers—22 warships in all. The Imperial Navy's losses were somewhat lighter: two battleships, one aircraft carrier, two heavy cruisers, two light cruisers and 12 destroyers—a total of 19 warships.

But under the surface, Japanese losses in this critical five-month period were far heavier than the American. Between August 7 (the day the Americans landed on Guadalcanal) and January 1, 1943, the enemy lost eight submarines in the South Pacific area. Not a single United States submarine was lost through enemy action in this theater, or elsewhere in the Pacific, during this period. GRUNION, lost in the Aleutians, was last heard from on July 30, and probably went down shortly thereafter. Sole loss in the South Pacific, S-39 was abandoned without a personnel casualty, after stranding. Silhouetted against the violence of the Guadalcanal conflict and the extensive submarine participation, these statistics speak volumes for the skill of the U.S. Submarine Force and the capabilities of the submersible.

Chapter 14

The Empire Blockade

(with Side Glances at Radar, Mines and Atlantic Operations)

☆　　☆　　☆

Tourniquet on Tokyo

During the summer and autumn of 1942 the Pearl Harbor submarines clamped and tightened a blockade on the home islands of Japan. This blockade amounted to a submarine offensive—the one offensive which the Navy was able to launch in the Central Pacific in 1942.

The continuous submarine blockade delivered upon the enemy's home front a series of blows that landed with increasing frequency and impact as the war went on. And while the spectacle of these sinkings was not described by the "Silent Service" for the edification of the American home front, it was not missed by the Emperor's subjects who witnessed the destruction at their maritime doorstep and saw their beaches littered with the iron bones of broken vessels and the sea-bleached bones of brother Japs. The Empire blockade, therefore, was a dual-purpose which placed a drain on Japan's shipping resources and a strain on Papa San's mystical belief in the Empire's invulnerability.

Long before the Japanese strike, it had been evident to American naval leaders that a submarine blockade of Japan should counter that nation's plunge into World War II. The monstrous Japanese offensive had delayed blockade operations, and in the spring of 1942 Pearl Harbor submarines had been deployed on a wide front, engaged in reconnaissance and other special missions which took precedence over the patrols planned for Empire waters. Large expanses of ocean were added to the Central Pacific operating area as the enemy drive rolled forward. When the SubsAsiatic Force fell back to Australia a portion of the northern part of its operating area was shifted into the SubPac orbit. In April 1942, when the Japanese offensive was at its height, the Central Pacific operating area was expanded to include Formosa and Palau. In May, ComSubPac recommended, and CinCPac approved, a plan whereby submarines en route to or from the Southwest Pacific could be ordered to reconnoiter in the Marshalls, Carolines or Gilberts. This fitted into the program devised for the supplying of submarines for the Southwest Pacific Force through Pearl Harbor. In accordance with directives from CinCPac and Cominch, ComSubPac maintained submarine strength in the Southwest Pacific at the level necessary to meet the demand in that area, and SoWesPac submarines slated for major repairs were returned to SubPac for overhaul on the West Coast.

The Battle of Midway interrupted Empire patrols in early June. And immediately following the Midway engagement, a number of Pacific Fleet submarines were sent to reinforce the Aleutian front. Then the South Pacific crisis developed, and Pearl Harbor submarines were drawn into that area as "loans" to the Brisbane Force. These emergency moves reduced the number of submarines available for patrols off Japan and temporarily weakened the grip of the blockade.

In the summer of 1942, however, the blockade took hold. A priority patrol plan gave areas off Honshu, Shikoku and Kyushu precedence over others covered by the SubPac Force. Top priority went to the Honshu area which embraced the approaches to Tokyo and Yokohama.

As submarines were not immediately available for continuous patrol of these areas, the recommendation was made to CinCPac that the number of submarines patrolling the Mandates be reduced and their weight shifted to the Empire blockade. But the pressure had to lessen in the Aleutians and the Solomons before the SubPac Force could go "all out" in applying the vise to Japan.

Submarine Tactics—The Radar Attack

The air search radar (SD) installed on a number of submarines at the beginning of the war, had little or no effect on the offensive tactics of submarining. As suggested by its name, this "aircraft warning installation" was used only to supplement lookout detection of enemy aircraft. Even there it often served in a supernumerary capacity, for its radar "pips," revealing the presence of aircraft and their distance from the submarine, failed to indicate the direction from which the planes were flying. Stormy seas interfered with the operation of this instrument. Traversing the hills and valleys of a roughened ocean, the rolling submarine could not depend on the SD, and the lookout in oilskins or the watch at the periscope remained the submarine's best eyes.

However, technicians of the Western Electric Company had long been working to develop a radar device which could locate surface vessels and indicate directional bearings as well as range. Result was the SJ radar which was ready for installation in submarines by the summer of 1942.

The SJ's operation was independent of visibility conditions. Raised into daylight or pitchy dark above the surface, the parabolic antenna would continue to register "sweeps" so long as it was revolved by the operators.

Obviously many ships which would otherwise have "passed in the night" undetected, were now exposed to the submarine equipped with search radar. Moreover, having

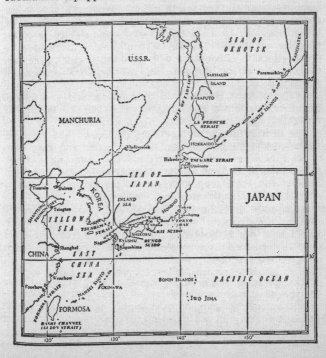

picked up the target, the SJ could guide the submarine's approach. Radar replaced the inaccurate, night-blind periscope stadimeter and eliminated the necessity for continuous sonar "pinging." For the first time the submarine had an efficient and accurate ranging device, available for tracking as well as detecting.

Thus the SJ's installation resulted in a marked increase of night attacks. Concurrently the night-surface approach came into its own as the favored night tactic.

This tactical trend did not develop until after 1942, for only a few submarines were equipped with search radar that year.

HADDOCK left Pearl Harbor on August 12, 1942, with the Force's first SJ aboard. The instrument embodied mystery as well as novelty. The idiosyncrasies of radar along with its capabilities had yet to be understood.

Lieutenant Commander Taylor and crew also had to learn of the capabilities and idiosyncrasies of the Japanese in the East China Sea area north of Formosa. Pioneering in two activities—warfare and search radar—HADDOCK's maiden patrollers were disposed to be conservative in regard to tactics. When, en route to the area, the submarine sighted a loaded freighter on August 12, Taylor conducted a daylight periscope attack in accordance with established rules. One torpedo hit the target. But the damaged vessel corrected a list and kept on going.

Taylor ordered HADDOCK to the surface, and gave chase. The race ran into a dark and moonless night, and the SJ was called upon to demonstrate its capabilities.

The instrument and its operators performed like veterans. Radar picked up the target at 13,600 yards, and gave continuous ranges and bearings for the T.D.C. from there on in. Information is lacking on the range at which the target became visible, but HADDOCK overhauled her swiftly, and Taylor opened fire at 1,300 yards on a 180° track.

Apparently the submarine was sighted. Blowing a frantic whistle, the freighter started a turn to starboard which would have put HADDOCK in line for a shot from the stern gun. Taylor ordered submergence. Two timed hits were heard as HADDOCK slid down under. Taylor reported a sinking. Although Japanese records failed to provide a name for the abolished vessel, it was eventually credited to HADDOCK as a nameless transport.

On August 26 while still patrolling in Formosa Strait, HADDOCK picked up a radar contact at 12,000 yards. There was a full moon and a cloudless sky which made an undetected surface approach impossible. The enemy's course and speed were plotted by radar. Taylor sent HADDOCK to full speed to gain position ahead for an early morning attack. At daybreak Taylor submerged the submarine on the target's track. It was 0820 in the morning before the target was sighted for the first time. (All previous tracking had been by radar.) Taylor fired four torpedoes from the stern tubes. All missed. The submarine was swung hard under full rudder, and the bow tubes were brought to bear. Two more torpedoes were fired. One of these hit, and the freighter was seen to sink. She was TEISHUN MARU, 2,251 tons.

HADDOCK's first patrol may be remarked as a historic episode in submarining and an important turning point in the Pacific War. Search radar expanded the horizon of submarine warfare by many leagues, and its successful introduction dated the beginning of the end for thousands of tons of Japanese shipping, which, in pre-radar days, might have reached its intended destination.

Links in the Chain

GUARDFISH set the seasonal pace for the Empire blockade. Returning to home base in mid-September, Klakring and crew turned in one of the most dramatic patrol reports to date. Only DRUM and TRITON the previous spring had sunk more tonnage in Empire waters. But in accounting for five ships, a trawler and a sampan, and hitting two freighters for heavy damage, GUARDFISH was not far behind these tonnage leaders. In battle action (twelve attacks) she was not behind at all. And her patrol, herewith related in some detail, contained another of those episodes that keeps the "Silent Service" talking over its coffee.

Guardfish Goes to the Races

On March 4, 1942, Lieutenant Thomas Burton Klakring, captain of S-17, attempted to ram a U-boat raider in the Virgin Islands. Six months later (August 6, 1942) Lieutenant Commander Thomas Burton Klakring took his new submarine GUARDFISH out of Pearl Harbor, T.H., to conduct a raid of his own off the home islands of Japan.

The northeast coast of Honshu had not previously been visited by a patrolling submarine. GUARDFISH's visit was to come as a surprise—one the natives were going to remember. GUARDFISH's submariners were going to remember it, too. They were going to remember that patrolling without benefit of search radar they made 77 enemy-ship contacts in half as many days. And they made some other contacts never to be forgotten.

After running out a storm en route to the area, GUARD-FISH made her first contact on August 19. At 0625 an 8,000-ton naval auxiliary was sighted, and shortly thereafter an escorting destroyer poked its nose out beyond the target. Fifteen minutes after first sighting the target, Klakring fired three torpedoes from 1,300 yards. Three explosions were heard, but the ship in question merely put on steam and turned away. The torpedoes may have missed and then detonated, or one warhead might have gone off magnetically and set off the others.

The destroyer promptly headed for GUARDFISH. Klakring held the submarine at periscope depth, hoping for a shot. At 2,000 yards the DD wheeled, dropped two depth charges, and steamed off to join her cohort. GUARDFISH went down to 180 feet for a reload. That evening she quietly entered her area.

After sighting three freighters, which she was unable to close on the 24th, GUARDFISH struck a merchantman coming out of Kinkasan Harbor. At 1657 three torpedoes netted two hits on the unwary vessel. The third torpedo exploded against the bluff of the island. The ship's bow was blown almost completely off, and she nose-dived with her screws still turning. That was the last of SEIKAI MARU, 3,109 tons.

This sinking put an end to ship operations in the vicinity of Kinkasan Harbor for the rest of the day. A ship GUARD-FISH had sighted coming out of Kinkasan just before the attack decided discretion was the better part of valor, and retreated into the harbor. GUARDFISH evaded a patrol boat and stood northward.

The next morning Klakring directed a submerged attack on another freighter. Of two torpedoes fired, one proved a dud and the other porpoised and failed to explode. A third torpedo appeared to premature, for the target, apparently undamaged, was seen to head for the beach. About to surface in pursuit, GUARDFISH made four plane contacts on her SD. Not long after that, one of GUARDFISH's torpedoes drifted into view, floating vertically, without its warhead. This depressing sight was followed by a sound of fast screws which, together with the previous plane contacts, left no doubt in Klakring's mind that GUARDFISH was "it" in a fast game of hunt-the-submarine. He ordered her down to 120 feet, at which depth she eluded the hunting party.

Followed a week of heavy seas and thick fog in which GUARDFISH made no contacts. Then, on September 2, while patrolling on the surface, she sighted a freighter eight miles distant. Directing a submerged attack, Klakring fired three torpedoes for two smacking hits on the target. The ship took a 50° starboard list, but did not appear to be sinking. So another torpedo was fired. No torpedo wake was seen in the rough seas, and no explosion was heard, but the freighter's crew began to abandon ship, and ten minutes later the vessel broke squarely in half and sank. She was TEIKYU MARU, 2,332 tons.

Around midday, September 4, GUARDFISH sighted three freighters heading northwest about half a mile offshore. At 1246, with GUARDFISH unable to close to less than 5,000 yards submerged, Klakring wound up and let one torpedo loose at this range. The forward room reported hearing an explosion, and one of the AK's turned beachward, belching smoke. She was probably damaged, and soon disappeared in the offshore haze.

Klakring assumed the freighter trio might be the advance section of a convoy. At 1634 his hopes were confirmed by the appearance of two large ore ships. He sent GUARDFISH boring in. At 1744 he fired one torpedo at the leading ship, range 500 yards. The torpedo hit 27 seconds later with a terrific explosion. Two shots at the second target resulted in another thunderous blast. Both vessels sank spectacularly while the submarine's crew took turns viewing the scene through the periscope. The obliterated ore ships were CHITA MARU, 2,276 tons, and TENYU MARU, 3,738 tons.

During the attack on the ore carriers, Klakring had spied two more AK's heading out of Kuji Wan. These, in turn, spied the submarine's handiwork, and thereupon reversed course. One anchored off the town of Minato, while the other remained on the move in the bay. Clearing the rocks to seaward of the bay, GUARDFISH stalked in to a point 6,500 yards from the anchored ship, and fired a long shot. Seven minutes and 27 seconds later an explosion, probably in the vessel's boiler room, flung a spout of smoke and steam several hundred feet in the air. A bull's-eye at over three miles! This was one of the longest torpedo shots of the war. Klakring and company watched the ship sink stern first until she rested on bottom with 100 feet of her bow slanting up out of water.

At this juncture another ship was sighted, steaming into view from the southeast. Klakring sent GUARDFISH racing to meet this newcomer. The submarine closed at high speed, submerged, and Klakring fired two torpedoes from 1,000 yards range. One hit—another GUARDFISH-shaking explosion—and the target began to settle by the bow. To hurry the settlement, Klakring fired another torpedo. It missed, but a moment later the target, KEIMEI MARU, 5,254 tons, went nose-diving to the bottom.

As darkness fell, the patrol boats came out in force. Concerning the end of this epic day, Klakring wrote, *"Propellers could be heard starting and stopping at frequent intervals until 2042 hours, when, it being all quiet and pitch black, GUARDFISH surfaced and cleared out on three engines. 2112: Two patrols sighted. 2220: A third patrol vessel sighted. Steered semi-circular avoiding course and left them all astern."*

Brazen submarine! But boldness justified by the confirmed sinking in one day of three enemy ships, and the probable sinking of another.

For the next two days, GUARDFISH was plagued by patrol vessels that hunted her in swarms. She made 19 patrol-vessel contacts in this time, and avoided all. Then, on September 9, with two torpedoes forward and one aft, she sighted a northbound freighter in the mid-morning seascape. At 1103 she fired her two bow tubes. No explosions. The torpedoes probably ran deep, for the range was only 500 yards, and Klakring felt that they couldn't have missed. The "fish" may not have reached set depth after the initial dive. It proved impossible to maneuver submerged for a stern-tube shot, and when target opened fire with a deck gun, Klakring sent GUARDFISH down to 150 feet. As she climbed to periscope depth some time later, a heavy explosion was felt—probably a bomb from an unseen aircraft. Klakring called off the approach, and took her down to let the situation cool off. That evening he headed her for Midway. As she left the area she was forced down and held down for nine hours by three more patrol boats. She won the endurance test, and arrived at Midway on September 15.

It was an excited complement of submariners who climbed out into the sunshine. They knew they'd sunk a lot of Jap tonnage and made a lot of attacks and survived their share of "goings over." But the topic for general discussion—the episode for remembrance—concerned the day GUARDFISH, investigating the coast of Japan, drew so near to land that captain and crew were able to watch a horse race.

In jockeying GUARDFISH into twelve attack positions that ended in the sinkings enumerated, Klakring and crew won for their submarine her first Presidential Unit Citation. They would win for her a second! GUARDFISH was one of the two United States submarines so honored during the war.

Submarine Mine Plants

As early as July 1941 plans had been made to lay submarine minefields in the event of war with Japan. When the Pearl Harbor attack crippled the U.S. Pacific Fleet an unanticipated workload gave the Submarine Force little opportunity for minelaying. Not until the autumn of 1942 did the force commanders feel that submarines could be spared for mine plants.

Paradoxically, the torpedo shortage that developed as the war expanded implemented the long-awaited opportunity for minelaying. As there were not enough torpedoes to fully load all submarines going out on patrol, space became available for mines.

The first submarines sent out to mine the enemy's waters were THRESHER, TAMBOR, GAR, TAUTOG, WHALE and GRENADIER. All plants except WHALE's were to be made in the Southwest Pacific. WHALE's destination was the Kii Suido—the eastern entrance to the Inland Sea—deep in the inner ring of the Japanese homeland sea frontier.

THRESHER (Lieutenant Commander W. J. Millican) steamed west to the coast of Asia to lay her mines in the Gulf of Siam. October 16 she was on location. There, in the northernmost waters of the Gulf at the doorstep of Bangkok, this submarine made the first mine plant of the Pacific War.

Three days later, GAR (Lieutenant Commander Donald McGregor) laid mines in waters adjacent to the THRESHER field.

On October 29, GRENADIER (Lieutenant Commander B. L. Carr) sowed the waters in the heart of the Gulf of Tonkin with mines.

TAMBOR (Lieutenant Commander S. H. Ambruster) repeated the performance on November 2, laying her mines in the eastern waters of the Tonkin Gulf.

And on the same day, TAUTOG (Lieutenant Commander Willingham) planted a field in the waters off Cape Padaran, French Indo-China.

These strategic plants covered important Japanese shipping lanes which had previously been patrolled by submarines of the SoWesPac Force. A minefield could scarcely pinch-hit for a wide-ranging submarine, but it did constitute a standing menace that forced the enemy to search, sweep or detour. Armed with the element of surprise, it could exact a sizable shipping toll.

In respect to surprise, the submarine mine plant has a decided edge on the field sewn by surface or aircraft. On the other hand, observation of the minefield's "activities" remains difficult. After planting mines in some remote area deep in enemy waters, a submarine could not loiter at leisure in the neighborhood to watch results. Eye-witness, on-the-spot reports of minefield sinkings are few and far between. In the case of the pioneer plants enumerated, observations were sketchy.

THRESHER reported two prematures. GAR reported four. GRENADIER and TAMBOR reported singles. Three prematures were reported by TAUTOG. WHALE was the only pioneer who did not report a premature. The mines she laid had contact exploders.

Completing the war's first mine plant in Empire waters, WHALE turned in an interesting and informative report. Under Lieutenant Commander John B. Azer, the mine-loaded submarine had headed out for Japan on her maiden patrol.

Pre-war shipping curves had indicated the Kii Suido passage as a main line for Japanese maritime traffic. WHALE's periscope watch confirmed the pre-war indications. Merchantmen and naval vessels were seen hugging the shoreline, running parallel to the coast about one mile off the beach. Evidently the pioneer raids earlier in 1942 had alarmed the local authorities.

Azer determined to alarm them further. Orders called for the mine plant in waters near the Kii Suido entrance but farther offshore. But at the suggestion of Executive Officer Lieutenant Fritz Harlfinger, WHALE's skipper decided to act on the initiative permissible in such circumstances.

"If we move in closer and plant the mines across their track just off the beach in that cove near the lighthouse, we'll scare them into a conniption," Harlfinger pointed out. "They'll never expect a sub to get in that close, and afterwards, they'll have to sweep every foot of the coastline."

Azer liked the idea. Throughout that day of October 25, he held the submarine offshore, making periscope observations. The Japanese shipping path was carefully plotted and alternate routes were noted. Three minefield locations were chosen—one on the main line and two to cover possible detours.

At moonrise WHALE moved in warily. Azer himself was on the lookout for mines, aware of the irony involved in a mine-planting submarine creeping through a minefield to lay mines. One Japanese mine was detected. The Imperial Navy had laid its specimens well offshore, however, and there was little danger of mines close in where the Jap ships were traveling.

Under a full moon the first field of Mark 10-1's was planted. The second was laid closer to the shore, and the third was sewn across the traffic lane that paralleled the beach. With ships in the immediate vicinity, she had to do some expert maneuvering to extricate herself from the area. Thanks to Japanese navigation lights, she was able to grope her way out across the channel.

Just before sunrise the following morning, the lookout sighted a Jap convoy. Azer rushed the crew to battle stations and sent WHALE boring in on the attack. Torpedo fire was answered by a bedlam of explosions, but it was too dark for positive identification of the targets, and no sinkings could be ultimately confirmed.

Two of the ships were damaged, however. In the morning light these were seen limping off, surrounded by swarms of sampans which had scuttled out from shore to rescue survivors. WHALE'S periscope watch was fascinated. The damaged vessels were caught between Scylla and Charybdis—either they veered in and grounded on a rocky shore, or they ran into the Mark 10-1 minefields.

Before WHALE could observe the outcome of the situation, she was driven under by a destroyer that came tearing out of the harbor on the hunt. While the submariners were under, making a reload, two heavy explosions rumbled from the direction of the minefields. Presently there were two more explosions. Busy with evasive maneuvers, Azer and company were unable to determine the upshots of these detonations. But all were convinced the mines had finished off a freighter or two, if not the pugnacious DD. After the war the Japanese admitted the sinking of a cargo ship by a mine in this area.

WHALE remained for several days in these dangerous waters, taking periscope pictures of headlands and beaches, gun emplacements and naval installations, anything of value for the Navy's future reference. In the teeth of Jap flying boats, sampans and harbor patrols, camera shots were made of the shoreline between Ashizuri Zaki and Murato Zaki, WHALE poking up her periscope at some points only 500 yards offshore.

In leaving for home she encountered a CHIDORI patrol boat just outside the 100-fathom curve, and the craft gave her a strenuous "going over." The first spread of depth charges flooded the inductions, opened valves and sent WHALE plunging toward sea-bottom with a 20° up-angle. As the blasts went off around the submarine, her light bulbs were pulverized, glass and paint chips flew into the faces of the men, and the boat pitched like a wild seesaw.

Harlfinger reported afterward, *"We barely held our own with the leaks. All available spare men were sent to the forward part of the boat in a desperate effort to regain an even keel. Charge after charge was dropped. We were pursued by the patrol boat for seventeen hours. The Nips were a little mad, I suppose, because we'd invaded their home territory."*

Finally the submarine shook her hunter and headed seaward. Azer and crew spent a night on the surface, repairing damage. Then they hit for home, photographs secure and minefields planted for the harvest season.

Aided by the experiences of the first six mine plants, a second group of submarine minelayers headed for Japan in December 1942, in compliance with a request from CinCPac. The submarines in this second group were SUNFISH (Lieutenant Commander R. W. Peterson), DRUM (Lieutenant Commander B. F. McMahon) and TRIGGER (Lieutenant Commander R. S. Benson).

SUNFISH planted mines in Empire waters at the entrance to Iseno Imi, completing the operation on December 17. DRUM, on the 17th, laid mines in the Bungo Suido passage between Shikoku and Kyushu. TRIGGER placed a mine pattern off Inubo Saki some 60 miles east of Tokyo on December 20.

TRIGGER's experience was unique in that she was able to witness some of the results of her handiwork. She arrived on station off Inubo Saki on December 16. Her orders were to conduct a reconnaissance mission a few days to determine the traffic route and then to lay two minefields along that route.

TRIGGER performed the preliminary reconnaissance. On the night of the 20th TRIGGER submerged in bright moonlight, and began her nocturnal planting. The first field had been sown, and the second one started when a ship was sighted approaching from the southward, heading almost straight for TRIGGER.

The mine plant was discontinued and TRIGGER hauled clear. As the ship approached it was seen to be a large freighter accompanied by a small escort vessel farther inshore. The ship passed astern in perfect position for a torpedo attack. But Benson allowed it to pass as he had been given to understand that TRIGGER's primary mission was to plant a minefield before risking detection.

About five minutes after the freighter passed astern, the submarine heard a violent explosion. A moment later the freighter, turned 90° from her course, was seen lying in the sea, helpless, with a broken back. She sank rapidly, folding up like a jackknife, with her bow and stern in the air. Score one for the mines.

Three days later, TRIGGER was patrolling outside her mine-field in order to intercept any ships that might be detoured around it. In the middle of the afternoon, smoke was sighted to the northwest. TRIGGER commenced an approach on a southwesterly course which would pass her well to the south-ward of her mines. The smoke broke up into four separate columns, advancing toward Inubo Saki.

At this instant [Benson wrote in his patrol report] the leading ship which had reached the exact bearing of our mine plants, commenced smoking at least five times as great as before and the three other ships scattered to the northward. The smoke of our mine plants lasted only a few minutes while the other three columns of smoke disappeared to the northward. Consider that a freighter of at least 5,000 tons was damaged, if not sunk, by this mine.

Such long-distance observation could not be conclusive. But about two hours later, after nightfall, a searchlight opened up on Inubo Saki and began to sweep the water off the point. The submariners noted another aftermath resulting from their mine plant. Coastwise shipping hugged the shore-line with greater tenacity than before.

While observing these phenomena, Benson and company took the opportunity to attack several convoys. On December 22 they sank TEIFUKU MARU, freighter, 5,198 tons. And before quitting the Empire area they downed the Imperial Navy destroyer OKIKAZE, 1,300 tons. These torpedo sinkings caused TRIGGER's sharpshooters to regret that they had passed up three good targets before making their mine plant. In consideration of this lost opportunity, and the fact that the minefield drove ship traffic inshore where the shallow water made submarining overly hazardous, TRIGGER's experience created some doubt as to whether such a mine plant was worth the effort.

Blockade Statistic

"*Submarines initially did great damage to our shipping, and later, combined with air attack, made our shipping very scarce.*" Admiral (former Ambassador to the United States) Nomura speaking. "*Our supply lines were cut and we could not support these supply lines. . . . Our experts knew that it was necessary to have 3,000,000 tons of shipping just for civilian living in Japan.*"

Sum total: 48 Japanese merchantmen sunk by SubPac submarines on Empire patrol, July-December, 1942. Perhaps as many ships damaged and sent hobbling into harbor for costly repair. Estimated tonnage sunk: 203,000 tons.

Thousands of tons of cargo irretrievably destroyed, and hundreds of Japanese seamen irretrievably "lost at sea."

United States submarine losses in area: None.

In the light of this war effort accomplished by some 16 submarines (approximately 1,000 officers and men) a layman might logically wonder why the U.S. Navy was not ordered lock, stock and barrel to the shores of Japan.

There were arm-chair and even editorial-chair strategists who made such proposals, forgetting that the submarine's singular ability to operate unseen behind enemy lines was a feature not enjoyed by surface and air craft. The undersea blockader could get in where battleships, like angels, might fear to tread.

Finally, the Navy did not yet have the forces available for a mass attack on the enemy's homeland in the Pacific. Yamamoto's battle fleets remained to be dealt with. Japan's air arm was formidable. The citadel's outposts would have to fall before its bastions could be stormed—an offensive that would demand an army. And before this all-out offensive could be launched in the Pacific, there was "unfinished business" elsewhere on the Navy's agenda. The United States was engaged in a global conflict—the Navy was fighting a two-ocean war.

In the autumn of 1942 Nazi U-boats were making a fight of it in the Battle of the Atlantic. Behind the U-boat front lay Hitler's Festung Europa with its monstrous West Wall reared as a battlement against the Allied world. England was only holding on. France was prostrate under the rule of Vichy. Russia, locked in a death-grip with the German invader, was holding on in the bloody welter of Stalingrad, but the outcome was far from decided. Fascist Italy still held a club over the Mediterranean, and Nazi legions stood in North Africa.

As decided by the Allied leaders at the war's beginning, the defeat of Nazi Germany and Fascist Italy was the immediate objective. To this end, American forces were assembled in England in the autumn of 1942, others were concentrated at Hampton Roads, Virginia, and the invasion of North Africa was mounted.

Submarines of the Atlantic Command were slated to light the way in "Operation Torch."

North African Invasion—Operation Torch

Submarine Squadron Fifty was formed on September 3, 1942, at New London, Connecticut, with Captain N. S. Ives in command. It consisted of the tender BEAVER, under Commander M. N. Little, and the following submarines:

BARB	*(Lieutenant Commander J. R. Waterman)*
BLACKFISH	*(Lieutenant Commander J. F. Davidson)*
SHAD	*(Lieutenant Commander E. J. MacGregor, III)*
HERRING	*(Lieutenant Commander R. W. Johnson)*
GUNNEL	*(Lieutenant Commander J. S. McCain, Jr.)*
GURNARD	*(Lieutenant Commander C. H. Andrews)*

In late October the tender departed in convoy for U.S. Base Two, Roseneath, Scotland. With the exception of GURNARD, all submarines in the squadron proceeded for the coast of northwest Africa as part of the "Torch" movement.

The success of the amphibious Anglo-American landings in Morocco depended in a large degree on the weather. Arriving on station four days preceding D-Day, the five submarines participating in "Operation Torch" conducted reconnaissance patrols off the northwest African coast and furnished the Allied fleet with weather information. SHAD patrolled off Mehediya, BARB off Safi, GUNNEL off Fedala, and HERRING off Casablanca, French Morocco. BLACKFISH patrolled the coast of Senegal, off Dakar. In addition, the submarines were to act as beacons to mark the exact location of the landings which were made on November 8th. They also served as a potential intercepting force against possible enemy breakout. A British naval officer and a British radioman were placed on each submarine to assure that communications with the British forces engaged would function without any hitch.

On November 6, heavy seas off the Moroccan coast caused Admiral Hewett, in command of the Western Naval Task Force, to consider an alternate plan for shifting the landings to the Mediterranean. Thanks to information from the submarines, and other meteorological data, the task force aerologist, Lieutenant Commander R. C. Steere, was able to predict that the high seas would moderate and the Moroccan landings would encounter better weather. On November 7 the submarines reported calm sea and a moderate ground swell. The task force advanced as planned.

The position of the submarines standing as twinkling beacons between the Moroccan shoreline and the oncoming Allied invasion fleet was not exactly comfortable. This was the first major amphibious operation of the war and every gun involved was hair-triggered. Morocco was a mystery, French reaction another unpredictable. Token resistance by the Vichy command at Casablanca was expected. But if the resistance were more than token, the French fleet lying in the harbor—battleship JEAN BART, light cruisers GLOIRE and PRIMAGUET, three flotilla leaders, six destroyers and twelve submarines—could put up a savage battle. Particularly dangerous were the twelve French submarines which might sortie and invite American and British gunners to shoot at every periscope in sight. In addition, a U-boat or two might have crept into the area. The situation had volcanic possibilities, and the U.S. submariners, maneuvering between the French coastal batteries and the guns of Task Force Thirty-four, were in something of a spot.

There were some tense individuals aboard BARB as darkness blacked out the evening of November 7th. Hallowe'en had been a week ago, but some of its atmosphere lingered in this gloom off the beaches of Safi. Tomorrow was D-Day and anything might happen tonight.

Waterman's submarine had a special mission to perform. BARB carried a group of four Army scouts under command of Army Lieutenant W. G. Duckworth. Duckworth and scouts were to disembark in a rubber boat, and paddle in to the Safi Breakwater Buoy with a radio and blinker. There they were to coach in the two assault destroyers BERNADOU and COLE, assigned to seize the harbor off Safi early the next morning.

Waterman took BARB shoreward on the surface, and at 2200 the scouts disembarked. Unfortunately the distance to the breakwater, estimated as three and one-half miles, was miscalculated, or the Army scouts miscalculated the current-and-paddle equation. At any rate, the rubber-boaters failed to reach the breakwater until six hours later, just as the firing began. Machine-gunners blazing away from shore peppered the rubber boat as the group dived overside. Luckily the beach was not far, and Duckworth and his scouts survived the incident with nothing much worse than a hair-raising scare and a ducking.

As the naval bombardment opened up and the landings began, the submarines withdrew to relatively secure positions. However, in the Casablanca area where all hell was breaking loose and the approaches were congested with landing craft, transports and maneuvering warships, no water was overly secure for submarining.

Here communications and recognition became a life-and-death matter, and in this respect GUNNEL's submariners had a hair-raising experience. Surfacing off Fedala, McCain's submarine stood by to watch the shooting at Casablanca. Suddenly they were under the guns of a passing cruiser—so obviously under the cruiser's guns that McCain, with no chance to exchange signals, had to bellow his submarine's identity through a megaphone.

"And if those boys shoot," he shouted down the conning tower, "we'll give them a torpedo!"

Happily the megaphone carried the word to the cruiser's bridge and GUNNEL was recognized. A close call! It seemed the British Admiralty had changed the recognition signals during the night, and the beacon submarines were not advised of the switch!

The Squadron Fifty submarines were ordered to patrol areas in the Bay of Biscay. That Franco was working hand-in-glove with Hitler became plainly apparent to the submariners who saw the evidence through their periscopes.

According to Submarine Squadron Commander Captain Ives: *"As many as six hundred contacts, of which two hundred were vessels of over one thousand tons, were made by a single submarine during one patrol. There was obvious violation of neutrality by Spain in permitting German air patrols and A/S vessels to operate in her territorial waters. This use of the Spanish flag was common, as might be expected. Positive identification was difficult for the commanding officers, as both identification data and intelligence of neutral movements were lacking or late."*

Throughout the winter of 1942-1943, SubRon Fifty continued to operate in the Biscay area.

Thus in the Atlantic as well as the Pacific the U.S. Submarine Force was carrying the torch.

End of 1942

The submariners watch the departure of 1942 without regret. It has been a bitter year—a year of smarting disappointments, frustrating shortages, desperate makeshifts—of one-sided battles against long odds—of galling retreats in which the Manila veterans, falling back from the Philippines and Netherlands East Indies to Australia, perhaps suffered most.

But the school of hard knocks issues a *cum laude* diploma —its graduate submariners have learned much, and profited thereby. Confidence has been gained in the fighting and staying qualities of the submarine. New tactics have been developed to exploit those qualities. The enemy's measure has been taken, and the submariners have "learned their own strength."

Three fleet-type submarines—SEALION, SHARK and PERCH —and two S-boats have been lost in the Southwest Pacific. GRUNION and S-27 have been lost in the Aleutians, and S-26 off Panama. In the Philippines, the tender CANOPUS is a memory.

But not a single U.S. submarine has been lost in Central Pacific waters. Meantime, new-construction submarines from the States have been arriving in Pearl Harbor with almost week-in week-out regularity—a total of 37 since the war's December 1941 outbreak. In addition, three new tenders— GRIFFIN, FULTON and SPERRY—have arrived to ease the burden borne by the veterans PELIAS, HOLLAND and OTUS.

As the year ends, ComSubPac has 51 fleet-type submarines and eight S-boats under his operational control. Eight fleet-type submarines are operating out of Fremantle. The Brisbane task force, composed of "loans," remains a variable figure due to the constant shifting of its units and interplay of commands, but it contains the remainder of the 80 U.S. submarines now fighting in the Pacific.

Between January 1 and December 31, 1942, United States submarines alone have sunk a total of 147 Japanese vessels (including such naval auxiliaries as aircraft ferries, ex-gunboats and patrol craft) of over 500 tons.

These figures loom as a shadow over Japan—a shadow in the shape of things to come.

As the Old Year moves out, making way for 1943, United States Submarine Forces in the Pacific are ready for an all-out offensive. The days of testing are over. The days of exploratory reconnaissance and pioneering are ended. The submariners are now in waters they know.

Given the tools—in particular, a reliable torpedo—they will do the job!

PART THREE

All-out Attrition

(1943)

Swift flame—then shipwrecks only
Beach in the ruined light;
Above them reach up lonely
The headlands of the night.
RIDGELY TORRENCE

Chapter 15

Battle Beneath the South Seas

Wrestler vs. Judo Expert

One of the livelier debates which entertained sports editors in the placid pre-war era concerned her relative merits of wrestling and jiujitsu.

In January 1943 a cartoonist might have pictured the Pacific struggle as such a match. Japan, the judo expert, agile, guileful, highly skilled in the twists, dodges and jabs of jiujitsu, locked in mortal combat with Uncle Sam, sinewy athlete in Navy tights.

This illustration would depict something of the character of the fighting and suggest the weight, size and make-up of the opposing forces that battled it out in the opening weeks of 1943 in the Bougainville-Bismarck-New Guinea area.

On January 1, 1943, Japan had an estimated 500,000 gross tons of merchant shipping over and above the minimum requirement necessary to maintain the Empire's war economy. Despite losses sustained in the previous year, the Japanese were still able to handle the logistics problem.

They handled it by moving their cargoes in relatively small convoys—four or five ships to a convoy with from one to four DD or DE escorts. As at the war's beginning, these convoys traveled close inshore wherever possible, and ran from port to port down through the island archipelagoes, whenever practicable making long runs at night.

In the New Guinea-Bismarck-Solomons area convoy units were often dispersed to travel under strong air cover or powerful individual escort. Cargoes were frequently trans-

190

shipped from major bases in barges and small coastal craft which moved beetle-like along the shoreline, usually at night. It was up to the Allies to break up this transportation system. Land-based aircraft, striking from Guadalcanal and Allied bases in eastern New Guinea, handled some of the job. But essentially it was up to the United States Navy.

The war of attrition, featuring the campaign to cut down the enemy's South Sea supply, was prosecuted largely by U.S. submarines. Week in, week out, the submariners fought the Battle of the South Seas against the Jap. At stake were Japan's forward bases—the chief prize, Rabaul, a gateway to the Philippines. Defending Rabaul, the enemy employed every stratagem at his command.

To counter the Jap's jiujitsu, Uncle Sam, Submariner, developed some shrewd stratagems of his own. One of these, a maneuver which came to be known as the "end-around," was the tactical innovation of 1943. The Jap hit back, striking painful blows.

Nautilus Celebrates New Year's

At that midnight moment when 1942 passed into history, submarines were laying for the convoys retiring from Guadalcanal. GRAYBACK was on her way to Munda Bar off New Georgia where she was to play beacon-ship for the task force due to bombard Munda airfield. Other Brisbane-based submarines were engaged in performing special missions. Coast watchers to be transported—spies to be carried to enemy beaches—airmen to be rescued from hostile jungles—refugees to be evacuated. Such missions had become commonplace to the submariners.

Typical was the one performed by NAUTILUS in the opening hours of the year. Ordered to Bougainville to rescue 29 refugees, the submarine captained by Lieutenant Commander Brockman crept into the very heart of the enemy's upper-Solomons territory.

"My first greeting to these people when they came aboard," Brockman related, "was Happy New Year!"

To the fourteen nuns, three married women, three children and nine men who comprised the refugee party, NAUTILUS' arrival came as a deliverance from the jaws of a concentration camp.

The baby of the party, aged three, was one of the youngest individuals ever to cruise the ocean at a depth of 150 feet.

The voyage to Australia was accomplished without mishap.

Loss of Argonaut

Deep within this same area bored ARGONAUT, hunting the enemy in the vicinity of Rabaul. ARGONAUT was making her third war patrol—her second under Lieutenant Commander J. R. Pierce, veteran of the Aleutian campaign.

On August 10, ARGONAUT made contact with a Japanese convoy. The convoy—five vessels escorted by three destroyers—was sighted some time later by a U.S. Army plane which was returning with empty bomb racks to its base. This aerial observer saw one of the destroyers hit by a torpedo—flash!—and immediately the two other DD's raced across the water, releasing depth charges.

As the furious barrage blasted the surface, a submarine's bow broke water and remained thrust above the waves at a steep up-angle. The plane could only watch helplessly as the destroyers circled, pumping shells into their obviously disabled foe. After several smashing hits, the submarine was gone from view.

In the weeks that followed, all efforts to contact ARGONAUT by radio proved fruitless. Japanese records corroborated the evidence, reporting a submarine sunk between Lae and Rabaul on January 10, 1943.

ARGONAUT'S loss was a hard blow to the Submarine Force, and indicative of the desperate fighting to come.

Searaven Develops a New Tactic

In the second week of January 1943, SEARAVEN was patrolling off Palau, keeping a watch on the approaches to Toagel Mlungui Passage—that recently disclosed "secret door" for Japanese shipping in the Pelews.

Both the submarine and her skipper, Commander Hiram Cassedy, were veterans from Manila—old hands at this deep-sea game of hide-and-seek. SEARAVEN, making her sixth war patrol (her fourth under Cassedy), had been through her share—perhaps more than her share—of action. Cassedy had attacked when opportunity presented, fired long shots and short shots, and scored many hits. But the RAVEN had yet to score a confirmed sinking. Such were the shortcomings of the Mark 14 torpedo and the hit-or-miss workings of chance.

Now, on station off Toagel Mlungui—after the successful accomplishment of a mission ended on December 30, when she landed seven agents and a British officer on Ceram Island—SEARAVEN'S luck was to change. The change came on the morning of January 13th.

About 0900, when the submarine was patrolling submerged, a periscope sweep picked up several columns of smoke to the southeast, distance about 10 miles. Cassedy attempted to close, but was unable to get much nearer than 7,000 yards. He decided to trail submerged and ascertain the convoy's base course and speed. The chase was on.

By noon Cassedy had figured out that the convoy was on base course 300° and making a speed of 9 to 10 knots. It was out of the question for SEARAVEN to surface and chase during daylight with the convoy in sight. Cassedy therefore held the submarine submerged until dusk. He now calculated the convoy would be 54 miles ahead, and given good luck he could overtake it by morning.

On the surface, SEARAVEN got underway at three-engine speed with the fourth engine charging batteries. By 0200 the next morning Cassedy reckoned he was again within ten miles of the convoy. He changed course six degrees to the right of the convoy's estimated base course, intending to pass to starboard. Two hours later he figured SEARAVEN was abeam, and came back to the base course of 300°. All this was done on dead reckoning. SEARAVEN was not equipped with search radar, and nothing had been sighted since the previous afternoon.

And at dawn nothing was in sight. However, Cassedy estimated that the convoy was bearing 161°, distance about 15 miles. He brought SEARAVEN to a normal approach course based on that assumption. An hour later the convoy was still nowhere in sight. Cassedy slowed to 12 knots and changed course to run for the 8-knot position circle of the Palau-Surigao route. If contact had not been made by the time SEARAVEN reached that point, Cassedy decided he would make a try at the 10-knot position circle. Then, at 0740 smoke was sighted bearing 160°, distance 15 miles.

SEARAVEN built up speed to 16 knots and ran for position ahead. At 0907, with the convoy 15 miles away, Cassedy took her down to commence a submerged approach. Two hours later SEARAVEN was in attack position with her torpedo tubes trained on a large cargo ship (AK).

Early in 1942 a number of submarine captains had employed this stratagem of running ahead of a target at night to dive on the target's projected route and launch a morning attack. The maneuver invalidated a tenet of peacetime training which held that a submerged approach which failed to close the target's track was an opportunity irretrievably lost. The tenet holds good for high-speed targets—task forces which move through submarine danger zones at top speed and may not be overtaken. But the slow-speed Japanese convoy presented the submarines with a different tactical set-up. To the captains it was soon apparent that when contact was made on a train of slow merchantmen, it was possible to make a surface run to a position ahead—a point on the track where the target might be "ambushed" and the submarine enjoyed positional advantage. The maneuver was in the experimental stage at the time Cassedy put Searaven through its paces.

Attempted at night without radar the tactic was comparable to a fast game of blind-man's buff. It demanded astute guesswork as well as expert mathematical calculating. Cassedy was able to meet both requisites.

At 1132 he opened fire at the freighter—the largest vessel in the convoy. Three shots were fired at the AK, and one at an anti-submarine vessel in line with the target. Timed explosions boomed in Searaven's sound gear as she went deep. There followed the electronic pandemonium caused by the crumpling of steel plates and machinery deep under the sea.

Forty minutes later Searaven returned to periscope depth. Nothing in sight but an anti-submarine vessel which appeared to be picking up survivors. The victim, later identified, was Shiraha Maru, 5,693-ton cargo carrier. In sinking this vessel Cassedy provided the submarine forces with a peerless demonstration of that new tactic, soon to be perfected with the benefit of radar—the "end around."

Sound Attack—The "Single Ping" Range

While the end-around was in the developmental stage, another tactic was becoming popular.

On practically all submerged attacks (and throughout the war the majority of submarine attacks were in this category), Sound was the first to make contact with the target when the submarine was patrolling submerged. The sound men did more than to keep tabs on the target while the periscope was down. Having detected the target's maneuvers, they reported on changes of the escort's disposition. Listening to the throbbing of a ship's screws, the trained operator could count the turns, make an independent check of the vessel's speed, and advise of any changes in speed. Thus the approach officer was able to follow the maneuvers of target and escorts without making an undue number of periscope exposures.

And if sound gear aided and abetted an approach, it was

essential during retirement. Once below periscope depth, sound was the sole means by which the enemy's moves could be ascertained.

Sea water lies in strata of varying density, a phenomenon which has to do with temperature. Currents may be involved, but as a rule surface water is warmer than the water 50 feet down. Varying with the gradient is the water's density.

Evading at deep submergence, then, the submarine seeks the protection of a "density layer." Such a layer, determinable by the temperature gradient, serves to deflect or "bend" a probing sonic wave. If the wave is deflected, it may not find the submarine. Or the "echo" may richochet at a tangent that deceives the enemy sender in regard to the submarine's range and location. The sound men in the submarine concentrate on listening to the enemy's "pings." The commanding officer, following what might be called "sound advice," maneuvers to put the submarine's attackers astern. Gradually the submersible withdraws from the danger area.

Sound can also play a leading role when the submarine does the attacking. By bouncing a supersonic echo off the target, the sound man could obtain the range with the nicest degree of accuracy. This method of range-finding had undergone pre-war experimentation. Opinion had differed concerning its practicability. Some believed it a resort that jeopardized the submarine. Others thought there was little chance of the enemy's locating a submersible which sent out one darting "ping." So the "single ping range" was a moot question at the war's beginning. However, several of the pioneer skippers tried it, among them Lieutenant Commander Warder taking SEAWOLF into action in Davao Gulf.

A few weeks later TAUTOG in the Southwest Pacific neatly demonstrated the technique. Closing in on the attack, she bounced a "ping" off the target to obtain a check on the firing range. After which she bounced two torpedo explosions off the target's hull.

This successful performance, following SEAWOLF'S, established the "single ping" as a handy aid for fire control.

Loss of Admiral English

Returning from patrols late in January, the submariners who had been at sea during the first weeks of the year found changes in each of the Force Commands.

Routine advices had conveyed word of the change at Brisbane where, on December 23, 1942, Captain James Fife, Jr., had relieved Captain Ralph Christie as Commander Task Force Forty-two. But the word from Pearl Harbor came to returning submariners as a shock. On January 19 Admiral English had been killed in a plane crash near San Francisco.

Rear Admiral Charles A. Lockwood succeeded Admiral English as ComSubPac, and left Fremantle for Pearl Harbor that same month. Captain Ralph Christie was promoted to rear admiral and ordered back to Australia to replace Admiral Lockwood at Fremantle.

Lesson in Logistics

The Japanese General Staff had long been worried about the transport problem resulting from the advance to the Solomons. It may be recalled that Yamamoto sponsored the Solomons drive against the advice of conservatives who foresaw the logistic difficulties involved. Yamamoto, of course, would never have to crouch hungry in a foxhole, waiting for a bowl of rice that wouldn't come. Nor would the Japanese admiral stand lookout on the bow of a rusty freighter crawling through a submarine zone. Militarists, like mathematicians, sometimes lack imagination. Yet the starving trooper and the sweating lookout are figures as intrinsic to the logistics equation as the numerals that add up into miles or tonnage. Raiding the shipping routes to Rabaul and Bougainville, American submarines were bent on animating these logistic figures.

There was WHALE, making her second patrol under Lieutenant Commander Azer. Cruising off Kwajalein, she sighted an old freighter outward bound for Truk. Promptly she smashed the AK's bottom out with four torpedoes. Down at sea January 13 went IWASHIRO MARU, 3,550 tons, the crew pulling away in lifeboats to report another hole in the Emperor's merchant marine.

Some time later, WHALE sighted a Jap patrol boat which was making squares around an apparently defined latitude and longitude. After watching this antic for awhile, Azer decided the craft was waiting for another vessel. From the patrol boat's location, he deduced that the other vessel was heading down from Saipan. Actually it was more a hunch than a deduction, but some submariners acquire a seventh sense for such things. Azer was such a submariner. He directed WHALE up the hypothetical track, and on January 17 a large passenger-cargo ship loomed on the horizon and advanced toward WHALE's periscope.

A transport! A big one. Rushing the crew to battle stations, Azer sent the submarine boring in on the approach. As the liner grew on the periscope lens he could see the decks crowded with brown troops, helmeted gunners lounging at the gun-mounts, officers in white on the bridge. He could almost see the course worked out in the chart room. There could be no doubt about it, these reinforcements were on their way to Bougainville.

"This sinking which would save the lives of our own Marines was a pleasure," Azer wrote in his patrol report.

Closing the range, he maneuvered WHALE into attack position. The patrol report vividly describes the action:

Fired three torpedoes. Three hits. One hit aft of his stack, the second blew wreckage up through forward hold; and the third hit aft. Target started turning toward us. Swung hard right and set up for a stern tube shot.

Fired single stern shot at range of 600 yards. Hit aft. This was a good hit, stopping the target cold. The target was sinking by the stern, taking considerable port list and smoke billowed from after part of the ship. Took pictures, firmly convinced this was the graveyard of another Japanese ship. Many of the crew had an opportunity to view the sinking ship through the periscope.

Crew and passengers abandoned ship, although gun crews remained at posts. Target settled about ten feet over-all and then maintained its depth. Closed and fired sixth torpedo from bow tubes. This hit aft of super-structure deck.

Target still floating. Fired seventh torpedo from bow tubes. This hit with terrific concussion, but did not change trim or draft of ship appreciably.

Fired eighth torpedo from stern tubes. This was heard to hit, but very little concussion was felt.

Getting dark. Target sinking slowly on an even keel, but still looks salvageable. Wishing to dispose of it before arrival of planes or rescue ships, fired ninth torpedo. This hit right under stack and the explosion rippled away both sides of vessel about ten feet below the main deck.

Target now settled more rapidly, the main deck being few feet from wash condition at last observation. Target was identified as the HEIYOU MARU, 9,815 tons.

On retiring we found ourselves in the midst of eight boats full of survivors, approximately fifty men to each boat. These men were dressed in both white and blue uniforms. One boat was passed close aboard, and survivors made ready to hit the periscope with their oars.

Wahoo vs. Convoy

Lieutenant Commander Dudley W. Morton had commanded his first submarine, the R-5, in the Atlantic, and was transferred to the Pacific after two fast-action patrols.

Nothing particularly uncommon about this A. & P. routine. But Morton, endeared to his Annapolis classmates as "Mushmouth" (abbreviated "Mush") because of a knack for yarn-spinning, was an uncommonly talented submarine officer. Torpedoings were guaranteed when he assumed command of WAHOO early in 1943 and took her out of Brisbane on her third war patrol with orders to patrol off Palau. WAHOO was en route to the Pelews when she received orders to investigate Wewak Harbor on the northeast coast of New Guinea. Wewak lies between two small islands. One is named Kairiru. The other—odd coincidence—Mushu.

"Mush" was confident he could locate any island named Mushu. But Wewak could be found on no available American chart. This made an approach exceptionally hazardous for a submarine, especially as the harbor was suspected of being strongly fortified. While WAHOO's officers puzzled over the problem of exploring an uncharted port, someone remembered that D. C. Keeter, MotorMac 1, had a grade-school atlas in his sea bag. From this pocket edition Morton contrived a navigational chart by tracing the map on a slide and projecting the same, by means of a camera and signal light, upon a large-scale chart. There might be hidden reefs and shifting bars in the harbor mouth; if so, they could be located by sonar search. Wewak, at any rate, was charted.

Early morning, January 24, WAHOO was off the dark coast of New Guinea. And there, as specified by the atlas, was the "off the map" harbor. Were Japanese ships in port? WAHOO's periscope found the answer in a pair of CHIDORI torpedo boats and a couple of snub-nosed harbor tugs.

"This was encouraging," Morton noted, "because patrol boats were likely to mean shipping." But Wewak's bay proved disappointing. Morton determined to go five miles farther down harbor—there might be something to shoot at near Mushu Island. There was. It looked like a DD. Although the submarine was deep within the harbor when the periscope found this warship, Morton kept WAHOO going. Her excursion down the harbor covered about seven miles, a long run for a submarine in enemy water guarded by sharp-eared patrol vessels and men-of-war. Slowly the submarine bore down on the quarry. Cautiously Morton raised the periscope for another look. This time he was able to identify the target as a FUBUKI-class destroyer. A curl of white froth at the warship's bow told Morton she was under way.

Obviously the DD was on the hunt, and Morton could only believe she was hunting a submerged submarine named WAHOO. Hastily lowering the periscope, he swung WAHOO into attack position and fired four torpedoes at a range of 3,000 yards. The four torpedoes missed! But the DD's look-outs did not miss the four torpedo wakes. The destroyer, having veered to avoid, now rushed straight for the submarine, a bone as big as a gorilla's shin in her teeth. With but two torpedoes remaining in the bow tubes, Morton had to do some lightning calculating.

Reporting this climax, he observed: "In order not to lose the initiative we continued to be aggressive. So we decided to shoot the remaining torpedoes down the enemy's throat as he came in to depth charge us."

WAHOO retained the initiative. Morton opened fire at a range of 1,200 yards. This torpedo missed. The range had dwindled to 800 yards when he fired the remaining torpedo. WAHOO dug under as the blast of a hit rolled its thunder down the channel. On the way out of Wewak, Morton raised the periscope for a parting look. The destroyer no longer had a bone in her teeth. Her bow was completely blown off and she had come to a stunned halt. Sailors clung to her turret tops and swarmed monkey-fashion up her rigging.

Japanese naval records do not list a DD sunk on that date in Wewak Harbor—evidently the enemy was able to beach and salvage the torpedoed vessel. Maimed as she was, she must have remained out of action for a long period.

Two days after the Wewak raid, WAHOO was about 450 miles off the New Guinea coast. The day, January 26, brought a morning benign with sunshine and a sea as calm as peace. At 0800 the lookout reported smoke on the horizon. Morton began tracking. He held the submarine on the surface, and drove ahead of the smoke to dive for a periscope attack. The smoke branched into two plumes—a two-ship convoy. A freighter and a transport, the two vessels were steaming in column. Morton rigged the set-up for a double salvo from the stern tubes. When WAHOO gained attack position, he fired two torpedoes at the leading ship and two at the ship astern. Two explosions stopped the first ship dead. The fourth torpedo struck the second ship in the quarter.

Swinging WAHOO to bring her bow tubes to bear, Morton raised the scope to check on the targets. The second ship wheeled and headed for the submarine to ram. At this juncture a third ship was sighted. Morton had to do some fast sharpshooting with the rammer heading for WAHOO. He fired three torpedoes at the newcomer, stopped her with a hit, then turned and fired two down-the-throat shots at WA-HOO's nearing assailant. Explosions rumbled in a spreading wave of sound as WAHOO went deep.

Eight minutes later Morton ordered her back to periscope

depth. A swift look showed the first ship had gone under. The second was crawling away. The third ship was at a standstill in the water like a model stuck in a sea of papier-mâché. "This ship was quickly dispatched and hundreds of Japs, evidently soldiers, were jumping over the sides like ants off a hot plate," Morton described the sinking. WAHOO stood by long enough to certify the transport as a goner. Then Morton ordered the submarine to the surface and set off in pursuit of the wounded freighter.

WAHOO was overtaking the fugitive when a fourth ship appeared on the horizon. A tanker. This was almost an embarrassment of riches. But before an attack could be made on either of these vessels a battery charge was necessary.

The tanker was then selected as the immediate target. The approach consumed most of the remaining day as Morton maneuvered to get ahead of the two vessels which were drawing together. At sundown WAHOO was in attack position, and he fired three shots at the tanker. The torpedoes hit, but the tanker kept on going.

Taking WAHOO to the surface, Morton closed the range. The tanker zigzagged frantically. A study of the zigzag plan ended in its frustration. An hour and a half after the first salvo, WAHOO had another bead on the target and Morton fired another torpedo. The shot struck home and the tanker folded at the middle like a closing jackknife.

This left WAHOO with but two torpedoes, and the crippled freighter seemed aware of the fact. Like a cornered badger, the AK turned to fight. Jets of flame spurted from her deck guns, and shells began to smash the water around the submarine. One shell ricochetted over the conning tower. Morton ordered WAHOO under, brought her back to the surface when the freighter ceased fire, and headed her toward the enemy.

As the submarine closed the range, a ghostly spoke of light rayed up on the horizon and fanned back and forth across the night sky. The crippled freighter had summoned an escort, and WAHOO would have to finish this target in a hurry. The freighter was already headed for the searchlight.

Morton sent WAHOO racing in to cut her off. Range 3,000 yards, he fired the last two torpedoes. Both hit the mark.

Later that night, Morton dispatched this crackling message:

IN TEN HOUR RUNNING GUN AND TORPEDO BATTLE DESTROYED ENTIRE CONVOY OF TWO FREIGHTERS ONE TRANSPORT ONE TANKER . . . ALL TORPEDOES EXPENDED . . . RETURNING HOME

There was a third act to this WAHOO drama. The morning

after the convoy battle, WAHOO sighted another convoy! Six ships! Without a single torpedo left, and no more than 40 rounds of 4-inch ammunition aboard, Morton headed the submarine toward the train of freighters, hoping to pick off a straggler by gunfire. He was maneuvering into position for a gun attack when a Japanese destroyer steamed over the horizon. The convoy's lookouts had sighted WAHOO, the ships were stampeding, and the DD opened fire at the submarine without ado. As shells ripped up the sea directly ahead, Morton gave the order to go deep and rig for depth-charging.

The DD came over and dumped her bombs. For an hour she continued the search while the submariners lay low, holding their breath. Finally the enemy departed, and Morton dispatched his famous curtain-line:

ANOTHER RUNNING GUN FIGHT . . . DESTROYER GUNNING . . . WAHOO RUNNING

So WAHOO ran home to Hawaii with a broom at her masthead. Discussing this 22-day patrol which took his submarine from Brisbane to Pearl Harbor, Morton said the nerves in his necknape spent a week untangling themselves. A fortnight later WAHOO was off again, on a warpath that was to go like that of a tornado through the Japanese merchant fleet. Few skippers equalled Morton's initiative, and none had a larger reserve of nerve.

Commander Howard W. Gilmore

GROWLER'S fourth patrol was nearing its conclusion. She had departed Brisbane on New Year's Day to harry the enemy's traffic lanes between Rabaul and the Western Solomons. No sooner had she reached this area than her periscope was up to its neck in torpedo attacks.

GROWLER downed a transport on January 16 and another on the 19th. Then she headed westward toward New Hanover to waylay traffic from Truk and Palau.

On January 30 she attacked and damaged a freighter. During this action she was driven deep by a tempest of gunfire and depth charges. The following day she struck at a heavily armed gunboat, only to have her life endangered by a defective torpedo.

The area seethed with enemy shipping and pugnacious patrol craft. At this date the Japanese were making a last desperate effort to evacuate the remnants of their Guadalcanal garrison. To the storm center the Imperial Navy was rushing

every gun, bomb and depth charge it could muster. As
GROWLER continued to contact enemy vessels on every hand,
it was apparent to her captain, Commander Howard W. Gilmore, that the anti-submarine measures were boiling the
water off the Bismarcks. The skipper who had invaded an
Aleutian harbor to sink a Japanese destroyer was undismayed
at this display of enemy force. Patrols meant convoys. Convoys were GROWLER'S business.

On the night of February 4, south of Steffen Strait, Gilmore put GROWLER on the trail of a convoy which was heading for Gazelle Channel, probably en route to Rabaul. Two
merchantmen under escort of two patrol craft. Estimating
their speed and course, Gilmore sent his submarine on a fast
run southward—a run calculated to give GROWLER an ahead
position on the convoy's projected track. True to Gilmore's
estimates; the convoy came steaming down the track about
0300 the next morning. Gilmore had accomplished a perfect end-around.

Two ships were sighted. Poor visibility necessitated a surface attack, and Gilmore directed a wary approach. Radar
went into action to guide the submarine and coach fire control. GROWLER was closing the target, and the torpedoes
were ready to go when the lead ship suddenly opened fire
at 5,000 yards.

Gilmore ordered a quick dive, and the submarine went
under. Almost as soon as she coasted beneath the waves,
Sound reported high-speed screws closing in on either bow.
The submarine was rigged for depth-charging, and the submariners braced themselves for a blasting. They got it for
about an hour.

Sometime between 0402 and 0413 a concussion ruptured a
manhole gasket in the forward main ballast tank. Water
sprawled into the forward torpedo-room at the rate of 1,000
gallons an hour. Emergency repairs stemmed this flood, but
the damage control party would be a Dutch boy with finger
in a crumbling dyke until the submarine could surface for
an adequate repair job.

At 0539 the patrol boats seemed to have withdrawn, and
Gilmore sent GROWLER to periscope depth. A sweep of the
scope disclosed the presence of a vessel about five miles distant. The convoy's smoke was visible against the sky beyond.
The torpedo-room bilges were being held at a reasonable
level by the drain pump, and the damage control party had
managed to cover the leaking manhole with sheet rubber and
deck plates held in place by shores and jacks. The violent
hemorrhaging had stopped, but the leakage remained dangerous.

With a patrol boat lurking in the vicinity, Gilmore held the submarine under and headed her westward to evade. At nightfall he brought her to the surface. The ruptured manhole was opened and a new gasket installed. Midnight found GROWLER once more roaming on the hunt.

At 0110 on the morning of February 7 a ship was sighted on the starboard bow, on an opposite course, range 2,000 yards. Gilmore turned the submarine away, ordered all tubes readied, and then swung about to close for an attack. As GROWLER reduced the range to 2,000 yards on a 130° starboard track, she was sighted. The enemy, a 2,500-ton gunboat, reversed course and rushed. Radar immediately detected the gunboat's course-change, but poor visibility screened the enemy's attack maneuver and it was not at once discerned by the bridge personnel.

On GROWLER'S bridge were Commander Gilmore, the officer of the deck, the assistant O.O.D., the quartermaster and three lookouts. At 0134 radar indicated that the range was too short to allow the torpedoes to arm. From the bridge came the order, "Left full rudder!" A moment later the collision alarm sounded. Then GROWLER crashed into the Jap gunboat head on at 17 knots. The impact was stunning. Every man in the submarine was thrown off his feet. GROWLER heeled over, and as she righted like a rolled log, the gunboat opened fire at point-blank range.

A whip of .50-caliber machine-gun bullets lashed across the submarine's bridge. Ensign W. W. William, assistant officer of the deck, was killed. W. F. Kelley, Fireman 3, standing lookout, died at his post. Commander Gilmore, badly wounded, clung to the bridge frame.

Gunfire blazed in the night; dark spray showered the bridge; steel whined and moaned, skimming the conning tower. Above the slam-bang of the guns and the deeper roaring of the sea, the commander's shout could be heard.

"Clear the bridge!"

Officer of the deck and quartermaster descended, followed by two bleeding lookouts who were pulled through the hatch.

Then came the order, *"Take her down!"*

At the aperture the men hesitated. Seconds ticked by—the commander did not appear. A hurricane of machine-gun fire was sweeping GROWLER'S super-structure. They closed the hatch and took her down.

A bullet punctured the conning tower as the submarine went under, and a stream of water shot into the hatch, forced through the bullet-hole at fire-hose pressure. All gyro, inter-communication, lighting and heater circuits were put out of commission by the spurting flood.

Lieutenant Commander A. F. Schade, who had been Gilmore's second, now assumed command. The collison with the gunboat had thrown him from the conning-tower hatch to the deck of the control room. Painfully bruised, dazed, he forced himself to meet the emergency. With water in the control room and the pump room half flooded, GROWLER was levelled off, and Schade held her submerged while temporary repairs were contrived. Some 30 minutes after the smashing dive, Schade gave the order to "battle surface." It was a crippled submarine that went up to fight it out with the enemy. Eighteen feet of her bow was bent at right angles to port. The outer doors of two torpedo tubes could not be closed. About 35 feet of the bow, including the bow buoyancy tank, had been crumpled like so much cardboard.

Fortunately the enemy was nowhere in sight. In the night the rammed gunboat had gone—presumably to the bottom. Gone, too, were those who had been on GROWLER's bridge— the dead, and Commander Gilmore.

Schade put the battered submarine on a home course at dawn. Endorsing GROWLER's fourth patrol report, Commodore Fife commended: *"The performance of the officers and crew in effecting repairs and bringing the ship safely back to base is one of the outstanding submarine feats of the war to date...."*

Admiral Halsey wrote: *"The force commander is proud to extend his congratulations and commendation to this valiant ship and her courageous crew."*

To Commander Howard W. Gilmore went the first Congressional Medal of Honor to be awarded a submariner. *"For distinguished gallantry and valor, above and beyond the call of duty,"* the posthumous citation read. *". . . Commander Gilmore, refusing safety for himself, remained on deck while his men preceded him below. . . ."*

Gilmore and GROWLER. Mention either, and submariners think of gunfire and chaos in a roaring sea—a submarine's life threatened—and a voice speaking out of the night.

"Take her down!"

Chapter 16

Japanese Anti-submarine War

☆   ☆   ☆

Japanese Counter-attack

Guadalcanal was declared secured on February 7, 1943, and Japan had suffered her second catastrophic defeat since the war's beginning.

The little man in the breech-clout did not take the setback sitting down. Wheeling to defend his Upper Solomons front, he struck back hard. His blows fell hardest on that inexorable antagonist pursuing him from corner to corner of the South Seas arena—the United States Submarine Force.

At the beginning of 1943 the U.S. Submarine Force knew just about what it could expect in the way of Japanese anti-submarine (A/S) measures. The Japanese Grand Escort Fleet, organized convoying, and aircraft equipped with radar and *jikitanchiki* (magnetic airborne submarine detector) were still in the future. However, the basic ingredients of the Japanese anti-submarine effort were in the pot. And there was no indication that the cooks would or could contrive a more lethal broth for Allied consumption.

Japanese ineptitude in this field of undersea warfare was, of course, recognized by the submarine Navy and exploited. The war was not many weeks old before the Americans realized "those guys up there" were setting their depth charges too shallow, breaking off their A/S attacks too soon and indulging in heady optimism concerning the results. Japanese airmen were not the only wishful thinkers. Imperial Navy men aboard destroyers, gunboats, sub-chasers and escort vessels frequently secured and sailed away in a glow of triumph entirely unjustified by the facts. A cheerful battle report always made good reading at Headquarters and enabled Tokyo Rose to broadcast an auspicious list of U.S. submarine obituaries. Many an embattled submarine owed its deliverance to Japanese presumption. And more than one submarine skipper could have quoted Mark Twain's, "The reports of my death are greatly exaggerated."

Although the Japanese anti-submarine effort was haphazard and at times almost lackadaisical, it managed to exact a punishing toll. Inferior though they were in many respects, the component A/S forces constituted a menace that meant trouble whenever encountered. The heavily armed destroyer, the ugly CHIDORI "pinger," the lethal mine and zooming plane could be as deadly as lightning which strikes at random but kills when it hits.

In February, March and April 1943, Japanese A/S forces struck with tempestuous violence and ferocity.

Loss of Amberjack

AMBERJACK—the submarine that had substituted for an oil tanker—went back into the Solomons from Brisbane on her third war patrol. She could have used a longer stay in port, but the Japanese were not taking a holiday, and neither were the submarines of Task Force Forty-two. So the crew had hardly got around to "Waltzing Matilda" before the skipper had his orders and AMBERJACK was off again.

She started out on January 24th; had to put back into Brisbane for repairs. She was at sea again on the 26th, and five days later she was patrolling the western approaches to Buka Passage.

On February 13 AMBERJACK was notified that her patrol was to include the entire Rabaul-Buka-Shortland Sea area. The next night she reported that she had plucked a half-drowned Japanese aviator from the sea during the afternoon and had been attacked and forced down by two destroyers that evening. This was the last message received from AMBERJACK.

Eventually it was learned that the Japanese torpedo boat HAYODORI, in company with Sub-chaser No. 18, attacked a U.S. submarine on February 16 in the area assigned to AMBERJACK. The submarine had previously been bombed by a Japanese patrol plane. Oil and wreckage swirled to the surface, and the Jap A/S vessels reported a sinking.

Loss of Grampus

Under the captaincy of Lieutenant Commander J. R. Craig, GRAMPUS, on February 14, was directed to patrol in the Buka-

Shortland-Rabaul area. On March 2 she was told to proceed toward Vella Lavella and enter Vella Gulf on the afternoon of March 5th. Her mission was to sink enemy shipping which might try to run westward through Blackett Strait. GRAY-BACK was to team up with GRAMPUS in this operation, and each was informed of the other's assignment.

Both submarines were warned on the evening of March 5 that two enemy destroyers had been spotted heading from Faisi, off southeastern Bougainville, toward Wilson Strait, the passage between Vella Lavella and Canongga. GRAYBACK was apparently unable to contact this pair of destroyers. But on the night the warning was radioed, she sighted a silhouette in that part of Vella Gulf assigned to GRAMPUS. Assuming it was her sister submarine, GRAYBACK gave the silhouette a wide berth. She was unable to exchange recognition signals. Whether the vessel she sighted that night was Craig's submarine remains a mystery.

On March 7, Brisbane Headquarters ordered GRAMPUS to report her position. No answer. Again on the 8th Brisbane requested word from GRAMPUS. The submarine made no reply. She was officially reported lost on March 22nd.

It seems possible, that GRAMPUS was caught and sunk by the two destroyers which passed through Blackett Strait on the night of March 5th. An ominous oil slick was sighted in Blackett Strait the following day. Submariners believe that GRAMPUS went down fighting in a night-surface action with these men-of-war en route to their own destruction in Kula Gulf.

Loss of Triton

Captained by Lieutenant Commander G. K. MacKenzie, Jr., TRITON left Brisbane on February 16 to hunt enemy traffic running between Rabaul and the Shortland Basin. On March 6 she reported a battle royal with a Japanese convoy of five ships escorted by a destroyer.

The last message received from TRITON reached Brisbane on March 11th. *"Two groups of smokes, 5 or more ships each, plus escorts. . . . Am chasing."*

The submarine was told to clear her area on March 25 and return to Brisbane. When TRITON made no reply to this order, and did not reach Australia on the date expected, the Brisbane Task Force realized it had lost another hard-fighting submarine.

Information made available after the war's end leaves little doubt as to the time and place of TRITON's last battle. Just north of the Admiralty Islands she went down fighting on March 15, in combat with three destroyers. Their battle reports described a depth-charge barrage as strewing the ocean's surface with "a great quantity of oil, pieces of wood, cork and manufactured goods bearing the legend, 'Made in U.S.A.' "

"Made in U.S.A." Epitaph for a valiant submarine.

Loss of Grenadier

In April 1943, GRENADIER, under Lieutenant Commander J. A. Fitzgerald, was patrolling in Malacca Strait. Early in the morning of the 21st, a few miles off Penang, GRENADIER's lookouts reported, "Plane on the port quarter." Fitzgerald gave the order to dive.

A few seconds after GRENADIER submerged, the executive officer remarked, "We ought to be safe enough now. We're between 120 and 130 feet." His statement was punctuated by the blast of a bomb which exploded near the bulkhead between the maneuvering room and after torpedo room. In the conning tower the lights blacked out and power was lost. GRENADIER heeled over about 15°, and coasted helplessly—down—down—coming to rest on the sea floor under some 270 feet of water.

Communication with the after compartments went out of kilter. Then the alarming word came through, "Fire in the maneuvering room!" Smoke surged from the compartment, men groped about blindly, coughing, and as the fire got out of hand, Fitzgerald ordered the compartment sealed.

Some 30 minutes later the compartment was opened and entered by a damage control party using "lungs" and respirators. Flames were eating into the hull-insulation cork, cables, stores and cleaning rags. The main motor cables had been gashed when the submarine heeled over, and arcing and sparks from the resulting short circuit had started the blaze.

Two fire fighters were overcome by the suffocating smoke. Crew members went about their duties, tight-lipped, or sat staring dazedly at the overhead. Fitzgerald spoke quietly over the inter-com, "Steady men. Everything is under control."

But when the fire was finally smothered, the maneuvering room was a wreck. The induction valve had been knocked off its seat, and a two-inch stream of water was pouring in. The hard patch above the main motor-controller had ruptured, admitting a spray that soaked the maze of electrical apparatus. Short circuits and grounds started a pyrotechnic sputter, and no sooner was one blaze extinguished than another cropped out.

Meantime, a bucket brigade hustled between the maneuvering room and the forward torpedo room, trying to keep the water level below the main motors. In the fouling air, men slumped from heat prostration and physical exhaustion. Eventually a jury rig was installed between the main battery and a drain pump, so that the pump could be put on the motor room bilge. The bucket line was secured, and the submariners turned to other emergency repair tasks.

GRENADIER had suffered serious internal injuries. In the forward end of the after torpedo room the hull on the starboard side had been dished in from four to six inches. The after tubes had been forced to port; bending the main shafts. All the hull frames in the maneuvering room and the after torpedo room were bent inward. The door between the maneuvering room and the after torpedo room was sprung and would not close properly. The strongback in the after torpedo room loading hatch was bent. Water sprayed in through the damaged hatch. Later the crew discovered that about two-fifths of the gasket in this hatch was chopped up. The hatch had been wrenched into an elliptical shape, and a man could put his hand between the knife-edge and the hatch cover.

All hydraulic lines to the tubes, vents and steering mechanisms in the after torpedo room were broken. Many of the gages in the after room were knocked acockbill. In the maneuvering room the control gage was twisted askew. Deck plates and supporting frames were warped. The engine room had also suffered damage, and hydraulic lines to the main vents were discovered broken.

The radio transmitter in the conning tower had been jarred from its foundation and the insulators in the antenna trunk were fractured. The SJ radar appeared to be unharmed, but it could not be tested. Minor damage extended all the way to the forward battery room where dishes and phonograph records had been shattered.

GRENADIER's company worked throughout the day, laboring to regain propulsion. Electricians did everything they could to shield vulnerable equipment from the salt bath showering from the maneuvering room overhead, but intermittent electrical fires and persistent leaks frustrated their best efforts. The motors were at last revived. At 2130 the submarine struggled to the surface. Somehow Lieutenant H. B. Sherry, the diving officer, managed to keep her on an even keel.

Fitzgerald had hoped that on the surface they could stem the leakage and restore the electrical equipment. The submarine was cleared of smoke, and the engineers and electricians got to work on the damaged power plant. By means of jury rigs they finally managed to turn over one shaft at slow speed. But the shaft was badly bent and it was impossible to get the contact levers into the second stage of resistance. Approximately 2,750 amperes were required to turn the shaft, whereas the normal was 450. After a heart-breaking attempt, the engineering officer, Lieutenant Alfred J. Toulon, and the electricians reported to Fitzgerald on the bridge that their efforts were stymied. Everything possible had been done to establish propulsion, and it was literally no go.

With her deck gun out of commission, GRENADIER could neither fight nor run away—a desperate situation. Morning was coming, and it would certainly bring with it a horde of Japanese sub-hunters. In this extremity Fitzgerald was not for sitting on his hands. He soon had the crew working on a sail which might take GRENADIER in closer to the beach where the crew could be disembarked and the submarine blown up. But the sail proved useless in the breathless doldrum of a tropic sunrise. As daylight burned through the eastern mists Fitzgerald decided it was high time to scuttle the helpless submarine and strike out for shore.

All confidential papers were destroyed. Radio, radar, T.D.C. and sound gear were demolished. While these acts of abandonment were in progress a merchant ship and an escort vessel hove in sight. A few minutes later a Japanese plane came droning over the horizon.

The plane made a beeline for the stricken submarine. But GRENADIER was not entirely paralyzed. Withholding fire until the position angle was about 65°, Fitzgerald ordered the gunners to open up with two 20-mm. and two .30-cal. machine guns. The attacking plane was hit. It pulled up sharply and the pilot changed course to the left to try a run up GRENADIER's port side. Again the embattled submariners blazed away as the plane roared in. The pilot dropped a bomb that exploded in the water about 200 yards from GRENADIER. The miss cost the airman his life—he died that night as a result of bullet wounds and a crash landing when he returned to base.

The enemy surface vessels were not to be thus driven off. Closing in relentlessly, the Japanese saw GRENADIER's crew lined up with life jackets on her forecastle. Fitzgerald moved among the men, stalwart and reassuring. "Take it easy, boys. We'll come through." Those who were sick or unable to swim were assigned to rubber lifeboats. The chief of the boat,

W. C. Withrow, was below, manning the vents. Fitzgerald gave the order to abandon. The crew went overside. The chief opened the vents. GRENADIER began to sink by the stern. Fitzgerald waited for Withrow to come up from below, then he and the chief went over.

The Japs circled GRENADIER taking pictures. Lieutenant Kevin D. Harty clung to a mattress and read aloud to the crew from a popular magazine. All hands, and presumably the periodical, were picked up by the enemy.

GRENADIER's submariners were more fortunate than some. Despite long imprisonment and barbarous treatment at the hands of frustrated inquisitors, all but four survived and were recovered from Japanese prison camps at the end of the war.

Battle without Quarter (Gudgeon Gets a Liner)

GRENADIER's story serves to illustrate the point that the random bullet which hits can be as fatal as the sharpshooter's. And the Japanese A/S effort, although inconsistent and disorganized, constituted a standing menace which never permitted any relaxation of vigilance. From the war's first day until its last the submarine on war patrol could not let down its guard.

The submariners tightened their belts and set out with renewed determination to paint the conning towers with Japanese flags. To hell with the A/S war! Throughout the worst of it in the Southwest Pacific, they continued to excursion through the enemy's lines on special missions that were Odysseys of daring and adventure.

On February 20 ALBACORE (Lieutenant Commander R. C. Lake) hit a bull's-eye in the Admiralties and downed the Imperial Navy's destroyer OSHIO. On April 9 TAUTOG (Lieutenant Commander Sieglaff) overtook the destroyer ISONAMI off Boston Island, Celebes, and three torpedoes sent this Japanese warship sloughing to the bottom. The 5,214-ton freighter PENANG MARU followed as a chaser.

Elsewhere in the Southwest Pacific the attrition war against the Japanese merchant marine went on full blast. One of the loudest blasters in the Southwest Pacific that spring was GUDGEON. Skippered by Lieutenant Commander W. S. Post, Jr., the submarine from Fremantle staged a ravaging raid on the Greater East Asia Co-Prosperity Sphere. GUDGEON's seventh war patrol—her first under command of "Bill" Post —was a short one of three weeks' duration. In this brief excursion, which took her into the Java Sea and Makassar Strait, she sank a freighter and an oil tanker, damaged two luckier merchantmen and engaged in a running gun battle with a sub-chaser.

The sub-chaser fight occurred off Great Masalembo Island. When sighted by GUDGEON's bridge lookout, the enemy patrol vessel was strolling along at some 15 knots. Post put four engines on the line, aiming to close on the enemy's starboard quarter, sweep her deck with 20-mm. fire and then sink the vessel with a shelling from the three-inch gun. Which was all very well until the range shortened to 1,900 yards, the sub-chaser made a sharp veer to the right and the submariners got a good look at their target.

"That Jap patrol boat seemed to open up like an accordion," one of GUDGEON's officers recalled. GUDGEON was chasing a powerful CHIDORI "pinger."

"The CHIDORI seemed undecided what to do," Post related. "So we took the bull by the horns and turned to starboard to keep our battery bearing on his broadside. I hope we scared him as much as he scared us."

Sub and sub-chaser then did a simultaneous ships right, and now the sub-chaser was chasing the sub. As the range closed to a dangerous 1,800 yards, Post fired four torpedoes at GUDGEON's pursuer. Because of the high-speed turn, the helmsman was unable to steady on the firing course, and the torpedoes missed. The salvo forced the CHIDORI to swerve, however, and this gave GUDGEON a moment's initiative. As the enemy hauled over to the submarine's port quarter, the GUDGEON gunners brought their battery to bear. Four times the three-incher flamed and slammed. The CHIDORI retorted with lashing machine-gun fire. But the Japanese were slowed by the shelling. "And just by luck," Post reported, "our fourth shot silenced the Jap's 37-mm. twin mount."

On her next war patrol—a run from Fremantle to Pearl Harbor—GUDGEON blew the largest hole yet blown in the Japanese transport service.

GUDGEON's homeward journey was by way of the Philippine area where she combed the Sulu Sea between Negros and Palawan. On the eve of April 28 she was driving through dark water tumbled by gusty winds and whisked by intermittent rain squalls. Post had just about decided to write off an uneventful day when—the time: 2345—things began to happen. Lightning splintered in the sky, and there was a ship silhouetted across the water. An ocean liner!

Post and company shocked into action. Headed south, the liner was traveling at racing speed. A radar sweep showed she was unescorted, and it was a good guess she was carrying troops and depending on big engines to get her clear of submarine attack. GUDGEON, already abeam, would have to rely on four Diesels to overhaul this fast transport.

The pursuit lasted a little over an hour. As GUDGEON closed in directly astern, Post saw the only chance was an up-the-kilt shot, and at 0100 the thumb of the firing officer itched at the key. Four minutes later, Post opened fire— four torpedoes aimed directly at the fleeing liner's rudder. If those fish missed, counter-mined, or prematured—! The ticking seconds seemed to march on to infinity, and then three explosions jolted the night. A distant flash across the sky showed the big liner dragging her stern.

Believing the ship merely damaged, Post sent the submarine to periscope depth and drove forward to deliver the *coup de grâce*. Then, watching through the periscope, he glimpsed the ship's black bow up-angled against the sky— the silhouette slid from view—another burst of eerie light revealed a heaving carpet of water. The radar watch saw it too. A dwindling pip on the magic screen—then nothing.

"Skipper! That baby's gone!"

This was one of the classic up-the-kilt sinkings of the war —all over exactly 12 minutes after the first torpedo was fired.

The transport, identified as KAMAKURA MARU, was the largest in the Japanese service. She was the former passenger liner CHICHIBU MARU, 17,526 tons.

Later in that patrol, GUDGEON caught a Japanese trawler in the Sulu Sea, sank the craft by gunfire and recovered three Filipinos who had been held captive by the enemy. GUDGEON concluded in the Sulu Sea May 12 by sinking the 5,862-ton freighter, SUMATRA MARU. In something more than two months' time, Post and his sharpshooting GUDGEON crew demolished 38,819 tons of Japanese shipping.

For the reasons discussed in this chapter, the enemy was unable to maintain the anti-submarine offensive launched in the Rabaul area in the first quarter of 1943. And the Japanese anti-submarine war was as unsuccessful as the related attempt to cope with the logistics problem. The deficiencies in the Japanese A/S system are clearly seen in the demise of the unescorted KAMAKURA MARU. When the Imperial Navy rushed anti-submarine forces to the front, American submarines struck at weakened sectors behind the front. Concentration of escorts in one area left the sea lanes of another exposed. GUDGEON's raid far west of the Solomons could have another lesson for impetuous Admiral Yamamoto had he lived long enough to study it.

The Admiral did not live that long. The Allies learned that Yamamoto and members of his staff were flying to Bougainville. Accordingly, the Japanese admiral was struck and killed by American aircraft as his plane came in for a landing.

In any event, he would have arrived too late to turn the South Seas tide. By April the Upper Solomons front had begun to crumble. Already the U.S. Submarine Force was withdrawing some of its units from the South Pacific and aiming their torpedo tubes toward Japan.

Chapter 17

Drive on Dai Nippon

Portrait of a Submarine Admiral

In a well-known Stateside Bureau during the war, an irreverent naval officer parodied the song, "Don't Fence Me In," with the words, "Don't Ship Me Out!" This pasquil may have pricked a conscience or two on the banks of the Potomac. But at Sub-Lant, SubPac and SoWesPac bases force commanders had to fight to keep their staff members out of the pressure hulls, and on several warm occasions fleet commanders had to fight to keep their submarine force commanders ashore. A recalcitrant force commander in this respect was Admiral Lockwood who (the story is off the cuff) engaged in a number of vigorous arguments with the Powers that Be, insistently requesting permission to lead a war patrol.

One of the first new fleet submarines to leave Pearl Harbor after Admiral Lockwood became ComSubPac was the USS SCAMP. Departing on her maiden patrol for a run in Empire water, SCAMP, captained by Commander W. G. Ebert, carried a distinguished passenger. The passenger was Admiral Lockwood.

It has been remarked that submarines are informal naval vessels—for who can strike an attitude in sweat-shirt and shorts? Abilities count for more than epaulettes when the plug is pulled. In the democracy of danger submariners learn a mutual respect, and performance is more important than punctilio.

Even so, a submarine crew with an admiral at close quarters could become a little tense during a voyage. True, Admiral Lockwood was a submariner. All in SCAMP could see that. Still, he was an admiral, a stranger to most of SCAMP's personnel. And his nickname spoken around Pearl, a shade formidable at first hearing, was "The Boss."

For his part, an admiral in a submarine might be a little sticklish were he newly appointed ComSubPac with Cominch and CinCPac watching him and the weight of one of the war's most important Force Commands on his shoulders. But, sitting on SCAMP's cigarette deck when she was drumming along on the surface, Admiral Lockwood looked as relaxed as a suburbanite spending the evening on a porch.

The cigarette deck is a pleasant place to relax. That is, until the diving alarm goes off, and then the occupant has to make the longest jump of anyone topside to reach the hatch. While enemy aircraft were not expected between Pearl Harbor and Midway, war admits to no certainties, and a submarine nearing Midway had to keep an eye peeled. A dive might be practice, or it might be the real thing.

"One day I was sitting in the wardroom and the diving alarm sounded," Commander Ebert related: *"I eased back to the control room. The boat made the usual dive. Only after we were well down did it suddenly occur to me that there was no admiral around. There was a moment of panic, to say the least. I asked the officer of the deck, and he said he was sure the admiral hadn't been on the bridge when he gave the alarm, although he had been there a few moments before. Well, we finally found the admiral, sitting on a bucket in the after torpedo room, shooting the breeze with one of the torpedomen!"*

The admiral left the submarine at Midway—which was as far as CinCPac would permit him to go—and SCAMP, after topping off, went on to the Empire. She later acquired a name for herself by sinking the converted seaplane tender KAMIKAWA MARU in the Southwest Pacific in May, downing the Japanese submarine I-24 in the Admiralties in July, and accounting for two passenger-cargomen and a large tanker before the end of her first fighting year.

Admiral Lockwood, too, acquired a name. The name of the force commander who guided SubPac to victory through the scalding tempest of the Pacific War's height. But Admiral Lockwood fought something more than a war. He fought rule-book thinking and hidebound conformity. He was the implacable foe of "stuffed-shirtism." He found time to congratulate a sailor for a job well done, to see that good transportation and quarters were provided for shore-coming submarine personnel, to assure men and equipment everything needed for the maintenance of efficiency. Lockwood saw to the preservation of *élan*, the upkeep of good spirit and good heart.

By the summer of 1943 the patrol-wearied crew putting in at Pearl Harbor or Midway could enjoy a boxing match, a bit of "rug cutting" or a clambake, as taste dictated. This program was continued at such advanced bases as Majuro and Guam. No wearisome setting-up exercises. No compulsory games. Admiral Lockwood sponsored informal recreation and entertainment.

The force responded with *ésprit de corps*—and gratitude. To his friends in the pressure hulls, from mess attendants to captains, Admiral Lockwood was "Uncle Charlie."

New-construction Submarines

At Groton, Connecticut, at Portsmouth, New Hampshire, at Manitowoc, Wisconsin, and several other construction yards, fleet submarines on the GATO model were coming off the line. Here American engineers and artisans, electricians, draughtsmen, mechanics and welders were winning the production war.

Shift the submarine production picture to Nippon—an I-boat launched in one of the Emperor's shipyards. Here is a cruiser submarine, and in many respects a good one. Somewhat bigger, perhaps, than the American of the GATO class. With powerful, modern Diesels, heavy armament, excellent sea-keeping qualities.

Toward the building of this boat Japanese engineers, draughtsmen, artisans, welders have contributed great technical skill and fanatical loyalty to Hirohito. But: whereas an American submarine may start its voyaging at the headwaters of the Mississippi, the Japanese must fetch their building materials from foreign lands and by many sea routes longer than the Mississippi. The new-construction I-boat is not indigenous to Japan.

United States submarine and Japanese I-boat furnish a miniature of the entire production war. A miniature, perhaps, of all the wars in modern history in which one opponent had to import in order to produce, while the other, self-sufficient, had but to stop the enemy's imports in order to put him out of the war-business. Those "made in America" submarines were specifically dedicated to stopping Japanese imports.

Tokyo began to feel the pressure early in 1943. Japanese imports were going down, Japanese marine insurance rates were going up, Japanese war production was falling off and some of the local *geisha* girls were beginning to wonder what had become of all those sailors.

Empire Blockaders (Tarpon's Foray)

Some of those sailors and the cargoes they carried went down to torpedoes fired by PORPOISE, TRIGGER, TARPON and HADDOCK operating in Empire waters early in 1943.

TRIGGER (Lieutenant Commander R. S. Benson) tangled with the destroyer OKIKAZE off the coast of Honshu on January 10, and three torpedoes buried the Jap man-of-war in a salty grave. TARPON got two big ones in February. Captained by Lieutenant Commander T. L. Wogan, she overhauled these targets on the Tokyo Road, and her torpedoes went straight to the mark. To the bottom on February 1 went FUSHIMI MARU, passenger-cargoman, 10,935 tons. One week later and not far from her first success, she overhauled an ocean liner. Accurate torpedo fire put an end to this queen of the transport service, and down at sea went TATSUTA MARU, 16,975 tons.

The Japanese did not possess many liners of that size. And by this sinking, which preceded the March demise of KAMAKURA MARU in the Sulu Sea, Wogan and his TARPON crew established a precedent and a record. Only three larger merchantmen would be sunk by American submarines in the Pacific War.

Wahoo on the Warpath

WAHOO's fourth war patrol began on February 23, 1943, when she struck out from Pearl Harbor for the East China Sea and the Yellow Sea. After a week at the Royal Hawaiian, Morton and crew were wound up for action. WAHOO ran on the surface all the way to the Nansei Shoto chain, skirted the north end of this dangerous archipelago and headed up the East China Sea straight for the Yellow.

Morton knew the shallow sea between China and Korea, having cruised it on a tour of duty several years before the war. Submariners called it the "Japanese wading pond." A pond does not give an undersea boat a great deal of depth for diving. But Morton did not intend to spend much of WAHOO's time hugging the bottom. He planned to spend it cutting the sea lanes to Tsingtao and Tientisin, Dairen and Seoul—lanes which linked the conquered China coast, Manchukuo and Korea to Japan.

To match this daring raid an enemy submarine would have had to enter the Gulf of Mexico or the Gulf of Saint Lawrence or some other body of water recessed in the American sea frontier, and run a 1,000-mile round trip through naval defenses. They never approximated WAHOO's ship-smashing invasion.

WAHOO's northbound run in the Yellow Sea proved disappointing. Morton began to wonder if the enemy's merchant marine had migrated to Nowhere. Not a single target worth the price of a torpedo was sighted until 0800, March 13, and on that date the submarine was off Wung Island, a scant 35 miles from the port of Dairen.

Even then, the target sighted was an inferior article—a small, inter-island steamer which the submariners dubbed "Smoky Maru" because of the black smudge surging from her stacks. Morton pronounced it, "worth one torpedo if you sink it, but not worth two under any conditions." WAHOO bored in, and Morton fired a single. The torpedo missed by a couple of feet, SMOKY MARU being stubbier than estimated. Better wait for bigger game and let this smudge-pot go.

So four more inter-island steamers were allowed to pass. Morton headed WAHOO for Kayo To lighthouse, hoping to come upon the main line from Tsingtao to Shimoneski. Here, too, the pickings were picayune, so he moved WAHOO into the coastal waters of the Shantung Promontory. Off this peninsula the submarine found targets!

The shooting began on March 19th. First victim was a NANKA MARU-type freighter which sank in three minutes, downed by a single torpedo. Morton brought WAHOO to the surface to hunt for survivors. No survivors were found.

Two hours later a medium-sized transport hove into view. Morton directed a high-speed chase that culminated in a torpedoing. The disabled ship spied the submarine's periscope and opened fire. A withdrawal seemed sagacious as the vessel was not far offshore and the water was too shallow to risk a scuffle with any patrol summoned to the scene by the transport's radio. Heading away, Morton took WAHOO across the pond to search the southern approach to the Korean port of Chinnampo.

March 21 brought a SEIWA MARU-type freighter into focus. WAHOO was maneuvered into attack position, and Morton fired three torpedoes at a range of about 1,600 yards. The first hit the target amidships, and there was a blast which knocked a wash basin from the bulkhead of the submarine's forward torpedo room. The Japanese ship was literally disemboweled.

So was another freighter WAHOO torpedoed later in the day. This sinking was less than a dozen miles offshore, and the action was hardly over before two junks came waddling out to investigate the matter. Morton ordered a battle-surface to attack these busybodies, and WAHOO chased them to within two miles of the beach. Returning to look for survivors, the submarine located four swimmers. The quartet refused assistance and there was no time to argue. However, two steamer trunks and a life ring were fished from the water. The life preserver identified the sunken vessel as the SS NITTSU MARU.

"There is never much water in this wading pond. . . . We have to be careful with our angle on dives to keep from plowing into the bottom. Aircraft and patrols have been scarce, because we are in virgin territory. However, she ain't virgin now, and we are expecting trouble soon. We hope to get at least four more ships and then expend our gun ammunition on the way home."

The above was logged by Morton as he shifted WAHOO northward toward the Laotighashan Promontory, ducking sampans and trawlers most of the way. March 23, a freighter was sighted. WAHOO stalked craftily, and Morton fired one torpedo. The ship, a coal carrier, settled slowly while a great, circular film of bituminous dust expanded on the water around her, resembling the inky stain exuded by a wounded squid. Evidently the coaler cried an S.O.S., for as the submarine retired there was a thudding of depth charges in the distance and the angry patrols were out. By that time WAHOO was in open water, hitting a fast clip for Round Island, one of the flagstones on the doorstep of Dairen.

The submariners discovered that the Round Island navigation light had been blacked out. Morton surmised the Dairen shipping had been detoured, and he scouted the port's approaches in search of the evasive route. Its deepest water about 50 fathoms and average depth around 20 fathoms, the Yellow Sea was no place for a submarine to be caught unawares. In water that shallow, depth charges would go off like firecrackers in a bird bath. So WAHOO moved on the hunt with the stealth of a Cherokee. On the afternoon of March 24 the trail was found.

Down the trail came a ship with the lanky silhouette of a tanker. This vessel had to be sunk within an hour, for the port of call was only around the corner. Racing time and tide, Morton sent WAHOO wading in. Three torpedoes sped at the target. Two prematured. The third missed. Driving forward to an ahead position, Morton fired three more. Fragments of the vessel's stern went up like tossed confetti. Five minutes later the ship was under.

During a third gun battle, fought some time later with a 100-ton trawler, the submarine's three 20-mm's. jammed. Shot to sponge, the trawler refused to sink. Aboard WAHOO there was a crate of "Molotov cocktails" which Marines on Midway had given the submarine's crew when she stopped off there. Morton now brought the submarine alongside the riddled trawler and the WAHOO men hurled incendiary bombs at the craft. Although still afloat when the submarine departed, the trawler was reduced to a mass of trash spouting flame and smoke. Most of those aboard it had made their last trawl.

Clearing the area and heading south down the Yellow Sea, WAHOO had but two torpedoes left for her tubes. Morton saved them for the Formosa-Kyushu trunk line. Leaving the Yellow Sea, WAHOO took the opportunity to shoot up two fishing sampans.

The last two torpedoes were fired on March 29 at a freighter on the Formosa-Kyushu line. As this vessel sank with her stern blown off, WAHOO concluded a war patrol which topped the record to that date in number of ships sunk.

Loss of Pickerel

Captained by Lieutenant Commander A. H. Alston, Jr., PICKEREL left Pearl Harbor on March 18, 1943, to conduct her seventh war patrol. She topped off with fuel at Midway four days later and headed for her assigned area, the east coast of northern Honshu. From those waters she never returned.

Mine plants guarded the coast of Honshu, and small patrol boats roamed PICKEREL'S area. After smiting a freighter on April 7, she could have fallen victim to one of these foes.

She was expected at Midway on or about May 6th. When she failed to answer repeated radio calls from her home base, her loss was presumed. It was officially announced on May 12th. PICKEREL was the first U.S. submarine lost in the Central Pacific. In a cerement of silence, she went down with all hands. Time, place and cause unknown.

Loss of Runner

Heading for the cold seas of the Kuriles, RUNNER, captained by Lieutenant Commander J. H. Bourland, left Midway on May 28 to begin her third war patrol. She was to follow the archipelago down to the Hokkaido coast, and then spend about a month covering the eastern approaches to Ominato and Hakodate. She was to leave this area on the Fourth of July and return to Midway, where she was expected around the 11th. No word was received from her while she was on patrol, and she did not return to Midway. Efforts to locate her were unavailing, and on July 20 she was reported presumably lost.

Mines watched the Hokkaido coast, and a minefield may have been responsible for her loss. An unreported attack was another possibility. Japanese records did disclose the fact that RUNNER sank two ships on that patrol—the freighter SEINAN MARU, 1,338 tons, off Ominato on June 11, and the 4,936-ton passenger-cargoman SHINRYU MARU, off the Kuriles on the 26th. With all hands, then, she went down somewhere silently, claimed by the sea.

Pressure below Japan (Trigger vs. Hitaka)

The yield in waters north of Tokyo proved disappointing. Loss of RUNNER late in June decided the issue. ComSubPac withdrew most of his submarines from this northern Empire area.

Meantime, the submarine blockade increased the pressure on southern Honshu, Shikoku and Kyushu. Sharp-eyed periscopes kept the approaches to Tokyo Bay under constant surveillance.

Following through in those approaches, TRIGGER (Commander Benson) struck the Imperial Navy a jolting uppercut on June 10 when she torpedoed the aircraft carrier HIYO. This carrier, also called the HITAKA, would undoubtedly have gone down for the count had she been farther from the entrance of Tokyo Bay. As it was, the punch from TRIGGER sent her reeling. Disabled, she could barely hobble into harbor, and the damage dealt her was drastic enough to keep her out of commission for nearly a year.

SubPac Operational Plan (Target Priority)

On June 24, 1943, ComSubPac published the first Operation Plan drawn up by that command. Sponsored by Admiral Lockwood and devised by his operations officer, Commander R. G. Voge, the plan contained no basic changes in previously issued "Standard Patrol Instructions." But the precepts and missions of the Submarine Force were for the first time stated cogently in one document.

Target priority in relative order of importance was: Aircraft Carrier (CV); Battleship (BB); Auxiliary Carrier (ACV); Oil Tanker (AO); any man-of-war larger than a destroyer; Transport (AP); Freighter (AK); Destroyer (DD). Standard Patrol Instructions and the Communications Plan were included as annexes.

Invading the Sea of Japan

By July 1943 there was in the entire Pacific Ocean but one

area open to enemy shipping which had not been investigated by U.S. submarines. This was Japan's private highway to Asia—the Sea of Japan, lying between the Asiatic mainland and Honshu and Hokkaido.

With but four narrow entrances—one in Russian territory and unavailable, another frozen up for a good part of the year, and the other two guarded by minefields—the Japan Sea was well protected against submarine invasion. Secure behind geographic and military barriers, the traffic arteries which laced Korea and Manchuria to the islands of Nippon were feeding ton after ton of raw material to the voracious Japanese War Machine. In May 1943, ComSubPac produced a plan designed to slash these arteries.

The plan called for the penetration of the Japan Sea early in July. Three submarines were selected to do the penetrating. Those chosen for this perilous venture were PLUNGER (Lieutenant Commander R. H. Bass), PERMIT (Commander W. G. "Moon" Chapple), and LAPON (Lieutenant Commander O. G. Kirk).

The submarines were to make their entrance through La Perouse Strait, the passage between the northern extremity of Hokkaido and Sakhalin Island. Little was known of the waters in question, save that they were cold, often fog-shrouded, and in some places dangerously shallow. Shallow water suggested minefields, but as Russian shipping was permitted the use of La Perouse Strait, it was a hopeful guess that its channels were free of mines. The three submarine invaders were instructed to begin shooting at 0000 on July 7, and they were given but 96 hours for hunting. Thereafter they were to keep their fingers crossed and get out through La Perouse before the enemy plugged the exit with mines, bombs and depth charges. To create a diversion on the date of the submarines' exit, NARWHAL (Commander Latta) was dispatched to the Kuriles to make a show of bombarding the airfield on Matsuwa Island.

Salty sweat and exquisite care went into the preparations for this raid. PLUNGER, PERMIT and LAPON would be the first American submarines to enter the Sea of Japan. Somebody nicknamed it "The Emperor's Bathtub." No place for three U.S. subs to be caught short "pulling the plug."

In the last week of June, Skipper "Bennie" Bass took PLUNGER out of Pearl Harbor and headed, under sealed orders, for Midway. There she met PERMIT and LAPON. Captained by the veteran "Moon" Chapple, PERMIT was ready to start her ninth patrol. LAPON was a newcomer making her first war patrol, but her skipper, O. G. Kirk, was another old hand at torpedo warfare. ComSubPac had seen to it that the raider crews could take confidence in the captains leading this exploit.

As the boats ran westward across the summer seas, some of the lads within the pressure hulls must have been comparing their chances with those of the U-boaters who had invaded the Gulf of Mexico and prowled into the mouth of the St. Lawrence. Or perhaps an invasion of Long Island Sound was more like it, with Block Island comparable to those which squeezed the waters of Etorofu Strait. The American submariners knew what had happened to U-boats off Block Island. Of course, the Japan Sea was a lot bigger than Long Island Sound. But the entry and exit runs were many hours longer. If the invaders were detected by alert anti-submarine forces, a get-away would be nip and tuck.

The three raiders reached the Kuriles on schedule, and transited Etorofu on the surface at night, undetected. Heading southward in Japanese water, they pointed their bows for La Perouse. This unknown strait was the real problem. Entry to the Sea of Japan, it was a likely corridor for ship traffic—Russian, as well as Japanese. The American submariners had been instructed to watch out for the ships of their Soviet ally. But in a race across the foggy Gulf of Tartary, vessels might be hard to identify—especially if the enemy were in pursuit. This was another hazard to be dealt with.

The weather was chilly, but the submariners approaching La Perouse Strait did some discreet perspiring. Decision was made to dash through the strait at night and on the surface, four-engine speed and all hands at battle stations. Momsen lungs and lifebelts were given to those who felt uneasy about mines.

Racing southward from La Perouse Strait, the raider submarines headed for individual patrol areas. LAPON sprinted for the southern end of the Japan Sea. PLUNGER prowled into the middle sea area between Dogo Island and the northern end of Honshu. PERMIT covered the western coastline of Hokkaido.

The weather was propitious, the sea as flat as Lake Michigan, but the raiders found the shooting somewhat disappointing. Opening fire on the tick of the 7th, PERMIT sank the small freighter BANSHU MARU No. 33 off Hokkaido. A few hours later Chapple and company downed the 2,212-ton passenger-cargoman SHOWA MARU. Farther south, PLUNGER waylaid and sank NIITAKA MARU, a 2,478-ton passenger-cargoman. But LAPON, hunting off the coast of Korea, flushed no targets worthy of her steel. However, numerous contacts were made in the northern end of the Japan Sea, which fact was marked for future reference.

The invaders retired as swiftly as they had made their entry. Exit through La Perouse was accomplished at top speed. Like invisible fish the three submarines slipped out through Etorofu while NARWHAL's authoritative 6-inch guns created a diversionary uproar at Matsuwa Island. PLUNGER, PERMIT and LAPON drove into the free Pacific with exhilarating news. News that three American submarines could successfully invade the Sea of Japan! News that that body of water was no longer anybody's "private highway" or Imperial Tub.

Loss of Pompano

Under Lieutenant Commander W. M. Thomas, POMPANO left Midway on August 20, 1943, to start her seventh war patrol. She was to cover the east coast of Honshu. After leaving Midway, she was never again heard from.

But the Japanese heard from her—or at least saw evidence of her veteran handiwork. Two good-sized ships went down to torpedo fire in POMPANO's area that September.

As in RUNNER's case, POMPANO's loss was shrouded in the silence and mystery of "cause unknown." POMPANO may have struck a mine. An operational casualty was also possible, or an unrecorded attack. Leaving no trace, the submarine went down with all hands.

Loss of Wahoo

Fresh from a West Coast overhaul, WAHOO headed westward from Pearl Harbor on August 8, 1943, to begin her sixth war patrol. With Commander Morton on the bridge, she was primed for battle, and humming for an area which meant action—the Sea of Japan. Accompanying WAHOO on this foray was PLUNGER, under Lieutenant Commander Bass. Having pioneered the run with PERMIT and LAPON, Bass's submarine was out to show WAHOO the ropes. A *maru*-shooting contest was anticipated.

To the bitter disappointment of all concerned, this second invasion of the Japan Sea accomplished little. The fault lay in the torpedo. Targets were plentiful, and both submarines worked long and hard to deliver attacks that were destined to fail before they began.

WAHOO had the worst possible luck with her torpedoes. Within four days, 12 Japanese vessels were sighted. Nine were hunted down and attacked. To no avail. Morton and his crew were staking their lives in this most hazardous invasion effort. That investment was "honored" by 10 torpedoes that broached, made erratic runs, or thumped against target hulls like derelict motorboats. "Damn the torpedoes!" Morton wrote in wrath. WAHOO's radio crackled out the execrable torpedo's record, and ComSubPac recalled the luckless submarine from the area.

Returning to Pearl Harbor WAHOO took aboard a load of the new Mark 18 electrics, and Morton requested that his submarine be sent back to the Japan Sea for her seventh patrol.

WAHOO left Pearl Harbor on September 9, topped off at Midway on the 13th and headed for La Perouse to run the gantlet. She was trailed by SAWFISH (Lieutenant Commander E. T. Sands) bent on penetrating the Japan Sea in her wake.

Morton's submarine was to make her entry on or about September 20, and patrol the sea below the 43° parallel. SAWFISH was to enter some three days later and cover the area north of WAHOO's. At sunset, October 21, WAHOO was supposed to leave her area, and head for home. She was instructed to report by radio after she made her way out through the Kurile chain. This report was expected about October 23rd.

The transmission from WAHOO was never received. SAWFISH made no contact with her, and she maintained a radio silence that became the muteness of interminable tide and infinite sea.

Yet WAHOO was heard from during her seventh and last patrol. Indirectly, and through a foreign agent. That agent was Radio Tokyo, broadcasting to the world a Domei report that a steamer was sunk by an American submarine on October 5 off the west coast of Honshu. The broadcast stated that the vessel was torpedoed near the Straits of Tsushima and sank "after several seconds" with 544 people losing their lives as the ship went down.

This broadcast was reported by *Time* magazine of October 18, under the headline, "KNOCK AT THE DOOR." The magazine's readers were reminded that the torpedoing occurred in waters which were "Japan's historic door" to the mainland of Asia. The magazine "presumed" the submarine knocking at this door was American, and compared the Japan Sea penetration to Gunther Prien's invasion of Scapa Flow and the Jap raid on Pearl Harbor.

The magazine's presumption was correct. What its editors did not know was the fact that other U.S. subs had invaded this sea, and that the submarine in question knocked on the door more than once.

The Japanese recorded an anti-submarine action in La Perouse Strait on October 11, 1943. "Our plane found a floating submarine and attacked it with three depth charges." There could be little doubt that the patrol plane's target was WAHOO.

On November 9, WAHOO was officially reported missing. At that time her loss was attributed to enemy mines. (The Japan Sea was thereupon abandoned as a patrol area, and it was not again invaded until June 1945 when special mine-detecting equipment was available for submarines.)

So closed the book for one of the greatest submarine teams of World War II—WAHOO and "Mush" Morton. If the philosophy of a combat submariner could be summed up in a single word, one would certainly suffice for Morton's.

"Attack!"

Submarine Tactics—Wolf-packing

In the last year and a half of the war, American submarine operations were somewhat altered in character. The change was introduced in September 1943 by the formation of the first American "wolf-pack."

The military principle of concentration of force—"getting there fustest with the mostest"—motivated this attack-group experiment. Applied defensively, the principle had developed the convoy system, by way of concentrating friendly forces for mutual protection against submarines. Successful in World War I, this anti-submarine measure was countered early in World War II by German efforts to concentrate their U-boat forces against convoys.

By September 1943 there were enough SubPac submarines available to permit a wolf-pack trial. The enemy might have noted that this coordinated attack group came into being at the time he was frantically striving to organize his anti-submarine program and install a convoy system. Force was preparing to meet force, as the occasion demanded.

On September 26 two submarines left home base at Pearl Harbor and headed west for Midway. At Midway they were joined by a third submarine. The three departed together on October 1st—destination, the East China Sea.

The coordinated attack group consisted of CERO (Commander D. C. White), SHAD (Commander E. J. MacGregor), and GRAYBACK (Commander J. A. Moore). It was under group command of Captain C. B. Momsen. This was the first American wolf-pack of the war. By war's end many a wolf-pack would be at Japan's historic door.

Chapter 18

Aleutian Conclusion and Atlantic Tidal Turn

☆ ☆ ☆

Heating up the North Pacific

While the Japanese were in hot water in the Central and Southwest Pacific, the U.S. and Canadian forces were not permitting the Aleutian waters to freeze over. Throughout the winter of 1942-1943 constant pressure was applied to pinch off the enemy's bases at Kiska and Attu. Only the wildest weather interrupted the relay of submarine patrols.

At the time the fighting was hottest at Guadalcanal, two fleet submarines were dispatched to join the S-boat force at Dutch Harbor. CACHALOT (Lieutenant Commander H. C. Stevenson) had arrived at that base on October 2, 1942. DOLPHIN (Lieutenant Commander R. L. Rutter) put in there three weeks later.

Keeping the enemy's bases under surveillance and watching the sea lanes coming north from Japan was a trying task as the winter caterwauled into 1943. Not infrequently a submarine had to surface and charge batteries in the teeth of a ferocious gale. During one such instance, S-32 (Lieutenant Commander M. G. Schmidt) was driven into a trough that rolled her 65° to starboard at least three times. Such an experience is hard on the crockery—in a sailor's jaw as well as in the galley.

In mid-January—and no thaw to speak of—S-18, under Lieutenant Commander C. H. Browne, conducted a reconnaissance mission covering the Attu-Semichi Islands area. The mission, which lasted from the 11th to the 26th, could scarcely have been called a harbinger of spring. Yet the Japs, had they been informed, might have taken it as a hint of warmer weather to come.

A heavily screened Jap convoy succeeded in rushing re-inforcements from Paramushiru in the northern Kuriles to Attu. As a result of this action, several S-boats were dispatched to cut the Paramushiru-Attu sea lanes. Surface forces stopped the enemy's traffic, however.

It was the last Jap train for the Aleutians. After that fiasco, the Japanese depended on their submarines to supply Attu and Kiska. Thirteen of these had cooperated in the invasion of the Aleutians in June 1942. Now they were to cooperate again—in a reverse operation.

Nautilus and Narwhal to Attu

Japanese I-boats were not the only submarines to land troops on Attu. Early in April 1943, two U.S. submarines were practicing amphibious maneuvers for a scheduled Attu landing.

NAUTILUS was practicing at Pearl Harbor. Lieutenant Commander Brockman needed no indoctrination course in the business of preparing his big submarine for an amphibious operation. At Makin it had been Carlson's Raiders. Now it was 109 Army Scouts to be put ashore in Blind Cove, Holtz Bay, in the northeastern end of Attu.

While NAUTILUS was readying at Pearl Harbor, NARWHAL, under Lieutenant Commander Frank D. Latta, was rehearsing with 105 men and officers of the Seventh Scout Company at San Diego, California, 2,000 miles away.

On April 20, NARWHAL set out for Dutch Harbor. Like her sister submarine on this Aleutian mission, she was jammed to the gills with passengers.

The Army Scouts aboard NARWHAL and NAUTILUS were able to go briskly ashore when the submarines reached Dutch Harbor on April 27th. There, joint disembarkation exercises were conducted, and by May 1, the two submarines were on their way to Attu.

Also en route to Attu was a striking force consisting of battleships IDAHO, PENNSYLVANIA and NEVADA, the escort carrier NASSAU, a number of destroyers, and transports carrying Army troops. Rear Admiral Thomas C. Kinkaid directed the operation.

D-Day had to be postponed for three days due to foul weather. While the ships milled offshore in fog and snow-storms, the two transport submarines maneuvered to keep out of everybody's way. At one time NAUTILUS made a 4,000-

yard radar contact on an unidentified vessel, and Brockman jockeyed in for a stern shot. Seen at 1,000 yards, the target proved to be NARWHAL.

May 11 finally brought the order to go in. Around 0300 the submarines rendezvoused off Blind Cove and the Scouts were disembarked in rubber boats. The night was ink-black and the beach was barely visible. NAUTILUS stood by until 0450, showing an infra-red light toward the beach to assist the boats in holding a correct course. NAUTILUS then opened to seaward, following NARWHAL in a planned retirement. Both scouting parties had landed safely.

The battle to take Attu lasted for three weeks. At the end, out of ammunition, the Japs made a suicide charge, rushing the American line with knives and bayonets. The *hara-kiri* was all over by May 30th. Japan had lost her major base in the Aleutians.

Grand Finale

The next move was to take Kiska. Invasion was scheduled for August 15th. At Adak a force of some 100 vessels was assembled and 29,000 American plus 5,000 Canadian troops were embarked with full battle gear. The upshot came as the war's strangest denouement. When the occupation forces went ashore after a heavy preliminary bombardment, not a single, solitary Jap could be found on Kiska. On August 31, under cover of one of those impenetrable Aleutian fogs, the entire garrison had made a getaway. Japanese fast transports, assisted by 15 submarines, had evacuated it to Paramushiru.

Aleutian Aftermath

While the United States-Canadian forces had been capturing Attu and Kiska, the submarine force from Dutch Harbor was on the go out at sea. The S-boats contributed to the Japanese defeat by sinking several AK's and a number of patrol vessels off the archipelago and in the vicinity of the Kuriles.

With the ending of the Aleutian campaign, the "sugar boats" were on the verge of concluding their valorous careers. In October they were slated for retirement or service as training vessels. But they had not yet fired their final shot. One of the last S-boats to go out from the Aleutians on war patrol was S-44—renowned conqueror of the heavy cruiser KAKO. It was not her lot to end up as a training vessel or in retirement. It was hers to go down in the last S-boat battle of the Pacific War.

Last Shot (Loss of S-44)

On September 26, S-44 stood seaward from Attu, under Lieutenant Commander F. E. Brown, to begin her fifth war patrol—area destination, the northern Kuriles. Submarines had been busy wrecking the Japanese fishing business in those waters, and there was shipping to be found off Paramushiru.

On the night of October 7, the submarine made radar contact with what appeared to be a small merchantman.

Brown ordered the gunners out on deck and closed in to deliver a surface attack. S-44 was only a few hundred yards from the target when Brown opened fire. A stunning salvo answered the S-boat's deck gun—the ship she had attacked in the dark was a destroyer!

Brown shouted the order, "Clear the deck! Take her down!" The diving alarm sounded as the crew reached the conning tower. But S-44 failed to submerge. A shell smashed into the control room below the waterline. A second projectile exploded in the conning tower, and a third stove in the hull near the forward battery room. The S-boat rolled and lurched under another series of hits as Brown cried the order to abandon and someone flagged a pillow case from the forward battery-room hatch as a signal of surrender. Either the Jap destroyer-men failed to see it in the night, or they were indisposed to show mercy. The shells continued to smash into S-44 as she went down.

Seven or eight men escaped the sinking submarine, but only two were picked up by the destroyer. These were Chief Torpedoman's Mate E. A. Duva, and Radioman Third Class W. F. Whitemore. Sole survivors of the S-44, they were released by Allied forces at the end of the war.

Atlantic Tidal Turn

In the winter of 1942-1943 the Squadron Fifty submarines which had participated in "Operation Torch" patrolled the Bay of Biscay. The Bay of Biscay was a festering spot, but little could be done to squelch Franco Spain's efforts in behalf of Nazi Germany. Restricted to sinking only those vessels positively identified as blockade runners, the submarines had been frustrated at the start, and the six-week patrols off the Spanish coast proved more dangerous than productive.

Barb, Herring, Blackfish, Shad, Gurnard and Gunnel assembled at Base Two after nine Biscay patrols.

It had become apparent that the Squadron Fifty submarines were not being used to best advantage. Reason:

lack of targets in the Atlantic. Accordingly the squadron was returned to the United States, and the submarines were then dispatched to the Pacific where the undersea war was in full career.

The U-boat War

In one respect the Nazi Navy suffered a handicap in common with the Japanese. Vaunted scientists that they were, the Germans were unable to match the Allies in the field of technology and in the laboratory. From the Battle of the Atlantic, future historians may well conclude that the totalitarian state or government which demands "regimented thinking" shackles itself in the world of science. Certainly the government which forces its scientists to think in goose-step is on a back road, and during the early part of the war many German physicists, chemists and educators were literally set to marching in uniform. In December 1943 Admiral Doenitz issued a top secret order containing the appeal,

IT IS ESSENTIAL TO VICTORY THAT WE MAKE GOOD OUR SCIENTIFIC DISPARITY AND THEREBY RESTORE TO THE U-BOAT ITS FIGHTING QUALITIES

As a result of this entreaty, German scientists who had been drafted were recalled from the front to assist in the creation of the Naval Scientific Directional Staff. This body was similar to the Scientific Council which, organized by Admiral King and composed of civilian scientists, operated with the Tenth Fleet (the coordinating agency for anti-submarine warfare). Late in the field, the German Naval Scientific Directional Staff was unable to overcome the Allied lead, and the "scientific disparity" bemoaned by Admiral Doenitz contributed much to the Nazi defeat in the Battle of the Atlantic.

Hitler's scientists tried to frustrate radar detection by coating the U-boat hulls with rubber. They tried to defeat sonar by means of *pillenwerfer*—large chemical pellets which, discharged from a submarine, created in the water a bubbling disturbance calculated to confuse echo-ranging. These gimcracks were effective to some extent, but Allied sonar operators soon learned of the ruse and were able to probe through it.

Late in the war, German scientists developed the *schnorkel* extension stack. This was an air tube—in effect, a windpipe extending from the submerged submarine to the surface. Serving as an air intake and exhaust for the engines, it per-

mitted the U-boat to operate on Diesel propulsion at periscope depth, thus giving the submarine a higher submerged
speed, and eliminating the necessity for a surface-run battery charge. *Schnorkel* was a most important innovation in
submarining. But it came too late to rescue the foundering
Nazi Cause.

Between July 1943 and June 1944 some 199 U-boats were
sunk by Allied A/S forces. By superhuman effort the Germans might have been able to replace the submarines. But
no mortal effort could replace the many experienced U-boat
captains and skilled crews lost with these vanquished undersea boats. Before the Nazis capitulated on V-E Day, a total
of some 781 German submarines had been sunk and approximately 30,000 German submariners had been drowned
in action.

Seen in historical perspective, these figures will not de-
tract from the U-boat's reputation as an engine of destruction. In the Atlantic the U-boat force destroyed almost 3,000
Allied vessels—approximately 14,000,000 tons of Allied shipping. It did not do so well against Allied naval vessels,
although it smote the Royal Navy an excruciating blow at the
war's outset. American naval losses to the U-boat were the
destroyers JACOB JONES and LEARY, the destroyer escorts
FISKE and FREDERICK C. DAVIS, five Coast Guard cutters, and
the escort carrier BLOCK ISLAND.

Admiral Doenitz made some plaintive excuses at war's
end. Hitler, he said, had not prepared to fight a naval war
against the Anglo-Saxon powers. To do so, Der Fuehrer
should have had 1,000 U-boats available at the war's beginning. The Nazi submarine admiral described radar as the
U-boat's Nemesis. It was, he asserted, *next to the atomic
bomb, the most decisive weapon of the war.*

Loss of R-12

Only two United States submarines were lost in the Atlantic during World War II. Both were lost in 1943.

R-12 (Lieutenant Commander E. E. Shelby) was proceeding off Key West, Florida, on June 12th. She was underway
to take up her position for a torpedo practice approach.

The submarine was rigged for diving and riding the vents.
On the bridge were Lieutenant Commander Shelby, two officers and three men. About 1220, the collision alarm
sounded below and the word was passed to the bridge that
the forward battery compartment was flooding.

Shelby immediately gave the order to blow main ballast

and close the hatches. Water plunged up over the super-structure as he spoke. And then, with a hollow roar, the seas closed in and R-12 was gone.

The disaster occurred in a calamitous 15 seconds. With the exception of Lieutenant Commander Shelby and the two officers and three men who were with him on the bridge, all hands were lost.

The R-boat went down in 600 feet of water. A Court of Inquiry pronounced the cause of the sinking as unknown.

Loss of Dorado

DORADO, the second submarine to go down in the Atlantic, was lost some time in October. Newly commissioned, under Lieutenant Commander E. C. Schneider, she departed New London, Connecticut, on October 6, and headed for Panama. She was never heard from thereafter.

DORADO may have been bombed accidentally by a sub-hunting patrol plane. There was also the possibility that DORADO encountered a German submarine in the Caribbean. Chance meeting with a lurking enemy—a shot in the dark—a torpedo—such undersea battles had been waged in the area.

Lack of evidence forced the Court of Inquiry to adjudge the case of DORADO's loss as unknown.

Somewhere in the Atlantic—perhaps in action off Cuba—she went down with all hands.

Chapter 19

Torpedo!

☆　　☆　　☆

Malfunctions vs. Morale

In 1939 and 1940 the German Submarine Force was plagued by torpedo failures. Gunther Prien and other ace U-boat skippers reported prematures and duds—troubles which were seated in the German influence exploder. And because accurate depth control was not imperative if influence exploders operated properly, the German torpedo was wanting in depth performance. Both of these defective features had to be corrected before the U-boats could hope to win in the Atlantic.

Admiral Doenitz reported that torpedo failures seriously undermined the morale of the U-boat crews, and drastic steps were taken to restore their confidence in their chief weapon. The tricky magnetic exploder was withdrawn from service, and a dependable contact exploder was issued in its place. The torpedo's runnings faults were corrected. The German torpedo was scoring with appalling efficiency by the time the United States entered the war, and the morale of the U-boat force was correspondingly high.

The U-boaters were spared that concatenation of defects that made American experience with the cranky Mark 14 a two-year nightmare. Moreover, the German's torpedo troubles were alleviated by a general background of victory, whereas the American submariners had to sweat through their difficulties at a time when the enemy was winning one battle after another.

The Philippines invasion alone was sufficiently punishing. To the 28 submarines of the Asiatic Fleet had fallen the bulk of the northern Philippines defense. Twenty-eight submarines—a squadron against an armada. Yet, given a good weapon they might have seriously impeded the foe. But armed with a defective torpedo—

Lingayen Gulf—five submarines on hand—only one Japanese transport sunk out of an invasion fleet of more than 80 ships! January, and the seas around the Philippines aswarm with enemy shipping. Only three Japanese vessels downed by American submarines in the area! February, only three! Four in March! Almost four months of warfare in the Southwest Pacific, and a scant 13 vessels sunk by the hard-fighting American submarines!

It remains for some future statistician to analyze the dozens of torpedo shots fired in those four desperate months. To sift through the maze of controversial reports—separate the wheat of verifiable torpedo hits from the chaff of prematures which looked like bull's-eye explosions—trace the deep-runners which missed the mark—estimate the number of duds which thumped in futility against stout targets. Due to the confusion of those early war reports and the fantastic difficulties involved in tracking down torpedo failures, such an analysis probably defies the making. But the historian may refer to the experience of SARGO's captain, Lieutenant Commander Jacobs (13 shots for zero hits), for a clue to the agonizing situation. Certain it is that the entire Philippines defense, from the day of the enemy strike to Wainwright's surrender, was hampered by the wretched performance of American submarine torpedoes equipped with a defective magnetic exploder.

As for submarine force morale—

There were casualties. Not many. Not as many as might have justifiably been expected. But a few commanding officers, introspective after repeated failures to score, asked to be relieved of command so that others might try where they had failed. And those skippers who were determined to hit it out and grit it out were burdened by the knowledge that they fought with a blunt weapon. Or was the fault really theirs? Had they missed those shots, fired too early or too late, miscalculated? Honest self-confidence forced to fence with a haunting ghost of doubt.

Hard on the submarine captain, the situation was equally hard on the crew. The crew of a submarine is a team—perhaps more interdependent than most. One fumble on a football field may not lose the game, but a fumble aboard a submarine can cost the life of all hands. The captain directs the approach, is responsible for the attack and gives the order to fire the torpedo. Often he alone sees the target.

Those in the conning tower, in the engine room, in the torpedo room must rely on his ability and his judgment. He in turn relies on the crew to perform ably each duty which is demanded during approach and attack maneuvers. The torpedo fails to hit? The captain at the periscope, the sound man who checked the range, the officer at the T.D.C., the chief torpedoman's mate—any one of a dozen men may have been responsible.

Repeated and unexplained failures invite mutual mistrust, engender suspicions that can break down the solidarity of a team. The commanding officer who sees a torpedo miss under circumstances that favored a hit is compelled to investigate the performance of his torpedo crew. The torpedo crew that knows its work has been ably performed is led to suspect the control room. If nothing succeeds like success, nothing is more depressing than continued and inexplicable failure.

Throughout the long retreat to Australia, the period of pioneer Empire patrols, the Solomons struggle, the Aleutian battle, the efforts of the submarine forces were consistently sabotaged by torpedo troubles. But morale stood on its feet and shook its fist. That some of the pioneer submarine teams did not disintegrate, that the force held together as solidly in the trough of adversity as on the crest of the wave is testimony to the courage, resolution and resourcefulness of the men who commanded and served in the Navy's submarines.

Prematures

Worst morale saboteur was the unexplained miss caused by erratic depth performance or failure of the torpedo to explode. These malfunctions often defied detection. Fired in battle, the guilty torpedo could not be hauled in for examination, and the miss could be blamed on innocent parties.

Less sinister, although equally baffling, was the premature —the torpedo that exploded too soon. When a premature blasted the water there was no mystery about what had happened. "Why" might remain an unanswered question, but it could generally be assumed that the fault was the torpedo's.

But the premature could be far more dangerous than a miss. They warned the enemy of the submarine's attack. Opportunity, knocking but once, might blow sky-high in a geyser of water well off the target ship's beam. Not only could the vessel then maneuver to evade, but the submarine's approximate position was revealed to the escorts. Proof is unobtainable, but it is entirely possible that prematuring torpedoes contributed to the loss of one or two American submarines.

The submarines were made disagreeably aware of prematures in the opening months of the war. However, the percentage seemed small, and it was not until after the depth-control difficulty had been corrected that the extent of the premature problem became apparent. When running deep, torpedoes were unaffected by the action of surface waves. Also, some of the early torpedoes ran so deep that the anti-counter-mining device kept the firing pin locked during the run and while the torpedo passed under the target. But when these malfunctions were corrected and the torpedoes began to run at shallower depths, the perturbations caused by the motion of the sea or by surges in the torpedo power-plant sometimes activated the delicate exploder and caused the torpedo to premature. Thus the percentage of prematures was abruptly increased by the correction of the depth-control difficulty.

In the magnetic exploder lay another cause for prematures. When set to run at a depth which was less than the draft of the target vessel, a torpedo entered the horizontal component of the ship's magnetic field some distance from the vessel's hull. Under certain circumstances, the exploder would go into action at that instant when the torpedo entered this magnetic field, and the torpedo would blow up about 50 feet from the side of the ship. These prematures, seen through a submarine's periscope, looked like perfect hits. The explosions were correctly timed, and an eruption of water, directly in line with the target, obscured the vessel from view. More than one Japanese ship was found to be undamaged after its sinking was reported by a submarine skipper who had been deceived by a premature.

Emerging in the wake of the depth-setting trouble, the premature problem raised its ugly head in the autumn of 1942, and the submarine forces found themselves confronted by another bugbear. By year's end the bugbear was full grown, and it pursued the submariners well into 1943. One of the submarines badgered by this difficulty was SCAMP. In March 1943, while on her first patrol and making her first attack, SCAMP fired a three-torpedo salvo in which all three torpedoes prematured shortly after arming. Of SCAMP's first nine torpedoes fired on that patrol, five prematured.

The premature problem was a heartbreaker for the force which had battled it out with deep-running. To Admiral Lockwood and all those who had pitched in to correct the torpedoes' depth performance, this new wrench in the machinery was beyond endurance. And what couldn't be endured had to be cured with the greatest possible dispatch. What prematures could mean to a superlatively able captain

and top-notch submarine crew is revealed between the lines
in TUNNY's report of an attack on a Japanese aircraft carrier
formation southwest of Truk on April 9, 1943.

Tunny vs. Carrier Formation

In April 1943, TUNNY was patrolling in the Caroline area.
During her first war patrol, concluded in February 1943, she
had experienced torpedo troubles which included a dud and
a premature. Now she was hoping for better luck. And it
seemed to be coming her way when, at 2100 on the night of
April 8, she received information that a convoy had been
sighted trucking southwest of Truk. TUNNY's skipper, Lieutenant Commander J. A. Scott, lost no time in putting the
submarine between the reported convoy and its destination.

At 2228 the following night, TUNNY made radar contact
with the convoy at a range of about 1,500 yards. Using radar
ranges and bearings, Scott plotted the enemy's course as
060° and his speed as 18 knots. This high speed served to
identify the contact as the carrier group which had been reported.

Scott ordered the submarine trimmed down to awash conditions to reduce her silhouette, and put her on four-engine
speed to pull ahead of the convoy. At 2237 the convoy
changed course to 085° T, which placed the submarine
dead ahead. Scott slowed TUNNY to two-thirds speed and
headed in to attack with decks awash.

On TUNNY's starboard bow was a large carrier or auxiliary
carrier. On her port bow two escort carriers were in column.
There was a destroyer on each bow of the formation. TUNNY
still on the surface, headed for the center of the enemy disposition. Scott intended, upon reaching attack position, to
swing left, fire the six bow tubes at the two-carrier column,
and the four stern tubes at the single carrier. This plan was
thwarted when the submarine suddenly picked up a group
of three small boats, apparently motor torpedo boats, about
one point on the port bow. The range to these craft was only
300-500 yards. TUNNY had to turn away and dive to avoid
detection.

Making a swift change of plans and equally rapid changes
in his firing set-up, Scott came right to a course that gave
him a 90° track, and ordered TUNNY to 40 feet. The T.D.C.
set-up was for a stern tube shot at the leading ship of the
two-ship column. At 2248, Scott fired four torpedoes from
the stern tubes, range 880 yards. Four hits were heard shortly thereafter.

In the meantime, the executive officer, Lieutenant Commander R. M. Keithly, was on the periscope, trying to pick up the single carrier for the bow tubes. He was encountering some difficulty because the recent course-change had left the convoy formation a little ragged and the ships were not in their correct relative positions. The periscope was almost blind in the night's blackout, and practically nothing could be seen unless the target were first approximately located. However, this game of blind man's buff did not last long. Some obliging Jap on the carrier came to Keithly's assistance by opening up with a signal lamp. Keithly was thereby enabled to get a periscope bearing, and it gave the radar a nice check just before the bow tubes were fired. Six torpedoes were shot at the target, range 650 yards, zero gyro angle, longitudinal spread. The first three sounded like smashing hits.

As an example of expert technique in approach and attack, TUNNY's performance had everything. This was probably the first time in history that a submarine had been presented with the opportunity of making a simultaneous bow and stern tube attack, with aircraft carrier targets for both tube nests. Many submarine officers had dreamed of such a situation, but here was the first time it materialized. It was also the last.

Scott proved himself more than worthy of the situation. When the torpedo boats unexpectedly appeared and Scott was suddenly forced to change his plans, TUNNY's fire control party proved sufficiently flexible to follow the abrupt transition without confusion. Ten torpedoes were properly fired at minimum ranges, and the crew operated as smoothly as a synchronized set of precision machines.

"In the history of the war," wrote a critic, *"probably in the whole history of submarines, this attack stands out as tops. It was art for art's sake."* But unfortunately it went for naught. The Japanese escort carrier TAIYO (OTAKA) received some damage which did little to interfere with her schedule. Apparently no other Japanese ships were damaged. The blasts TUNNY heard and reported as hits were undoubtedly prematures caused by defective exploders.

The Exasperating Mark 6

So confidence in the reliability of the Mark 6 exploder waned rapidly during the first six months of 1943. As the intricacies and behavior characteristics of the previously secret mechanism became known to many, many were the theories and suggestions for its improvement. Everything possible, short of designing a completely new influence-exploder, was done. And still torpedoes blew up shortly after arming or exploded at harmless distances from targets. Thanks to Admiral Lockwood, the SubPac Force finally got rid of the faulty magnetic exploder in July 1943. But on July 11, Admiral Ralph Christie, then in command of SubSoWesPac, directed that the magnetic exploder be retained by his force.

GROUPER'S captain recommended the inactivation of the Mark 6 exploder with this comment: *"It would appear far better to sink the enemy vessels encountered—when targets in certain areas are so hard to find and attack—than to continue spoiling good chances just to prove that a really useless mechanism can be made to function a fair proportion of the time."*

But it was not until March 1944, after all attempted remedial action had failed and prematures had become the bane of the Southwest Pacific Force, that SoWesPac submarines were ordered to inactivate the magnetic feature of their exploders.

Duds

When Admiral Lockwood, in June 1943, ordered the inactivation of the magnetic exploder device, his force believed that its torpedo worries were all but over. Submarine commanders were more than willing to forego the advantages claimed for the magnetic exploder, in order to obtain torpedo hits against the sides of enemy ships. There was at that time no reason to doubt that the contact mechanism of the exploder was anything less than reliable.

A small percentage of duds had been previously observed, but these deadhead torpedoes which hit and failed to explode were comparatively rare. A few failures of even the simple contact exploded had to be expected. Although less complex than the magnetic device, the contact device was still an intricate mechanism. Any mistake in its final check and installation might result in a flooded exploder or one that otherwise failed to function.

The dud was a hard offender to track down. Its extensive delinquency became apparent only when the other torpedo "bugs" had been exterminated and enemy ships continued to survive what should have been fatal submarine encounters. But the dud was to be smoked out, and the smoking began in earnest on July 24, 1943, when the submarine TINOSA had a chance to play Annie Oakley with a "sitting duck."

Tinosa vs. Tonan Maru

The "sitting duck" was TONAN MARU No. 3—a prize

long coveted by American submarine captains. She and her sister ship, TONAN MARU No. 2, had been built as whale factories for processing whales and rendering the blubber at sea. They had later been converted into oil tankers for government use. With a gross tonnage rating of 19,262 tons, each was a whale of a tanker. About twice the size of the average merchant oil carrier, they were the largest tankers that Japan possessed.

Imaginative submarine skippers liked to study this mammoth in the silhouette book and dream of her coming within attack range. TINOSA, captained by Lieutenant Commander L. R. "Dan" Daspit, was patrolling westward of Truk when the dream became a reality. For there was the giant tanker, unescorted! Steaming across the seascape with all the complacency of an ocean monster that believed itself a king among minnows.

When contact was made with this tremendous target, TINOSA had 16 torpedoes on hand—all that remained to her after several previous encounters with enemy shipping. Daspit lost no time in bringing his submarine to attack position. He opened fire on the tanker with a spread of four torpedoes, using a large track angle. The range was high—about 4,000 yards—but TINOSA had been unable to close the target's track, and Daspit was forced to accept the unfavorable track angle and lengthy range.

Two torpedoes of the salvo hit near the tanker's stern. The vessel stopped dead in the water and veered in a manner which placed the submarine about two points on her port quarter. Daspit quickly fired two more torpedoes. Both exploded resoundingly. TONAN MARU No. 3 belched smoke and settled slightly by the stern.

Here was a situation almost too good for verity—the big ex-whale factory dead in the water like a mired hippopotamus—not an A/S vessel in the vicinity—submariners with plenty of time at their disposal to finish off the target at will.

Carefully Daspit selected a position 875 yards off the tanker's beam and fired one torpedo. The torpedo was heard by Sound to make a normal run. At the moment when the sound of the torpedo's screws stopped abruptly, Daspit at the periscope saw a fishy splash at the point of aim. There was no explosion. A dud.

Deliberately Daspit lined up for another attack, fired another torpedo. Again the torpedo's run trailed off into silence. Two more torpedoes were fired with great care and precision. If silence was golden (under the circumstances it was not!) TINOSA had hit the jackpot. Certainly she was hitting the target—at that range a blind man could not have missed. But Tonan Maru No. 3 remained as fixed in the scene as a taxidermist's exhibit in a showcase. For all their content of T.N.T., the warheads of Tinosa's torpedoes might as well have been stuffed with sawdust.

So the submarine skipper's dream distorted into a nightmare of impotence. Another skipper thus foiled by duds and robbed of one of the war's great trophies might, himself, have blown up from spontaneous combustion. But Daspit held down the safety valve on his temper. After the first dud he had resolved to get to the bottom of the matter. And as it turned out, his investigative procedure produced results of greater import than the demolishment of this one fat Japanese target.

What Daspit demolished was any lingering question as to the culpability of the Mark 6 exploder. Altogether he fired eight torpedoes, launching them one after the other from a theoretically perfect position—on the target's beam, using a 90° track angle. The shooting extended over a period of several hours. Before each torpedo was fired it was withdrawn from the tube and all adjustments were checked. Fire control was methodical, as cool as leisure could make it. Working the T.D.C., Lieutenant C. E. "Ebbie" Bell, another calm and capable young officer, did his job with surgical precision. The Torpedomen operated as a well-disciplined unit, and Tinosa played her part as an excellent submarine. Eight hits were scored (including that made by the first dud). And eight times the shots ended in deafening silence where there should have been thundering explosions.

Daspit's careful and finely calculated selection of the best possible track angle was later proved as a reason for the exploder failures. Had the torpedoes struck the target glancing blows, as was the case in the first two salvos, the exploders might have worked. Fired at a 90° angle, whereby they struck the target squarely with normal impact, they failed to work. One torpedo was seen to hit the tanker, jump clear of the water like a playful bass, and sink. The tanker sat there like the broadside of a barn as Tinosa pelted her with eight duds.

Daspit ceased shooting when a last torpedo remained on board. He wanted to take that torpedo back to Pearl as a sample for magnifying-glass analysis. Fifteen torpedoes expended on a single target—twelve hits—and Tonan Maru No. 3 remained obdurately afloat.

Japanese rescuers raced out and towed the great tanker safely into Truk. But the big oil carrier had served the U.S. Submarine Force well. Tinosa mourned the fact that the ex-whale factory was not sunk. But the story that Daspit brought back with him from the Carolines contributed more to the ultimate defeat of Japan.

Shooting the Trouble

When TINOSA reached Pearl Harbor, and a thorough examination of her remaining torpedo failed to disclose any errors in adjustment, the fat was in the fire. Admiral Lockwood decided to dispense with unheeded dispatches and tackle the Medusa-headed torpedo problem himself. His first act was to order the firing of two torpedoes against the submerged cliffs at Kahoolawe.

The test shots were fired, and one of the two torpedoes proved to be a dud. This Mark 14 blank was recovered and examined. The examiners found that the exploded mechanism had released the firing pin, but the pin had not hit the primer cap with sufficient force to set it off.

What next occurred was an exemplary demonstration of what could happen when a complex technical problem, hitherto bottled up in a jar labeled "Secret," was uncorked for the analysis of many able minds. All the available talent at Pearl Harbor joined in cooperative effort to solve the problem, bringing to its solution a variety of skills and techniques. Commander Service Force loaned an ordnance technician, Lieutenant Commander E. A. Johnson. Johnson, working with Commander A. H. Taylor and Lieutenant Commander H. A. Pieczentkowski, devised a unique test procedure. Warheads loaded with cinder concrete in place of torpex, but equipped with exploders, were dropped on a steel plate from a height of 90 feet. This duplicated the forces generated by a torpedo when it struck the side of a steel ship. And seven of the first 10 warheads dropped duplicated the performance of duds by failing to explode. Seven contact duds out of 10—and the war already in its twentieth month!

The impact test corroborated the findings at Kahoolawe. The exploder's firing pin would release, but it would strike with insufficient force to set off the primer cap. However, if the steel plate were set so that the warheads struck it a glancing blow, the exploders invariably functioned properly. This explained why some ships were sunk by torpedoes which struck them glancing blows at the turn of the keel or against the side, whereas solid and normal hits might fail.

With that much information in hand, the inquiry concentrated on the exploder's firing pin. This was a mushroom-shaped device weighing several ounces. When released, spring action forced the pin to move in a direction at right angles to the torpedo axis. Two guide studs controlled the direction of motion which brought the pin into contact with the firing cap. The force of deceleration when the torpedo struck a solid blow was found to be in the neighborhood of 500 times the force of gravity. This force, acting on the firing pin, produced a frictional component of approximately 190 pounds on the guide studs. The firing spring was unable to overcome this friction and drive the pin with adequate force against the cap.

Three corrective measures were tried. Some firing pin modifications did the trick.

On September 30, 1943, BARB left Pearl Harbor for patrol, carrying 20 torpedoes equipped with the modified firing pin. The Gordian knot had been cut, and the faulty exploder had been corrected. At last—almost two years after the beginning of the war—U.S. submarines went to sea with a reliable torpedo.

The Electric Torpedo

Early in 1942 a German electric torpedo was captured. This torpedo was turned over to the Westinghouse Electrical Manufacturing Company which was asked to produce a Chinese copy for American use.

Many difficulties were encountered. The production of a Chinese copy was not feasible. Several parts of the German torpedo were not adaptable to American manufacturing procedure. The functions of other parts were not fully understandable.

The program for the development of the electric torpedo presently stalled. But in April 1943, the Naval Inspector General was called upon by the Commander-in-Chief U.S. Fleet to investigate electric torpedo development and determine the reason for the delay in getting that weapon into production. The Inspector General reported:

"The delays encountered were largely the result of the manner in which the project was prosecuted and followed up. These difficulties indicate that the liaison officers of the Bureau of Ordnance failed to follow up and to properly advise the Westinghouse Company and the Exide Company. . . . The Torpedo Station had its own electric torpedo, the Mark 2, and the personnel assigned to it appear to have competed and not cooperated with the development of the new Mark 18. . . . Failure to provide experienced and capable submarine officers to the Bureau for submarine torpedo development . . . has contributed largely to the above deficiencies."

The electric torpedo had been favored by the Germans

primarily because it was "wakeless"—a feature that made its detection difficult and gave the target little chance to evade. Moreover, the depth control of the electric torpedo was superior to that of the steam torpedo. Also the electric torpedo did not go deep on its initial dive after being launched, and the impact exploder was free of the "bugs" which infested the steam torpedo's exploder. In the bargain, the electric torpedo could be manufactured at a fraction of the cost of the steam torpedo, and with a great saving in manhours. Its chief disadvantage was slow speed—28 to 30 knots as compared with 46 for the steam torpedo in high power. Nevertheless, submarine officers who assisted in proving the first electrics were enthusiastic.

The electric torpedo was subject to its share of infant diseases. There were some erratic runners, sinkers, and slow runners. The torpedo's tail vanes were found weak and had to be strengthened. Cold water and consequent low-battery temperature caused the torpedo to run slow. But these difficulties, encountered through experience, were relentlessly tracked down and swiftly eliminated. Much of the corrective work on the electric torpedo was accomplished in the torpedo shop at the Submarine Base, Pearl Harbor.

The electric torpedo did not meet with the instant favor of the submariners. But it steadily acquired popularity. Admiral Lockwood enthusiastically pushed the torpedo's employment. Thirty per cent of the submarine torpedoes fired in 1944 were electric. In the last six months of the war the percentage rose to 65.

So the history of the American submarine torpedo came full-circle. The name "torpedo" was bestowed upon the invention by Robert Fulton, who borrowed the term from the *torpedo electricus*—the cramp fish which kills its prey by electrocution. At long last, with the launching of the electrical Mark 18, the "tin fish" had come into its own.

Situation Summary

The war would have been foreshortened and many American lives saved had a reliable American torpedo been available from the beginning. That was the consensus of the veteran U.S. Submarine Force, of the officers and men who fought the undersea war in the Pacific. American submarines dealt a sledge hammer blow to the Imperial Japanese Navy. Yet of the grand total sunk, less than 15%—just three major warships—were sent to the bottom before the defective exploder was corrected late in 1943.

Some say the Philippines defense might have held had the

submariners been provided with a decent weapon. Some say the American torpedo effort was hamstrung by a super secrecy, which prevented even the torpedomen from knowing how to service the torpedo. And some say a rigid military protocol which prevented early criticism of the weapon's defects was responsible. Whatever the basic ailment, the cure came just in time.

Chapter 20

Southwest Pacific Push

Navy's Move

Admiral Halsey's Third Fleet began its drive for the Upper Solomons on June 30, 1943, with the capture of Rendova Island. New Georgia, farther north, was next. Then came Kolombangara, Vella Lavella and Bougainville. Smashing Japanese naval opposition, Halsey's forces drove relentlessly forward.

Some 27,000 Japanese troops were on Bougainville, but they might as well have been in Alcatraz. American aircraft controlled the sky over them, and the U.S. Navy controlled the surrounding seas. Isolated and trapped, the Japanese on Bougainville were as helpless as POW's. Military action against them was not worth the effort, so they were bypassed. The Upper Solomons campaign was over.

While Admiral Halsey's Third Fleet was expelling the Imperial Navy from the Solomons, allied forces were not neglecting the enemy in New Guinea. September 1943 found Vice Admiral Kinkaid's Seventh Fleet operating in New Guinea waters (under area command of General MacArthur) to the detriment of Japanese communication lines around such outposts as Lae, Salamaua and the Trobriand Islands.

Lae and Salamaua were occupied by American-Australian troops in mid-September. By November the Japanese positions on the northeast coast of New Guinea were completely neutralized.

The Seventh Fleet now participated in an amphibious move on New Britain—a thrust calculated to paralyze the enemy's naval base at Rabaul. Seventh Fleet forces spearheaded the invasion, blasting at Arawe on the south coast of New Britain in mid-December. There was surprisingly little resistance.

Marines were soon ashore on the north coast at Cape Gloucester.

The Japs continued to hold their Rabaul citadel and the neighboring base at Kavieng, New Ireland. But these strongholds were like stymied castles on a chessboard—major pieces which had been outflanked and reduced to impotence and were no longer worth the taking. Like Bougainville, they could be by-passed. The game was over for the Japanese in the South Seas.

So the long arm of Japan, which had encircled the Bismarcks and reached through the Solomons, was amputated in the last quarter of 1943. Where were the Japanese hopes of yesteryear?

Where was the Imperial Army? It had taken American ground forces almost seven months to win Guadalcanal—Rendova was little more than a skirmish. New Georgia was mopped up in six weeks, and Bougainville was neutralized in a month. Where were the Emperor's troops, the antiaircraft weapons, the planes?

Answer: Japan had been unable to solve the transport problem. The Japanese lost the Battle of Logistics long before they lost the battle of the Upper Solomons. Long before they were plucked by the Allies, Japan's South Seas bases were pumpkins dying on a vine of withered supply lines.

Much of that blight was inflicted by the U.S. Submarine Force.

Transportation Torpedoed

Seizure of the Upper Solomons and of footholds in the Bismarck-New Guinea area pushed the SoWesPac submarines to advanced fueling stations that saved the subs many leagues of travel. Simultaneously came the new SJ search radar that extended the search range. And better torpedoes.

But fueling stations, SJ radar and better torpedoes did not decrease the SoWesPac workload—only increased the submarine's capacity to tackle the job. As the submarine became more capable, more work was loaded on its shoulders. During the Upper Solomons campaign, the Task Force Seventy-two submarines were variously employed (at Admiral Halsey's direction) in support of fleet operations. Fremantle submarines participated in Seventh Fleet operations in the New Guinea-Bismarck area. These duties, in addition to the undersea war of attrition—the campaign that torpedoed the enemy's transportation system in the South Seas.

That campaign went on without a slow-down. It went on

while submarines performed all manner of special missions and duties. A submarine might lay mines, transport coast watchers and intelligence agents, evacuate refugees, rescue marooned aviators, go out scouting or prowl on reconnaissance. But the submarine's chief job was to sink enemy ships. In the South Seas battle the SoWesPac submarines remained on the job.

They did not fight the South Seas undersea war of attrition without assistance. The traffic lanes coming southeast from Palau, south from Truk, southwest from the Marshalls and Gilberts were covered for many miles by submarines from Pearl Harbor under operational control of Admiral Lockwood. And many a ship with cargo intended for the South Seas front was stopped north of the Mandates and in the waters off Japan—at the very roots of the transport-system vine.

When the war ended, the Japanese troops on Bougainville meekly surrendered. Toward the last, facing starvation, they had gone in for gardening. Their little vegetable patches (they could hardly have been called victory gardens) were all that kept them alive. In western New Guinea some of the Japanese garrisons were in similar straits. In other corners of the Southwest Pacific there were little outposts where the enemy, by-passed, was left marooned.

Some of those Japanese Crusoes awaited a triumphal relief. They were in for a long wait.

Submarine Support of Fleet Operations (Solomons-Bismarck-New Guinea Drive)

During the Upper Solomons drive every special assignment that could possibly be carried out was undertaken by the Brisbane Force and the submarines based at Fremantle. During the May-December period of the South Seas push, So-WesPac submarines accomplished the following typical missions:

May 25, 1943: TAUTOG (Lieutenant Commander Sieglaff) landed two Mohammedan agents on Kabaena Island.

May 25: GATO (Commander R. J. Foley) made sounding reconnaissance of Numa Numa Bay, near Choiseul in the Solomons. The previous month-end she had landed 16 coast watchers and Australian intelligence troops on Teop.

June 4: SILVERSIDES (Lieutenant Commander Burlingame) planted a minefield in Steffan Strait between New Hanover and New Ireland.

July 31: GUARDFISH (Lieutenant Commander N. G. Ward) landed a survey party on the west coast of Bougainville.

September 1: GREENLING (Lieutenant Commander J. D.

Grant) landed survey parties in the Shortland Islands and in the Treasury group.

September 20-28: GUARDFISH (Lieutenant Commander N. G. Ward) landed a reconnaissance party on the west coast of Bougainville.

September 29: GATO (Commander R. J. Foley) landed a reconnaissance party on the east coast of Bougainville.

September 29: PETO (Commander W. T. Nelson) concluded an unsuccessful two-day search for a Fifth Air Force crew lost somewhere off Wewak, New Guinea.

October 30: TAUTOG (Lieutenant Commander W. B. Sieglaff) bombarded Fais Island.

Practically all amphibious landings were preceded by submarine reconnaissance or by exploratory parties landed by submarine, or both.

Strategic employment of submarines as a task force scouting line below Truk had come as a result of conference with Admiral Halsey and his staff, who apparently considered it the most direct way submarines could support the fleet. Zero accomplishment emphasized the submarine's limitations in the field of open-sea scouting. Undoubtedly the same number of submarines deployed on the enemy's known traffic lanes would have inflicted great damage on his shipping, and so have been of more value to the fleet.

The only enemy naval vessel sunk by a SoWesPac submarine in the South Pacific during the Upper Solomons campaign was the Japanese submarine I-24. She was sunk off New Hanover on July 27 by SCAMP (Lieutenant Commander W. G. Ebert).

To the South China Sea in 1943 (Bowfin's Patrol)

After the retreat to Australia in 1942, the South China Sea had been too remote, submarines too few and torpedoes too scarce for anything like adequate area coverage. In the autumn of 1943, however, the South China Sea came in for more attention. The enemy was sending an increasing number of convoys down the Asian coast and into the Philippines. An increasing number of oil tankers traveled the sea lanes from Singapore and Borneo. These tankers were upped on the submarine priority list and the growing mechant marine activity was marked for diminution.

In September 1943, BOWFIN was sent out to the South China Sea under Lieutenant Commander Willingham to look over the situation. Covering the northern part of the area, this submarine—it was her maiden patrol—demolished KIRISHIMA MARU, passenger-cargoman, 8,120 tons.

Two days after the sinking of KIRISHIMA MARU, the Japanese lost a large transport in the same area. She was KASHIMA MARU, 9,908 tons, torpedoed and sunk by BONEFISH, under Lieutenant Commander T. W. Hogan.

Having destroyed this troopship, BONEFISH went on to sink a bigger one. On October 10, Hogan tracked down and sent down the 10,086-ton transport TEIBI MARU. The South China Sea was becoming unsafe for troop carriers.

KINGFISH (Lieutenant Commander V. L. Lowrance) took up the South China Sea patrol in October. She began by planting a minefield off the southwest corner of Celebes Island, squarely across a Japanese shipping lane from Makassar City. She continued on to land six British agents with 4,000 pounds of radio equipment on a hostile Borneo beach. On October 20, in South China Sea water, she sank SANA MARU, freighter, 3,365 tons.

With KINGFISH ending her patrol, BOWFIN was sent out again, this time under Lieutenant Commander W. T. Griffith. Bound for the South China Sea, she left Exmouth Gulf on November 4, her prospective course charted along the usual route through Lombok and Makassar Strait, Sibutu Passage and Balabac Strait. Five days out, not far from Makassar, she battle-surfaced to shoot up a convoy of five schooners.

BOWFIN was only warming up. Entering Sibutu Passage on the night of November 11, she battle-surfaced again to set fire to a pair of small oil tankers. This gun action was fought in bright moonlight within a range of Japanese shore batteries on Sibutu Island, but the shooting was over and BOWFIN was under before the coast artillerymen knew what it was all about.

BOWFIN cruised for a short time in the waters off Mindanao, found no targets, and proceeded west across "Dangerous Ground" toward Cape Varella. Midnight, November 25-26, she was approaching Fisherman's Islands in the sort of weather that makes a poor sailor wish he'd never heard of a foc's'le head and "graveyard watch." Sheeting black rainstorm and seas of India ink. Blindfold for a ship's lookout —worse for a wave-smothered periscope—but nothing to stop radar.

At 0200, BOWFIN'A SD picked up several large "pips." Three minutes later the inquiring SJ contacted something off in the night, 1,000 yards distant.

"I first thought I had blundered into the beach or some small islands, although I had 75 fathoms of water," Griffith noted in the log. *"Came hard left to clear out to seaward, and backed emergency to keep from ramming an enormous tanker!"*

A few minutes later the submarine backed full to keep from ramming another big tanker. Griffith realized he was in the midst of a Japanese convoy, northward bound. Five ships showed up on the radar screen with visibility practically zero and a blind spot ahead on the SJ due to improper tuning. However, after an hour and a half of tracking, Griffith knew the disposition of these targets. The ships were moving by two's in parallel columns 4,000 yards apart, the fifth ship trailing between the columns with an escort.

Griffith directed an approach on the leading vessel in the nearest (the starboard) column. At 0351 he fired three torpedoes. One struck the tanker's bow, and in the glaring blast the ship's bow section and foremast disintegrated. A second torpedo exploded amidships. As the tanker settled by the head a tide of liquid flame spread across the water. The men on Bowfin's bridge could see the tanker's broken silhouette and smell the burning gasoline. The vessel's deep-toned whistle wailed a disaster call in the night.

Meantime, Griffith had shifted the submarine for a torpedo shot at the second ship. As the volcanic blast of a hit lit up this second target, Bowfin had to back emergency to keep from ramming the torpedoed tanker which had veered around broadside within 300 yards of the submarine.

Griffith did some fast maneuvering. Explosions that sounded like depth charges were going off to starboard. The torpedoed tanker, its foredeck awash, was almost on top of Bowfin. The second vessel, damaged, wallowed in the sea about 1,500 yards beyond. Deciding to finish off the tanker before the escort could arrive on the scene—the other ship could wait—Griffith swung Bowfin for a stern-tube salvo, and fired three torpedoes at 1,200 yards. One hit under the tanker's stack, and the whistle choked off as if its throat had been plugged.

Bowfin was steered off into darkness for a quick reload, then Griffith skirted the scene of action for a last look. Rain was smothering the gasoline fires, and in the dim and smoky light the big tanker was slowly sinking in a sea of fumes. The second vessel was gone—like Charon's ferry in the night-draped Styx.

Griffith headed Bowfin toward Cape Varella to search for the rest of the convoy. At 1050 a periscope sweep brought a 5,000-ton freighter into view. Attempting a submerged approach, Griffith encountered trouble with depth control, and surfaced to accomplish a fast end-around. Four torpedoes scored four hits, blowing the AK completely to pieces.

As Griffith maneuvered the submarine over to the flotsam-strewn water where the freighter had exploded, a small

OTORI escort vessel came climbing over the waves about 1,500 yards away. The seas were too rough for the six-foot depth-setting required for a torpedo shot at this A/S craft, and Griffith headed BOWFIN away.

The following day, BOWFIN found another target—a small coastal steamer—which was disposed of with three torpedo shots. Then, early on the morning of the 28th, BOWFIN received a contact report from the submarine BILLFISH operating in the area—a convoy was in the vicinity. Shortly after the reception of this news, BOWFIN was on the track of five large ships which were steaming under escort.

Griffith directed a surface approach, and at 0313 making a surface attack, he fired four torpedoes at the leading (and largest) target. Four hits sank the ship in as many minutes.

At 0317 Griffith fired two more bow torpedoes. These smashed into the second vessel, leaving her awash to the bridge. At this juncture the third vessel of the convoy, which had been moving in column off BOWFIN's beam, turned and headed straight for the submarine. Gunfire blazed as the ship opened up with a 5-incher at 500 yards. The second shot hit the submarine. The shell ricocheted from the deck into the superstructure and exploded between the pressure hull and the starboard induction pipe. The blast carried away the low-pressure air lines aft, ripped open part of the main induction pipe, and destroyed the ventilation lines.

Griffith fired two stern-tube shots at the attacking ship. That ended the Japanese gunnery. Both torpedoes hit, and the vessel went down, sagging in the middle like a weighted hammock. With this target out of the way, Griffith sent BOWFIN in pursuit of the remainder of the convoy.

While the last two torpedoes aboard were being loaded, the submarine overhauled the quarry. Griffith drove in for an attack on the largest vessel, calculating the set-up carefully. At 0353 he fired the torpedoes. The first prematured at 500 feet, and its explosion deflected the second, sending it on a course wide of the mark.

"This premature cost us two sure hits and a 7,000-ton vessel," Griffith commented afterwards. (The submarines of SoWesPac were still using the Mark 6 exploder.)

So BOWFIN headed home from the South China Sea. But her war patrol was to have a P.S. On December 2 BOWFIN sighted a 75-ton oil-carrying yacht in Makassar Strait. Griffith ordered a gun attack, and BOWFIN's sharpshooters destroyed this unwary craft.

Her main induction patched and her patrol report crammed with action, BOWFIN arrived at Fremantle on December 9th. Hers was one of the season's high-scoring patrols. This patrol, with that of BONEFISH, marked the beginning of the end for Japanese merchant shipping in the South China Sea.

Submarines to the Philippines

The campaign to reoccupy the Philippine Islands began long before American landing craft nosed up against the Leyte beaches. United States submarines had never surrendered the usage of Philippine waters, and early in 1943 they began to visit the islands on special missions that were as intriguing as the "sealed orders" under which the captains sailed. The guns were still slamming on Guadalcanal when the first of these missions was undertaken by GUDGEON. January 14, 1943, this submarine, under Lieutenant Commander Stovall, landed a party of six Filipinos captained by Major I. A. Villamor, and one ton of equipment near Catmon Point on the island of Negros.

TAMBOR (Lieutenant Commander S. H. Armbruster) landed a Lieutenant Commander C. Parsons, USNR, and party, with 50,000 rounds of .30-cal. ammunition and 20,000 rounds of .45-cal. ammunition, plus $10,000 cash, near Pagodian Bay, Mindanao, on March 5th.

In April, GUDGEON was back again, this time under Lieutenant Commander W. S. Post, on a mission to land an officer, three men and three tons of equipment near Pucio Point, Panay. Post was never the man to let a mission interfere with the war of attrition. Putting first things first, on April 28 he drove GUDGEON in to attack a target no submarine would wish to overlook. So the Japanese lost KAMAKURA MARU, 17,526-ton transport—the biggest to go down to date in the Philippines. This sinking had a sequel on May 12, when GUDGEON, her mission completed, torpedoed and sank SUMATRA MARU, 5,862-ton freighter. The dead as well as the quick were making quiet landings on the beaches of the Philippines.

May 26, TROUT (Lieutenant Commander A. H. Clark) landed a party of agents with $10,000 and two tons of equipment on Basilan Island, P.I. On June 12 she was in Pagodian Bay on the south coast of Mindanao, unloading 6,000 rounds of .30-cal. ammunition, 2,000 rounds of .45-cal. ammunition, and a party of five under Captain J. A. Hammer, USA. From this hidden cove TROUT evacuated five officers. One of these, Lieutenant Commander C. Parsons, USNR, seems to have had a peculiar penchant for submarine rides in the Philippines. Revisiting Mindanao on July 9, TROUT picked up Parsons and carried him on another inter-island excursion.

On July 31, GRAYLING (Lieutenant Commander J. E. Lee)

delivered a ton of supplies and equipment to certain parties at Pucio Point, Pandan Bay, Panay. Under Lieutenant Commander E. Olsen the same submarine arrived in Pandan Bay on August 31 with two more tons of cargo.

And on October 20, CABRILLA (Commander D. T. Hammond) was at Negros to take aboard four men and the aforementioned Major Villamor.

These activities, had they been noticed, would have led the Japanese to suspect that things which did not meet their eyes were happening in the southern Philippines. Who, they might have asked, was this Major Villamor? And the busy and mysterious Lieutenant Commander Parsons who rode submarines around the Philippines as though they were taxis around Times Square! Presently, reports did begin to filter into General Homma's Headquarters—a Japanese scouting party shot down—an outpost raided—a motor convoy ambushed in the jungle. Homma was aware that all the Americans in the Philippines had not been captured, and native guerrilla fighters were beginning an organized resistance. It took him longer to learn that undersea boats were supplying the "underground" war.

Loss of Grayling

The Imperial Navy lost I-182 on September 9, and on that same day a U.S. submarine was seen in Lingayen Gulf, and the Japanese passenger-cargoman HOKUAN MARU reported fighting a submarine action in the "Philippine area." The submarine seen in Lingayen Gulf may have been GRAYLING, ordered to patrol the approaches to Manila on that date, or the submarine driven off by HOKUAN MARU may have been GRAYLING. On August 23 she had completed her special mission to Pandan Bay, Panay, by delivering a cargo of supplies to the local guerrillas. Then she left to reconnoiter Tablas Strait and hunt traffic off Manila. Pandan Bay was the last anchorage she ever made.

Apparently GRAYLING went down some time between the 9th and 12th of September. Commander Task Force Seventy-one requested a transmission from GRAYLING on the 12th. Her radio spoke no answer. On September 30, 1943. she was officially reported "lost with all hands."

Narwhal Enters the Guerrilla Movement

Of all the submarines that left Australia to go to the Philippines on special mission, the veteran NARWHAL engaged in the greatest number of these "cloak and dagger" exploits.

Late in October she headed out on her first secret mission —a run to the island of Mindoro with peripatetic Lieutenant Commander Parsons, 46 tons of stores and two parties of specialists. Captain of NARWHAL was Lieutenant Commander F. D. Latta, who had been on her bridge when she transported a company of Army scouts to Attu.

NARWHAL was in good hands. Any naval captain who could name a submarine's four engines "Matthew," "Mark," "Luke" and "John" was an officer of unusual capacities. The Biblical Diesels responded by outrunning two Japanese A/S vessels in the Mindanao Sea. And presently NARWHAL was moored alongside a Japanese registry schooner, the DONA JUANA MARU, unloading part of her stores.

This extraordinary business was followed by a junket even more remarkable. Leaving Mindoro, NARWHAL proceeded coolly to Nasipit Harbor, Mindanao (where she went aground in 20 feet of water, and got off not quite so coolly), then tied up at Nasipit dock where a Filipino band played "Anchor's Aweigh" as the supplies brought in by the submarine were unloaded. If the strains of "Anchor's Aweigh" marching off in the Philippine sunshine sounded a little fantastic to the invading submariners (where was the war?) the 32 evacuees, including baby, who came aboard for the return voyage to Australia, could assure NARWHAL's crew that Jap soldiery cracked the whip in Manila. Someone brought aboard a copy of the Manila *Tribune,* dated November 11, 1942, featuring a story that the old SEALION had been raised and was in Dewey Drydock, her interior dismantled and her hull undergoing study. SEALION—that must have been a century ago. And Wainwright's men—or what was left of them—were still in the prisons and stockades in the interior. But help was on the way, coming aboard such submarines as NARWHAL.

In Australia NARWHAL received another set of sealed orders. Again she headed for the Philippines, this time loaded with 90 tons of ammunition and stores, and carrying a party of eleven Army operatives. "Matthew," "Mark," "Luke," and "John" made the run in good time, and on December 3 the submarine was unloaded near Cabardaran, Mindanao. There, a party of eight (including Lieutenant Commander Parsons) was picked up for the return trip. NARWHAL then proceeded to Alubijid, Majacalar Bay, to take aboard three women, four children and two men. Latta stepped up the four engines to 17 knots as the submarine left this bay—the place had an unhealthy look. Latta noted, "These special missions are trying."

Fought by Filipinos and Americans of the "underground," the guerrilla war spread through the Philippines in the winter of 1943-44 like a brush fire eating through a forest. Landing arms, equipment and secret agents on isolated beaches, U.S. submarines supplied the guerrilla forces with the wherewithal for war. Information brought out by these secret mission submarines implemented and influenced invasion operations when the drive to retake the Philippines was finally launched.

Loss of Cisco

The Japanese High Command did not remain impervious to the increasing submarine activity in Philippine waters and the adjacent South China Sea. Guerrilla endeavors and shipping losses in these areas were countered by tightened coastal patrols and anti-submarine reinforcements.

On September 28, patrolling Japanese aircraft spotted a shimmering oil slick in the Sulu Sea, due west of Mindanao. Submarine with leaking fuel tanks! The planes flashed the word to A/S surface craft and roared down on the attack.

By this it would seem that the Japanese A/S attack was persistent and deadly. Surface vessels joined the planes in the bombing, and the spot where the submarine lay was watched for twelve days. So was lost the USS CISCO and all hands, under Lieutenant Commander J. W. Coe.

There is little doubt about the submarine's identity. Venturing out on her first war patrol, CISCO had headed west from Port Darwin, Australia, in September 1943. Nothing was heard of CISCO after she left Port Darwin. But on September 28, the day of the Japanese onslaught on the oil-leaking submarine in the Sulu Sea, CISCO was due to be covering that lap of her westward journey. No other United States or Allied submarine was scheduled in those waters at that time.

In the submarine forces, "Red" Coe had made a name for himself as one of the ablest and keenest submarine commanders. He personified the type of leader who held the line when the going was worst in the undersea war. A submarine could always be replaced. Ace skipper and crack crew—these were personnel losses far more costly than the material.

Depth-charging of Puffer

PUFFER came back from the East Indies-Philippines front in late October with a depth-charging story long to be remembered in the Submarine Service. Even in the formal language of a naval report the narrative packs a dramatic punch, and the episode remains a notable example of Japanese attack and submarine reaction in the A/S war. Between the

lines one sees a vivid picture of a submersible under fire—
the doings within the pressure hull—the reflexes of assailed
machines and men. Perhaps the most extraordinary feature of
the detailed experience is the psychological footnote at its
conclusion. Here is the story:

On October 9, 1943, PUFFER, under Lieutenant Commander M. J. Jensen, was patrolling the northern waters of Makassar Straits. Mid-morning she was on the track of a large
Japanese merchant ship. At 1110 she hit the merchantman
with two torpedoes. The target stopped dead in the water
and assumed a list, but refused to sink. Thereupon, at 1119
Jensen fired two well-intended torpedoes from the stern tubes.
One of these prematured. The other torpedo missed or was a
dud. So Jensen maneuvered for another attack.

The merchantman's escort, a CHIDORI-class torpedo boat,
had been seen earlier in the morning, but was at this time
nowhere in the offing. Left to defend herself, the damaged
merchant ship opened fire on the submarine, blazing away
with small-caliber guns.

Then, at 1125 three distant depth charges were heard by
PUFFER'S sound operator, and a few minutes later there was
"pinging" and Sound reported fast screws approaching. Jensen decided to clear the vicinity. He still hoped to finish off
the merchantman, however, so he did not order deep submergence. Then the attack came, unexpected as a rain of
lightning bolts.

At 1145 six depth charges exploded near the submarine.
During this barrage, the conning-tower hatch and the conning-tower door lifted off their seats and reseated, admitting
a shower of water as they did so. A plug in a sea-valve cast-
ing in the after torpedo room was loosened, and water
spurted from this leak, jetting from under the plug in a flat
stream the size of a knife blade. The submariners were afraid
to tighten the plug, for if it were broken instead of only
loose, any attempted repairs would worsen the fracture.

PUFFER'S rudder and the stern planes had apparently suffered damage, for their operation was noisy and the motors
appeared to be overloaded. Gaskets were found blown out of
the main engine air-induction valve and the ventilation supply valves. Considerable miscellaneous and minor damage
was reported. PUFFER went deep.

Ten minutes later another depth charge slammed near-by.
Fifteen minutes after that, four depth charges went off
overhead, staggered in depth. It was evident the enemy was
able to follow the submarine. The slow venting of the main
induction and air supply trunk, as they flooded past the ruptured gaskets, may have been leaving a trail of air bubbles.

Or there might have been oil leaks. The current interfered with evasive maneuvers (when PUFFER'S ordeal was finally over, she surfaced in the same place where she submerged—all her underwater running had been just enough to overcome the racing current).

Practically all of the damage done to PUFFER was inflicted during the first attack. Thereafter she remained at a deep submergence, pinned down by the obdurate tenacity of the CHIDORI "pinger." The enemy's depth charges were not set deep enough to crush the submarine with their explosions. But the torpedo boat was not to be easily eluded. After dropping a string of charges, she would sidle off, only to return an hour or two later to make another try. Her perseverance and the ease with which she located the submarine were most unnerving.

PUFFER'S crew had difficulty with her depth control. The leak in the after torpedo room continually added to the weight aft, and the trim pump was unable to pick up a suction on the after torpedo-room bilges. Gradually the submarine worked her way deeper until the control room was at an alarming depth level. There was a 12° angle on the boat when the motors moved her at slow speed. Few submarines had ever gone so deep—and the fact provided a mental hazard hard to overcome.

Meantime, the air conditioning was stopped to conserve power and prevent noise. A bucket brigade was formed to control the bilge water and forestall the grounding out of the electrical motors. After PUFFER had been submerged about 12 hours, CO_2 absorbent and oxygen were used. The specific gravity of the battery electrolyte went so low it could no longer be read on the hydrometer.

PUFFER had not been severely damaged. She had no insoluble problem of ship handling. Jensen's evasion maneuvers were conventional and correct. The anti-submarine attack made upon her was unique only in the stubborn perseverance with which it was conducted and the consistency with which the enemy tracked PUFFER and depth-charged her position. The submarine had been submerged since 0525, and it was late in the day when a second anti-submarine vessel joined the first at 1820. These enemies hammered at PUFFER until well after midnight. The last depth charges were dropped at 0115 on the morning of October 10, but the Japs remained over PUFFER making "dry runs" until 1225 that day. Thirty-one hours after PUFFER first submerged, and more than 25 hours after her attack on the merchantman, the enemy finally left, and the counter-attack was over.

After Sound reported "pinging" had stopped, Jensen de-

cided to remain at deep submergence until after nightfall.
PUFFER was in difficult trim, and an immediate attempt to
rise to periscope depth might have ended in loss of control.
Safety tanks, negative, auxiliary tank, and after trim had
been blown dry and had pressure in them. There was a 12-
inch pressure in the boat already, which practically prevented
the venting of these tanks into the boat. The submariners
endured until 1910 when PUFFER surfaced direct from deep
submergence into bright moonlight, almost 31 hours after
diving. She surfaced with a sharp port list, caused by the
free water and the flooded induction lines, and it was nearly
an hour before the crew could bring her to an even keel.
Contact with an enemy patrol was made about 15 minutes
after surfacing. Jensen maneuvered to evade, and PUFFER
was not attacked. At 0450 on the morning of October 11,
she was able to make a trim dive, and no serious leaks were
found. Jensen held her down all that day to rest the crew
and then headed PUFFER for home.

The mechanical features of PUFFER's experience—what
happened to her machinery, and the measures taken to keep
her going—these were not the chief items of interest in her
report. Submarines had endured worse "goings over," suffered
more damage, gone perhaps as deep. What was of paramount
concern to the Force Command was the reaction of PUFFER's
personnel—how the submariners stood up under it, how
they behaved, what they were thinking about during the
long ordeal. New machines and new techniques would enter
submarining in the next decade. But the mechanics of the
human mind vary little with the passing of generations—men
reacted to stresses and strains yesterday much as they will
tomorrow. So the conduct of PUFFER's crew was carefully
studied for clues in behaviorism.

The mental can never be divorced from the physical, and
the reactions of PUFFER's crew can be seen as intimately
related to the submarine's condition—particularly its air conditioning. When that was shut off, the heat became insuffer-
able. Temperature of 125° F. was reported in the maneuvering room. The forward torpedo room was suffocatingly
hot. The after torpedo room and the engine room were the
coolest compartments in the submarine, but the almost glu-
tinous humidity was higher in the cooler rooms than in the
hot spots, and the steam-room atmosphere was like a drug.
Decks and bulkheads became clammy with condensed moisture. The men gasped for breath and slipped on the greasy
decks.

Although the temperature in the after torpedo room was
probably well over 100° F., men going from the maneuver-

ing room reported that they shivered and shook as with a chill. The human body possesses no mechanism for reducing its temperature below ambient wet-bulb temperature. It was therefore probable that in such places as PUFFER'S maneuvering room the men developed a high fever. While there were no reports of delirium, the sudden chill indicated that such fever did exist.

Sweating like boxers, the submariners thirsted for cool drinks. The men were constantly drinking, vomiting, drinking again. Profuse sweating and inability to keep down liquids produced many cases of severe dehydration. No one in the submarine cared to eat anything.

The bucket brigade, fighting the mounting water in the motor room bilges, struggled against extreme fatigue. Hourly the air in the submarine worsened. Despite the use of CO_2 absorbent and oxygen, the atmosphere was utterly foul toward the end of the dive. Breathing was sluggish and resultant headache was severe. An officer making the rounds from control room to after torpedo room had to stop and rest several times on the journey. He found a number of the men in a state of physical collapse. From the stupor in which they sank, it became impossible to rouse them to go on watch. As the hours wore on, stations were manned by volunteers. Some of the crew were past the stage of caring what happened.

Both officers and men stated that their first mental reaction to the enemy attack was anger. They were infuriated at everything and anything. They were particularly angry at themselves for having allowed themselves to be caught in such a predicament. Anyone compelled to take a beating without being able to fight back finds it one of the world's hardest punishments to endure, and the submariners who stood it for 31 hours would not soon forget the experience.

The suspense proved the hardest thing to bear. PUFFER'S officers stated that because of this fact, the ordeal was harder on the men than on the officers. When on watch, the officers were in the conning tower or control room. At such times they knew the proximity of the enemy, the state of the battery, what was being done to evade. Many of the men, however, not engaged in some useful task, could only sit and think, and imaginations were fed by lack of information. To remedy this, the officers occasionally went through the boat and described what was happening overhead. Use of the public-address system proved annoying, as the feeling existed that its noise might disclose the location of the submarine. The conning-tower telephone talker passed information to the other talkers on the fire control telephone circuits.

PUFFER'S crew recorded a word of solid advice for those who might have to go through a similar experience: "Find something to do, and keep busy." Men who were idle suffered more from the imprisonment. Then to hear the approaching vessel, the "pinging" of her echo-ranging as she deliberately and methodically probed for the submarine, followed by the rush of racing screws and the thunderous detonation of a depth-charge salvo—this repetitious build-up and climax, worsened by anticipation, resulted in the hardest sort of nerve strain.

None of the officers reported any difficulty in reaching decisions, but they pointed out that no involved or rapid-fire calculations were called for. The major issue was whether or not to surface and fight it out with the gun—a desperate resort when the opponent was a heavily armed CHIDORI. Another question concerned the choice between speeding up the motors for evasive action, or conserving the remaining battery and waiting where they were until dark. In this connection, one of the enlisted men reported that he was asked to vote for or against an immediate rise to the surface. He expressed himself as willing to go along either way, but he refused to commit himself one way or the other. Apparently few of PUFFER'S company advocated a gun action in daylight. The submarine carried a 3-incher. But a submarine in PUFFER'S situation could not well have risked a gun duel with a CHIDORI.

As time went by, dragging leaden minutes into endless hours, as the air fouled into a sewerish gas, as men's sweating bodies weakened in the enervating heat, morale wilted, and in some cases expired. One man suggested flooding everything and getting it over quickly with mass suicide. Another, who had received a minor but most painful injury, appeared incapable of understanding what went on about him. Toward the end of the long submergence, officers as well as men apparently reached the conclusion that they would never come out of it alive. The ease with which the enemy repeatedly located the submarine forced them to this depressing conclusion. Pessimism was climaxed when, after remaining at deep submergence for many hours, all hands were ordered to put on life jackets.

In the engine room a man broke out of his locker three cans of pineapple juice and passed them around. It seemed no longer necessary to save anything "for when things got worse." Everyone questioned had a vivid recollection of the tremendous psychological blow that was dealt by the order to don life jackets. The order was given to provide against a sudden contingency which might force PUFFER to the surface.

But the adverse reaction in PUFFER'S case suggested that a crew should be prepared for such a seemingly drastic eventuality before the order is given. All critics of PUFFER'S report pointed out that the mental state of a submarine's crew is the determining factor in a life-or-death issue under the sea. Deterioration of crew morale can be as disastrous as damage to the submarine's machinery. For this reason, critics considered it a mistake to shut down PUFFER'S air conditioning. A submarine crew in a tight situation is exceedingly allergic to noise—a squeaky pair of sandals was recalled by one of PUFFER'S crew. Nevertheless, the crew would have accepted the noise of the air-conditioning machine and ventilation blowers in preference to the stupifying heat and humidity.

Despite the fact that there were few duties to perform, PUFFER'S company got little sleep. An officer stated that in four hours off watch he napped for about 15 minutes. He recalled this with bitterness because the nap was broken by the order to don life jackets. The steaming, hothouse atmosphere was at once a soporific and a narcotic. Huddled around anything that seemed cool—an uninsulated portion of the hull, or an exposed circulation water pipe—the submariners panted, muttered and stirred as though in the grip of somnambulistic nightmare.

After the submarine surfaced and was out of danger, its crew recovered physically with great rapidity. Within 24 hours, all were physically normal. But for days thereafter, there was evidence of mental strain.

PUFFER'S officers arrived at a number of conclusions, and these were noted by the Force Command. When a submarine had gone through such an experience, its crew should be broken up. The sharing of PUFFER'S ordeal welded her men together in a fraternal, almost mystic bond, and no newcomer was able to penetrate the inner circle. Men who subsequently made several successful patrols on PUFFER were still "outsiders"—not members of the gang. They hadn't been through THE depth-charging.

Another observation was recorded for submariners of the future: "Be slow to form an estimate of a man's value before you have seen him under stress." Most of the men who were on their feet, working to save themselves and the ship when PUFFER'S long dive was over, were not the previous "leaders" of the crew. Those who lasted out were of a more phlegmatic disposition—the ones who didn't bother too much when things were running smoothly.

PUFFER'S report left for the submarine force this curtain

line: *"The worriers and the hurriers all crapped out, leaving the plodders to bring home the ship."*

Loss of Capelin

CAPELIN was the last submarine to be lost to the Southwest Pacific Force in 1943.

One of the newcomers to the Pacific, CAPELIN had set out on October 31 to conduct her first war patrol. She was captained by Commander E. E. Marshall. On November 11 she sank the 3,127-ton Japanese freighter KUNITAMA MARU. Five days later she returned to Port Darwin with a defective conning-tower hatch mechanism, troublesome bow planes and a bad radar tube.

Repairs at Darwin were quickly made—Commander Marshall was satisfied that the submarine was in fighting trim—and CAPELIN once more stood seaward.

Nothing was heard from CAPELIN after her belated leavetaking of Darwin.

BONEFISH reported sighting a U.S. submarine on December 2, just north of the equator in waters assigned to CAPELIN on that date. But all attempts to contact her by radio failed. The ocean closed over her. Somewhere she went down with all hands.

Chapter 21

Central Pacific Offensive

☆ ☆ ☆

Operation Galvanic

The young men with fur on their chins and chests could feel a bristling in the air. Coming back from patrol, they could scent it in the atmosphere. Things were looking up at Pearl Harbor.

"I tell you, Joe, these fast carrier task forces are going places. What with a new YORKTOWN and this ESSEX and LEXINGTON—"

"Telling me? Listen, sailor, I got the word this morning from a buddy at the U.S.O. He—"

"Scuttlebutt! But Nimitz has got something cooking. This big stuff isn't here for nothing."

The big warships were gathering, and the submariners were glad to see it. And if the above dialogue is fictional, the fact that Nimitz had something on the fire in the autumn of 1943 is history. While Halsey's Third Fleet was starting the Upper Solomons campaign, Admiral Nimitz was completing plans for "Operation Galvanic"—the drive to take the Gilberts.

Ten submarines cooperated with the carrier task forces and amphibious landing forces in "Operation Galvanic. Long before D-Day submarines reconnoitered the target islands, investigated the fortifications, studied the approaches and hit at the Japanese traffic. Two months in advance of D-Day, NAUTILUS was in the Gilberts at Apamama on a mission intimately connected with the projected offensive. Details of this drama-packed Apamama mission will presently be recounted.

As seen on the chart the Gilbert Islands (Makin, the Tarawa Group and Apamama) lie like a cluster of fruit on the end of a laden branch. Other clusters are the near-by Marshalls and Carolines, and the branch—conceive it as composed of sea lanes—comes down from the Marianas in the northwest.

Key islands of the enemy's Central Pacific transport system, the Marianas (Guam and Saipan) were the distributing point for war supplies freighted down from Japan and destined for the Mandate outposts. From Saipan and Guam the cargoes followed the southeast sea lanes to the Carolines, Marshalls and Gilberts.

Here, then, in the Central Pacific, as in the South and Southwest Pacific, the submarines on patrol, fighting the war of attrition, supported fleet operations by intercepting Japanese convoys, damaging or sinking Japanese troop and cargo transports and otherwise disrupting and destroying Japanese shipping. While it is impossible to estimate the tonnage which left the Marianas for the Gilberts in the spring, summer and autumn of 1943, it is certain that a considerable share of the shipping sent southeast from Saipan and Guam was tagged for delivery to Makin or Tarawa. After the Makin raid, the Japs made a determined effort to reinforce the Gilberts (an effort that showed in the Tarawa defense) and the guns and men came by way of the routes described. It can therefore be assumed that many of the ships sunk by U.S. submarines patrolling off the Marianas, Carolines and Marshalls in the first nine months of 1943 carried cargoes and troops for Tarawa and Makin. In this respect the attrition war fought by SubPac contributed to the ultimate success of "Operation Galvanic." Over the sunken skeletons of dead supply ships the American invasion forces drove to the Gilbert beachheads.

Pre-Galvanic Attrition War

Unlike the South and Southwest Pacific, thickly strewn with islands and stepping-stone archipelagoes, the Central Pacific has far horizons and endless reaches of latitude and longitude uninterrupted by any landfall. Island groups are as few and far between as oases in the Sahara. Shipping lanes, like caravan lanes, follow established navigational routes—in peacetime. In wartime, with oceans of latitude for evasive routing, a convoy may travel in as many roundabout directions as there are points on the compass. This open-sea shipping presents the hunting submarine with a problem not unlike the Touareg Saharan raider's. The raider may roam the great open spaces for days, and then miss his quarry over the next dune. The Touareg, therefore, lies in wait near a terminal oasis. So it is with the hunting submarine.

The vast expanses of the Central Pacific were not patrolled in haphazard, hit-or-miss fashion. There was the Empire blockade and the Truk blockade—submarine concentrations on shipping focal points. Around the Pelews, the Marianas, the Marshalls and Gilberts the SubPac patrols were blocked out as part of a carefully designed pattern. Seven patrol areas boxed in the Marshalls and Gilberts. The waters off Saipan and Guam were similarly covered. Pacific Fleet submarines traveled in these designated areas with much the same regularity as planets in their orbits.

"Operation Galvanic" struck at the Gilberts on November 21st. From the previous spring to that date, SubPac submarines operating in the Central Pacific between the 10° and 24° parallels, in an oceanic belt which embraced the Marianas and northern Marshalls, waylaid, sank or damaged dozens of Japanese merchant ships.

These spring-to-December attrition sinkings deprived the enemy in the Gilberts of thousands of rounds of ammunition, thousands of pounds of food, thousands of items of war gear. At the easternmost end of the Central Pacific transportation vine, the Gilbert Islands were "out on a branch." Tarawa proved thorny and poisonous. But the vine in this area, even as in the Solomons, had been blighted by the fire of submarine torpedoes. Tarawa's fall was assured.

Preliminary Operations (Submarine Lifeguarding)

In August, 1943, the new Pacific Fleet aircraft carriers and light carriers with their supporting cruisers and destroyers were organized into Task Force Fifteen, under Rear Admiral Charles A. Pownall. This fast carrier task force (nucleus of what later became Task Force Fifty-eight) was to pull the trigger of "Operation Galvanic." But by way of preparatory overtures, it was to conduct a series of hit-and-run raids.

In planning these raids, Admiral Pownall considered the problem of rescuing airmen who might be downed at sea. Could ComSubPac furnish a submarine to be stationed near each target island for the purpose of rescuing downed airmen? Admiral Lockwood not only could, but did.

As a result of Admiral Pownall's requests, SNOOK (Lieutenant Commander C. O. Triebel) was on station off Marcus Island when the planes of Task Force Fifteen roared out of the blue on September 1st. There was no need for submarine rescue work, as American losses were unusually light.

STEELHEAD (Lieutenant Commander D. L. Whelchel) was

on duty off Tarawa on the 20th when Navy planes dropped bombs on this Gilbert Island base. Again there was no occasion for submarine rescue work.

The first successful submarine lifeguard mission was performed during the strike on Wake, made October 6-7 by Task Force Fourteen, under Rear Admiral A. E. Montgomery. This strike, a combined aircraft-cruiser bombardment, hit the island with hurricane fury. While the battle was at its height, the submarine assigned to lifeguard duty in the area accomplished several daring rescues. She was SKATE, under the captaincy of veteran Commander E. B. McKinney.

SKATE's lifeguard patrol did not begin happily. At dawn on October 6, the day of the first strike, she was savagely strafed by an enemy plane. In this action, Lieutenant (jg) W. E. Maxon was seriously wounded. His wounds did not appear fatal, however, and SKATE continued her patrol.

At 0545 on the morning of October 7, SKATE sighted several squadrons of American planes which were searching for the target island. Signals were exchanged, and the dive bombers were informed as to Wake's direction.

On the search for downed aviators, McKinney moved the submarine on a line about six miles offshore. At 1043 several heavy shells landed in the sea close by, and McKinney ordered SKATE under. When the submarine again surfaced at 1128, she received the word that three airmen were down.

McKinney trimmed down and headed SKATE shoreward in the direction given. The rescue party—Ensign Francis Kay; William A. Shelton, Gunner's Mate 3; and Arthur G. Smith, Torpedoman's Mate 3—crouched on SKATE's bow as the submarine moved in. Japs on the beach opened fire, and shells began to drop around SKATE, but the aviators were there in the water and the submarine lifeguard swam resolutely to the rescue.

Lieutenant H. J. Kicker was plucked from a rubber boat. A few minutes later, SKATE was alongside an aviator who was struggling in the water. As the swimmer appeared exhausted, Torpedoman's Mate Smith swam to him with a life ring. The rescued airman was Ensign M. H. Tyler.

Search for a third airman off Peacock Point was interrupted by an attacking Jap dive bomber. A bomb shook the submarine as she dived, smashing her searchlight and damaging the bow-buoyancy vent-operating mechanism. Repairs were quickly made, and SKATE surfaced after eluding the planes.

Meantime Lieutenant Maxon's condition had worsened. This casualty presented ComSubPac with a difficult question for decision. When Maxon's condition was first reported,

ComSubPac requested that a Task Force Fourteen destroyer rendezvous with SKATE and take off the wounded officer. SKATE was directed to attempt this rendezvous.

On the afternoon of October 7 the air strike was over. Unable to rendezvous with the destroyer, McKinney headed SKATE for Midway at top speed as directed. Maxon was now in a most critical condition, and all hands were pulling to save his life.

But the ruthless urgency of war intervened. As SKATE was stepping out for Midway, a message came in from Admiral Montgomery—nine aviators were adrift on life-rafts in the vicinity of Wake. The decision was up to ComSubPac who had to weigh the prospects of Maxon's chances for life against the equally slim prospect of locating nine airmen adrift in the open sea. The decision was made, and SKATE was ordered to return to Wake and hunt for the nine until all chances of rescue were exhausted.

On the morning of October 8, Lieutenant Maxon succumbed to his wounds—two days before SKATE could have reached Midway, had she continued the homeward race at top speed. On October 9, off Wake, SKATE picked up another aviator and three more were recovered the next day, to bring the total to six aviators rescued.

After this successful rescue effort, the commanding officer of LEXINGTON radioed to SKATE: "*Anything on LEXINGTON is yours for the asking. If it is too big to carry away, we will cut it up in small parts.*"

From that time until V-J Day no important carrier strike was made without one or more submarines on the scene of action as lifeguards.

Submarine Photographic Reconnaissance (Nautilus with a Candid Camera)

In planning for the Gilbert Islands campaign, Rear Admiral R. K. Turner, who was in command of Amphibious Forces, requested photographic reconnaissance of Makin, Tarawa and Apamama by submarine. Admiral Nimitz approved the request, and Admiral Lockwood picked NAUTILUS as the submarine to do the job.

Periscope photography had been under consideration before the war, and steps had since been taken to obtain suitable cameras and adapt them for periscope use. But little experimental work in reconnaissance photography had been done. Lieutenant Commander Parks, pioneering one of the first reconnaissance missions, had taken photographs of enemy shorelines. Other captains had photographed sinkings with notable success. Periscope cameras had been designed primarily for the photographing of enemy ships and action scenes.

However, reconnaissance photographs must contain exact and minute detail if they are to prove of any value for intelligence purposes. The picture, taken from a range of several thousand yards, must be clear enough to reveal the presence or absence of machine-gun positions, artillery, or other defense installations on enemy beachheads. Camouflage could not fool a sharp-eyed camera. But the techniques of periscope photographic reconnaissance were wartime developments. A major portion of the credit for their successful development goes to NAUTILUS—the first submarine to conduct a full-fledged photo reconnaissance mission.

In selecting her for the task, Admiral Lockwood made a fortunate choice. Her captain at this time, Commander W. D. Irvin, was unusually painstaking in everything he undertook. Moreover, unknown to ComSubPac when the choice was made, her executive officer, Lieutenant Commander R. B. Lynch, was a camera enthusiast, experienced in the art of photography.

At Pearl Harbor Submarine Base, brackets for the mounting of the camera on the periscope were built. The necessary photographic supplies were taken aboard NAUTILUS, and an enlisted rated photographer was assigned to the submarine for temporary duty. (The photographer could have used six hands, and on all subsequent photo reconnaissance missions two enlisted photographers were aboard.) The lower sound room was fitted up to be used as a darkroom and photographic laboratory for processing the exposed film. Processing on board was necessary in order to permit the retaking of any pictures which did not turn out satisfactorily. Thus equipped, on September 16, 1943, NAUTILUS departed on her mission.

Brady, setting out with his little black wagon to photograph the battlefields of the Civil War, was no more of a novice than Irvin, setting out with NAUTILUS to photograph the beachheads of Makin, Tarawa and Apamama. In either case the venture was dangerous, the camera work untried and the ultimate outcome uncertain.

NAUTILUS was equipped with several cameras. The Eastman Medalist was standard issue, and NAUTILUS also carried a National Graflex, Series II, and an "Eastman 35" which was specially designed for periscope photography. The Medalist camera was considered the finest in the field, but it lacked a reflex viewfinder. The "Eastman 35" and the Graflex had this feature, but it was soon apparent that all of these cameras were inadequate for the job at hand.

The submarine periscope embodied a number of peculiarities which made periscope photography difficult. When the periscope was raised, vibrations within the submarine or the movement of the periscope through the water caused the periscope's head to vibrate. These vibrations, magnified as the light strikes the lenses and passes down the tube, created a blurred photograph unless high-speed camera shutters were used. However, the efficiency of light transmission through the periscope was something like 35% in high power, and this "dim view" necessitated low shutter-speeds.

Lacking a viewer, the Medalist camera proved impractical. The "Eastman 35" produced too small a picture. The Graflex, which caught the first and one of the finest submarine combat pictures of the war, was not suitable for the present operation. Fortunately for the NAUTILUS mission, Lieutenant Commander Lynch happened to have his own camera aboard.

This camera, a Primarflex, had a single-lens reflex viewfinder and a focal-plane shutter which was ideal for the work in prospect (a focal-plane shutter stops action better than a between-lens shutter). Lynch's Primarflex was pressed into service, and NAUTILUS' camera problem was over. In fact, the Primarflex solved the periscope photography problem for the U.S. Submarine Force. All subsequent submarine photo reconnaissance missions were performed with this type of camera. Ironically enough, it was of German manufacture. It could not be imported for love or money, but the Bureau of Aeronautics (in charge of all matters pertaining to photography in the Navy) could and did advertise for the camera in various photographic trade journals. These unusual "want ads" netted ten Primarflex cameras. Stored at PRISIC (Photographic Reconnaissance and Interpretation Section, Intelligence Center) the second-hand cameras were eventually issued to the submarines sent out on photo reconnaissance missions. Thus a camera made in Germany contributed to the downfall of Japan.

The tactical problems which had to be solved by NAUTILUS were difficult. Reefs around the atolls prevented camera work at short ranges, and the danger of detection by enemy lookouts or sentries limited the raising of the periscope head to a height of about six feet. A mental hazard was introduced by the possibility of minefields along the coastline. But these were perils incident to any submarine reconnaissance mission off an enemy base.

Procedure on this first photographic reconnaissance mission set the pattern for those that followed. A whole roll of 12 pictures was taken at each periscope exposure. The field being eight degrees in high power, the periscope was rotated about four degrees after each camera shot to give a picture overlap of three or four degrees. Before the exposure of each roll of film, the position of the submarine was accurately fixed by landmarks. This position was marked on the chart, and a notation of the number of film roll exposed in that position was made. Also vectors were drawn to show the included angle covered by the film roll. Following the exposure of each roll, the submarine moved down the coast a short distance to repeat the process. An overlap of about fifty per cent on each successive roll insured against leaving "holidays."

After the film was developed, each photo was mounted so as to match with the next. In this manner, a continuous panorama of the coastline was obtained.

The work of NAUTILUS on this Gilbert Islands mission did more than solve the problems of technique and procedure. It also established the value of this type of reconnaissance. As a consequence of the standards set by Irvin and crew, every amphibious operation in the Pacific thereafter was preceded by submarine photographic reconnaissance.

Submarine Support of Fleet Operations (Galvanic Campaign)

For "Operation Galvanic" the United States assembled the largest armada yet seen in the Pacific. The naval force totaled 118 warships (including 13 battleships and 19 car-

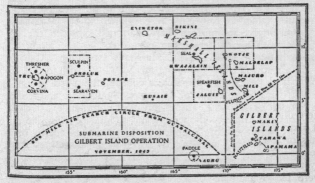

SUBMARINE DISPOSITION
GILBERT ISLAND OPERATION
NOVEMBER, 1943

riers of various types) plus a fleet of transports, supply ships and auxiliaries. Vice Admiral R. A. Spruance, recently appointed Commander of the Fifth Fleet, was in over-all command of the armada.

Capture of Tarawa was the major objective, with Makin

and Apamama as secondary objectives. Unfortunately the strength of Tarawa, the central stronghold, was under estimated, as was that of Makin in the north.

Ten submarines cooperated with the carrier task force and the amphibious landing force in "Operation Galvanic." These submarines were THRESHER, APOGON, CORVINA, SCULPIN and SEARAVEN (stationed in the Carolines); SEAL, SPEARFISH and PLUNGER (in the Marshalls); PADDLE (stationed off Nauru); and NAUTILUS (operating in the Gilberts).

Controlling factors during this operation were weather conditions for the carrier strikes and surf conditions on the beach at Tarawa on D-Day. Weather in the Pacific moves from west to east. There were no Allied weather stations which could supply the information required. The submarine forces took over this task.

PADDLE (Commander R. H. Rice) was assigned an enlisted aerologist and furnished with weather observing instruments and pibal balloons for taking upper air soundings. She took station to the north of Nauru Island (about 300 miles west of Tarawa) where, each sunset from D—5 day until D+4 day, she sent a weather report which included wind direction and velocities of the upper air.

The tactical disposition of submarines supporting "Galvanic" was based on two general assumptions. The first: Any enemy naval interference with the landing would probably emanate from Truk. The second: Enemy forces would choose a northerly route to avoid detection by land-based search planes from Guadalcanal, and would probably fuel en route, either at Eniwetok or Kwajalein in the Marshalls.

Accordingly, submarines were stationed close to the entrances of Truk to detect any enemy sortie, and along the routes between Truk and the Marshalls (see map). Captain J. P. Cromwell was embarked in SCULPIN, with orders to form, if so directed by dispatch, a coordinated patrol group— a wolf-pack—consisting of SCULPIN, SEARAVEN, and either SPEARFISH or APOGON. The enemy fleet commanders decided to avoid the Gilberts altogether, and submarine offensive operations were therefore confined to the sinking of enemy merchantmen bringing supplies to Truk. Two submarines were lost during this operation, and NAUTILUS had a narrow escape.

Nautilus at Apamama

Commander Irvin's NAUTILUS was handed a complicated set of instructions in connection with the amphibious detail of "Operation Galvanic." NAUTILUS' primary mission was to transport to Apamama and put ashore a Marine detachment —eight officers and 70 men of the Amphibious Reconnaissance Company, Fifth Amphibious Corps. This was to be accomplished while Tarawa and Makin were under attack.

In conjunction with this transport operation, NAUTILUS had several secondary missions.

A sea-bag full of orders—but submariners were becoming inured to multiple operations. NAUTILUS had carried Marines to the Gilberts before. She had already reconnoitered Apamama with a candid camera. Lifeguard duty and surf observation were relatively easy assignments compared with the business of transporting and landing troops. However, to engage in all these tasks, she would have to look lively and shake a leg.

NAUTILUS left Pearl Harbor on the morning of November 8 with the Marines. Eight days later she was in the vicinity of the Gilberts, and she received a message that she might expect to find Japanese troops on Apamama. Two days later (November 18) she was on lifeguard patrol off Tarawa. The sky roared. Planes from Admiral Pownall's carriers raced in from the horizon to blast Tarawa with load after load of bombs. All that day and the next the aerial bombardment continued. NAUTILUS maintained a sharp lookout, but no downed aviators were sighted.

At sundown of the 19th (the eve of the amphibious landings) Irvin moved his big submarine shoreward to observe surf conditions, as directed. Night closed in, and with it a horde of surface ships converging on Tarawa from all directions.

The commander of the assault force had been previously asked to prescribe the exact route for NAUTILUS to follow at this time. The night was as black as an old-time kitchen range—Tarawa glowing like a red-hot stove lid in the dark —and flitting silhouettes were everywhere. Heading for her next objective, Apamama, NAUTILUS followed the specified route with pencil-line exactitude.

At 2154 Irvin was maneuvering NAUTILUS to clear a reef. Radar contact was made with the warship approaching at a businesslike 25 knots. The battery was low, the air supply was low, the reef was too near for comfort and submergence seemed the worse of two evils. Unlikely the oncoming vessel was a Jap, although its approach was decidedly belligerent. Irvin readied the recognition signals. Then—2159. A blaze of gunfire from the warship. From the submarine the green flare of the recognition comet. Too late —the salvo landed. Smash! NAUTILUS was hit by a 5-inch shell from the Destroyer USS RINGOLD.

The projectile struck the conning tower, ripping into the superstructure. Perfect fire control and perfect marksmanship! The projectile failed to explode. Not so perfect ordnance!

But this imperfection—one fluke in a thousand—saved NAUTILUS. Sparks spurted from the conning-tower bilges, but there was no blast and resulting fire. The concussion caused damage, however. And another salvo was heard as the submarine went deep. One close explosion ruptured a water line to the port main motor cooling system and started leaks in the bilges. Water streamed in torrents down the conning-tower hatch, the gyro went out of commission, the main induction flooded and only fast and efficient damage control prevented serious trouble.

As it was, it was serious enough. Irvin decided to work the submarine slowly southward, making the most of a favorable current. The unexploded projectile was too lucky for any further favors from the gods, and everyone aboard, including the Marines under Captain J. L. Jones, USMCR, was doing some industrious sweating. To quote Commander Irvin's log:

"We felt time was running out fast. . . . The 78 Marines we had aboard were stoic but they were unanimous in the attitude that they would much prefer a rubber boat on a very hostile beach to their present predicament."

By early morning of November 20, NAUTILUS was on the surface and running for Apamama. She reached her destination that afternoon. Convinced that torpedo rooms on assailed submarines were not as comfortable as foxholes, the Marines went ashore with a will.

NAUTILUS remained at Apamama that night and for the next several days, during which time she took off two wounded men and supported the landed company with a shore bombardment of enemy positions. With the occupation of Apamama accomplished, the submarine headed back for Pearl Harbor—mission successfully completed.

In the Officers' Club of the Submarine Base, Pearl Harbor, there was on display an unexploded 5-inch shell. Those best acquainted with this eccentric projectile tipped their hats each time they passed it. As one would to an acquaintance—but not exactly a friend.

Loss of Corvina

To participate in the Gilbert Islands campaign, CORVINA (Commander R. S. Rooney) left Pearl Harbor on November 4 to take her station directly south of Truk. Her mission was to intercept and attack any enemy naval force which might sortie and attempt to rush to the defense of the Gilberts. This was CORVINA'S maiden patrol.

On November 30, after the surface force operations in the Gilberts had been completed, CORVINA was transferred to the Task Force Seventy-two (Brisbane) Command. Dispatches to this effect were radioed to the submarine on two successive nights. There was no acknowledgment by CORVINA.

On December 23, CORVINA was officially announced as lost with all hands.

According to Japanese records, one of their I-boats encountered an American submarine directly south of Truk on November 16. Three torpedoes were fired at the American, and two hit, "causing a great explosion sound." There was a swirl of water, and the submarine was gone. CORVINA'S war patrol was ended. So far as is determinable, she was the only United States submarine sunk by a Japanese submarine during the war.

Loss of Sculpin—Captain John P. Cromwell

The destruction of SCULPIN, the second submarine lost during "Operation Galvanic," was soon suspected by the Force Command, although details were not known until her survivors were recovered from the Japanese prison camps. Then it was discovered that SCULPIN'S loss had a tragic aftermath—an epilogue which only Fate could write as the conclusion for a chain of events.

The day following CORVINA'S departure, SCULPIN (Commander Fred Connaway) headed out of Pearl Harbor. After "topping off" with fuel, she left Johnston Island on November 7. She replied to no radio transmissions thereafter.

SCULPIN'S patrol station was directly north of Truk—her mission to intercept and attack any Japanese force which sortied from Truk's northern gateway during the Gilbert Islands campaign.

On the possibility of tactical advantage, a plan had been devised whereby three of the submarines stationed in the Carolines and Marshalls could combine forces as a wolf-pack and deliver a coordinated attack on the enemy. Aboard SCULPIN was Captain John P. Cromwell who was to take charge of the coordinated attack group if the wolf-pack were formed.

The group was to consist of SCULPIN, SEARAVEN and APOGON. On the night of November 29, ComSubPac ordered its formation.

Forty hours later (and no word from SCULPIN) ComSub-Pac sent new orders, directing SCULPIN to proceed to Eniwe-tok and observe enemy shipping in the Marshalls. These and other orders for SCULPIN were transmitted during the next several days. From the submarine—silence. On December 30, SCULPIN was announced as presumably lost.

After the war her survivors told the story. On the night of November 18, she made radar contact with a fast enemy convoy, and her commander directed an end-around at full power. Closing in at dawn on the attack, the submarine was detected and the convoy zigged toward her, forcing her deep.

About an hour later, surfacing to start another end-around, she was sighted by a rear-guard destroyer. She made a quick dive and was depth-charged.

SCULPIN suffered only minor damage during this barrage. But SCULPIN broached. She went under immediately, but the enemy had sighted her, and the attack was at once resumed.

About noon, November 19th, a string of 18 depth charges exploded around her. SCULPIN was badly hurt. The blasts dented her pressure hull, started serious leaks, damaged her steering gear and diving planes. Commander Connaway decided to surface and fight it out with the deck guns. The order was passed, and SCULPIN battle-surfaced, rising from the deep like a wounded leviathan.

Attacking the Japanese destroyer, the submarine put up a furious battle. But she was no match for the heavily armed DD. A shell from the destroyer smashed into SCULPIN's conning tower, and another crashed through the main induction. On the bridge Commander Connaway and Gunnery Officer Lieutenant Joseph R. Defrees, Jr., were killed. Lieutenant N. J. Allen was killed by the explosion in the conning tower. Standing at their posts, men died on the bridge and in the control room as SCULPIN rolled in torment under the enemy's punishing fire.

Lieutenant G. E. Brown, the diving officer, succeeded to command. With shells bursting around the submarine and the conning tower torn open, he decided to scuttle and gave the order, "All hands abandon ship!" The crew struggled into life jackets and clambered out of the hatches. Vents open, the submarine plunged from sight, making her final dive.

About 12 men "rode the ship down." Among them were Captain Cromwell and Ensign C. G. Smith, Jr., who refused to leave the stricken submarine. Forty-two of SCULPIN's crew, including three of her officers, got overside and were taken prisoner by the Japanese destroyer. One of the men was immediately thrown by his captors back into the sea because he was badly wounded. Another man escaped this diabolical treatment by wrenching free of the sailors dragging him to the rail, and joining his companions.

It was said that Captain Cromwell, who went down with the submarine, did so because he possessed vital information concerning "Operation Galvanic" and other war plans—information which might be extracted by torture. SCULPIN would keep these secrets well, and her captain chose to confide them into her keeping rather than risk the extraction of the

information he possessed. For this action, he was posthumously awarded the Congressional Medal of Honor.

SCULPIN'S survivors were taken to Truk. After grilling, they were embarked on two carriers (21 on one, and 20 on the other) and started for Japan. Only one of these parties reached Japan. It was the fate of these SCULPIN survivors to start for Japan aboard the carrier CHUYO.

Torpedoing of Liscome Bay

Although the Imperial Navy's surface forces at Truk were not sent out to contest the Gilbert Islands occupation, the American assault forces met savage resistance.

The Navy's surface forces at Tarawa were to suffer their share of the casualties. Japanese opposition in the air was negligible, but one Jap torpedo bomber damaged the light carrier INDEPENDENCE. Japanese submarines wreaked greater havoc. The destroyer FRAZIER sighted, rammed and sank an attacking I-boat. But another enemy submarine succeeded in torpedoing the escort carrier LISCOME BAY. LISCOME BAY exploded like a powder-box. Over 700 died in this sinking, those lost including the commander of the escort carrier support group, Rear Admiral H. M. Mullinnix.

In the sinking of CORVINA and LISCOME BAY, the Japanese Submarine Force was nearing the conclusion of its prowess. It would down but one more major United States warship in the Pacific. But United States submarines had barely begun their war against the warships of Japan.

Attrition Continued (A David Meets a Goliath)

While the Fifth Fleet was concentrating on the Gilbert Islands area and ten Pacific Fleet submarines were operating in "Galvanic," the remainder of the SubPac Force was hitting the enemy's shipping closer to home. Torpedoes crashed in the waters off Japan while the guns were thundering at Tarawa, and as the echoes from the Gilberts died away in December, explosions were booming along the Marshall and Caroline sea lanes to the north, and there were oceanic blasts below Dai Nippon.

SKATE (Commander McKinney) was hunting just north of Truk. December 21 she sank TERUKAWA MARU, a 6,429-ton freighter. Christmas Day she sighted bigger game, and forthwith slammed a torpedo into the superbattleship YAMATO.

Flagship of the late Admiral Yamamoto, this 63,000-ton monster was game of overwhelming size. Packing 18.1-inch guns, vitals shielded by a "torpedoproof" underwater protection system, she and her twin sister, MUSASHI, were the world's biggest battlewagons. There were to have been triplet giants, but the third behemoth, SHINANO, was converted during construction into a 59,000-ton aircraft carrier. YAMATO, the first-born (commissioned in 1941), had been at Midway, where she had circumspectly retired without firing a shot. Now, off Truk, the pride of the Imperial Navy was damaged by an undersea torpedo.

SKATE—a submarine David, indeed—was unable to down this mighty Goliath. But the big BB's "torpedoproof" underbelly was not quite so invulnerable as her sponsors had hoped. Staggering away, she lived to fight another day, but her time would come. A time was coming for all three of these colossal sisters.

Sailfish vs. Japanese Escort Carrier

1745: Surfaced in typhoon weather. Tremendous seas, 40-50 knot wind, driving rain, and visibility, after twilight, varying from zero to 500 yards.

2348: Radar contact bearing 11°T (154° relative), range 9,500 yards. Commenced tracking (ship contact #1).

2352: Radar contact on another and smaller target just to right of and 900 yards closer than first contact (ship contact #2).

2353: Radar contact on a third target about same size as first contact and located 1,000 yards beyond the first contact (ship contact #3).

2355: Radar contact on a fourth target smaller than the other contacts and 900 yards closer than No. 2 contact (ship contact #4).

2356: Have still only managed to build up speed to twelve knots since initial contact. With these fast targets at close range, have abandoned any idea of a methodical approach, the seas are mountainous with a driving rain. Can't see a thing but blackness and water with the water mostly in my face.

So reads Lieutenant Commander R. E. M. Ward's report, SAILFISH's tenth war patrol; date: December 3, 1943; time: early evening until midnight.

On the stroke of midnight the log continues:

0000: Near target close aboard on starboard quarter turned on what appeared to be a good size searchlight with a greenish tinge to it, directed at us and apparently signalling. He could not have seen us so assume he was signalling to someone else near us or he had a doubtful radar contact.

0001: Dove to 40 feet and came right to course 340°T for bow shot at biggest pip. We are 400 yards off track of near destroyer. All targets seem to be in line of bearing, roughly 280-100 degrees true with 900-1,000 yards between targets. Although initial radar contact was not made until a range of 9,500 yards, the picture looks as though we are on the left flank of a fast group of men of war, consisting of a destroyer, then possibly a cruiser, then a carrier or battleship, then another carrier or battleship with possibly something beyond that. Selected nearest of the two largest pips as our target.

0012: Fired tubes 1, 2, 3, and 4, by radar setup, range 2,100 yards, gyro 53° to 37° right, track 108 to 120 port, torpedoes set at 12 feet, using spread of 1¾° right, 1¾° left, 5° left, and 5° right. Times of hits indicate torpedoes one and four were the hitting torpedoes. Commenced swinging left to bring stern tubes to bear. Heard two torpedoes hit.

0230: Radar contact bearing 310°T, range 8,400 yards. Commenced tracking (ship contact #5).

0240: Tracking shows target to be circling. The pip is small, yet can't believe radar would pick up a destroyer at 8,400 yards tonight.

0430: Target settled down on a northwesterly course, speed 2 to 5 knots. Radar pip now looks like we may have two targets very close together.

0550: Morning twilight and visibility improving fast, rain has stopped, but bridge is still shipping water, targets tracking with speed varying from 1 to 3 knots, range 3,500 yards. With visibility improving so rapidly must fire soon, hence have decided to fire three bow tubes on the surface and then attack again in daylight by periscope, making reload during approach.

0552: Fired tubes 1, 2, and 3, range 3,200 yards, gyros 002°, 00-½°, and 004-½°, estimated track 148 starboard, TDC speed 1 knot, torpedoes set at 10 feet, spread of 0°, ½° right, and ½° left.

0557: Observed and heard two torpedo hits. First hit looked like a momentary puff of fire, second hit looked like and sounded (on the bridge) like a battleship firing a broadside—even with the locomotive rumble so characteristic of sixteen inch shells. Commenced swinging ship to bring stern tubes to bear in case if target started going somewhere.

0558: The nips started celebrating by firing star shells and heavy AA tracers from at least a dozen guns located at the point of the torpedo explosions, but didn't seem to know where we were because the shooting was directed everyplace but towards us. It's a good show but despite the illumination I can't see the target.

0748: Finally see something—*Aircraft Carrier, range about 10,000 yards,* dead in water (ship contact #6). Nothing else in sight.

Impatiently continuing check of torpedoes. All tubes were flooded during each preceding attack. Gyro pots of one torpedo aft and one forward are flooded necessitating reload.

The carrier, stopped dead in the water, had been hit by two torpedoes

Ward himself was not sure he had scored a hit in that wild typhoon. But the captain of the Japanese carrier was sure. At once he had flashed the message, "We are torpedoed."

The destroyer URAKAZE noticed from maneuvers that one of the vessels in the convoy was apparently in trouble, but she received no instructions and continued on her course.

At 0030 the carrier radioed a dispatch to Tokyo. *"Hit by one torpedo at 0010. Fire in crew's quarters forward. Able to proceed. Position 3230 N., 14350 E."* In reply, Japanese Headquarters ordered URAKAZE to escort the damaged carrier and the other carrier in the convoy.

This message did not get through. A tow was then ordered for the crippled vessel, but the storm apparently canceled this assistance.

Then, at 0600, the damaged carrier was struck by another SAILFISH torpedo.

"Hit by torpedo," she radioed frantically. *"Can make no*

headway. Position 3155N., 143E." Far distant, the carrier ZUIHO received this message and ordered the warships in the damaged carrier's vicinity to go to her assistance.

One of these, apparently URAKAZE, was sighted by SAILFISH,

0748: Momentarily sighted tops of a destroyer apparently standing by the carrier (ship contact #7). The picture now indicates that we have a badly damaged carrier plus one destroyer. If there were a cruiser here with 85 foot tower and 125 foot mast he'd show up like a sore thumb compared to the carrier's 60 foot flight deck. Depth control is extremely difficult due to mountainous seas. . . . I am convinced that the carrier is a dead duck but there should be someone else around besides a single destroyer, yet there is nothing else in sight from 55 feet and no screws on sound. Am passing carrier down port side from aft forward, range about 1,500 yards. He has many planes on deck forward and enough people on deck aft to populate a fair size village. The only visible evidence of previous hits is a small list to port and a small drag down by the stern. The number of people on deck indicates they are prepared to abandon ship—a reassuring picture.

Ward maneuvered SAILFISH abeam of the stalled carrier. As there were still no other Japanese ships in sight, he steered the submarine around into position to aim the stern tubes at the target for a straight stern shot.

0940: Fired tubes 5, 6, and 7, TDC range 1,700 yards, gyros 182° 185¾°, track 88 port, torpedoes set at 12 feet, using a spread of 0°, 8° right, and 2° left. All torpedoes heard running normal.
0942: Two hits (time indicates 2,700 yard torpedo run) heard on sound and throughout the boat, followed by a very heavy swish on sound then by exceptionally loud breaking up noises heard not only on sound but also very clearly throughout the boat. . . .
0951: At 55 feet for a look. Nothing in sight on, or either side of, generating bearing. Made sweep to look for the destroyer and sighted a heavy cruiser of the TAKAO or NACHI Class. Commenced swinging hard left to bring bow tubes to bear (ship contact #8).
0952: Angle on the bow 10 starboard and he is still swinging towards, range 3,300 yards. Between my surprise at having underestimated the range to the carrier (2,700 yard torpedo run instead of 1,700), the fairly

close depth charges from a destroyer I still hadn't been able to see, the surprise sighting of the cruiser racing our way with her forefoot showing over the waves, and the boat starting to broach with her left full rudder, I ordered 90 feet, and thus threw away the chance of a lifetime. . . . The Monday morning quarterbacks can have a field day on this attack! To top it all off, I have personally criticized the sinking of the SORYU, where the towing cruiser could have been gotten first, then the carrier at leisure—yet, I didn't go up ahead of the carrier and make *absolutely* certain that this wasn't a similar set up. This cruiser was undoubtedly on the off bow of the carrier. . . .

1330: Periscope depth. A careful fifteen minutes look at depths between 52 and 60 feet reveals nothing. I am convinced the carrier has been sunk and the cruiser has gotten clear.

The carrier, hit a third time at 0942, had gone down at 0948. Conducted from start to finish in a dragon-toothed typhoon, the battle had lasted ten hours. Ward had no need to worry about the comments of the "Monday morning quarterbacks." Vice Admiral Miwa, Commander Japanese Submarines, cited the SAILFISH performance as a striking example of what submarines could accomplish by relentless and persistent attacks.

Malign fate. A favor on one hand, and cruel deprivation on the other. Veteran of the Pacific War, the escort carrier sunk by SAILFISH had been one of Japan's busiest—made frequent runs as an aircraft ferry to Truk. She was CHUYO. And aboard her on this fatal return trip to Japan were the 21 SCULPIN survivors who had been placed in her hold at Truk.

Only one of these SCULPIN men survived the sinking of CHUYO. A final irony—that SCULPIN should have been the submarine which stood by during the SQUALUS rescue in 1939 when SQUALUS sank off the Isle of Shoals. SQUALUS—raised and renamed SAILFISH.

1943 Summary

As 1943 draws to a close, the Pacific submarine war is roaring into high gear.

Limited offensives are ended, and the big push is begun. There are, at the end of 1943, some 75 fleet submarines in the Central Pacific, representing a net increase of 22 during the year. Three new tenders—BUSHNELL, ORION and EU-

RAYLE—reported for duty in 1943, and two of these have been serving in the Central Pacific, thus making a total of six tenders operating with SubPac. Material shortages and consequent deprivations are over.

The sinking of CHUYO appears as handwriting on the wall for the Imperial Navy. With dependable weapons, new tactics, new capabilities, the submariners are far ahead of New Year's Day, 1943. As one man, the submarine forces in the Pacific speak up for the forthright and inspiring leadership of Admiral Lockwood.

The success of the submarine attrition war against the Japanese merchant marine may be seen in the table below (statistics from the U.S. Strategic Bombing Survey). Note the

Month	Jap Merchant tonnage sunk by U.S. Submarines	Jap Merchant tonnage afloat
December 1941 through February 1943	717,708	6,076,553*
1943		
March	109,447	5,771,398
April	105,345	5,732,762
May	122,319	5,630,243
June	101,581	5,536,304
July	82,764	5,487,600
August	80,799	5,465,238
September	157,002	5,430,804
October	118,847	5,320,196
November	231,684	5,262,937
December	131,531	5,034,778
10-month total	1,241,319	

* Japan needed 6,000,000 tons to maintain war effort.

mounting tonnages beginning in March 1943, and that summer's increase in "days on offensive patrol." Note, too, the bulky tonnage-total subtracted from the enemy's merchant shipping in November.

"Submarines," admitted Admiral Nomura, under post-war interrogation, "*initially did great damage to our shipping. And later the submarines, combined with air attack, made our shipping very scarce. Our supply lines were cut and we could not support these supply lines. . . .*"

PART FOUR

Pacific Sweep

(1944)

Then rose from sea to sky the wild farewell—
Then shriek'd the timid and stood still the brave—
Then some leap'd overboard with dreadful yell,
As eager to anticipate their grave. . . .
And first one universal shriek there rush'd,
Louder than the loud ocean, like a crash
Of echoing thunder; and then all was hush'd,
Save the wild wind and the remorseless dash
Of billows. . . .

BYRON

Chapter 22

Oceanic Housecleaning

(January-June 1944)

☆ ☆ ☆

Attrition vs. Japanese Empire

The attrition war waged by U.S. submarines against Japanese shipping can be seen as a triple-purpose operation. Its moves were aimed at three elementary objectives. First: the cutting of supply lines between Japan and the Empire's outlying military bases—a move obviously related to military strategy. Second: the cutting of transportation lines between conquered territories and the home Empire—a move to prevent the exploitation of those territories and thus deprive the Japanese homeland of foodstuffs and vital raw materials. Third: the cutting of transportation lines between the home Empire and colonial and other foreign markets—a move to liquidate the enemy's overseas commercial enterprises. To some extent, all three objectives were related. But the last two, calculated to disrupt Japan's foreign trade and stifle her domestic industries, blended to achieve an ultimate and most important objective—the ruination of the Empire's economy. This, it might be said, was the chief objective of the submarine attrition war.

Since the Japanese Empire was a maritime empire, one might think the Tokyo war lords would have recognized the supreme importance of salt-water shipping. While export trade was an economic imperative, imports were absolutely vital for survival. More than 50% of the iron ore, petroleum, scrap iron, coking coal, lead and tin—items paramount to the war-manufacturing effort—had to be shipped in. In the matter of food alone, Japan had to import a good 20% of the total supply needed to feed the home populace. The war lords (mostly army bred) were near-sighted about the need to maintain the merchant marine.

Warning for Japan

In January 1944, U.S. submarines swept some 50 Japanese merchant vessels into oblivion. Into oblivion with the 50-odd merchant vessels went cargoes which included everything but the proverbial kitchen sink—and it may be that even that homely item was on one of the manifests.

Total merchant tonnage lost to U.S. submarines that month approximated 240,840 tons. This topped the tonnage sunk by U.S. submarines in any previous month of the war. And reference to the table in the Addenda will show that in January 1944 the American submarines sank a greater tonnage than they downed in the first seven months of the Pacific conflict.

Worse, from the Japanese standpoint, was yet to come. Improved torpedoes, better radar, new submarine tactics— these were factors calculated to make the war entirely uneconomical for an Empire dependent on shipping. Another and most important factor was the increasing number of U.S. submarines in the Pacific—submarines with well-trained crews and experience-trained skippers.

February Sweeping (Introducing Some Champions)

SNOOK, PLUNGER, POGY, FLASHER, RASHER and PUFFER all accomplished some vigorous sweeping during the second month of 1944. There were others—the Pacific's Oriental carpet was broad enough for all the brooms available. But the forenamed were among the busiest. POGY's work can stand as exemplary.

POGY (Lieutenant Commander R. M. Metcalf) found all the sweeping she could handle off Formosa. Japan's second largest colony (Korea being the largest), this big island lying at the toe of the Nansei Shoto chain was an important source of food for the home Empire. About 80% of the sugar consumed in Japan was imported from Formosa, as was some 38% of Japan's rice imports.

On February 10 POGY made contact with a convoy in Bashi Channel off the southern tip of Formosa. Riding herd was a Japanese destroyer. To Metcalf and his crew this was so much "pogy bait," and they lost no time in maneuvering to attack. For its part, the Imperial Navy lost the destroyer MINEKAZE, and the Japanese merchant marine lost the 5,500-ton passenger-cargoman MALTA MARU.

Metcalf headed the submarine northward up the east coast of Formosa, and on the 20th of February she caught a convoy on the Tropic of Cancer. Skillful approach and sharp-shooting attack sent torpedoes slamming into TAIJIN MARU, freighter, 5,154 tons, and NANYO MARU, freighter, 3,610 tons.

Three days later, in Nansei Shoto waters, POGY blew the bottom out of another freighter—HOREI MARU, 5,888 tons. With a DD and four *marus* to their credit, Metcalf and company headed homeward. This submarine's February patrol cost the Japanese some 21,000 tons of Formosa shipping.

February's returns were not all in before ComSubPac and ComSubSoWesPac knew their submarines were setting a new record. From the North Pacific to the Java Sea, Japanese cargoes were going down in wholesale lots.

Loss of Grayback

Success demands its price, however, and the submariners paid it. Radar, electric torpedoes, night camouflage and other boons did not eliminate operational hazards or end the danger of counter-attack. They gave the submariners a chance to fight harder, to strike the enemy more often—and to risk their lives more frequently in mortal combat.

One of February's high-scoring sweeps was staged by GRAYBACK, under the leadership of Commander J. A. (Johnny) Moore. Pioneer veteran of the first war year, GRAYBACK was on her tenth patrol. Dispatched to the East China Sea, she received orders to conduct an eight-day patrol in the broad strait between Luzon and Formosa before proceeding to her East China Sea area.

GRAYBACK sank four ships in these enemy waters. She was expected at Midway on March 7th. She did not come home. On February 27 a Japanese carrier plane had discovered a submarine on the surface, lat. 25-47 N., long., 128-45 E. According to Japanese report, the attacking aircraft "made a direct hit on submarine, which exploded and sank immediately."

GRAYBACK was gone. But when the final count was in, her name was still "up there" among those of the high-scoring leaders. Fourteen enemy ships had been downed by her torpedoes, and the vanquished included a submarine, an ex-light cruiser and a destroyer.

Loss of Scorpion

Early in 1944, perhaps on a day in February, the Submarine Force lost SCORPION. Captained by Commander M . G. Schmidt, she had departed Pearl Harbor on December 29,

1943, and headed for a patrol area in the northern East China Sea and Yellow Sea. This was SCORPION's fourth war patrol.

On the morning of January 5, Schmidt reported that one of the crew had fractured an arm, and requested a rendezvous with HERRING, at that time in SCORPION's vicinity. The rendezvous was made, but heavy seas prevented transfer of the injured man. The following day Schmidt reported the case "under control." SCORPION went on.

She was never seen or heard from again. Somewhere in the Pacific?—the East China Sea?—the Yellow Sea?—SCORPION went down with all hands. Japanese records give no clue to the submarine's fate, although a Japanese I-boat was known to have been in SCORPION's area on February 16th. The sea closed in around her—where and when remain unknown.

Loss of Trout

On February 29 a Japanese convoy was waylaid by a submarine at lat. 224 N., long. 131-45 E. During the ensuing battle, a ship was badly damaged and the 7,126-ton passenger-cargoman SAKITO MARU was sunk.

TROUT was the only U.S. submarine operating in that vicinity at that date. Under Lieutenant Commander A. H. Clark she had left Pearl Harbor on the 8th to conduct her eleventh war patrol.

She did not report the SAKITO MARU sinking and it was not known to SubPac Headquarters until after the war. TROUT was due to return to Midway about April 7th. She never made port. Her loss remained a mystery until war's end, and then a search of Japanese records disclosed the convoy attack and the counter-attack which must have been TROUT's final battle.

If she were, indeed, struck down by an A/S hunter-killer group on February 29, TROUT ended her war career as she began it—fighting.

Loss of Tullibee

Late in March TULLIBEE was lost in a manner at once singular and tragic. Under Commander C. F. Brindupke, she had left Pearl Harbor on March 5 to conduct her fourth war patrol.

TULLIBEE's area was in the open sea north of Palau where she was to cooperate as a unit in "Operation Desecrate," the carrier-air strike scheduled to hit Palau on March 30th. But after her departure from Midway TULLIBEE was not heard from again. Her loss was officially announced on May 15th. The circumstances of the TULLIBEE disaster were not known until the end of the war, when C. W. Kuykendall, Gunner's Mate 2, was released from the Ashio copper mines in Japan. He was the lone survivor of TULLIBEE.

He told a heartbreaking story. TULLIBEE had reached her station off the Pelews on March 25 (five days before the carrier strike at Palau) and on the night of the 26th she had made radar contact with a convoy. Brindupke ordered a surface approach. Rain squalls obscured visibility as TULLIBEE stalked her quarry, which proved to be a transport, three freighters, two A/S vessels and a destroyer.

Brindupke twice started to close for the attack, but withheld fire because of the blinding rain. Meantime the escorts, detecting a submarine in the vicinity, were dropping random depth charges. As the sea boomed and spouted, Brindupke drove TULLIBEE in a third time, and fired two bow torpedoes at the invisible target—the big Jap transport.

Kuykendall was among the lookouts on the bridge at this time, peering blindly into the gusting rain. Perhaps a minute and a half after the torpedoes were fired, a stunning explosion rocked the submarine. Kuykendall was hurled into the sea.

Struggling in the water, he could hear men shouting and crying out in the night around him. There was a last shout or two in the darkness—then the crushing silence of rain and sea. Kuykendall swam alone throughout the remainder of the night. He never again saw anything of TULLIBEE and his companions.

At 1000 on the morning of March 27, an escort vessel spied the swimming gunner's mate. The Japs fired on him with spiteful machine guns, and then, tiring of the sport, sidled over to pick him up. Kuykendall learned from his captors that the transport TULLIBEE had fired upon had been hit by a torpedo. After the usual grilling and brutal third degree, he was sent to Japan to sweat it out as a prisoner of war.

TULLIBEE had not been sunk by the Japanese. Of that, Kuykendall was certain. Range and bearing of the enemy escorts put them out of position for an immediate counterattack, and they could not have spotted the submarine on that squally night. There could be but one explanation for the explosion which downed the submarine, and the timing of the blast substantiated it. TULLIBEE had been hit by one of her own torpedoes which had made a circular run.

Scamp Gets Home

On the morning of April 7, 1944, SCAMP (Lieutenant Commander J. C. Hollingsworth) was patrolling south of Davao Gulf. In those hot waters she sighted some big game—an enemy task force of six cruisers, screened by destroyers and aircraft. The sea was blue glass, and while attempting to reach attack position SCAMP was detected. Down she went, and down came the depth charges—a barrage of 22 blasts. She remained at deep submergence for several hours and then returned to periscope depth. Finding the horizon clear of enemy ships, Hollingsworth surfaced the submarine at 1423 in order to send out a contact report.

At 1543, a float plane was sighted coming directly out of the sun at an altitude of about 1,500 feet. Hollingsworth immediately gave the order, "Take her down!" followed by "Rig ship for depth charge!" and "Left full rudder!"

A moment later there was hell to pay. The payment was recorded as follows in Hollingsworth's patrol report:

Boat had seven degree down angle and was passing forty feet with rudder full left when bomb or depth charge landed port side of frame seven seven. Terrific explosion jarred boat. All hands not holding on to something were knocked off their feet. All power was lost. Emergency lights turned on. Boat began to take a large up angle and settle fast. All main vents were open at the time of the explosion, and failed to close by hydraulic power. The diving officer noted the hydraulic controller was on the "off" position having jarred to "off" by the explosion. The hydraulic plant was started and the main vents closed. Diving officer began blowing everything.

Boat had slowed only slightly when passing 280 feet. With all tanks dry—a large up angle and still going down at 320 feet. Boat settled finally, hung for a time and started up rapidly. During this time the following reports were being received. "Fire in maneuvering room!"—"All power lost!"—"Thick toxic smoke in maneuvering room and after torpedo room!"—"All hands aft sick!"—"Forward engine room pressure hull dished inboard!"—"Pressure hull crews wash room dished inboard!" "Rudder jammed hard port!" —"Motor room taking water fast!" "Main induction drains showing a full stream!"

Decided: the section watch would have to fight it out—we would not go to battle stations or fire quarters—that if we passed fifty feet going up we would surface and fight it out with deck guns. . . . The control-room watch was having trouble keeping up with the orders, and doing a marvelous job. The diving officer ordered men not required elsewhere to the forward torpedo room to help take the angle off the boat. The men came through the control room like fullbacks and arriving in the forward torpedo room were packed between the tubes like sardines. By venting and flooding everything the boat was caught at fifty-two feet and started down again.

We went down and up three times and had started down a fourth time before power was regained. Lieutenant T. S. Sutherland had charge in the maneuvering room. The situation there was bad. All hands were violently sick but sticking it out trying to get main power. The angles the boat was taking did not help them. (Later figured we were 20 tons heavy aft during this time.)

As the boat started down for the fourth time and with air banks getting low the maneuvering room reported they were making two thirds on the starboard shaft, and five minutes later two thirds on the port side. Never received a happier report. Shortly afterwards the diving officer leveled off at one fifty feet. The rudder was finally placed amidships by hand.

This thrilling battle report concludes:

We had made one complete circle before the rudder was placed amidships. Seven thousand gallons of Diesel oil which had been released from No. 5B, plus the blowing and venting of main ballast tanks, must have convinced our aviator friend that we were sunk—or else he did not have another bomb. There were no bombs during above period, approximately fifteen minutes. The commanding officer takes pleasure in making the following two statements. *There was no confusion! All hands did their job well and silently!*

Depth charges were still thudding to eastward at 1830, as SCAMP moved off, traveling deep. Once in the clear, Hollingsworth headed for the Admiralty Islands. Accompanied by DACE, the injured submarine limped into Seeadler on the morning of April 16th. Tough submarine and tough submariners.

Loss of Gudgeon

Leaving Pearl Harbor on April 4, 1944, GUDGEON (Lieutenant Commander R. A. Bonin) was beginning her twelfth war patrol.

She entered the Valley of the Shadow. In the seas north of the Marianas the Japanese were rushing troopships, munition convoys, all available reinforcements to Saipan and on down to Truk and Palau. Admiral Toyoda, new Commander-in-Chief of the Combined Fleet (Admiral Koga had been killed late in March in a plane crash), was determined to hold the Marianas line. Into these perilous waters went GUDGEON.

On April 18, Japanese planes sighted a submarine some 166 miles off the island of "Yuoh." The aircraft attacked and dropped bombs. "The first bomb hit bow. Second bomb direct on bridge. Center of the submarine burst open and oil pillars rose." So reported the Japanese.

There is no island of "Yuoh" in the Pacific. The Japanese may have erred in decoding, or there may have been error in subsequent translation. At the time of the attack GUDGEON was due off the island of Maug. GUDGEON could have been the reported target.

On May 14 GUDGEON was ordered to return to Midway. She never returned. She was lost with all hands.

Submarine Operational Plan, 1944

In 1944 a new submarine operational plan was devised to spread the attrition-war effort among the boats going out on patrol by equalizing the attack opportunities and dividing the burdensome runs, share and share alike.

The plan contained other important operational features and strategic elements.

To complement this plan, new names were given to patrol areas formerly designated by number. And submarines went out to hunt in the "Hit Parade," "Convoy College," "Dunker's Derby" and "Speedway." One area was most appropriately titled "Maru Morgue."

Sponsored by Admiral Lockwood and his operations officer, Captain R. G. Voge, the plan met with the instantaneous approval of the force. That the plan worked is evident in the havoc dealt the enemy by U.S. submarines in the remainder of 1944.

Lapon vs. Raton

By the spring of 1944, U.S. submarines were cruising in good hunting areas like schools of fish. One consistently good hunting ground was the South China Sea. Early in the war, the western reaches of this great sea had been relatively secure for Japanese ship traffic. That security no longer existed.

LAPON (Lieutenant Commander L. T. Stone) left Fremantle on April 25 to conduct her fourth war patrol in a South China Sea area below Saigon. Her previous patrol in March, reported earlier in this chapter, was a high-scoring 19,000-tonner. A new-construction boat out of Groton, Connecticut, in 1943, LAPON was keeping up her end of the undersea war. When she reached her patrol area early in May she was on her mettle.

Three weeks of combing the southern approaches to Saigon provided little action. Then on May 24, with about a week of time-in-area remaining, she picked up a Japanese convoy. A slam-bang torpedo attack spelled finish for WALES MARU, a 6,586-ton passenger-cargoman, and BIZEN MARU, freighter, 4,667 tons. Having sent some 11,000 enemy tons to sea bottom, LAPON reloaded and looked around for other *marus* to conquer.

While she was looking, she received the news that game of another caliber had been sighted in her area—a Jap submarine was in the vicinity! These were fighting words to Stone and company. The watch was alerted and all hands strained at a leash of anticipation.

Enter RATON (Lieutenant Commander J. W. Davis) also hunting the South China Sea for bear. Like LAPON she was conducting her fourth war patrol. She, too, had set herself a mark to shoot at by downing some 18,000 tons during a three-day fracas the previous December. Commissioned at Manitowoc in 1943, with Davis on her bridge, she, too, was a newcomer out to give the enemy battle.

She had left Australia on the 10th of May, and had reached her patrol area a few days later. That area was located almost due south of LAPON'S.

Surface and undersea areas may be marked on charts. But the water, weather and other physical characteristics of the sea have a way of blending at the boundary lines. The waves that washed LAPON'S area rolled on into RATON'S. The vista was all one. Even the time of day may seem common for adjacent sea areas although man-made clocks declare it otherwise. RATON, it should be noted, was keeping time an hour later than LAPON. Thus the morning of May 27 bathed both submarines with dawn's early light, but at 0500 for LAPON, it was 0400 for RATON.

What time was it, then, for the Japanese submarine reported in this vicinity? The answer must remain insoluble, for it depends on the whereabouts of the submarine in question, and at 0500 on the morning of the 27th, LAPON was still looking. At that hour she was about 200 miles southeast of Saigon, cruising submerged and making wary periscope sweeps. The Jap was presumably anywhere.

And while time was of the essence in one respect, in another it was of little consequence. No matter how one's chronometers are set, a torpedo is a torpedo. Whether it strikes at 0515 (Hypo) or 0615 (Item) is a matter of small moment. LAPON's chronometers indicated the time at 0503 (Item) when, according to Stone's patrol report:

> Sighted submarine identified as enemy on base course about 035°. Determined to be of the I-68 Class as found in ONI-14.

0504: Turned away for stern tube attack.

0513: Fired first of two torpedoes at range of 1,400 yards, track 53° port. Before firing the last two torpedoes, the previous certainty that this was an enemy submarine was lessened in the mind of the Commanding Officer, and fire was checked. Between the time of sighting and firing the submarine changed course to to the west about 60°, either on a zig or on a broad sweep.

0517: Went to 200 feet.

0518: Heard two explosions as of torpedoes exploding at end of run.

Meanwhile RATON's skipper (Lieutenant Commander Davis) was jotting down some observations of his own. These were timed according to chronometers set for "Hypo"—an hour behind LAPON's "Item." But the date was May 27, and the morning was young.

0430: Interference on SJ radar screen. Appears to be another SJ and on bearing 290°—300 T. Lat. 7°-32′ N Long. 108°-51′E.

0535: Lost interference on SJ radar screen.

0615: Ship shaken up considerably by either two underwater explosions or by striking submerged object. People in forward torpedo room thought we had struck something or had been struck by something. Commanding Officer was in control room at time, en route to the bridge, and it appeared to him to be two heavy muffled explosions nearby on port side. Went hard right and steadied on course 035°T (at time of explosion we were on course 350°T going ahead full on three main engines, 17 knots). After making turn the

J.O.O.D. reported thin oil streak about 1,000 yards on port beam. No other disturbance sighted in water. . . .

LAPON arrived home at Fremantle on June 6th. RATON came indignantly into harbor on the 23rd. No one who compared reports could doubt that she had been fired upon by LAPON. The positions checked within two miles, and the timing was all too simultaneous.

Undoubtedly RATON's crew had some comments to make, and submariners acquainted with Davis were careful not to jostle his elbow for a long time afterward. RATON an I-boat! But LAPON could be forgiven under the circumstances—with an enemy known to be in the vicinity, and torpedo warfare what it was.

So far as is known, the LAPON-RATON case was the only shooting of its kind in World War II. In numerous instances, U. S. submarines were tracked by U. S. submarines—and finally identified as friendly. This single brush in the South China Sea was the only time an American submarine fired at one of its own family.

The wonder is that undersea warfare did not generate a whole series of Hatfield-McCoy embroglios. When one considers the difficulty of submarine identification—the submarine concentration in areas that contracted as the war progressed—the record seems remarkable. Mix Japanese submarines into the picture, and it is apparent that American submarine skippers were masters of the fine art of "recognition."

Loss of Herring

HERRING (Lieutenant Commander D. Zabriski, Jr.) left Pearl Harbor on May 16 and set out for the Kuriles to conduct her eighth patrol. On May 31 she made rendezvous with BARB (Lieutenant Commander E. B. Fluckey) in anticipation of a cooperative patrol. The submarines exchanged information and parted company.

A few hours after leaving HERRING, Fluckey's submarine made contact with a Japanese convoy. As BARB was starting an approach, she heard distant depth-charging and assumed HERRING had attacked and was under counter-attack. Some time later BARB picked up a prisoner who revealed that HERRING had sunk an escort vessel of the convoy.

HERRING later tackled a freighter and a passenger-cargoman lying at anchor off Point Tagan, Matsuwa Island, in the Kuriles. According to Japanese records, this attack was made on June 1st. It resulted in the sinking of two Jap vessels. During the action, a shore battery spotted the invading submarine and opened fire. The Japanese gunners reported two direct hits on the conning tower. "Bubbles covered an area about 5 meters wide and heavy oil covered an area of approximately 15 miles."

If the Japanese report were accurate, she was the only U.S. submarine sunk by a land battery during the war.

Loss of Golet

GOLET (Lieutenant Commander J. S. Clark) left Midway on May 28 and headed for an area off the northeast coast of Honshu where she was to conduct her second patrol. A door of silence closed quietly behind her, and SubPac Headquarters never heard from her again.

The time and place of GOLET's final battle remained a mystery until war's end. Then Japanese records disclosed an A/S attack, dated June 14, 1944, made on a submarine at lat. 41-04 N., long. 14-130 E. "On the spot of fighting we later discovered corks, raft, and so on, and a thick pool of oil. . . ."

GOLET was the only U.S. submarine at that time in the immediate area. Evidently she went down with all hands in this battle off northern Honshu.

Cutting the Japanese Oil Line

During the first quarter of 1944, U.S. submarines concentrated on an attrition operation that was to drain the vitality of the Japanese war effort.

Life blood of the Imperial War Machine was oil. Without oil the Imperial Navy would rust at anchor, the Army and Air Force would jolt to a halt, the merchant marine would be stranded. Without oil the whole, great, glittering War Machine would stall with all the futility of a flivver out of gas. Any motor mac could see it. Obvious to a schoolboy. Yet Japan's military leaders were as strangely remiss regarding oil requisites as they were in other similarly obvious matters —for example, the need for a convoy system.

During the first year of the war, the Japanese tanker fleet had been remarkably immune from submarine attack. There were reasons for this immunity. The average tanker is faster on its feet than the lumbering cargo vessel, and its comparatively high speed makes it an elusive target. Undoubtedly many tankers were spared in 1942 by defective torpedoes. And in that year there were not enough submarines available to cover the remote zones of tanker operation.

With their sources in Sumatra, Java and Borneo, the main oil arteries pulsed northward into the South China Sea where they joined the big Singapore trunk line for the run to Japan. Northward up the South China Sea, northward past Formosa, northward up the East China Sea ran the line. Probing submarines had been too few in number to put a drain on this vein in 1942. Nevertheless, they had pricked it. And in 1943 they went on probing.

With an extraordinary lack of foresight, Japan's war lords seem to have assumed that the immunity enjoyed by their tanker fleet would continue for the war's duration. Had they glimpsed the Operation Plan published by ComSubPac on June 24, 1943, they might have furrowed their brows over the tanker situation with some concern. As rated by this revised plan, the oil tanker (AO) stood a high No. 4 on the priority parade, outclassed as a target only by aircraft carriers, battleships and auxiliary carriers, and outclassing heavy cruisers, light cruisers and everything else afloat. The Japanese were, of course, in the dark concerning this arrangement. They were soon to see the light.

Long and rakish with lean flanks and funnel aft, the AO has vulnerable characteristics. Her low freeboard may serve to reduce her silhouette, but there is no mistaking her for what she is, once sighted. Moreover, low freeboard puts the great bulk of her under water where the torpedo is in its element. High speed gives the tanker a margin of safety, but her volatile cargo means a holocaust when she is hit, and the odds make six of one or half a dozen of the other. They began to show up in the autumn of 1943.

Three tankers went to the bottom in September. Two went down in October. Seven were sunk in November. And three were downed in December. Thus in the last four months of 1943 a goodly 15 tankers were obliterated—more than Japan had lost in the previous 20 months of warfare.

Then the calendar turned on 1944. U.S. submarines bristling with brooms were prepared for a big spring housecleaning. Or—to rig a more appropriate metaphor—U.S. submarines had their razors sharpened for that jugular vein which carried the lifeblood of the Japanese war effort—petroleum.

Jack the Tanker Killer

Out of Groton, Connecticut, in the spring of 1943 had come the submarine USS JACK. Typical of the new-construction boats, she went out to the Pacific armed with the latest in modern battle equipment—new radar devices—new supersonic gear—new everything including a splendid machine for the manufacturing of ice cream. Surely her captain, Lieutenant Commander T. M. "Tommy" Dykers, had reason to be proud of this spanking undersea warship as he brought her into Pearl Harbor for her battle orders.

On her maiden patrol conducted in Empire waters, she waded in two-fisted and sank some 16,000 tons of Japanese merchant shipping. Her next patrol, made in the autumn of 1943, was luckless, and she returned home empty-handed. She was then dispatched to Fremantle to join the Southwest Pacific Force. And from Fremantle, on January 16, 1944, she was dispatched to a patrol area in the South China Sea.

So her big moment arrived—at four o'clock in the morning of February 19, 1944, as she cruised along the Japanese traffic lane which connected Singapore with the distant Empire. The sea was a heaving carpet of warm velvet, softened by the dim light of a quarter moon. Faint starshine added to the luminescence, but it took strong binoculars to pick up anything on the horizon's curve. The lookouts on the submarine's bridge and up in the periscope shears were straining their eyes at the glasses. Wait—what was that off there? At 0358 one of the watch had spotted something.

Black as a cat the silhouette crept into view—a long, rakish craft with funnel aft—a tanker unmistakably. Then as JACK's bridge personnel went tense, another tanker was outlined on the horizon. Then another! And still another! And then one more! And there was JACK with her sights trained on five black tankers all in one picture—an oil convoy! Dykers and company went into action as one man.

During the approach, the convoy's formation shaped up. The ships were moving in two columns—four tankers in the main column, and one tanker leading three escort vessels on the flank. One of the escort vessels was a destroyer.

The submarine concentrated on the high-priority targets. By 0442 JACK had reached attack position, Dykers opened fire with a spread of three bow torpedoes aimed to catch the third tanker in the near, main column as it overlapped a target in the far. He fired a fourth torpedo at the last tanker in the main column. This target was struck by two torpedoes. The hits flared at the waterline, there was a dazzling spurt of flame, and then the tanker exploded like a colossal bomb, hurling up a tower of blazing gasoline that seemed to spatter against the ceiling of the night.

Two of the three torpedoes fired in the first salvo were heard to strike something in the far column, but the blinding blast of the tanker prevented identification of these hits. A lake of burning oil spread across the scene of the tanker's demise, and skirting this fiery lake at top speed came the destroyer, shooting wildly. Dykers pulled the submarine away from the milling convoy and started an end-around to make another attack.

Daylight found the tanker convoy once more under way, and through the heat of morning JACK raced at four-engine speed, traveling in an arc that would bring her out in front of the quarry. At 1445, some 42,000 yards out in front, she submerged. Three hours later, the four tankers hove into view, traveling in box formation with no escorts anywhere in evidence.

Down the track they came, like pins irresistibly drawn toward a magnet. Four Japanese ships whose masters, disregarding all warning, seem to have determinedly set a course for Avernus. By what reasoning had they dismissed an escorting destroyer? Why, having suffered one submarine attack, dd they suppose they could escape another? The answer to this enigma is sealed somewhere in the Japanese mentality.

In no mood to look gift oilers in the teeth, JACK accepted the situation and bored in with a ready will. At 1849 Dykers fired four torpedoes from the stern tubes at two of the tankers which were overlapping. Two shots hit the leading target, and one torpedo smashed into the tanker in the background. Fifteen million gallons of gasoline went up with a fiery roar. Two tankers went down, incinerated under a mountain of greasy smoke.

An hour later, Dykers surfaced the submarine. The two remaining tankers had separated. One, standing off to the north, had picked up an escort. The other, running westward into dusk, was alone. Dykers sent JACK on a race to catch the lone tanker. The fugitive was zigzagging desperately—which slowed its escape—and the submarine soon overhauled. At 8,000 yards, Dykers fired three bow torpedoes at the galloping target.

Things went askew. The first torpedo failed to run. The second missed the mark. The third ran erratically and passed astern of the tanker. As JACK turned away after this futile salvo, the Japanese tankermen opened fire with a 5-incher. Some of the shells fell close aboard as Dykers once more closed the range and the bow tubes were being reloaded.

The tanker was zigzagging wildly, but by carefully tracking the target on each of its radical twists and turns, Dykers presently had its number. At 2233 he fired a salvo of four torpedoes which scored three hits. Flame exploded from the tanker's vitals and rolled across the seascape like incandescent surf. JACK headed away from the red glare in the night.

High jinx in the Court of Neptune—ice cream—fireworks —the submarine, it would seem, had nearly everything. Sailing home over the bounding main, she could be confident that she had distinguished the name of JACK. At war's end that name was going to stand among the top 10 on the scoreboard recording tonnages sunk by individual U.S. submarines. But perhaps JACK would be best remembered as the submarine which downed four Japanese tankers in one day —a feat of AO attrition unequalled by any other U.S. submarine in the war. Here is the record:

Date	Tanker	Tonnage	Location
Feb. 19, 1944	Kokuie Maru	5,154	1434N., 11411E.
Feb. 19, 1944	Nanei Maru	5,019	1434N., 11411E.
Feb. 19, 1944	Nichirin Maru	5,162	1545N., 11535E.
Feb. 19, 1944	Ichiyo Maru	5,106	1545N., 11548E.

Only one other submarine extracted a heavier tonnage from the Japanese tanker fleet in a single patrol. That submarine was FLASHER, in December 1944. But JACK's blow was perhaps more excruciating, landing as it did in the wake of the Truk debacle.

Submarines vs. Oil Imports

JACK's foray of February 19 did not conclude the tanker attrition for that month. On the 23rd, 24th and 25th, three more Japanese oilers were subtracted from the tanker fleet by submarines COD, GRAYBACK and HOE.

It must have come over the Japanese, then, that in the first eight weeks of 1944 they had lost a total of 21 oil tankers —almost as many as they had lost in all of 1943. Tanker losses for the year's first quarter totaled 235,000 tons. Of this tonnage, submarines had sunk 130,421; the air strikes at Truk and Palau had accounted for 99,501; Army aircraft had sunk 5,461. (Other losses were operational.)

Import statistics can be brief. At the start of the war, Japanese oil imports averaged 300,000 barrels a month. By the end of 1942 oil imports were well over a million barrels a month. This supplied the War Machine with a sufficiency during that favorable year.

Then, in the first quarter of 1943 Japanese oil imports slacked off. But in the second quarter they rose to a monthly high of 1,500,000 barrels. This would have looked gratifying on the graph had not the War Machine been gulping oil at a rate which accelerated as the conflict heightened. Like the inebriate whose thirst increases after a couple of beers, Japan's military effort was demanding more and more fuel. When oil imports dropped to 1,200,000 barrels a month in the last half of 1943, consumption was threatening to drink up importation and drain the reserves.

The shortage caused sobriety in Tokyo on New Year's Eve. And by the end of January 1944, sobriety had become anxiety. In that month oil importation had fallen under a million barrels. In February the figure dropped to 900,000 barrels. In March it was still only 900,000. And in April—despite tanker construction—despite convoys—despite everything the oil authorities could do—oil importation dropped to 700,000 barrels!

Now this drop in oil imports in the first quarter of 1944 hit the Japanese military effort at the heart. Of course, any stricture in the oil system affected the enemy's military effort. A pinch in the Admiralties or a smash at Truk and Palau caused wrenches and recoils. But the heart of the military effort was the home Empire. Reduction of the supply of life-blood oil to that heart could cause a convulsion. Such a reduction—and submarines were largely responsible for it—convulsed Japan's whole military effort in the spring of 1944. And in one specific instance it forced the Imperial Navy to make a move which was to change the whole face of the war.

After a smashing American air raid on Rabaul in November 1943, Admiral Ozawa's carrier fleet, bereft of planes, retired to Japan. There Ozawa's carriers intended to pick up and train new aircraft squadrons. But when Ozawa arrived in Japan he found a serious oil situation. Tanker losses caused by U.S. submarines had so reduced the flow from the Netherlands East Indies that the home islands were running out of gas. With a fuel famine threatening, the Imperial Navy's High Command thought it best to dispatch Ozawa's carriers to Singapore, where they would be nearer the wells of Borneo, Sumatra and Java.

Thus the spring of 1944 found Ozawa's carrier fleet training at Singapore—far from the Second Fleet of Admiral Kurita which had been driven from Truk to Palau. The oil emergency then compelled these fleets to base at Tawi Tawi in the Sulu Archipelago. Their effort to reach the Marianas from that recessed base resulted, as will be seen, in the Battle of the Philippine Sea and a catastrophic defeat for Japan.

Between January 1, 1944, and June 30, 1944, Japan had lost 43 tankers. Of these, U.S. submarines downed 27, for approximately 189,000 tons of oil tankers. Additional tonnages sunk by naval aircraft and other agents raised the tanker loss to an approximate 335,000 tons.

However, tanker tonnage was not the critical figure. The critical figure concerned the quantity of oil reaching Japan.

And the table below was the one which chilled the heart of oil headquarters in Tokyo.

Japanese Oil Imports: First six months of 1944

January	1,000,000	barrels
February	900,000	barrels
March	900,000	barrels
April	700,000	barrels
May	600,000	barrels
June	600,000	barrels

In these declining importation figures the evidence was plain. The oil was not getting home to Japan.

To quote *The War Against Japanese Transportation*, published by the United States Strategic Bombing Survey (1947): *"Had submarines concentrated more effectively in the areas where tankers were in predominant use after mid-1942, oil imports probably could have been reduced sooner and the collapse of the fleet, the air arm, merchant shipping and all other activities dependent upon fuel oil hastened. . . . And the fuel shortage might have been acute at the end of 1943 rather than a year later."*

The criticism does not take into account the torpedo difficulties and other harassments which badgered the submarine forces in 1942 and 1943. But it does underline the importance of the tanker attrition drive which went into high gear in the first half of 1944.

That drive was continued throughout the ensuing summer and autumn, with such drastic results that at year's end the Japanese Total Mobilization Bureau reported to the Emperor's War Cabinet: *"The preservation of liaison between the southern occupied territories and Japan is an absolute necessity . . . It is recognized that if the resources of the south, especially petroleum, are abandoned, with the passage of time we will lose our ability to resist attack."*

The Emperor's Total Mobilization Bureau was a little late in its observation.

Chapter 23

Convoy and Wolf-pack

(Spring and Summer 1944)

☆　☆　☆

I Went to Convoy College

Two U.S. submarine wolf-packs loped out of Pearl Harbor in mid-June 1944 to take up the attrition war. These were "Parks' Pirates" under group leadership of Commander L. S. Parks, and the "Mickey Finns" under Captain W. V. O'Regan.

A patrol area set up in accordance with the newly devised plan had been established in the waters lying between Formosa, Luzon and the Asiatic mainland. This area was known as "Convoy College." Both wolf-packs were now to enter "Convoy College" where they would major in torpedo warfare.

One submarine that graduated with a *summa cum laude* was PARCHE, under the captaincy of Lawson P. (Red) Ramage.

Parche vs. All Hell (Commander Lawson P. Ramage)

PARCHE, HAMMERHEAD and STEELHEAD ("Parks' Pirates) were off Formosa on the morning of July 30, going about their business like any well-organized submarine wolf-pack. So far, business had been slow and pretty much routine—that is, slow and routine so far as submarine warfare is concerned.

Then, at 1030 in the morning of the 30th, STEELHEAD (Commander D. L. Whelchel) sighted a convoy's smoke. STEELHEAD trailed. The convoy was under an umbrella of air protection, and Whelchel's submarine was unable to attack during the day. But at 2015 STEELHEAD got off a message to pack-mate PARCHE, giving the course and speed of the Japanese ships. Ramage put PARCHE on the estimated track and sent her plunging along the surface, top speed.

Midnight, and the two submarines were overhauling the quarry. By 0300, morning of the 31st, STEELHEAD was boring in on the attack. At 0332 Whelchel opened fire, aiming six torpedoes at a tanker and a large freighter. One torpedo was seen to hit the freighter, and a few moments later a mushroom of black smoke surged up from the tanker. Whelchel maneuvered to fire four stern shots at another freighter. Two Japanese rockets soared in the night, signaling the convoy's alarm.

These flares were seen by PARCHE. Ramage's submarine had made contact with one of the convoy's escorts about 30 minutes earlier, and was driving forward with crew at battle stations to strike the convoy's flank. Glare of the rockets now revealed several large ships in silhouette and three escorts rushing about. One of the escorts was ahead of PARCHE and to the starboard. Two were on the submarine's port, between PARCHE and the convoy. As one of these was bearing down on Ramage and company, Ramage decided the pattern needed some fast alteration.

Running the submarine at full speed, he started a circular swing to draw away from the oncoming escort. The A/S vessel continued on its course while PARCHE continued her circle which brought her in behind the stern of the second port-side escort.

"This reverse spinner play apparently confused the opposition," Ramage recalled afterward. "PARCHE was now between the escorts and their convoy, but while this maneuver was going on, the entire Jap convoy had reversed its field and was now headed directly for PARCHE."

Ramage picked out the closest target for the first shot—a medium-sized freighter. But the range had been overestimated. Before the set-up could be made, the ship was only 450 yards away. Sharp full right rudder slid the submarine out of the freighter's path, and PARCHE's bridge personnel could almost feel the breeze as the freighter went by at a scant 200 yards.

Ramage swung the submarine and opened fire with two bow shots. The alerted freighter managed a lucky zig. But the freighter's swing blocked the rush of an escort, and a moment later PARCHE's lookouts spotted two tankers off to starboard. Starting a run for these targets, Ramage got in a stern shot at the freighter, and a thumping explosion registered a hit. A five-minute dash brought PARCHE within torpedo shot of the tankers.

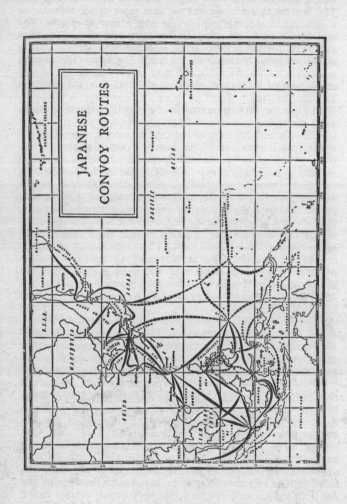

JAPANESE CONVOY ROUTES

Ramage fired four torpedoes at the leading tanker, then swung PARCHE hard right to fire three at the second tanker. The leading tanker collected the first salvo from cutwater to wake. The first torpedo blew the ship's bow to pieces. The next three ploughed into the tanker's mid-section, quarter and stern. The ship went under immediately, leaving only a small patch of burning oil to mark the spot. The second tanker, struck near the bow by two torpedoes, staggered and slowed down, but kept on going. So did PARCHE, and she didn't slow down.

Every escort in the convoy and all of the remaining ships were now wheeling and milling. As though his submarine were a PT-boat; Ramage drove PARCHE into the center of the traffic jam, shooting everything. The convoy shot back everything. Weaving and dodging through the convoy like a rodeo broncho attacking a herd of wild bulls, PARCHE struck at one *maru* after another, fired torpedo after torpedo as the enemy returned fusillades of glowing tracer and screaming shells. The seascape blazed and roared. Hard right, hard left, the submarine swerved and veered. In her forward and after torpedo rooms the sweating men grunted, swore and labored to load the tubes. Above, the T.D.C. operator "played the organ" at pinwheel pace, somehow keeping up with the spate of target data which came down from the bridge. On the bridge, at 0423, Ramage and companions were watching two A/S vessels close in—and Ramage was planning the next dodge—when a small, fast *maru* loomed up on the starboard bow, rushing to ram.

Halfway across the rammer's bow, Ramage ordered PARCHE's rudder full right. Ship and submarine passed in the night with elbow room at less than 50 feet. This, as any navigator knows, is the width of a safety-razor blade. The shave left PARCHE boxed in by small craft on both sides and an on-coming passenger-cargo vessel looming up like the Flatiron Building dead ahead. Left with no alternative but a down-the-throat salvo, Ramage fired threw bow shots at the advancing menace. The first torpedo missed. The next two were on the nose. The ship came to a rumbling stop as if she had run her bow into a mud bank. Ramage drove the submarine forward, then swung hard left to bring the stern tubes to bear. Firing a single, he saw the torpedo strike the vessel amidships. At 0442, as Ramage was maneuvering in for a final shot, the ship put its heavy head under the sea. Then, with a rush, it was gone.

Ramage glanced about for something else to shoot at, while the residue of the convoy, firing indiscriminately, looked for the submarine.

"There were still several small craft and escorts around, but no worthwhile targets that we could see. I decided to put some distance between us and this hornet's nest."

As PARCHE hauled clear, distant explosions could be heard. STEELHEAD was attacking a remnant of the convoy which had run in that direction. At 0449 Whelchel fired four torpedoes at a large passenger-cargoman, and another salvo of four at a big freighter. The freighter was seen to sprout lifeboats and then go under. Whelchel "pulled the plug."

PARCHE, in the meantime, was putting the "hornet's nest" astern. As she hauled away, one of the A/S vessels challenged her by searchlight, sending "AA-AA." This somewhat surprising flash was noted by a PARCHE signalman, Courtland Stanton, with the comment: "Those Japs probably have a lot of forms to fill out, too."

Doubtless one of the forms filled out by the Japanese convoy's survivors reported the loss of some 39,000 tons of merchant shipping. As determined by post-war inquest of the Joint Army-Navy Assessment Committee, STEELHEAD was responsible for the sinking of the 7,169-ton freighter DAKAR MARU and the 8,195-ton transport FUSO MARU. Both submarines were credited with the destruction of the 8,990-ton transport YOSHINO MARU. And PARCHE was credited with the sinking of KOEI MARU, a 10,238-ton tanker, and MANKO MARU, passenger-cargoman, 4,471 tons.

The Submarine Service credited Commander Lawson P. Ramage with something more. Commander Ramage was recommended for the Medal of Honor. Queried about the action later, Ramage made brief reply to an interviewing journalist: "I got mad."

Commander Lawson P. Ramage received the Medal of Honor.

Tang Rings the Bell

In the old days, Lloyd's of London made it a practice to ring a solemn bell whenever word of a ship's loss reached that insurance office. During the War of 1812, Yankee privateers all but wore out the clapper, so consistently did they arouse the bell's doleful bonging. Had the custom persisted and been adopted in Tokyo for World War II, the Japanese capital in the summer of 1944 would have resounded with a ceaseless tolling. In the last week of June and first of July, one submarine alone sank ships enough to sound the tocsin of a great marine disaster.

The submarine was TANG. And the disaster began on June 8 when, under captaincy of Commander Richard H. O'Kane,

TANG slid away from Pearl Harbor to begin her third war patrol. East China and Yellow Sea areas were her destination. Her patrol was one of the great convoy-smashers of the war.

TANG made her first target contact in the East China Sea, night of June 24th. Two weeks later she had sunk 10 Japanese ships. O'Kane headed the submarine home for just one reason. She was out of ammunition.

So TANG concluded the most destructive anti-merchantman patrol of the Pacific conflict. Officially credited with 10 sinkings, O'Kane and company set a record. No other U.S. submarine sank as many ships during a single war patrol. No other, in one patrol, sank a greater merchant tonnage. And only three other submarines—RASHER, FLASHER and ARCHERFISH—downed heavier tonnages of Japanese shipping (merchant tonnage plus naval) in one war patrol.

Loss of S-28

On July 3, S-28 (Lieutenant Commander J. G. Campbell) left the Submarine Base, Pearl Harbor, to conduct training exercises with the Coast Guard cutter RELIANCE.

S-28 made two practice torpedo approaches on RELIANCE, and the following day (July 4) these exercises were continued. At 1730 the submarine dived to begin a submerged approach. RELIANCE lost sound contact with the submarine, and was unable to pick it up thereafter. No distress signals had been heard, and there was no echo of an explosion. S-28 had suddenly gone deep.

The alarmed Coast Guard vessel summoned other vessels from Pearl Harbor. Search for S-28 was begun. The submarine could not be located.

As S-28 went down in 1400 fathoms of water, salvage would have been impossible.

The sea closed over the S-boat quietly, and she went down with all hands.

Loss of Robalo

On July 2, ComSubSoWesPac received a contact report from ROBALO stating that she had seen a FUSO-class battleship with air cover and two escorting DD's just east of Borneo. It was the last message received from this submarine which had left Fremantle on June 22 to patrol in the South China Sea. It was ROBALO's third war patrol. Her captain was Commander M. M. Kimmel.

When she did not reply to inquiring transmissions, she was presumed lost. It remained for Philippine guerrillas and a

U.S. Navy man, who had been held prisoner at Puerto Princessa Prison Camp on the island of Palawan, to report ROB-ALO's story. On August 2, an American soldier on a work detail in the prison yard picked up a note dropped from the window of a cell. The soldier passed it to a fellow prisoner of war, a Navy yeoman, who succeeded in conveying the information to Mrs. Trinidad Mendosa, wife of the guerrilla leader, Dr. Mendosa. The note had been dropped by a survivor of ROBALO. It disclosed the fact that the submarine had gone down on July 26, two miles off the west coast of Palawan. The survivors believed ROBALO had been sunk by the explosion of her after battery.

An officer and three men managed to swim ashore from the stricken submarine. The four were captured by Japanese M.P.'s. The Japs had imprisoned them as guerrillas. Their note stated that they were the only survivors of ROBALO.

Headquarters doubted that a battery explosion could have sunk the submarine, and it seemed probable that ROBALO had struck a mine. The four who survived the disaster were never recovered. After the war it was discovered that a Japanese destroyer had removed them from Palawan on August 15th. The destroyer's destination was unrecorded. Apparently it never reached its intended destination.

Pintado Gets the Whale

While wolf-packs were ganging up on "Convoy College" and roaming the waters of "Hit Parade," lone submarines were on the prowl in many areas. These "lone wolves" continued to operate throughout the war, and in numerous instances they did so much damage to convoys that the enemy took them for wolf-packs. Outstanding example was TANG. Another "lone wolf" that blew a big hole in Japanese merchant shipping in the summer of 1944 was PINTADO.

Captained by Commander B. A. Clarey, this submarine headed westward from Pearl Harbor on July 24 to conduct her second war patrol. Area assigned: the northern waters of the East China Sea.

Late in the afternoon of August 22, her periscope picked up a target that looked a whole lot bigger than average. A bulge of smoke coming up from the southwest sent PINTADO tracking forward. By 1800 Clarey had the periscope trained on a large Japanese convoy which was traveling in three-column formation. Two anti-submarine vessels paced along on either flank of the convoy, and a CHIDORI torpedo-boat "fish-tailed" in the lead, "pinging" this way and that like a cocky drum major performing at the head of a band. But

Clarey was not interested in the escorts. What fascinated Clarey was the convoy's center column—a transport led by an oil tanker. An abnormally large oil tanker with two big smoke stacks abreast of each other aft—a silhouette as unmistakable as Noah's Ark!

Clarey and company could not have been more elated. Here was one of the largest oil haulers in creation—perhaps the biggest Japanese merchantman on the sea! Here was that great ex-whale factory twin of the monster which once escaped TINOSA. Here, marching in this convoy's center column, was TONAN MARU No. 2.

Commander B. A. Clarey had seen this "dream boat" before That was on October 10, 1942, when AMBERJACK (Lieutenant Commander J. A. Bole, Jr.) made a periscope inspection of the Imperial Navy's harbor at Kavieng. Executive officer of AMBERJACK at that time was Lieutenant Commander B. A. Clarey. And there in Kavieng Harbor was this same ex-whale factory in service as a plane-carrier hauling aircraft to the Bismarck Archipelago.

AMBERJACK had fired four torpedoes. Hits thundered under the whale factory's stern, and TONAN MARU No. 2 sat in Kavieng Harbor with her rump in the mud. Eventually the Imperial Navy raised her and she was laboriously towed to Japan where she was refitted and put into service as an oil tanker. And now she was in front of PINTADO's periscope and Clarey's eyes—the revivified TONAN MARU No. 2, as big as life and twice as handsome.

"It was difficult for me to believe that this could possibly be the same ship," Clarey wrote afterwards. But the vessel was undoubtedly the ex-whale factory whose twin had been sunk by Navy bombers at Truk. And it was time the whole family was exterminated. Commander Clarey described the action as follows:

We maneuvered into position ahead of the center of the convoy because we wanted to attack and sink, if possible, the largest ship. Evidently the Nips believed this position to be the safest place for the most valuable ship in the convoy. By six o'clock we had attained position directly ahead of the convoy, right on the track of the whale factory which was zig-zagging alternately to the right and left. At 6:15 we ordered "battle stations submerged," at which time we took a sounding obtaining a depth of 210 feet, rigged ship for depth charges, and proceeded to a firing position. During these maneuvers a CHIDORI torpedo boat anti-submarine vessel, the leading escort, was coming in our general direction and at one time passed about 75 yards ahead of our periscope. He finally passed clear, not having detected us and, about 11 minutes later, we fired four torpedoes from the stern tubes at the whale factory from a range of about 1200 yards. About a minute and a half after firing, two torpedoes were heard and observed to hit the target. One hit forward and one amidships. Immediately after firing we turned in order to bring the bow tubes to bear and at one minute after seven fired six more torpedoes at the whale factory and the overlapping tankers in the port columns. All torpedoes were set at six feet. Two of the torpedoes from this last salvo ran erratic. One circled and crossed twice over the PINTADO; it could be distinctly heard as it passed over the engine room. The other torpedoes ran straight. About 2½ minutes later two more hits were heard and the leading tanker in the far column burst into flame over its entire length like an ignited, gasoline-soaked log. The second of these hits was obtained in the tanker next astern.

On again looking at the whale factory it was, by this time, burning briskly from bow to stern. The sun had set about ten minutes past six and it now, being a little after seven, became quite dark. We decided to seek deeper depths and pull away from this area in order to surface as soon as possible, reload our torpedoes and try to attack this convoy again that night. . . .

Shortly before 10 o'clock we surfaced and started our search for the remainder of the convoy. As we skirted the area of the damaged ships we could see three enormous and very distinct fires at a range of about five to six miles. A pall of dense, black smoke covered the entire sky, darkening the area around the scene. We continued to search for the remainder of the night and all of the next day but were unable to again locate the convoy.

The convoy's biggest ship was gone for good. The elephantine vessel, identified after the war as none other than TONAN MARU No. 2, was from that date forward an ex-ex-whale factory.

Loss of Flier

To conduct her second war patrol, FLIER (Commander J. D. Crowley) left Fremantle on August 2 and headed for area waters off Saigon, French Indo-China. On the evening of August 13 she was transiting Balabac Strait, traveling on the surface when a thunderous explosion rocked the submarine. Oil, water and debris showered the bridge. Crowley was thrown from his feet and several others on the bridge were injured. Lieutenant J. W. Liddell, the executive officer, was blown through the hatch. Men struggled up the ladder behind him. FLIER, still making 15 knots, sank a minute after the explosion.

Thirteen survivors, including Commander Crowley, started a desperate swim in the direction of land. At first they tried to keep together. Then the tide swept some of the weaker swimmers away from the others. Crowley decided the best chance was to strike out for coral reefs northwestward.

But a little while later, Lieutenant J. E. Casey, who had been blinded by oil, quietly slipped away. Realizing it had to be every man for himself, Crowley told all hands to swim on as best they could toward the land which was now in sight.

The sun came up in a crimson welter and the sky blazed. All morning the swimmers labored on. At 1330 five of the group, including Crowley, caught a floating palm tree. Clinging to this flotsam, they succeeded in reaching the beach of Mantangule Island. There they found Quartermaster J. D. Russo, who had swum the entire distance. And later they were delighted to encounter two others.

On this jungly island, FLIER'S survivors lived like Crusoes for five days. On August 19 they found friendly natives who guided them to a U.S. Army Coast Watcher Unit on Palawan. The coast watchers provided communication facilities, and arrangements were made for evacuation by submarine. They were picked up by REDFIN.

So concluded one of the most harrowing submarine adventures of the Pacific War. The survivors who made the long swim were grateful for the luck and stamina that kept them going after FLIER struck the mine.

Prisoner-of-war Rescue by Submarines

In March 1944 the Japanese at Singapore were cheering the completion of a railroad which had been built by the slave labor of British, Australian and native POW's. This iron trail had cost the lives of 22,000 prisoners. The survivors of this barbarous railroading were to go to Japan to slave in the Emperor's factories and mines.

On September 6, a convoy of six ships with five escorts left Singapore for Japan. Crammed aboard RAKUYO MARU were 1,350 English and Australian captives. Some 750 of their fellows were stuffed like cattle into the holds of another ship. Several days after sailing, this group was joined by three passenger-cargomen and two more escorts from the Philippines. On the night of September 11-12, the convoy was proceeding northward in three columns, three ships to a column, the DD SHIKINAMI leading the center column and three small escort vessels riding herd on each flank.

This convoy fell prey to an American wolf-pack called "Ben's Busters"—GROWLER, PAMPANITO and SEALION. Between 0100 and 0130 on the 12th, all three submarines contacted the convoy by radar some 300 miles off Hainan. The submarines swung into action.

At 0155 GROWLER attacked from the convoy's starboard side, and put a torpedo into HIRADO, the leading escort vessel on the starboard bow. This craft, a frigate, blew up amidships, burst into flames and sank within a few minutes.

At 0524 Commander E. T. Reich drove SEALION into attack on the convoy's starboard side. In two minutes' time, Reich slammed two torpedoes in the passenger-cargoman NANKAI MARU in the center of the formation, another torpedo into a large transport leading the right column, and two more into the transport RAKUYO MARU. The Japanese aboard RAKUYO MARU immediately abandoned. The unfortunate prisoners, left to fend for themselves, somehow got free of the ship and into the water.

At 0653 GROWLER attacked and sank the destroyer SHIKINAMI. RAKUYO MARU sank late in the afternoon.

During the day, most of the Japanese were picked up by escorts, while the prisoners in the water were held at bay by rifles and pistols. By nightfall the miserable men, abandoned, were swimming desperately, or clinging helplessly to mats of wreckage. Nearly all were smeared from head to foot with the crude oil which covered the water's surface. After sundown the prospect of survival seemed slim indeed. But these castaways were to have an unexpected deliverance.

Throughout the day PAMPANITO tracked the convoy, which had changed course and fled toward Hong Kong. PAMPANITO hung on doggedly as her captain, Lieutenant Commander P. E. Summers, directed the chase. At 2240, the submarine was in position for a surface attack. Seven torpedoes hit home. One salvo sank the 10,509-ton passenger-cargo carrier KACHIDOKI MARU. Now more prisoners of war struggled desperately in the water.

On September 14 GROWLER departed the area. But SEALION and PAMPANITO remained. On the afternoon of the 15th, PAMPANITO, passing through the waters where she had made her attack, discovered a crude raft loaded with men. Summers sized up the situation at once and PAMPANITO began picking up survivors as fast as she could locate them.

Her patrol reports tells the dramatic story:

As men were received on board, we stripped them and removed most of the heavy coating of oil and muck. We cleared the after torpedo room and passed them below as quickly as possible. Gave all men a piece of cloth moistened with water to suck on. All of them were exhausted after four days on the raft and three years' imprisonment. Many had lashed themselves to their makeshift rafts which were slick with grease; and had nothing but life belts with them. All showed signs of pellagra, beriberi, immersion, salt water sores, ringworm, malaria, etc. All were very thin and showed the results of undernourishment. Some were in very bad shape, but with the excitement of rescue they came alongside with cheers for the Yanks and many a curse for the Nips.

At 1710 of that day (the 15th) PAMPANITO sent a message to SEALION asking help. From that hour forward the submariners raced with darkness. SEALION gave a hand, and the two submarines combed the area, picking up survivors. By 2000 no more men could be safely accommodated aboard the over-crowded submarines. The two headed full-speed toward Saipan. Lieutenant Commander Reich expressed the feelings of the submariners as he wrote, "It was heartbreaking to leave so many dying men behind."

PAMPANITO had rescued 73, and SEALION 54.

As soon as he received the word, ComSubPac ordered BARB and QUEENFISH, then in Luzon Strait, to proceed to the rescue area and hunt for survivors. By the afternoon of September 17, these two submarines were combing the waters where the derelicts had last been seen. BARB had sunk a Japanese escort carrier the day before. But Lieutenant Commander Eugene B. Fluckey was always ready for the sort of assignment involving a rescue. He wrote:

0100 (17th). Received orders from ComWolfPack to proceed to survivor area. I heartily agree. As an after thought inserted here, having seen the piteous plight of the 14 survivors we rescued, I can say that I would forego the pleasure of an attack on a Jap Task Force to rescue any one of them. There is little room for sentiment in submarine warfare, but the measure of saving one Allied life against sinking a Jap ship is one which leaves no question, once experienced.

Rescue parties, consisting of crack swimmers, and hauling-out, delivery, and stripping parties, had immediately been organized. BARB and QUEENFISH ran a race against the threat of enemy attack, heavy seas, and wind which was whipping up to typhoon velocity. Incredibly enough, survivors were found and picked up. The search went forward until the afternoon of September 18, when a 60-knot wind forced the two submarines to discontinue and head for Saipan. By that time it was certain that no living survivors remained.

When BARB and QUEENFISH completed their rescue mission, 32 more British and Australian survivors had been rescued. Altogether 159 were picked up by the four submarines but seven died before the submarines reached port. Concerning their condition and the care given them, Lieutenant Commander Summers of PAMPANITO wrote:

We had an acute problem with the seventy-three survivors aboard plus our complement of eighty officers and men, but by careful planning and supervision the situation was kept under control and all hands fared very well. The survivors were long used to being in cramped space and even the small space allotted them brought no complaints. The crew was crowded too but cheerfully stood their regular watches and "nurse-maid watch." All survivors, except six of the more critical cases, were berthed in the after-torpedo room. . . . All men were infected to various extents with beri-beri, scurvy, malaria, and other skin irritations. Strict segregation from the crew was necessary. Two officers were assigned to manage the problems and a two-man "nurse-maid watch" was kept in the after torpedo room in addition to the Pharmacist's Mate and two volunteer assistants (one Ship's Cook and one Seaman) who were working continuously. The first problem was getting the men on board. In their weakened condition and due to the fact that they were covered with heavy crude oil, the actual recovery was quite a task. Many of the men could help themselves but the majority had to be lifted bodily on board. . . .

Several required hypo shots but for the most part a little oil wiped from their eyes and mouth, a wet rag to cool their parched salt-sore lips and throats, and a strong "Yankee" hand to help them get below was sufficient. While still topside their clothes were cut away and they were given a diesel oil sponge bath to remove most of the heavy crude oil. Getting the weakened ones down the hatch was quite a job. . . . Water was their most acute need and they were given plenty (in small amounts at first). Hot soup, tea, and broth followed, and they were soon sleeping the sound sleep of thoroughly exhausted men.

BARB's Commander Fluckey, inimitable stylist, wrote:

A word on the survivors. . . . They were in the water or on their small wooden life rafts for a period of 5 days before being picked up. This in addition to 3 years of prison life under the Japs which included bashings, beating, starvation, malaria, dysentery, pellagra, sores, ulcers, etc., had left them in terrible physical condition. The at first dubious, then amazed, and finally hysterically thankful look on their faces, from the time they first sighted us approaching them, is one we shall never forget. Several of them were too weak to take the lines thrown them. These were rescued by the valiant efforts of Lieutenant Commander R. W. McNitt, Lieutenant J. G. Lanier, and Houston, C. S., MoMM2c who dove in after them. . . .

The appreciation of the survivors was unbounded. Even those who couldn't talk expressed themselves tearfully through their glazed, oil-soaked eyes. We regret there was no more, for we had found it possible, by taking over every square foot of space aboard ship, sleeping three to a torpedo rack, etc., to accommodate a hundred.

Last of the Convoy Routes

In July the Japanese convoy run from Formosa to Palau was abandoned and Palau-bound convoys were routed through Manila. In August, when the United States offensive struck the Pelews, all runs to Palau were abruptly terminated.

In August the convoy run from Hong Kong to Hainan was ended. The ships were transferred to the hard-pressed Singapore run.

In September the convoy run from Formosa to Hainan went out of operation. The route lay athwart the "Convoy College" area. The closure imposed a severe deprivation on Japan's iron-mongers, for a sizable percentage of Japan's iron ore imports had come from Hainan.

By the end of summer, 1944, Japanese shipping was almost entirely confined to the South China Sea, the East China and Yellow Seas and Empire waters.

The torpedo warfare which raged in "Convoy College" inspired in Japanese mariners a pessimism which spread throughout the merchant service. Concerning the submarine's responsibility for the deterioration of morale in the Japanese merchant marine, the post-war United States Strategic Bombing Survey had this to say:

Inquiry into the greatest fear of merchant seamen produced various answers. The consensus of opinion appeared to be that crews in general feared air attack the most, but ship captains with a more realistic outlook on their chances of survival feared submarine attack the most.

By the autumn of 1944, Japan had lost shipping contact with all but a fragment of her conquered Southwest Pacific empire. U. S. submarines from Pearl Harbor and Fremantle were the agents chiefly responsible. Storming across "Convoy College" and ranging over the South China Sea, "lone wolves" and wolf-packs torpedoed the convoy system out of the heart of the Co-Prosperity Sphere.

Chapter 24

Submarine Support of Fleet Operations

☆ ☆ ☆

The Pattern

The pattern for submarine support of offensive fleet operations had been cut by the time the Gilbert Islands were secured. The scouting line in the Battle of Midway — reconnaissance before landings in the Solomons — weather reporting and beacon duty in the Solomons and off Morocco — troop transport at Makin and in the Aleutians—photo reconnaissance, lifeguarding and scouting patrols during the Gilbert strike — these established the chief elements of the design.

This chapter briefly reviews some of the moves made by U.S. submarines supporting the fleet as reconnaissance, scouting and fighting units during the 1944 Pacific push.

Spearheads for Big Drives

"Operation Flintlock" to seize the Marshalls—"Operation Hailstone" to knock out Truk—"Operation Desecrate" to hammer Saipan and Tinian—submarines spearheaded all these Central Pacific blows which sent the Japanese reeling. When Admiral Spruance's Fifth Fleet advanced, it entered waters long patrolled by SubPac submarines. When amphibs drove ashore, they landed on beaches reconnoitered by subs. When air armadas struck, they found subs on hand as lifeguards. And subs were in place to intercept the Imperial Navy as it retreated across the mid-Pacific.

Off Truk SKATE sank the Jap light cruiser AGANO. That was in February—only a hint of what was to come.

In the waters off the Pelews, the Imperial Navy got another hint. A loud one from submarine TUNNY.

At sunset on the eve of the Peleliu strike, TUNNY (Commander J. A. Scott) made contact with Japan's newest battleship and flagship of the Japanese fleet. This was the monster MUSASHI, 63,000-ton twin sister of the giantess YAMATO. Scott drove TUNNY in on the attack, and fired six expertly aimed torpedoes. But an alert escort warned the battleship just in the nick. As she swung to comb the tracks, MUSASHI was hit twice near the bow. Had the hits been aft or in the engine spaces, the huge BB would probably have been slowed, and Mitscher's carrier planes might have caught and sunk her the next day. Wounded in the head instead of the legs, she managed to get away. But her hour would arrive.

The Marianas Campaign ("Operation Forager")

Two thousand miles southwest of Pearl Harbor, Majuro Atoll provided the SubPac Force with a fine forward base and rest camp. The camp was built in 15 days by men of the tender SPERRY. The tender also put her wing over the incoming submarines that slid from time to time into the lagoon.

Early in June 1944, the blue lagoon was bustling with unusual activity. The Fifth Fleet was steaming out on "Operation Forager"—the invasion drive on the Marianas.

From the point of view of the submarine forces, the Marianas Campaign and the Battle of the Philippine Sea which followed were—so far as submarine support of fleet operations was concerned—the high points of the war. Some naval strategists consider the action history's outstanding example of the successful employment of submarines in a major fleet engagement. Effective scouting, efficient communications, intelligent handling and several smashing torpedo attacks combined to give the Submarine Force a leading role in a victory which meant the beginning of the end for the Imperial Navy.

The Marianas invasion promised action. Moving on Saipan, the U. S. amphibious forces would be entering the Japanese inner defense ring. The Japanese would oppose this amphibious move with every defensive weapon they could muster—of that Admiral Nimitz was certain. The Fifth Fleet's primary task was to support the Saipan landings and to protect the amphibious forces carrying out the operation. Enemy interference with the operation would come from enemy-held water considerably to the west, and scouting by planes which would have to leave Saipan and proceed to the Philippines area was practically out of the question. So submarines were once more called upon to serve as vedettes on guard against the possible sortie of a Japanese fleet.

The main Japanese fleet had concentrated at Tawi Tawi in the Sulu Archipelago. The enemy was expecting a thrust at the Marianas, and advices from Rabaul indicated a simultaneous Allied strike at Wewak, New Guinea. In an effort to base the fleet as close as possible to these scenes of impending action Admiral Toyoda had ordered Admirals Kurita and Ozawa to the Tawi Tawi anchorage.

Allied reconnaissance located the Japanese naval concentration, and ComSubSoWesPac sent HARDER, REDFIN and BLUEFISH to maintain a watch in the vicinity. HAKE, BASHAW and PADDLE were stationed southeast of Mindanao to cover that route to the Marianas. ComSubPac stationed PINTADO, PILOTFISH and TUNNY in Luzon Strait. FLYINGFISH was placed at San Bernardino Strait and GROWLER at Surigao Strait. Thus all avenues from Tawi Tawi to the Marianas were covered by submarines.

In addition, five SubPac submarines were placed north and west of the Marianas to watch the approaches from the Empire. And ALBACORE, SEAWOLF, BANG, FINBACK, STINGRAY, MUSKALLUNGE, PIPEFISH, SEAHORSE and CAVALLA were disposed to the westward of the Marianas, in waters lying between Palau and the 20° parallel. All were shifted from day to day as information on the Japanese fleet was received and ComSubPac moved his units into intercepting positions. This submarine disposal could not have been better conceived and it remains as an example of masterful submarine strategy.

The Palau Campaign ("Operation Stalemate")

"Stalemate"—the operation to capture Palau, with Yap and Ulithi as secondary objectives—was under the over-all command of Admiral Halsey. (For the remainder of the war, Halsey and Spruance would alternate as Fleet Commanders. When Halsey had charge of the Pacific Fleet it was designated the "Third Fleet." When Spruance was in command it was called the "Fifth Fleet.")

Halsey's method of submarine deployment differed considerably from Spruance's. Halsey would station submarines at such strategic points as Surigao, San Bernardino, Luzon Straits, and the Bungo Suido, but he also wanted a submarine reconnaissance line to cover a broad front which would extend across miles of open sea. Such a reconnaissance line was devised for "Operation Stalemate."

This line was designated as the "Zoo." It was occupied by three wolf-packs composed of three submarines each. The packs were called "Cats," "Bears," and "Dogs," with Captain C. W. Wilkins in SEAHORSE, Commander A. H. Holtz in BAYA, and Commander R. S. Benson in RAZORBACK as pack commanders. Captain Wilkins was in over-all command of the "Zoo."

Halsey's Third Fleet (some 800 ships) drove at Palau on September 15th. After a scorching three-day bombardment, the Marines went ashore. The 12,000 Japanese defenders put up a tooth-and-nail fight, and Marine casualties were severe. But with the fall of Palau the last main central Pacific gate to the Philippines was crashed.

"Zoo" was maintained from September 13 until September 25th. But the wolf-packs were unable to make contact with the enemy during this time. Thereafter, the submarine reconnaissance line was not used in the Central Pacific. Admiral Nimitz reasoned that submarines patrolling the sortie routes from known enemy bases had more opportunity to inflict damage on the enemy.

The Leyte Campaign ("King Two")

The terms "Stalemate" and "King Two" were borrowed from chess.

"King Two"—the opening move of a fast gambit—started a swift game that was to cost the enemy the Philippines. The success of the mid-September raids convinced Halsey that the central Philippines were ripe for a smash. His conviction was supported by information from a number of sources. One source was photographic reconnaissance. Another was the patrol report of submarines such as NARWHAL, NAUTILUS, ANGLER and REDFIN.

The landing of secret agents and guerrilla supplies supported the amphibious Philippines offensive. By the autumn of 1944, the guerrilla war was going like a forest fire on Mindanao, Negros and Samar. The submarines which stoked this fire with incendiary war materials blazed the trail for MacArthur's invasion forces.

CREVALLE, BONEFISH, NARWHAL, NAUTILUS, SEAWOLF, STINGRAY and REDFIN conducted guerrilla supply missions in the Philippines in the spring and summer of 1944. They went in with weapons and war gear and came out with evacuees. All these missions were dangerous ones for submarines. Above all, they were dangerous for the Japs.

During 39 such missions, over 1,325 tons of war supplies were placed in the hands of guerrilla fighters. The word to them was, "Very soon now, Joe."

Chapter 25

Submarines vs. the Japanese Navy

☆ ☆ ☆

Marked Men-of-war

American submarines were pitted against the Imperial Navy from the first. They might have hit it harder and sooner had they been armed with a dependable torpedo. The defective magnetic exploder was particularly prone to err when it entered the expansive magnetic field which surrounded a battleship or an aircraft carrier. Early submarine attacks against vessels of that caliber were invariably frustrated.

The aircraft carrier SORYU, sunk during the Battle of Midway, was already on her last legs when NAUTILUS administered the *coup de gráce*. Sunk by S-44, the heavy cruiser KAKO was blown to the bottom by non-magnetic Mark 10 torpedoes. Sixteen months then elapsed before a U.S. submarine downed another Jap heavyweight. But attack after attack had failed to sink the enemy's larger men-of-war. Proof positive that the fault was the torpedo's became apparent when submarines carrying the rectified exploder began to demolish the Imperial Navy's capital ships. SAILFISH started the rally on December 3, 1943, when she downed the escort carrier CHUYO.

In the first quarter of 1944, the submarine drive against the Imperial Navy was getting under way. Straws in the wind, the sinking of the light cruiser AGANO by SKATE, and the sinking of the light cruiser of TATSUTA by submarine SANDLANCE.

The onslaught, unleashed by Admiral Lockwood when he corrected the torpedo's faults, developed during the summer of 1944 into a campaign of annihilation. United States sur-

325

face and air forces, aided by Allied elements, contributed their share to the extermination campaign.

Destroy the Destroyer!

The big submarine headline in April featured the news that it was now open season for DD's. How had the mighty fallen! Had been a time when the lusty destroyer was looked upon by the periscope as the most dangerous foes—an opponent to be avoided by the submarine unless combat were inescapable.

It was not the doctrine when the calendar reached 1944. By that date 14 Japanese specimens (9 modern and 5 old-timers) had been sunk by U.S. submarines and the depth-charge barrage was a blown-up bugaboo.

On April 13, 1944, the announcement was made that the destroyer season was open. The date was timed by various factors which indicated that the Imperial Navy's destroyer losses (from all causes) had created a serious DD shortage, and the enemy was having great difficulty in mustering these vessels for important convoy and man-of-war escort duty. The anti-DD campaign was designed to increase the shortage.

In the spring and summer of 1944, the Japanese destroyer hunt continued with a vengeance. The predatory DD that loomed up over the horizon and came rushing forward with a white moustache under its nose was liable to a down-the-throat shot that would stop it as an elephant gun would stop a hyena. Submarine torpedoes—electric and the revised Mark 14—downed a dozen Japanese DD's that spring and summer.

But the season's champion destroyer-killer was HARDER. Before Sam Dealey's submarine was through, she had set a world's record.

Official post-war assessment credited HARDER with downing three Japanese destroyers in a row and damaging at least two more. Extraordinary shooting for one submarine in a brief period of four days! Perhaps more remarkable than those torpedoings was their after effect—Admiral Toyoda's alarm and the Japanese fleet's precipitate departure from Tawi Tawi. The strategic consequences of HARDER's anti-DD drive could not be measured in destroyer tons. Nor were they fully known until after the war.

Loss of Harder (Commander S. D. Dealey)

HARDER left Australia on August 5, 1944, to conduct her

sixth war patrol. She was at that time leading a wolf-pack composed of herself, HAKE and HADDO. On the morning of August 21, HARDER joined RAY and GUITARRO in attacking a large convoy.

After the convoy battle, HADDO and HARDER made a combined attack on three Jap coast defense vessels off Bataan. These small vessels were speedily demolished, and by that time HAKE, the third submarine of the wolf-pack, arrived on the scene. The wolf-pack continued the hunt.

HADDO destroyed the DD ASAKAZE on the morning of August 23, and then, out of ammunition, headed for Australia. HARDER and HAKE headed for Caiman Point.

At 0453, on the morning of August 24, HAKE submerged not far from Caiman Point. HARDER was then in sight 4,500 yards south of her. Presently HAKE heard "pinging" to the southward, and her periscope picked up two ships against the morning sky. HAKE's captain, Commander Broach, sent the submarine boring in. The targets were identified as a Siamese destroyer, and a Jap minesweeper. Broach discontinued the attack when the destroyer zigged away. The minesweeper loitered off the bay.

At 0647, HAKE, coming to a northerly course, sighted HARDER's periscope dead ahead, perhaps 650 yards distant. Sound reported faint screws on this bearing, so Broach ordered a turn away toward the south. As HAKE turned, Sound heard three strong "pings." A periscope exposure showed the minesweeper veering toward the two submarines.

Broach suspected the enemy had made contact, so he ordered deep submergence. The minesweeper continued to "ping" uncertainly. Then at 0728, HAKE heard 15 rapid depth charges thundering in the distance. Two hours and a half later—silence.

That noon there was no sign of HARDER. She did not join HAKE that night.

The account of an A/S attack off Caiman Point was found in Japanese records. The report concluded, "Much oil, wood chips and cork floated in the vicinity."

So perished HARDER and Commander Sam Dealey—one of the greatest fighting teams of the Pacific War. Commander Dealey was posthumously awarded the Congressional Medal of Honor.

Submarines vs. Japanese Grand Strategy (Battle of the Philippine Sea)

Every war lord loves to devise so-called "grand strategy." Admiral Soemu Toyoda was no exception. For defense of the Marianas he came up with "A-Go Plan," whereby the Combined Fleet would slip out of Tawi Tawi in two sections. Admiral Ozawa's Carrier Force would steam north to strike at the invaders. A battleship force would circuit southward, then come up as rear guard. Simultaneously, Jap aircraft from the Bonin Islands were to hit the U.S. Fleet.

But what if the United States forces were warned about the Combined Fleet's departure from Tawi Tawi? Apparently, Toyoda, while worried about submarines, neglected that contingency. On the other hand, Admirals Nimitz, Spruance and Lockwood, planning "Operation Forager," had not overlooked the possibility of interference from Toyoda's fleet. Spruance did not intend to be caught flat by Japanese flattops. Therefore, as has been described, U.S. submarines were in the Philippines as well as on Toyoda's mind.

HARDER, REDFIN and BLUEFISH covered the Tawi Tawi exits. Three submarines were strategically placed on station north of Luzon—three south of Mindanao—one at the eastern entrance to San Bernardino Strait—one at the eastern entrance to Surigao Strait. Then HARDER, on the night of June 6, had staged her destroyer-shoot in Sibutu Passage.

Frightened by the HARDER foray, Toyoda pulled the trigger ahead of time on the "A-Go Plan."

Thus it was that HARDER, on the evening of June 10, reported the departure from Tawi Tawi of three battleships, four or more cruisers and some half-dozen destroyers, steaming southward in sortie.

The next information came from REDFIN (Commander M. H. Austin) also watching the Sulu Archipelago. Morning of June 13, REDFIN saw six Japanese carriers, four battleships, eight cruisers and a flock of destroyers head northward from Tawi Tawi. Austin's submarine got off this interesting report that evening. Then FLYINGFISH spotted the big group emerging from San Bernardino Strait.

The group was, of course, Ozawa's carrier force. Admiral Spruance now knew the Imperial Navy was on the move. But instead of striking straight for the Marianas where the offensive was now going full blast, Ozawa's armada proceeded to wander aimlessly around in the Philippine Sea.

Why? Because the fleet's sortie from Tawi Tawi was premature. As a result of Toyoda's jumping the gun on the "A-Go Plan," Ozawa's carriers raced across the Sulu Sea and out through San Bernardino Strait about 24 hours ahead of the operation schedule.

Meantime, where was the task force which HARDER had sighted? Spruance wanted to know. And the answer to this question came from SEAHORSE (Commander S. D. Cutter).

En route to a patrol station area in Luzon Strait, SEAHORSE was heading northwestward across the open sea between the Philippines and the western Carolines on the evening of June 15th. A hot news flash emanated from Cutter's submarine.

TASK FORCE IN POSITION 1011-N . . . 129-35E . . . COURSE NORTHEAST SPEED 16.5 KNOTS . . . SEAHORSE TRAILING

Unfortunately the HORSE developed motor trouble as she trailed, and presently reported that she had lost contact. But the two Japanese forces were now located—the main body east of San Bernardino Strait and the second section coming up from Surigao Strait. Spruance deduced they would rendezvous for fueling before striking for the Marianas. Where? The answer to this all-important question was provided by the submarine CAVALLA.

Cavalla and Albacore vs. Shokaku and Taiho

Captained by Commander H. J. Kossler, CAVALLA, on her maiden patrol, was heading westward to relieve FLYINGFISH at San Bernardino Strait when ComSubPac received the electrifying report from FLYINGFISH. CAVALLA was immediately ordered to scout across the estimated track of the Japanese carrier force.

On June 16 at 2300, CAVALLA's radar picked up a convoy of two tankers and three DD's traveling eastward at high speed. But the submarine was detected by one of the destroyers and forced deep. About an hour and a half later, Kossler ordered CAVALLA to the surface to transmit the contact report. He then headed her for the Philippines.

Kossler was unaware that this tanker convoy was the key to the puzzle concerning the Japanese fleet's rendezvous point. What was more, if those tankers could be destroyed, Kurita's battleships and Ozawa's carriers would be low on fuel— a shortage that would put a check-rein on their movements. This would give U.S. Navy aircraft a bonanza opportunity to locate and destroy them. ComSubPac lost no time in instructing CAVALLA.

DESTRUCTION THOSE TANKERS OF GREAT IMPORTANCE . . . TRAIL . . . ATTACK . . . REPORT

When these orders were received, Kossler reversed course and started CAVALLA after the convoy at four-engine speed.

But by morning of the 17th it was obvious that she could not overhaul the oil argosy. Accordingly, she was ordered to follow along the track at normal cruising speed.

CAVALLA lost the tankers, but she found something else. What she found was the task force which HARDER and SEA-HORSE had previously contacted. At 2000 on the evening of June 18, the Jap BB's came over the horizon like a herd of elephants. Kossler "pulled the plug." This was in accordance with an order to report before attacking. Results illustrated the wisdom behind this decree.

As CAVALLA lay low, the battleship force rumbled directly overhead like a munitions train going over a trestle. CAVALLA, far beneath, was undetected. Two hours later she climbed to the surface and transmitted a report which told Spruance that the Japanese Fleet was about 350 miles southwest of Mitscher's Task Force Fifty-eight.

CAVALLA was deprived of these big-game targets, but Fate was to present her with another, for the following morning she made contact with Ozawa's carrier force. And in the meantime ComSubPac had informed his submarines in the Philippines area that, the enemy task force having been reported, they now could shoot first and report afterward. This was just what Kossler wanted when, peering through the periscope at 1048, he found himself looking at the masts of a large ship under a parasol of Japanese planes. Now CAVAL-LA's periscope was focused on a Japanese aircraft carrier which was accompanied by two cruisers and a destroyer. The carrier was identified as one of the SHOKAKU class. Kossler directed a submerged approach on a 90° starboard track.

The carrier resembled a floating beehive. Planes hovered over her in swarms while others skimmed down to her flight deck. CAVALLA's approach was undetected. At 1118 Kossler fired a salvo of six torpedoes, range 1,200 yards. As the wakes went ribboning toward the target, the DD 1,500 yards away turned toward the submarine. It was time to flood negative and go deep if CAVALLA expected to live to report the attack.

Kossler flooded negative. CAVALLA went deep. The depth charges thundered down. But the submarine sidled out from under the barrage. Kossler was presently able to report the action.

HIT SHOKAKU CLASS CARRIER WITH THREE OUT OF SIX TOR-PEDOES AT ZERO TWO ONE FIVE . . . ACCOMPANIED BY TWO ATAGO-CLASS CRUISERS THREE DESTROYERS POSSIBLY MORE . . . RECEIVED 105 DEPTH CHARGES DURING THREE HOUR PERIOD . . . SUPERSONIC GEAR OUT OF COMMISSION . . . HULL IN-DUCTION FLOODED . . . NO OTHER SERIOUS TROUBLE . . .

SURE WE CAN HANDLE IT . . . HEARD FOUR TERRIFIC EX-
PLOSIONS IN DIRECTION OF TARGET TWO AND ONE HALF
HOURS AFTER ATTACK . . . BELIEVE THAT BABY SANK.

Kossler's belief was confirmed by fact. "That baby" went
down. And she proved to be SHOKAKU herself—30,000 tons.
One of the three largest Japanese aircraft carriers in commission!

But this torpedoing was not the only one dealt Ozawa's
carrier force on the 19th of June. Some three hours before
SHOKAKU was wiped out, ALBACORE struck an even larger
carrier. Sixty miles north of the CAVALLA-SHOKAKU battle, this
titanic encounter took place.

ALBACORE was at that time under the operational control
of ComTaskForce Seventeen—Vice Admiral Lockwood, who
served in dual capacity as ComSubPac and Commander
TF17. Lockwood's expert direction of his submarine task
force engineered the opportunity to win a smashing undersea victory.

When CAVALLA contacted and reported the convoy of tankers, Admiral Lockwood deduced that the Japanese fleet intended to refuel somewhere in the vicinity of 13 N., 137 E.
He immediately ordered four submarines—FINBACK, BANG,
STINGRAY, ALBACORE—to move 100 miles south and SEA-
WOLF 150 miles south of former station. This placed these
five submarines directly across the path of the oncoming
fleet. Chess pieces could not have been better deployed by a
Casablanca.

To ALBACORE fell the drastic play. A little after 0700 on
the morning of the 19th, she submerged to escape the eye of
an enemy plane. Her veteran captain, Commander J. W.
Blanchard, had an idea the plane meant something. It did.
About an hour later, ALBACORE's periscope was watching an
aircraft carrier, a cruiser, and the tops of several unidentified ships. Range was 13,000 yards, and angle on the bow
70° to port. Blanchard swung the submarine to a normal
approach course. While she was swinging, the periscope
picked up a second carrier group.

This group consisted of a flat-top, a cruiser, and several
destroyers. Angle on the bow was only 10° starboard—and
ALBACORE was in an excellent position for attack. Blanchard
promptly seized the better of two opportunities, and came
around to the course for a 70° starboard track. At 0801 the
submarine had closed the range to 9,000 yards, angle on the
bow 15° starboard and distance to the track 2,300. A moment later it was apparent that one of the escorting destroyers was going to run between ALBACORE and the target and

block the shot. Blanchard had to swing to a northerly course to let the destroyer pass beyond the line of fire.

At 0804 the range was 5,300 yards, and ALBACORE 1,950 yards from the target's track. The target's speed plotted at 27 knots. These data were fed into the T.D.C. A periscope exposure made at 0806 checked accuracy. At 0808 Blanchard was ready to shoot. And at that eventful moment, the world's best firing position seemed to fall apart! For as Blanchard ran up the periscope, it was evident that the T.D.C. was not indicating a correct solution.

Blanchard's feelings could be compared to those of a marksman who had drawn a bead on one of the largest rhinos in Tanganyika, only to discover the sights of his rifle were out of kilter. Blanchard pulled down the periscope, took a hasty look at the malfunctioning T.D.C.—and already the target had gone by the firing bearing.

Impossible to swing the submarine and keep up with the bearing rate-of-change. It was now or never—accept the solution as correct, and trust to a wide spread to catch the target with a chance hit. Up periscope! Bearings fed the T.D.C. by hand! Time 0809:32. Fire!

Six torpedoes raced at the target, and Blanchard ordered ALBACORE deep. As the submarine went down, a muffled explosion was heard, timed for the run of No. 6 torpedo.

In the submarine forces at this time, "seeing was believing." ALBACORE, deep under the sea, saw nothing. And Blanchard could not believe one muffled explosion meant a sunken carrier. Not until months afterward did the outcome of the encounter come to light. Then a Japanese prisoner of war disclosed that on the morning of June 19 the aircraft carrier TAIHO, torpedoed just as she was gassing planes, had gone down.

Eventually it was learned that the single hit by ALBACORE had ruptured the carrier's gasoline tanks. Aboard the carrier was Admiral Ozawa himself, who managed to transfer his person to the carrier ZUIKAKU. About six hours after the torpedoing, the gasoline fumes from TAIHO's hemorrhaged tanks ignited. And the 31,000-ton aircraft carrier—Japan's newest, and one of the largest in the world—went booming and bellowing to sea bottom. Down with her went dozens of planes and almost her entire crew.

Two first-line carriers sunk by submarines during one eventful morning! The loss of SHOKAKU and TAIHO was a stunner for the Imperial Navy. Toyoda's fleet was still reeling when U.S. Navy planes roared overhead on the evening of the 20th and gave it an unmerciful blasting.

By midnight of the 20th, the Japanese Combined Fleet was

retreating pell-mell across the Philippine Sea, fleeing for the relative security of Okinawa. Under the fire of submarine torpedoes and air bombs, the Marianas defense plan had disintegrated like a sheet of tissue in a furnace.

SubPac and SubSoWes Pac submarines, in intercepting, reporting and attacking the Japanese naval forces, unquestionably proved worth their weight in pressure hulls and permanently established the place of the submersible as a supporting pillar of the fleet. Sinking 61,000 tons of aircraft carriers in one lump, CAVALLA and ALBACORE won front-rank stations in the submarine hall of fame. Front-rank with them stands HARDER, the submarine that deranged Admiral Toyoda's operational plan.

Chapter 26

Submarines vs. the Japanese Navy

Overture to Leyte Gulf

Capture of Saipan, Tinian and Guam gave United States forces control of the Marianas bastion at the edge of Japan's "inner defense zone." From this Central Pacific stage the Navy could launch a smashing drive at the Philippines, the Nansei Shotos or the Japanese home islands. The Marianas airfields provided Army Air with springboards for the B-29 Super-fortresses that were soon to bomb the heart out of Tokyo.

Japan's military leaders were desperate. The flogging given the Combined Fleet in the Philippine Sea had sent it crawling to Okinawa in the Nansei Shotos—a whipped dragon with its tail between its legs. From there it dragged itself home to its lair in Japan's Inland Sea. It could not, however, curl up and convalesce in this hide-away. At once it had to recuperate for "Operation Sho-Go"—the defense of the Philippines.

Moreover, the dragon had arrived home with its fires almost out, and panting with thirst. Only to find drying oil tanks and dusty pumps. So it eventuated that once again the U.S. submarine attack on Japan's main oil line forced the Imperial Navy's strategic hand. From Kure, Japan, Admiral Kurita's Second Fleet was dispatched in July to the southern end of the South China Sea where it was to train near Singapore at the island of Lingga. Questioned later about this move, Admiral Kurita was explicit. *"The shortage of fuel in the home area required training operations at Lingga."*

Thus the main body of the Japanese dragon was compelled to detach itself from the crippled frame and run to a

334

remote haven for sustenance, leaving its wings and lesser members behind in Nippon. The quoted statement by Kurita dissolves any doubt that this cleavage of the Jap Fleet was not a forced move—an expedient to the Imperial Navy's disadvantage. Strategists might question that point, but there can be no gainsaying the crucial oil shortage in Japan and the fact that last-resort expediency is seldom advantageous.

Ozawa's carrier force—the "wings" which remained in Japan—had absorbed the bulk of the punishment given the Combined Fleet in the Philippine Sea. Bereft of three first-line carriers, most of its aircraft and nearly all of its complement of naval pilots, this force had reached home waters in deplorable condition. Fuel shortage or no, it could not put to sea until repairs and replacements were contrived. New ships and planes might be slapped together in time. But naval aviators were not so readily produced.

Then, while green recruits were being jammed through air schools, the summer burned away. Loss of the 20,000-ton escort carriers TAIYO and UNYO complicated the naval-air problem. The autumnal skies darkened and the glass fell in the Philippines before the Japanese carrier airmen were schooled. The dragon was called upon to fight with its wings clipped.

Halsey (and U.S. submarines) forced the Philippines showdown. MacArthur proposed a slow advance up from the south. But submarine reconnaissance convinced U.S. Navy leaders that the Philippines were ripe for a smashing assault. Navy aircraft confirmed the opinion. Halsey relayed the word to Nimitz. Nimitz advised Admiral King in Washington. Came the green light for Navy's plan to smash into the central Philippines at Leyte Gulf. D-Day was scheduled for October 1944. The U.S. forces braced for "Operation King Two."

According to Admiral Toyoda (post-war reminiscence) the Japanese Navy was hard put to carry out Defense Plan "Sho-Go" at the time the United States offensive struck the Philippines. "*We felt that to take the task force into Leyte was to take a big gamble; and while it would not be accurate to say that we were influenced by public opinion, questions were beginning to be asked at home as to what the Navy was doing after loss of one point after another down south. . . . But since without the participation of our Combined Fleet there was no possibility of the land-based forces in the Philippines having any chance against your forces at all, it was decided to send the whole fleet, taking the gamble.*"

A lesser Japanese naval officer put it this way: *"We had to do something, so we did our best. It was the last chance we had, although not a very good one."*

At any rate, Kurita was ordered to bring the battleships north from Singapore waters, and Ozawa with his four available carriers was ordered to race south from Japan. A third naval force, under Admiral Shima, was dispatched south from Formosa. The three Japanese forces were to converge on Leyte Gulf, but only Kurita's fleet and Shima's force were detailed to get there.

Ozawa's carriers were to perform a dual mission. The carrier aircraft were to strike at the United States Third Fleet and then (since the pilots were untrained in deck landings) proceed to the airfields of Luzon. The Japanese carriers, their planes gone, would remain in the Philippine Sea to lure the American fleet northward. As decoy ducks, Ozawa's carriers would probably be blown to Kingdom Come. That was realized. But the Imperial Navy—or, at least, Toyoda—was willing to make this sacrifice on the assumption that Kurita's Second Fleet and Shima's force would be able to run eastward through the Philippine straits and attack the American invasion shipping in Leyte Gulf.

Kurita was ordered to demolish MacArthur's transports in Leyte Bay, whatever the cost. Here was the Japanese Navy's last chance. The whole "Sho-Go" project was haphazard, mussy-minded and ambiguous. However—

Although destruction seemed in the cards for Ozawa's force, there was some chance that the carrier decoys might get away. And Kurita's force, built around seven battleships, was a formidable fleet. The battleship group included the monster twins YAMATO and MUSASHI, largest BB's in the world. Thirteen cruisers and 18 destroyers escorted these giants. When Toyoda gave the order to move, one of the world's decisive naval battles was in the making.

U.S. submarines were to have a four-ace hand in the decision.

Submarines Intercept the Enemy

Toyoda's plans were, of course, unknown to the American naval leaders. But much could be learned from putting two and two together, and more could be learned from SubPac and SubSoWesPac submarines patrolling off Luzon, off the Nansei Shotos and off Japan. By mid-October it was evident that the Japanese were mustering all available sea forces for a showdown battle in the Philippines.

Patrolling off Japan, submarines BESUGO and SKATE reported the sortie of Ozawa's carrier force. This flash told Nimitz the Japanese Navy was coming out to fight, and Halsey's Third Fleet steamed for an intercepting position.

Meantime Admiral Kinkaid, with the Seventh Fleet, was en route for Leyte Gulf with MacArthur's troop transports. On October 20, this armada reached its destination. As MacArthur put it, he had "returned."

D-Day landings were made on schedule. Losses were light, and General MacArthur announced:

OPERATIONS PROCEEDING SPLENDIDLY IN EVERY RESPECT.

But naval action was impending. On October 21, submarine SEADRAGON reported a Japanese carrier, two cruisers and six destroyers off the southern tip of Formosa.

In the same area SHARK II reported contact with four large vessels and three smaller ones on the same course, rushing at 22 knots. BLACKFISH reported one carrier, two cruisers, and six destroyers steaming toward Luzon. Off Kyushu, SEADOG reported a big convoy heading southeast under heavy escort. ICEFISH in Luzon Strait reported two heavy cruisers and three destroyers steaming on a run that would take them down the east coast of Luzon.

So SubPac periscopes watched the forces of Ozawa and Shima, and SubPac torpedoes struck at these ships as they raced down on the Philippines. But "King Two," although supported throughout by Admiral Halsey's Third Fleet, was entirely a Southwest Pacific operation. Thus the bulk of the submarine support for "King Two" fell to the SubSoWesPac Force operating with Admiral Kinkaid's Seventh Fleet.

Submarines DARTER, DACE, ROCK and BERGALL were stationed in the Palawan Passage area to block the enemy in those waters. BLACKFIN was stationed northwest of Palawan and GURNARD was stationed off Brunei Bay. COBIA was on watch near Sibutu Passage and BATFISH was in the Sulu Sea off northwest Mindanao. Guarding the approaches to Manila were ANGLER and GUITARRO. Farther north, off the west coast of Luzon, were BREAM, CERO, NAUTILUS and COD.

If the Imperial Navy courted a showdown, the United States forces on the sea, over the sea and under the sea were prepared to oblige. The submarines from Fremantle dealt the first hammer blows at the oncoming Japanese.

Dace and Darter vs. Maya, Atago, Takao

In the early hours of October 23 two SubSoWesPac submarines were bent on cruiser elimination. These were DACE

(Commander B. D. Claggett) and DARTER (Commander D. H. McClintock). The eliminating process began on October 10 when the pair, teamed up as a wolf-pack under the leadership of Commander McClintock, commenced combing the seas between northeast Borneo and that perilous patch of water off Palawan known as "Dangerous Grounds."

On October 11, McClintock was directed by ComSub-SoWesPac to conduct a dual patrol that would cover the western approach to Balabac Strait and the southern approach to Palawan Passage. DACE and DARTER were ordered to be on the alert for enemy naval forces which might be northbound from Singapore. DACE sank two freighters off North Borneo. But these vessels were small potatoes compared to what was coming.

Coming was the Imperial Second Fleet—Admiral Kurita's battleship force, led by super-battleships YAMATO and MUSASHI. Straight for Palawan this big-gun fleet was heading— an armada of juggernauts that, by comparison, reduced the two submarines in its path to a pair of toothpicks.

Upon reaching Brunei on the northwest coast of Borneo, Kurita's fleet divided into two task forces. Under Vice Admiral Nishimura, two over-age battleships, the rehabilitated cruiser MOGAMI and four destroyers were to pass south of Palawan Island, steam across the Sulu Sea and rendezvous with Shima's Formosa fleet in the Mindanao Sea. This group was then to strike for Leyte Gulf through Surigao Strait. The main body, under Kurita, was to pass north of Palawan, cross the Sibuyan Sea and head eastward through San Bernardino Strait. This force consisted of five battleships, including the two giants, a dozen cruisers and 14 destroyers. Defending Palawan water, DARTER and DACE were certain to contact either one task force or the other. They found themselves pitted against Kurita's main body.

Early in the morning of October 21, DARTER'S radio picked up a news broadcast of MacArthur's landing on Leyte. McClintock reasoned that the enemy fleet from Singapore would probably head for the short-cut route to Leyte Gulf—Balabac Strait. Accordingly, he headed DARTER for Balabac, and late that evening the submarine made radar contact with three large warships. DARTER tracked them for seven hours, reporting the contacts.

The ships were traveling at high speed, and the submarine was unable to overhaul. Morning of October 22, McClintock abandoned the pursuit and headed southward for a rendezvous with DACE. Midnight, October 22-23, the two submarines were within hailing distance of each other. McClintock's patrol report tells the story:

0000: Speaking to DACE, planning remainder of patrol.

0016: Radar contact.

0017: By megaphone to DACE—"We have contact. Let's go!"

0020: Targets headed up Palawan passage. [Both subs chased.] Between now and dawn sent out three contact reports, giving [as] final estimate task force of eleven heavy ships. Tracking party said that gaining attack position was hopeless due to high target speed (initial estimate, 22 knots). We managed to average about 19 knots. Estimates of enemy speed began to drop until finally it was 15 knots. We had them now! Did not attack in darkness, as it was considered vital to see and identify the force which was probably on its way to interfere with the Leyte landing. It was felt that there could be no radical dawn zig due to size of force and narrowness of Palawan passage. Targets did not zig during night.

0425: 20,000 yards dead ahead of port column of heavy ships. Slowed to 15 knots. Biggest ship is last in port column. Picked it as target.

0509: Reversed course, headed towards port column and submerged. (DACE had just passed us to dive to northeast.) DARTER planned to attack from west in half light of dawn at 0540.

0527: First four ships in column identified as heavy cruisers. Fifth one is probably a battleship.

0528: Range is 2,880 yards to first cruiser in column.

0532: Commenced firing bow tubes at leading cruiser. After firing two into him and one spread ahead, target was rearing by so close that we couldn't miss, so spread the remainder inside his length. Then swung hard left (to bring stern tubes to bear) while getting set up on second cruiser.

0533: Torpedoes started hitting first cruiser. Five hits. Commenced firing stern tubes at second cruiser. Whipped periscope back to first target to see the sight of a lifetime. She was a mass of billowing black smoke from the number one turret to the stern. No superstructure could be seen. Bright orange flames shot out from the side along the main deck from the bow to the after turret. Cruiser was already down by the bow, which was dipping under. Number one turret was at water level. She was definitely finished. It is estimated that there were few, if any, survivors.

0534: Started deep. Evaded. Heard four hits in second cruiser. Felt certain that four hits would sink this one too.

0539: Depth charge attack began. Four destroyers milling about overhead.

0540: Commenced hearing breaking up noises on sound gear, roughly where the targets should be stopped. They increased until they seemed to be right overhead and shook the submarine violently. Heavy rumblings and explosions.

0557: Heard four distant torpedo explosions in rapid succession. Probaby DACE firing. The Japs must think our submarines are everywhere at once. From 0600 to 0604 there were tremendous explosions, probably magazines. It is estimated that from 0600 on, our targets' breaking up noises began to combine with those of DACE's targets.

0605: Depth charges began again. Probably meant for DACE this time. A total of about 36 were heard. From this time on more distant breaking up noises and distant rumbling explosions (not depth charges) could be heard until about 0625.

0630: Last of depth charges.

0820: At periscope depth: One ATAGO-class cruiser sighted, range 12,000 yards, at our attack position, listing slightly to starboard and dead in the water.

1100: Started in towards cruiser.

1300: Range to cruiser 8,000 yards. Two destroyers patrolling on beam at range of 4,000 yards from target. Four planes circling overhead. Decided we would never get to fire from beam with destroyers where they were, so commenced working around to bow.

1430: Range 7,000 yards to cruiser. Coming in on port bow of target when destroyers both headed towards us. . . . Went deep and evaded. Could not attack destroyers since our torpedoes were for the cruiser. Decided to wait until tonight when combined attacks of DARTER and DACE would outwit the destroyers.

1500: Cruiser seen hoisting out a boat. He must have some steam now. Sunset—Too close to cruiser to surface for star sights.

1915: Surfaced. Cruiser in sight on radar. Proceeding to rendezvous with DACE. Sent contact report on the stopped cruiser and estimated composition of the remainder of the Jap force.

2100: Cancelled rendezvous because DACE not yet sighted and reduced visibility rendering immediate attack favorable. DACE ordered to take attack position ten miles from cruiser; bearing 150 degrees true; and DARTER ten miles bearing 050 degrees true from cruiser.

(Thought destroyers would attempt to tow cruiser in our direction towards Palawan Barrier Reef.)

2200: Cruiser underway, speed varied from four to six knots; course was erratic as though target was steering with screws. One destroyer patrolling on each beam.

2245: Started in for surface attack in very poor visibility. Told DACE we would attack in 90 minutes and to sink him if we were forced down.

2400: About one hour to run to gain attack position ahead. Making about 17 knots.

0005: (October 24th). Navigator plotting in conning tower. Grounded on Bombay Shoal with tremendous crash.

In the meantime, DACE, having contacted the enemy, was in the thick of it. Interesting to follow Commander Claggett's blow-by-blow account as it synchronizes with McClintock's. At 0532 on the morning of October 23, DACE heard five torpedo explosions and Claggett noted that "DARTER must be getting in."

0534: Four more torpedo hits. DARTER is really having a field day. Can see great pall of smoke completely enveloping spot where ship was at last look. Do not know whether he has sunk, but it looks good. Ship to left is also smoking badly. . . . There is much signalling, shooting of Very stars, etc. It is a great show. The big ships seem to be milling around. I hope they don't scatter too far for me to get in. Two of these large ships have been hit so far.

0542: The situation is beginning to clear up. I have now picked a target. It looks like a battleship. Range 7,000 yards.

0545: Have identified target as a heavy cruiser of the ATAGO or NACHI-class. There are two of these, but can now see a larger ship astern. Looks like a battleship! Famous statement: "Will let them go by . . . they are only heavy cruisers!" Shifted targets. . . . This is really a submariner's dream . . . sitting right in front of a task force! . . . Now with better light conditions I have seen the following: two ATAGO or NACHI cruisers leading a battleship or CA (my target); there are two other battleships believed to be the ISE-class in column about 1,500 yards to the westward, and behind my target presenting a zero angle on the bow. There are several destroyers milling around DARTER'S position about six miles away. There is one large unidentified ship well to eastward; this looks like either a carrier or perhaps another battleship. Total: eight heavy ships, four destroyers.

0552: The two cruisers passed ahead at about 1,500 yards. They were overlapping; appeared to be running screen for my target. My target can be seen better now, and appears to be a KONGO-class battleship.

0554: Commenced firing a salvo of six bow tubes. Fired One, Two, Three, Four, Five, Six. Took quick look around and saw next battleship still close, so started deep, turning into his wake.

0556: First hit! Second hit! Fourth hit!

0601: Heard two tremendous explosions. These explosions were apparently magazines as I have never heard anything like it. The soundmen said that it sounded as if the bottom of the ocean were blowing up.

0603: Heard tremendous breaking up noises. This was the most gruesome sound I have ever heard. Noise was coming from the northeast, the direction of the target, and it sounded as if she was coming down on top of us. I have never heard anything like it. Comment from Diving Officer:
"We better get the hell out of here!"

0605: First depth charge—not close, but they got progressively closer, and we received a severe working over the next half hour.

1100: At periscope depth. Nothing in sight. Commenced reload and served breakfast.

1425: Saw tops of masts, headed for same.

1510: Can now make out target as a damaged ATAGO cruiser guarded by two destroyers patrolling well out. He also has air cover. Decided that possibilities of getting in for a daylight attack are pretty slim. Cruiser is definitely stopped at scene of DARTER attack, and there doesn't seem to be much possibility of his getting away. Will make a submerged night attack.

2256: DARTER says she will try surface attack from quarter. If she is forced down or chased away by destroyers, we are to attack her [the cruiser's] bow.

2330: Received message that DARTER was making end around to west, was instructed to attack when ready. Commenced end around for better background for submerged attack. Night is dark, but have good horizon to east and will be able to make out target against it.

0007: (October 24th). Received message from DARTER saying she was aground.

Loss of Darter

DARTER was jammed, and in a most precarious position. Making 17 knots, she had ridden up to a draft of nine feet forward, and the reef held her in a relentless clutch. Desperate efforts to get clear were unavailing. The night roared with enemy aircraft. Any moment a Jap warship might come lunging from the dark. The submarine was trapped.

Parenthetically it should be remarked that Commander McClintock had fully realized the dangers involved in the end-around maneuver which had brought DARTER to grief. The incident is considered a classic example of calculated risk. It was regarded by the Submarine Command as one of the unfortunate tactical mishaps always possible in submarine warfare, and McClintock was not held in any way at fault.

DARTER's call to DACE brought Claggett's submarine maneuvering to her aid. Aboard DARTER all confidential papers were burned and secret equipment was smashed. DACE came nosing up through the gloom. Claggett's report of the rescue follows:

C153: Flooded down and approached DARTER. Got line over from bow to DARTER's stern and commenced rescue operations. Salvage impossible. Transferring DARTER personnel via two rubber boats, a slow task. Used up half the battery maneuvering to keep off reef. Current setting me on.

0439: Last boat containing Commanding Officer and Executive Officer of DARTER came aboard. Cast off and backed clear. Received word that demolition charges and warhead were set for 0455, so decided to wait until then before torpedoing.

0500: Heard slight explosion, but can see no damage.

0510: Fired two torpedoes at DARTER. Both exploded on reef.

0530: Fired two more. No apparent damage.

0545: Commenced firing with deck gun. Expended 30 rounds of ammunition. These appeared to do little damage.

0558: Caught by plane in the unenviable position of lying to with 25 men topside. Submerged with ammunition on deck and gun trained out. Heard two explosions which sounded like small bombs. Plane apparently picked DARTER for target.

0805: Surfaced to send message requesting assistance in destroying DARTER.

Redoubtable DARTER was not to be easily destroyed. In midmorning a Japanese DD prowled up to the reef and lay to. Aircraft hovered over the warship, but this protection was unnecessary as DACE was out of torpedoes. Forced to hold DACE at safe distance, Claggett and McClintock could only stand by helplessly while the enemy inspected the stranded submarine.

That evening Claggett brought DACE to the surface and headed her toward DARTER, intending to use his own demolition outfit for the necessary destruction. But as DACE was closing in on DARTER, enemy "pinging" was heard. It sounded like a Japanese submersible, and the American submariners turned to meet this unseen adversary. Later that night DACE received permission to leave the area.

While DACE was on her way home with DARTER's crew, the submarine ROCK was dispatched to Bombay Shoal to destroy stranded DARTER. But again destruction was frustrated as ROCK's torpedoes exploded in futile fury against the intervening reef.

Finally, on October 31, NAUTILUS arrived off the shoal with orders to destroy DARTER. Firing point-blank, NAUTILUS' gunners pumped 55 shattering 6-inch shells into the target. Her commander noted, *"It is doubtful that any equipment in DARTER at 1131 this date would be of any value to Japan— except as scrap."*

So a valiant submarine came to her end. She did not lie alone in those dangerous waters off Palawan. Not many miles from DARTER's shallow grave were the deep-buried bones of Admiral Kurita's flagship, the heavy cruiser ATAGO, sent to the bottom by DARTER's torpedoes. And not far from ATAGO's grave lay the remains of the heavy cruiser MAYA, torpedoed by DARTER's pack-mate DACE.

Hit by torpedoes from DARTER, a third Japanese heavy cruiser, the IJN TAKAO, a floundering cripple, limped to Singapore where she remained for the duration, paralyzed by a wrecked engine.

Whereas Japanese fatalities on board ATAGO and MAYA had been heavy, no American lives were lost through the DARTER grounding—thanks to expert seamanship on the part of the crew, high-caliber leadership on the part of her skipper, and courageous rescue work by DACE. All hands jubilant over the victory, the conquerors of ATAGO, TAKAO and MAYA made home port.

Sho-Go Showdown

While DACE and DARTER were knocking out three of the

Emperor's heavy cruisers off Palawan, U.S. submarine BREAM (Commander W. G. "Moon" Chapple) intercepted a Jap warship column off western Luzon. BREAM pumped six torpedoes at a heavy cruiser. A huge explosion lit the night as BREAM went deep. Jap CL AOBA managed to stay afloat, but her injuries kept her out of the Battle for Leyte Gulf.

With four heavy cruisers eliminated before the battle was even begun. Toyoda must have known the "Sho-Go" gamble was lost. The sinking of ATAGO, Admiral Kurita's flagship, messed up matters considerably. Kurita transferred his personage to battleship YAMATO. Afterwards he said the transfer was an improvement.

But in post-war retrospect, Admiral Koyanagi, Kurita's Chief of Staff, had this to say:

The most trouble we felt was communication. Half the personnel of the communication staff of the previous flagship was killed in the torpedoing, so lack of personnel caused communications trouble when we got aboard the YAMATO.

Kurita himself, when queried about communications, replied:

"I thought that the communications were not entirely adequate partly because, when I switched my flag from ATAGO to YAMATO, communications personnel were divided between two destroyers, one of which had to accompany the [damaged] TAKAO.

The admiral's reference to TAKAO puts another angle on the torpedoing of this second DARTER victim. TAKAO had to limp away on the arm of an escort, and the escort, as it happened, carried off half of Kurita's surviving communications personnel!

The U.S. Navy's submariners would be the last deponents to declare that DARTER'S torpedoing of ATAGO and TAKAO caused a communications foul-up that, in turn, cost the Imperial Navy the Battle for Leyte Gulf. But if the post-war statements of Admirals Kurita and Koyanagi can be trusted, the DARTER foray created much confusion.

As for the ensuing battle for Leyte Gulf details must be left to other naval histories, for the concern of this text is submarine operations. A brief sketch will suffice as a background for the undersea actions which followed in the surface-air battle's wake.

Off southeast Mindoro, Kurita's battleship fleet took a terrible blasting from U.S. Navy aircraft. By nightfall every BB in the armada had suffered at least one bomb hit. The monster MUSASHI, hit by a tornado of bombs and aircraft torpedoes, had capsized. Kurita, on a reversed course, was heading west.

Thereupon he received a message from Admiral Toyoda —an order which may have caused Kurita to regret that the communication channel between his bridge and the Commander-in-Chief's Headquarters was in any state of repair. The message was this: ADVANCE COUNTING ON DIVINE ASSISTANCE

It must have been with some misgivings concerning the assistance that Kurita once more headed his punished armada for Leyte Gulf.

Midnight, October 24-25, Kurita's force reached the Pacific end of San Bernardino Strait, six hours behind schedule. Steaming out of San Bernardino, the abbreviated battleship fleet raced southward along the coast of Samar, with big guns aimed for Leyte. And, as darkness grayed into morning of the 25th, it looked as though miraculous aid had, indeed, screened the movements of Kurita.

For Halsey had drawn off the carrier task groups of the U.S. Third Fleet and sent them racing northward to attack Ozawa's carriers. Thus all available Third Fleet forces were chasing Ozawa's "decoy ducks" at the hour Kurita's warships charged down on Leyte.

Halsey, of course, had no way of knowing Ozawa's carriers were mere decoys. Ozawa's fleet maneuvered erratically off Cape Engano, breaking radio silence, making smoke and doing everything possible to invite attention. Believing the Japanese carriers must at all cost be held away from Leyte Gulf, Halsey sent his task groups to engage Ozawa.

This move was subjected to much post-war criticism, chiefly because Admiral Kinkaid was not immediately notified of the Third Fleet's departure. Left to guard Leyte Gulf with the United States Seventh Fleet, Kinkaid was up against something of a power house. Down came Kurita with four battleships, eight cruisers, 11 destroyers. Another task force pressed on toward Surigao Strait, the warships having suffered no appreciable damage. At the same time Shima's task group from Formosa was heading for the strait. Had the three Japanese forces succeeded in reaching Leyte Gulf simultaneously, the Seventh Fleet might have been thrown back.

Again, it might not. Minus four heavy cruisers (thanks to submarine torpedoes) and several other big warships including mighty MUSHASHI (thanks to submarine reports which summoned Navy bombers to the attack) the Japanese Combined Fleet was seriously abbreviated when it reached Leyte.

Meantime, Admiral Kinkaid's Seventh Fleet was squared away for the show-down. One of the American escort carrier groups fought a whirlwind engagement to block Kurita's battleship force off the coast of Samar. In Surigao Strait the other advancing Jap naval forces were stopped dead and thrown back by Kinkaid's warships. When it was over, much of the Japanese Fleet was scrap iron on the bottom of the sea.

As for Ozawa's carriers, caught by Third Fleet aircraft off Cape Engano, four of the "decoy ducks" were dead decoy ducks.

The Japanese defeat was sufficiently catastrophic. American losses of one light carrier, two escort carriers, two destroyers and a DE, plus loss of the Australian cruiser AUSTRALIA (sunk by *kamikaze* attack during the Leyte landings) were minor compared to Japanese fatalities. These included three battleships, a first-line carrier, three light carriers, eight heavy cruisers (six sunk; two irreparably damaged), four light cruisers, nine destroyers and three submarines. Never in history had a nation lost so much warship tonnage in so short a time.

The Imperial Navy was done for.

The Philippines were lost.

The immediate submarine contribution was something more than the elimination of four heavy cruisers, a retreating light cruiser and a destroyer. And something more than the maladjustment of Kurita's communication machinery, as witness the endorsement of DARTER's fourth war patrol report by Admiral Kinkaid, Commander Seventh Fleet:

> The Fourth War Patrol of the USS DARTER embraces one of the most oustanding contributions by submarines to the ultimate defeat of the Japanese Navy. . . .

Sealion II vs. Kongo

As November waned, U.S. submarines were forced to hunt more and more assiduously for Japanese men-of-war. Big game had become conspicuously scarce. The surviving units of Kurita's Second Fleet, with the exception of some odds and ends at Singapore, had run northward in hectic flight. Principal fugitives were the super-battleship YAMATO and battleships NAGATO, KONGO and HARUNA. Their safest route home was by way of Formosa Strait and the East China Sea—the northern end of the trunk line which had once tethered the conquered southern territories to the home Empire.

This oceanic expanse between Formosa and Kyushu was a dangerous sea for American submarines. Access was difficult. On the west lay the Japanese-held coast of China. On the east lay a great minefield which extended almost all the way from Formosa to Kyushu. To reach the approaches to northern Formosa, a submarine had to skirt the northernmost islands of the Nansei Shoto chain and make the long run southward behind the mine barrier. Once the submarine gained the lower latitudes of the East China Sea, she found herself flanked by a hostile coast on the west and fenced in by mines on the east. This was not the most comfortable hunting ground in the book. But in November 1944 it was a likely area for home-running Japanese battleships. To intercept such anticipated fugitives, SEALION II (Commander Eli T. Reich) was dispatched to the southern waters of the East China Sea.

The LION left Pearl Harbor on November 1st. This was to be her third war patrol, and the success of her first two under skipper Reich undoubtedly lay behind her assignment to an unusually hazardous patrol area. Crew and skipper were just the submariners to handle the southern end of the East China Sea. A Japanese battleship? Why not? To date, U.S. submariners had sunk practically every type of Japanese vessel except a battleship. But they had dented one or two BB's.

At 0020 on the morning of November 21, SEALION was hunting on the surface some 40 miles north of Formosa in the East China Sea. Came the report of a radar contact. Target was unbelievably distant—so distant that the watch at first thought it was land. Probably the coast of Formosa.

Presently, radar reported again. Contact was several thousand yards nearer this time. Then came a report from the conning tower that banished all uncertainty.

"Two targets of battleship proportions and two of large cruiser size! Course 060 True! Speed 16 knots! Not zigging!"

SEALION's engine room got orders for flank speed ahead on all four main engines. The night was overcast and moonless, but the sea was calm and visibility was good for about 1,500 yards.

The targets had shaped up as a task force on the radar screen. What appeared to be a cruiser was leading the column formation. Then came the two battleships. Then a cruiser in the rear. Port side, flanking the leading cruiser, was an escorting destroyer. To the starboard, flanking each battleship, were two more destroyers. What the radar screen did not show was the massive tonnage of all this war-shipping in comparison with the weight of SEALION II. But submarines are no respecter of an opponent's size. Undersea torpedomen follow the adage: "The bigger they are, the harder they fall."

Reich decided to make a surface approach. This was a daring decision. The big warships were certainly maintaining an alert radar watch, and premature discovery would put SEA-LION on the receiving end of a colossal counter-attack. If she were forced to dive, the chances were she would have to go deep and stay deep until the battleships and their escorts cleared the area. However, if she could close in without detection and launch a surprise attack, she might be able to make several strikes before the escorts drove her under. Reich weighed the risks and accepted the odds.

Tracking the course, Reich deduced the Jap warships were bound for Sasebo. This was undoubtedly a unit that had fought in the Battle for Leyte Gulf and was now heading home to salve its scars. Reich and company were determined to interrupt this retirement. SEALION held a course to the westward, starting her end run.

At 0146 SEALION was on the enemy's starboard beam, slowly gaining. As she bent all speed to get ahead, a night wind entered the approach problem and the LION had to claw her way through rising seas. An hour later the submarine was out in front, and Reich picked the second ship in column—the nearest battleship—for his target. As he maneuvered the submarine into attack position the leading cruiser went by. Then an escorting destroyer threatened to intervene. This silhouette, dimly seen from the bridge, was the first visible contact with the enemy task force—until that moment the chase had been conducted entirely by radar. The destroyer, about 1,800 yards distant, was an unwelcome nuisance. Fearing the DD might overlap the battleship in line of fire, Reich set the Mark 18 electric torpedoes for a running depth of eight feet.

During the approach, all hands in SEALION had been elated over the prospect of attacking a Jap BB. Now, at close quarters, the mood changed slightly. This lone submarine, her bow pointing toward the battleship, faced a potential broadside of eight 14-inch guns, eight 6-inch .50-caliber guns, four 5-inch AA guns, and two torpedo tubes. And there was more where that came from, for SEALION faced all the firepower that could be amassed by the other Jap warships.

At 0256, as the destroyer passed the waiting submarine, Reich fired six bow torpedoes at the battleship, range 3,000 yards. As the last shot left the tube nest, he threw the rudder hard right. This brought the stern tubes to bear on the second battleship in the column. At 0259, range 3,100 yards, Reich fired three stern shots at this target.

Sixty seconds later the SEALIONERS on the bridge saw the mushroom fire of exploding torpedoes and heard three hits on the first battleship. A moment after that they saw at least one hit on the second target—a great sheet of flame that whipped skyward.

SEALION's bow was pointed away from the enemy, and the submarine ran westward at flank speed while the Jap destoyers charged eastward in pursuit of ghosts. Dull explosions echoed the torpedo blasts. Depth charges rumbled in the sea, and it was evident that the naval task group was as fuddled as the average merchant convoy. By 0310 SEALION was 8,000 yards west of the Jap task force, and Reich slowed the submarine to parallel the enemy's course and rush a torpedo reload.

Apparently the hits had only dented the armor belt on the battleships, and another attack was necessary. This would not be easy with the targets moving at 18 knots. To make matters worse for SEALION, the wind was caterwauling, and she was taking solid water over the bridge with plenty of it coming down the conning tower hatch. Traveling at top speed, the submarine held on.

A good break was urgent, and at 0450 it came. At that critical moment, the enemy column began to separate into two groups—the cruiser, a battleship and another cruiser in column was pulling ahead. The second group—two destroyers and the battleship which had suffered three torpedo hits —was dropping astern at 12 knots. This was more like it! The LION might get in another attack if she stalked this lagging group. Reich started another end-around, fighting weather that was swiftly developing a hurricane.

By 0512 SEALION was in attack position. Reich slowed her and turned in for the attack. It never eventuated. The battleship with its two escorting destroyers had stopped dead in the water 17,000 yards away. Suddenly the sea was hit by a horrendous explosion. A flash of light came down SEALION's conning tower hatch and illuminated the compartment below. Next came a concussion wave that plucked at breath and clothing like a vacuum cup. In the conning tower, tense submariners waited for word from the bridge. That explosion and flash suggested a big-gun salvo. The next one might be right on. Then came the word.

"Our damaged battleship just blew up!"

SEALION did not sit around licking her chops, but immediately took off at flank speed in an attempt to overhaul the warships to the northward. But the riotous weather slowed her, and she was forced to abandon the chase.

The battleship sunk by SEALION II was the 31,000-ton KONGO. Post-war investigation confirmed the sinking. And it added a postscript to the confirmation. Unknown to the

American submariners until war's end was the fact that a
torpedo from SEALION'S stern-tube salvo, instead of damaging
another battleship, had hit and blown to bits the destroyer
URAKAZE. A battleship and a destroyer sunk in one slashing
attack!

But the battleship alone would have been sufficient. In
sinking KONGO, Commander Eli Reich and crew destroyed
one of the most powerful warships in the Pacific and won for
SEALION II an enduring anchorage in the U.S. Navy's Hall of
Fame.

Archerfish vs. Shinano (No. 1 on the "Hit Parade")

ARCHERFISH (Commander J. F. Enright) left Saipan on November 11 to conduct her fifth war patrol. Out of Portsmouth
Navy Yard in 1943, the submarine had met with indifferent
luck thus far, and there was nothing in the cards to indicate
a change. From Saipan she headed north to patrol in the waters of "Hit Parade." Her assigned area lay about 150 miles
south of Tokyo—a stretch of water due north of Hachijo
Jima in the Nanpo Shoto chain.

ARCHERFISH'S primary mission was to act as lifeguard for
the first B-29 strikes on Tokyo. She was also to engage in
offensive patrolling and shoot at any targets that came her
way. But Enright was not anticipating much shooting. American Superforts droned in the sky. ARCHERFISH was not long
out before she made contact with three friendly submarines.
It could be assumed that Japanese shipping would avoid this
lively area.

Early in the morning of November 28, ARCHERFISH received word there would be no air raid that day and she was
therefore free from lifeguard duties until further notice. The
day was a round of routine monotony. But that evening, when
the submarine was about 12 miles off Inamba Shima, something happened. It happened at 2048—radar contact at long
range. Enright set the machinery in motion and started tracking from ahead.

Within an hour the target was identified as an aircraft carrier, on base course 210, making 20 knots and zigzagging.
Only one escort could be located. The sky was overcast but
bright moonlight seeped through the clouds, and visibility
was good for about 15,000 yards. The horizon was dark to
the north, so Enright started his approach on the enemy's
starboard flank.

At 2230 an escort was sighted on the target's starboard
beam. The position maintained by this escort conspired with
visibility conditions to rule out a surface approach on the tar-

get from that side. Enright therefore changed course back to the base course. At 2250 the range was decreasing but ARCHERFISH was too far off the track to close in with a submerged approach. Range to the escort was 6,100 yards, and the carrier was 15,000 yards away. So Enright held the submarine on the surface and drove in.

As the range shortened, he sent his lookouts below, and, awaiting gun flashes and splashes, braced himself on the bridge. He could now make out the target group as a large carrier in a cordon of four escorts—one on either beam, one ahead and one astern. A surface attack seemed out of the question, but there was little chance of the submarine's regaining the ahead position required for a submerged approach.

Enright sent out a contact report, hoping to guide some other submarine into an intercepting position. The carrier group was making one full knot better than ARCHERFISH could do at her best. Strive as she would, Enright's submarine was slowly falling behind, and it was evident to her skipper that she would end up far in the rear unless the enemy made an accommodating zig or zag. As it was, the enemy was doing his best to accommodate, but his zags and zigs were not angular enough. However, by careful maneuvering and paralleling the base course, ARCHERFISH managed to hang on.

Many are the pros and cons with regard to zigzagging as a submarine defense. Some say that zigzagging throws a continuous problem to submarine fire-control. Others say that a zigzag course keeps the ship longer in jeopardy—if the vessel made a bee-line to get away, she might have a better chance to escape. The chance seems to be about 50-50. Whatever the theoretical arguments, it remains a fact that ARCHERFISH's target would have escaped had the navigators maintained a straight course.

At 2340 the target group made a radical course-change—a change in the base course to the west. ARCHERFISH was now farther off the track than before. She hung on desperately as the "black gang" coaxed a few more turns from overloaded engines. The chase went on through midnight and into the morning of November 29th. It was obvious that if the carrier held to her base course of 275, the ARCHERFISH situation would be hopeless. Enright sent out a second contact report.

Then came the break. At 0300 the target group made another radical change in course, this time veering to the southwest. The range began to close rapidly, and ARCHERFISH was ahead.

At 0305 Enright ordered the submarine under. Range to

the carrier when ARCHERFISH submerged was 11,700 yards. At 7,000 yards the target could be seen through the periscope. Wait—that baby was going to pass too close! Enright changed course 10° to the left, and now the range shortened to 3,500 yards. At about this point the starboard escort approached the carrier to receive a blinker message. This caused the escort to pass ahead of ARCHERFISH at only 400 yards.

At 0316 the carrier zigged away from the submarine. This move put the queen right where Enright wanted her. ARCHERFISH had been a little too close to the target, and the zig gave her a nice position: 1,400 yards range with a 70° starboard track. Because of the late zig, Enright had to accept a larger than normal gyro angle. No matter. At 0317 he fired the first shot of a six-torpedo salvo—Mark 14's set for 10 feet and spread to smash into the target from stern to bow.

Forty-seven seconds later Enright saw and heard the first torpedo hit just inside the carrier's stern, near the propellers and rudder. A great, glowing ball of fire climbed the vessel's side. Then another torpedo smashed home. Enright ordered the submarine deep to evade the inevitable counter-attack. As ARCHERFISH went down, four more timed hits were heard. Breaking-up noises hissed and crackled in the sound gear. Fourteen depth charges boomed in the sea, the nearest some 300 yards away. Finally, silence.

At 0614, Enright put up the periscope for a look. Nothing in sight. Four hours later a thunderous explosion was heard, its source a mystery. Whatever its origin, it came as a salute to the victors of the greatest undersea battle fought in "Hit Parade."

Enright identified the target as a vessel of the HAYATAKA class and accordingly claimed credit for sinking a 29,000-ton aircraft carrier. The facts did not come to light until V-J Day. The Japanese super-battleships YAMATO and MUSASHI, mounting 18-inch guns, were the largest men-of-war ever built by any nation. The Allies were aware that the keel had been laid for a third behemoth of this class—a giant sister to accompany the other two. The name and whereabouts of this third monster remained unknown to the Allies until the cessation of hostilities. Then it was learned that the huge vessel had been converted into a super-aircraft carrier named SHINANO. And her whereabouts was latitude 32-00 N., longitude 137-00 E., where ARCHERFISH had caught and sunk her.

Commissioned on November 18, 1944, she was torpedoed just 10 days later while on her maiden voyage to a safe port for fitting out. SHINANO had a standard displacement of

59,000 tons. Enright and company sank the largest man-of-war ever downed by a submarine. ARCHERFISH leads the hit parade in world history!

The Score (U.S. Submarines vs. Japanese Navy, 1944)

In 1944, U.S. submarines established a championship record. Armed at last with good torpedoes, the SubPac Force and the SoWesPac Force smote the Japanese Imperial Navy a stupendous blow. In this one year, the American submarines sank 55 Japanese warships. The obituary embraced: 1 battleship; 4 aircraft carriers; 3 escort carriers; 2 heavy cruisers; 8 light cruisers; 30 destroyers; and 7 submarines. In addition the U.S. submarines permanently disabled 3 heavy cruisers, and 1 aircraft carrier.

Chapter 27

Bisecting the Empire

☆ ☆ ☆

Maru Morgue and Maru Cemetery

The last three months of 1944, bracketing the Philippines Campaign, sealed the doom of the Japanese merchant marine. While the Imperial Navy was doing and dying, the Japanese transport service was following suit, and its death throes were as violent as those which racked the IJN.

As of October 1, 1944, the Japanese merchant tonnage afloat totaled 3,474,008 tons. By November 1, the total had shrunk to 3,095,820 tons. On December 1, it was down to 2,847,534 tons. And by the end of December it had been further reduced to 2,786,407 tons.

Navy aircraft sank weighty merchant tonnages in the Philippines during October and November, and Army Air came to the fore in December. But submersibles retained the dominant role in the attrition war during the year's final quarter. In spite of intensified carrier and land-based air participation, 55% of the Japanese merchant ships downed in this period were sunk by SubPac and SubSoWesPac submarines.

As "King Two" hit Leyte and MacArthur's forces pushed from there to Mindoro, the SubPac submarines patrolling Luzon Strait and off southwest Formosa turned "Convoy College" into a potter's field for Japanese ships. The lucky *maru* that escaped this burying ground was slated for sinking in the South China Sea (SubSoWesPac Area below the 18°-30° parallel. In these waters, throughout October and November, the Japanese convoys went down like Oriental funeral processions, the burials clamorous with the cymbal-crash of torpedoes, the din of pagan whistles and bells, the

355

ruction of fireworks, the groans and wails of the mourners, the sepulchral rumble of vessels entering the grave. Day and night the Japanese ship burials went on.

Responsible for over 55% of the tonnage subtracted from Japanese merchant shipping during this period, U.S. submarines put a tremendous shoulder to the wheel of the Philippines campaign. No better example of submarine support for an amphibious operation can be found in World War II. And the submarines did more. Cutting the sea lanes to the Philippines, their October-November attrition drive tore to pieces the Empire's transportation system, severed the Singapore-Japan trunk line, and permanently broke the back of the Japanese merchant marine.

The airmen in the Philippines theater contributed their share, and a goodly share it was. But over the necropolis of "Convoy College" and the cemetery of the South China Sea the submariners reared a monumental score. Over 70 merchantmen downed in two months!

But the decimation of Japan's merchant marine had not been accomplished without painful submarine casualties. Seven U.S. submarines were lost in the autumn of 1944— three on one October day. Among those that went down, two were valiant veterans of the war's pioneer period when the Japanese War Machine was thundering down full-tilt on the Philippines instead of frantically retreating.

Loss of Seawolf (A Tragedy of Errors)

No submarine in the Pacific had fought harder in the war than SEAWOLF, pioneer veteran of the Asiatic fleet. Fourteen patrols and 56 torpedo battles had gone into her record since that long-ago day when Lieutenant Commander Warder took her around to Davao Gulf and poked her periscope into the vortex of the Tojo-Yamamoto offensive. By the autumn of 1944 she had sunk 71,609 tons of enemy shipping. Few submarines had downed as many ships and as much tonnage.

On September 21, 1944, SEAWOLF left Brisbane to begin her fifteenth patrol. She was captained by Lieutenant Commander A. L. Bontier. Eight days later she arrived at Manus in the Admiralties. At this base she received a special mission assignment—she was to carry Army stores and Army personnel to the east coast of Samar in the central Philippines.

While SEAWOLF was en route to Samar, MacArthur's forces were driving at the island of Morotai, the stepping-stone just north of Halmahera. A new submarine safety lane, wherein submarines would presumably be free from attack by friendly forces, had been established in the area directly north of Morotai. SEAWOLF made her passage in this lane.

On October 2, the WOLF notified ComTaskForce 72 that she was bucking heavy seas and running a day behind schedule. This information was promptly relayed to Commander Seventh Fleet.

At 0756 on October 3, NARWHAL sighted SEAWOLF and the submarines exchanged recognition signals. Not long after that a Japanese submarine attacked a Seventh Fleet task group which included two escort carriers and destroyer escorts EVERSOLE, EDMONDS, ROWELL and SHELTON. A torpedo struck SHELTON.

ROWELL was directed to stand by the sinking DE. While ROWELL was circling SHELTON, the damaged vessel reported "sound contact" with a submarine. Although ROWELL did not pick up this contact, depth charges were immediately dropped upon the supposedly detected Jap.

Meantime, the American task group commander dispatched a "hunter-killer" group to search out the Japanese submarine. At 1130 two planes were launched from carrier MIDWAY. One of these planes sighted a submarine. The submarine dived and the plane dropped two 335-pound bombs as the submersible went down. The plane had sighted no recognition signals, but this submarine was within the limits of the safety lane. However, the aircraft pilot did not know he was within an attack-restriction area at the time—his information on this detail had been faulty.

Upon receiving a report of this bombing, ROWELL raced to the position given (which had been marked with dye by the plane) and made sound contact on a submarine at 1310. ROWELL delivered six attacks—five with "hedgehogs" (ahead-thrown projectiles) and one with depth charges. After the first "hedgehog" attack, ROWELL heard the submarine send signals by sound gear. The stuttering transmission bore no resemblance to the proper recognition signal, and ROWELL considered it an attempt to "jam" her own sound gear. So she blasted the water with another "hedgehog" pattern. Following this second attack, four or five underwater explosions were heard. Debris was blown to the surface, and ROWELL's crew glimpsed what looked like a section of periscope. A Japanese periscope? Or was it American?

After the war it was learned that the Japanese submarine RO-41 was responsible for the SHELTON torpedoing off Morotai. RO-41 was not counter-attacked, and she eventually returned to Japan. The A/S attacks made by ROWELL were 18 miles from the point where SHELTON was hit, and they did not trouble RO-41. As a rule, neither Japanese nor American submarines attempted to "jam" an attacker's sound gear with sound signals. Undoubtedly the signals heard by ROWELL were from SEAWOLF, and the American submarine was desperately trying to establish herself as a friendly unit, in accordance with instructions prescribed.

In view of all the evidence, submarine authorities were practically certain SEAWOLF was sunk by American forces —either by ROWELL's "hedgehog" and depth-charge barrage, or by the bombing from the carrier plane whose pilot was uninformed about the submarine safety lane.

Commander of the task unit and all commanding officers of the ships involved in the "hunter-killer" operation knew they were in a submarine safety lane. They disregarded the provisions governing such a lane because of seemingly compelling circumstances. Three enemy submarine contacts had been reported in the Morotai area during the preceding two weeks. SHELTON had been critically damaged by torpedoes at 0807 on the day in question. According to the latest Daily Submarine Position Report for the area, the nearest friendly submarine was no closer than 70 miles from the position of the A/S attack that was made by the carrier plane and ROWELL.

However, had SEAWOLF's position been promptly reported to all concerned, the "hunter-killer" group would have known their contact was within 35 miles of a friendly submarine. In which case, they would have proceeded with more caution. But no correction to the October 3 Submarine Position Report was issued—the correction was incorporated in the Report promulgated the following day. The Navy has a saying for it. "Somebody always fails to get the word."

The SEAWOLF tragedy bears evidence to the jeopardy which threatened every submarine operating in a battle zone, particularly when enemy submarines were in the vicinity. Not only was the submersible imperiled by its undersea foe, but it risked accidental attack by friendly "hunter-killers". Yet, such sinkings by friendly forces were remarkably rare on the American side. So far as is known, the possible destruction of DORADO by friendly aircraft in the Caribbean and the probable destruction of SEAWOLF by ROWELL are the only cases of the kind.

SEAWOLF's loss was the first in a month that was to cost the Submarine Service grievous casualties. Five U.S. submarines would go down before the end of October, and on one dark day—the 24th—three of these would fight their last battle.

Loss of Escolar

Commander W. J. Millican took ESCOLAR out of Pearl Harbor on September 18 on her maiden patrol. At Midway, where she topped off with fuel, she joined CROAKER and PERCH II to form a wolf-pack. ESCOLAR'S captain commanded the group which was named "Millican's Marauders."

The pack put out from Midway on September 23 to conduct a patrol in the Yellow Sea.

On October 17, PERCH received a message from ESCOLAR stating that she was in position 33-44 N., 127-33 E., and was heading eastward. This was the last message ever received from ESCOLAR. She should have returned to Midway about November 13th. She did not return.

As was frequently the case with submarines which failed to come back from war patrol, ESCOLAR'S fate was to be recorded only in the invisible writing of mystery. No Japanese A/S attack was reported on a submarine in ESCOLAR'S area. The sea enfolded her, and she went down with all hands.

Loss of Shark II

Accompanied by SEADRAGON and BLACKFISH, SHARK II (Commander E. N. Blakely) left Pearl Harbor on September 23 to begin her third war patrol. The pack slipped in through Luzon Strait and ranged along the 20° parallel, covering an area about midway between Hainan and the western end of Bashi Channel.

On October 22 SHARK contacted and chased a convoy. The convoy got away. Then on the 24th SEADRAGON received from Blakely's submarine a message stating that she had picked up a lone enemy freighter and was going in on the attack. The Japanese reported this attack as made at 20-14 N., 118-27 E. Apparently SHARK's target was a prison ship carrying 1800 American prisoners of war. After this vessel was torpedoed, the Japanese escorts counter-attacked fiercely. Seventeen depth charges were dropped. "Bubbles, heavy oil, clothing and cork" came to the surface of the exploding sea.

Because many prisoners of war were being transported to Japan, U.S. submarines had been instructed to search for POW survivors in the vicinity of Empire-bound vessels which were torpedoed. SHARK II may have been sunk while attempting to rescue such survivors. She was the second

U.S. submarine lost on October 24th. The first was DARTER, stranded in the manner described in a previous chapter. The day's third submarine casualty was TANG.

Tang in Formosa Strait (Commander Richard H. O'Kane)

Late in September 1944, Vice Admiral Onishi, Commander-in-Chief of the Imperial Navy's First Air Fleet, proposed a suicidal tactic for his aviators. The Imperial Army in the Philippines was prepared to immolate itself with *banzai* charges. Admiral Toyoda was willing to sacrifice Kurita's Second Fleet and Ozawa's carriers. The Japanese merchant marine was dedicated to a *hara-kiri* performance. It was time for Japan's naval airmen to indulge the Code Bushido with appropriate ceremony. Whereupon Vice Admiral Onishi suggested the *kamikaze*.

The word means "divine wind." Perhaps this was the assistance Toyoda ordered Kurita to count upon when the Second Fleet's commander hesitated about proceeding to Leyte Gulf. However, the *Kamikaze* Special Attack Corps was held in check during the Leyte and Mindoro campaigns. Even suicide planes need gasoline to start with and a modicum of maintenance to put them in flying condition. The Jap planes at Manila were low on gas and in such bad condition they were too weak to "commit suicide." After the war, a Jap staff officer said spare parts for the planes were lacking because of production stoppages in Japan caused by lack of raw materials "principally caused by submarine attackers."

So the "divine wind" did not blow its fiery breath across Leyte and Mindoro. During those crucial campaigns it was throttled down to a puff. And the support given MacArthur's Manila-bound troops by *maru*-shooting submarines is re-emphasized.

One submarine that contributed Herculean support to the United States offensive was TANG (Commander R. H. O'Kane). By indirect contribution (cargo carriers sunk during previous patrols) she had helped bring about that raw material scarcity which resulted in a shortage of parts for *kamikaze* planes. More direct was the contribution of her October 1944 patrol in Formosa Strait—a patrol which went far to cut down the volume and the speed of Japanese reinforcements.

Commander O'Kane on the bridge, TANG set out from Pearl Harbor on September 24 to conduct her fifth war patrol in the southern reaches of the East China Sea between northwest Formosa and the China Coast. Here she would be on the inside of the Formosa Strait bottleneck, in that dangerous area which was hemmed by minefields to eastward and a hostile coast on the west. O'Kane was given the choice of making the long run down through the East China Sea alone, or joining a wolf-pack. O'Kane chose to go it alone.

TANG topped off at Midway on September 27, and neither the wolf-pack nor any submarine base heard from her or saw her thereafter. But the Japanese both heard from and saw her. First intimation that she was blockading their Formosa Strait traffic lanes came on the night of October 10-11 when O'Kane and company torpedoed and sank two heavily laden freighters. This was the beginning of a foray that was to be officially described as "the most successful patrol ever made by a U.S. submarine."

Following the action of October 11, the hunting slacked off, and TANG spent the next 12 days in routine search. Then, after a careful analysis of the shipping routes, O'Kane put a finger on the chart. TANG reached that point on October 23rd. And down the road as calculated came a convoy—three cargomen, a troop transport, a tanker or two and pugnacious escorts.

O'Kane decided to stop this convoy with a surface attack. Driving TANG into the center of the formation, he unleashed a series of ship-puncturing salvos that mangled the *marus* on all sides. Ensued a ferocious free-for-all—freighters blowing up, escorts dashing about in frenzy, the submarine weaving and dodging through a storm of bullets and shells. Looming up out of the battle smoke, the troop transport bore down on TANG to ram her under. Emergency speed and hard left rudder saved the submarine. Then she was boxed in with three burning vessels on one side, and a freighter, a medium transport and several infuriated destroyers charging in on the other. Holding the bridge, O'Kane swung the submarine to attack her attackers. A salvo tore into the freighter and disabled the transport. TANG'S tubes were now empty, but O'Kane aimed her bow at the nearest destroyer and sent her charging at the DD. The bluff worked. Unwilling to risk a possible torpedoing, the destroyer veered away. As the night flared and shook with the din of gunfire and shellbursts, TANG, her tubes unloaded, raced out through the cordon of escorts. Depth charges flailed the sea behind her. Unscathed, she reached quiet water and submerged.

O'Kane reported seven ships torpedoed in this battle. And

while the residue of this convoy limped off into some backwater, TANG returned to the surface of Formosa Strait to intercept another.

On October 24, exactly 24 hours after her previous encounter, she picked up this second convoy, another heavily escorted herd of *marus* steaming south to reinforce the Imperial troops on Leyte. O'Kane could make out tankers with aircraft on their lengthy decks and troop transports loaded like camels, their fore and after decks piled high with crated planes. Again O'Kane directed a surface approach. When the range was reduced to about 1,000 yards, O'Kane fired six torpedoes—two at a transport—two at a second transport—two at a near-by tanker. All torpedoes smashed home with a series of shattering blasts that tossed up clouds of fire and debris.

At once the night became livid with the glare of burning ships, spitting guns, larruping tracer and exploding shells. A large transport and a tanker were astern of the submarine, and off the beam a destroyer was charging in at 30 knots. Two DE's rushed at TANG from the other side. For the second time in 24 hours the submarine was boxed in. And again O'Kane's expert handling saved her from destruction by the enemy.

As on the previous night, he rang full speed ahead and sent TANG charging straight at her attackers. But this time the charge was no bluff. Closing the range, O'Kane fired three fast shots to clear the way. The first struck the tanker which promptly spewed a geyser of flame. The second hit the transport and stopped her dead in the water. The third struck the destroyer and stopped this foe with a thunderclap that shook TANG from stem to stern. Sprinting out through the gap, she dashed away from the Jap DE's.

O'Kane held the submarine at safe distance while the last two torpedoes were loaded in the tubes. Loaded into the tubes with these last two torpedoes was Fate, the one factor neither O'Kane, nor TANG's crew, nor TANG herself could dominate. What TANG, crew and O'Kane might have gone on to accomplish, had this factor taken a normal turn, can only be imagined in the light of what they had thus far achieved. Abbreviated as was TANG's fifth patrol, O'Kane and company had already sunk seven cargomen.

Now Fate was to cut down this fighting submarine at the very hour when she deserved the laurels of victory.

Loss of Tang

O'Kane picked the damaged troopship as the target for

a parting salvo. Rushing this way and that, the convoy's rattled escorts gave the submarine an opening. The crippled vessel was a set-up—as O'Kane gave the order to fire, there was no intimation of impending disaster.

The first torpedo found its groove and ran straight for the mark, trailing its luminescent wake. The second torpedo swerved sharply to the left, porpoised and made a hairpin turn. A circular run!

O'Kane shouted for emergency speed, and the rudder was immediately thrown over. Too late. Twenty seconds after firing, the terrible boomerang returned from the night and struck TANG in the stern. The blast flung O'Kane and his companions from the bridge. In the submarine's control room men were hurled against the bulkheads, a number suffering fractured arms or broken legs. Mortally stricken, TANG plunged 180 feet to the bottom. Her crew foughts it way forward from the flooded after compartments.

Nine submariners had been blown from the bridge into the boiling sea. O'Kane was among these four swimmers who were picked up by the Japanese the following morning.

The men trapped in the submarine looked Death squarely in the face. After code books and similar publications were burned, these crew members assembled at the escape hatch. Before the escape could be attempted, a Japanese A/S vessel roamed overhead and launched a depth-charge attack. Blast after blast hammered the sunken submarine, bruising her bow and starting a vicious electrical fire in the forward battery. To the men caught at sea bottom, this seemed the final extremity. But they did not yield to despair and abject resignation. Thirteen of these submariners escaped from the forward compartment. By the time the last man squeezed into the escape hatch, the electrical fire was melting the paint on the bulkhead. Eight of the 13 escapees reached the surface alive. Five were able to swim until morning, when they were picked up.

TANG'S nine survivors had to meet another ordeal after their escape from the sea. Aboard the destroyer escort which picked up the nine, there were Japanese survivors from the ships torpedoed by TANG. Blows, kicks and clubbings were dealt the American submariners until the punishment was almost beyond endurance. Yet the torment was suffered with stoicism and stamina.

"When we realized that our clubbings and kickings were being administered by the burned, mutilated survivors of our own handiwork, we found we could take it with less prejudice."

In that statement Commander Richard H. O'Kane displayed a magnanimity and sense of justice that characterized him as a naval officer of extraordinary stature.

After TANG'S survivors were recovered from Japanese prison camps at the end of the war, Commander Richard H. O'Kane was awarded the Medal of Honor.

FOR CONSPICUOUS GALLANTRY AND INTREPIDITY IN COMBAT, (reads the formal citation) . . . *AT THE RISK OF HIS LIFE ABOVE AND BEYOND THE CALL OF DUTY. . . .*

THIS IS A SAGA OF ONE OF THE GREATEST SUBMARINE CRUISES OF ALL TIME, THE FIFTH AND LAST WAR PATROL OF A FIGHTING SHIP—THE U.S.S. TANG—ABLY LED BY HER ILLUSTRIOUS, GALLANT AND COURAGEOUS COMMANDING OFFICER, AND HIS CREW OF DARING OFFICERS AND MEN. . . .

At the time TANG went down, only one other submarine (TAUTOG) had sunk as many Japanese ships. Only TAUTOG, fighting through to war's end, would sink more than TANG'S 24. O'Kane's submarine also had served with outstanding success as a lifeguard, with 22 rescues to her credit. But one other submarine (TIGRONE) would top this rescue score.

Three warships in the United States Navy were twice awarded the Presidential Unit Citation. Two of the honored three were submarines—GUARDFISH (Commanders T. B. Klakring and N. G. Ward) and TANG (Commander R. H. O'Kane).

The Saving of USS Salmon

In the last week of October 1944, SALMON (Lieutenant Commander H. K. Nauman) was patrolling in the lower latitudes of "Hit Parade." On the night of the 30th, Nauman directed an attack on a Japanese tanker which had been damaged and stopped by TRIGGER. When caught by SALMON off the southern tip of Kyushu, the tanker was guarded by four A/S vessels which were cruising back and forth some 1,000 yards from the crippled oiler, maintaining an alert watch.

Nauman sent his submarine boring in, and fired four torpedoes for two hits. The guards counter-attacked furiously, and SALMON went deep. She was leveling off at 300 feet when the enemy located her. Then came the depth charges, and for a few moments the submarine was on the receiving end of a terrific lambasting.

For 17 hectic minutes the assailed submarines fought their

battle damage, endeavoring to stop a score of leaks and trying to repair broken machinery. SALMON's hemorrhages could not be stemmed. With the sea gushing into the boat, she would only sink the deeper, and Nauman decided her best chance was to battle-surface and fight it out with the deck gun. The odds on the surface would be one against four, but the odds submerged were hopeless.

When SALMON broke water, she was up moon from the enemy, and the nearest escort was about 7,000 yards away. Either this escort failed to spot the submarine, or purposely delayed the kill until the three A/S vessels farther distant could close in. Whatever the enemy's reason, the attack on wounded SALMON was slow in coming. This unexpected respite gave the submariners time to correct a 15° list and start some of the machinery. Undoubtedly the dilatory onslaught cost the attackers their chance to finish off SALMON.

Nauman ordered the available guns manned and planned his strategy. When the nearest A/S vessel finally headed for SALMON, the submarine gunners held their fire. Every shot had to count, and Nauman was conserving ammunition. Equally wary, the enemy veered away, and then closed on a different tack. A fusillade from the submarine drove the vessel off.

After long minutes of this cat-and-mouse game, the Japanese decided to ram. At this point, Nauman countered with an old military strategem—a surprise offensive on the attacking enemy. The A/S vessel charged. Nauman snapped the orders. Wheeling on her oncoming foe, SALMON charged with all the velocity she could muster. Firing point-blank, the submarine gunners opened up. Her rush carried SALMON down the side of the A/S vessel, and at a range of 50 yards the submarine fire raked the enemy's deck. A spatter of gunnery came back, but it was nothing to bother SALMON. Her marksmen shot the fight out of the A/S vessel. The Japanese gunners were riddled at their posts and the patrol craft was slashed to kindling. When last seen in SALMON's wake, the target appeared to be sinking.

SALMON kept right on going. A second A/S vessel closed in. A few well-directed shots exploded this craft's ambition to duel. And at this climax the Jay Factor supplied a rain squall. It was all the luck needed by the hard-pressed submariners. Nauman sent SALMON racing into the squall, and behind curtains of blowing rain she swam away in the night.

As soon as repairs could be improvised, SALMON's radio called to the submarines in her vicinity. The next night TRIGGER, SILVERSIDES and STERLET were on hand to guard her with a protective screen. This screen was soon augmented by air cover, and the Mariana-based planes escorted SALMON all the way to Saipan. From there she went to Pearl Harbor, where repair engineers reported her damage too extensive to justify costly overhaul. So the submarine was retired from active service. Nauman and all of the SALMON crew were transferred to the submarine STICKLEBACK, then building at Mare Island Navy Yard. As in DARTER'S case, Submarine Headquarters wanted to retain this crack crew as a fighting unit.

Loss of Albacore

DARTER, SHARK II, TANG—October 24 was a black-letter day for the U.S. Submarine Service. Somber coincidence that ALBACORE (Lieutenant Commander H. R. Rimmer) should leave Pearl Harbor to begin her eleventh patrol on that ill-starred date. Veteran ALBACORE, whose combative captains and crews had sent more Japanese Navy vessels to lie down below than were sunk by any other single submarine.

Now she was to cover the Pacific approaches to Hakodate and Ominato. Because the coastal waters of this area were mineable, she was ordered to stay outside of water less than 100 fathoms deep. After her departure from Midway, ALBACORE was never heard from again.

Japanese records, examined after the war, suggested that ALBACORE struck a mine off northern Hokkaido. This disaster occurred on November 7, and was witnessed by an enemy patrol craft. The submarine, evidently detected by the patrol, was running submerged when the enemy heard an explosion under the sea. Thick oil, bubbles, cork, bedding and boxes of provisions swirled to the surface and drifted off on the tide.

ALBACORE went down with all hands, leaving a champion's record behind her.

Loss of Growler

Out of Fremantle on October 20 stood the submarine GROWLER (Commander T. B. Oakley, Jr.), leading a wolf-pack composed of herself, HAKE and HARDHEAD. The pack's destination was an area off southwest Luzon.

Oakley's wolf-pack reached the assigned area on schedule, and then GROWLER'S SJ radar developed trouble. Emergency repairs were managed, but spare parts were urgently needed. On November 7 a prospective rendezvous between GROWLER and BREAM was arranged, as BREAM would be able to furnish Oakley's submarine with the necessary spares.

Early in the morning of November 8, GROWLER was en route to the rendezvous point. Freakish luck that at this time her uncertain radar should make contact with an enemy convoy. Oakley directed HARDHEAD to track and deliver an attack on the convoy's port bow.

About an hour later, HAKE heard two far-off explosions. At the same time, HARDHEAD, approaching the convoy, heard a dull crash that sounded like a torpedo. The convoy zigged away from GROWLER's position, and a few minutes after that HARDHEAD counted three thudding depth-charge explosions.

Followed a silence that lasted for over an hour. During this interlude, HARDHEAD closed in on the convoy's port bow. When the submarine reached the specified attack position, she fired a hitting salvo.

The convoy's excorts rushed HARDHEAD, and she became the target for a whipping counter-attack which was frustrated only by desperately skillful evasion. HAKE, too, was subjected to a wicked depth-charging. It was obvious to both submarines that the enemy's "first team" was on the field. HARDHEAD and HAKE escaped, but the calls were close. And when the storm was over, they were unable to reestablish contact with GROWLER.

Had GROWLER been sunk by enemy depth-charges? Or had one of her torpedoes made a circular run? Japanese records did not reveal a submarine-sinking at that locale and date. Neither HAKE nor HARDHEAD could determine the answer.

So the manner of GROWLER's going remains conjectural. She fought her last battle on the night of November 8, and went down in the South China Sea with all hands. Cause unknown.

Loss of Scamp

SCAMP (Commander J. C. Hollingsworth) left Pearl Harbor on October 16, topped off at Midway and set out to conduct her eighth war patrol. The area assigned was in the vicinity of the Bonins. However, on November 9 she was ordered to stay clear of area waters south of the 28° parallel during raids on Tokyo by the Superforts from Saipan. SCAMP acknowledged the dispatch. And this acknowledgement was the last communication received from the submarine.

On November 14 SCAMP was ordered to proceed to the eastern approaches to Tokyo Bay where she was to station herself as a lifeguard. November 29, SubPac Headquarters received word that an enemy minefield had been planted in the waters off Inubo Saki. This was in the vicinity of SCAMP's lifeguard station. All submarines in the area were promptly warned, but for SCAMP the warning may have been too late. When she failed to return from her lifeguard mission, her loss was presumed.

Post-war inquest uncovered a report by a Japanese patrol plane which had sighted and bombed an "oil slick" in the Tokyo Bay area on November 11th. Guided to the scene by the plane, a coast defense vessel dropped 70 depth charges on the spot where the oil-trail originated. The barrage brought a black tide of oil welling to the ocean's surface.

Any or all of these attacks could have been made on SCAMP. At some final hour, following her message of November 9, SCAMP's time arrived. There was thunder—or perhaps no more than a murmur—under the sea. Then the silence beyond fathoming. SCAMP and all hands were gone.

"Burt's Brooms" ("Operation Hotfoot")

When Admiral Halsey was planning "Operation Stalemate" for the capture of Palau, plans were also projected for the first full-scale carrier-air attack on the Japanese mainland. The strike was to be made by Mitscher's Task Force Thirty-eight in November, and the operation was titled "Hotfoot." Mitscher's aviators, of course, wished to approach the Tokyo area undetected. The greatest obstacle to a surprise raid was the picket-boat line which the Japanese maintained several hundred miles south and east of the Honshu coast. Some of the pickets were sure to get off a warning, and Mitscher's punch would be "telegraphed."

So ComSubPac proposed an accessory plan. Why not have submarines sweep the strategic "Hotfoot" area as an overture to the delayed strike? CinCPac approved this plan, and the anti-picket sweep was ordered.

Seven submarines—RONQUIL, BURRFIS, STERLET, SILVERSIDES, TRIGGER, TAMBOR and SAURY—were organized into the wolf-pack. Commander T. B. "Burt" Klakring was placed in charge of the pack. And "Burt's Brooms" left Saipan on November 10, with orders to sweep an avenue approximately 180 miles wide, over which Mitscher's carriers could move toward Japan with relative safety from detection. The submarines were directed to sink by gunfire every picket boat encountered and to "leave no holidays."

The "Brooms" went out to raise a dust, but the sweeping

proved more of a task than expected. Buffeted by foam-capped seas, the "Brooms" ploughed into the Japanese picket line. The targets bobbed and jumped like bubbles in a kettle, and the submarines bounced, rolled and bucked like birch canoes in a rapids. Clutching their leaping mounts, the sub gunners saw black spots before their eyes. Only four picket boats were sunk, and those at considerable risk of life and limb. In the bargain, the operation backfired. Either the pickets were unduly alarmed by the sweep, or the Japanese coast guards grasped the opportunity to test their A/S system. At any rate, all available planes and patrol craft were rushed to the threatened area. Instead of clearing an avenue, the sweep attracted attention and multiplied the swarm of pickets in the target area.

As this result was the antithesis of the one desired, it was apparent that future sweeps would require different tactics. Submarines were not built to serve as gunboats. Their strongest punch was the undersea torpedo.

December Clean-up

A glance at the statistics concerning Japan's merchant marine losses during World War II will show that merchant sinkings tended to slack off in the last month of each war year. The reason varied with the year, but the cause of the slump in December 1944 is obvious. By that date Japanese merchant tonnage afloat had reached a new low—a level which could be represented as close to "sea bottom." Japan had begun the year with 4,947,815 tons of merchant shipping. As stated at the beginning of this chapter, Japanese merchant tonnage afloat on December 1, 1944, amounted to 2,847,534 tons. Statistics may prove anything in politics, but in war such figures as these prove a shrinkage of some 2,100,000 tons of shipping during a critical 11 months! The Empire's merchant marine was nearing the bottom literally as well as metaphorically. And so much of it was on the bottom geographically that the hunting submarines could find little to shoot at in December 1944.

SEA DEVIL sank two large merchantmen off Kyushu early in December. SEALION II gulped a big one off Hainan. TREPANG smashed up a small herd in "Convoy College." Other *marus* went down here and there. But the only record *maru*—shoot was scored by FLASHER.

But before that stupendous shoot, an epic of another kind went on record. The story came down from the Kuriles, and the name was DRAGONET.

The Saving of Dragonet

"Surface and bring home your submarine with her forward torpedo room completely flooded!"

Were a force commander to issue the above order to a "bottomed" submarine, he would undoubtedly be reported as a mental case. And were he to issue the order to a submarine operating within range of enemy shore batteries in the Kurile Archipelago his case would be considered serious. Of course, no force commander in his right mind would think of issuing such an order. No submarine skipper could be expected to accomplish such a dangerous and difficult feat.

Yet the order was issued by that most inexorable of force commanders—Fate. And skipper J. H. Lewis of DRAGONET carried it out. Moreover, he brought the submarine to the surface right under the eyes and guns of the Japanese Air Base at Matsuwa Island. Then, defying the wrath of a cyclonic storm, he ran her to Midway!

Drama began on the morning of December 15, when DRAGONET, on her first war patrol, was cruising submerged in the frigid waters off Matsuwa. Commander Lewis' patrol report narrates the highlights of Act One:

0717: In position Lat. 47-57.5N., Long. 153-08.5E., six miles south of Matsuwa To, returning to depth of 100 feet after a periscope observation. At 70 feet, course 090° (T); speed 2 knots, with 2° dive angle, a slight jar was felt and ship broached to 58 feet. This was thought

: to have been an aircraft bomb. Rigged for depth charge attack. Hung at 90 feet with 20° dive angle. Heavy grinding sounds forward and repeated jars. Realized we were aground. Forward torpedo room reported flooding. Collision quarters sounded, and abandoned forward torpedo room. Blew all main ballast tanks and put pressure on compartment salvage air to forward room.

Forward room reported completely flooded. Boat rose to 65 feet with very large dive angle and then began to sink again. Getting noplace, and afraid that stern would clear and be sighted from Matsuwa, ordered all main ballast tanks flooded.

Settled at 92 feet with 16° dive angle and pounding badly.

Could not obtain suction with trim pump on forward trim tank. We were greatly concerned with the heavy pounding and grinding sounds that continued. Essential we get off before ship breaks up.

Act Two of this tense drama follows immediately.

0732: Received report that water was receding in the forward torpedo room.
0735: Blew forward main ballast tank group and safety tank. Angle began to level off and ship rose slowly. Blew after main ballast tank group.
0738: Surfaced under the eyes of shore installations on Matsuwa, exchanged feel of temporary relief for one of shameful nakedness. Cut in all four main generators clearing area at best speed. With all the days of low visibility we have had, today *would* be one of unlimited visibility and ceiling. Shore installations clearly visible on Matsuwa as we ran for it.
0740: Steering normal escape course at emergency ahead speed about 17.3 knots. Large list to port and believe No. 2 main ballast tank has been holed.

The bringing of this water-logged submarine to the surface was a feat to rival the hydraulic wizardry of Houdini. But the escape was not yet accomplished. December 16 staged another climax. Act Three—The Storm:

1800: In cyclonic storm. Barometer dropped 0.13 in one hour. Gale winds and heavy seas. Slowed to 5 knots and changed course frequently to find best sea condition to ride out storm. Bowplanes are still rigged out and pounding continuously. Feels as though ship will come apart. Water rising in forward torpedo room. Leak around cable stuffing gland in bulkhead between forward battery and torpedo room causing water to enter pantry. Blew No. 1 normal fuel oil tank in No. 5A and B.F.B.T. in effort to obtain an angle and reduce water level in torpedo room. Developed 20° port list which settled down to a final 10 degrees. Rolling 40° to port. With the large free water surface in flooded compartment it felt that we would roll over. Opened No. 5B flood valve and blew this tank to sea. This leveled the list. Pumped No. 3 auxiliary dry. Taking fuel from the starboard side of No. 6.

Act Four: Morning of the next day. The seas had hauled around to the westward and DRAGONET'S bow was riding higher with some six inches of water sloshing over the torpedo-room floor plates. As two torpedoes had been half-way out of the tubes when the flood rushed in, and the bow planes were pounding heavily in the rough sea, Lewis sent an emergency squad forward to secure the torpedoes and rig in the bow planes by hand. Three officers and two men entered the compartment. The air was foul with the fumes of fuel oil, and oxygen was bled in to the gasping work party. The job was accomplished handily, but at this time the submariners learned that the pressure hull had been ruptured on the port side—a rent above the top level of the forward trim tank. This was dangerous damage, and DRAGONET's difficulties were far from over. On October 18 came the Act Four climax:

> Ship rolled 63° to port and hung there righting herself very sluggishly and settling down with a 20° port list. Mercury spilled out of master gyro and compass went out of commission. Personnel were thrown out of bunks, clear across compartments. Sea filled the port side of bridge, but fortunately did not reach the upper conning tower hatch.

After this barrel-roll in the Pacific, the seas flattened down and DRAGONET proceeded on an even keel to Midway. She arrived on December 20, and all hands went ashore to celebrate a Merry Christmas. The DRAGONET drama was over.

A Navy Yard overhaul was required to put the submarine back into fighting trim. That she reached the yard at all was phenomenal. Or call it a combination of submarine architecture, naval engineering and that amalgam of skill, trained reflexes and grit which made American submariners the sort who could surface a submarine with her forward torpedo room completely flooded and bring her home from the Kuriles in spite of Hirohito and high water.

Oil Fire off Indo-China (Flasher's Great Patrol)

By December 1944 the Empire's oil importation effort was expiring. It was expiring because U.S. submarines in the first half of 1944 had cut the main oil artery between the Netherlands East Indies and Japan. Paradoxically, the Japanese tanker fleet floated some 868,000 tons. Thus it had been reduced by only 5,000 tons since January 1944, and it was almost 200,000 tons heavier than it had been at the war's beginning. A break-neck building and conversion program had replaced the oil haulers almost as fast as submarines had sunk them. Yet Japan was almost out of gas.

For the Japanese tanker fleet, like the Italian Navy, constituted a fleet in being, rather than a fleet in action. The ships were there, but they could not get anywhere else—that is, with any reasonable degree of safety. And if they did get somewhere else, presumably some place where they could pick up oil, there remained the problem of getting back. Going or coming, this problem was well-nigh insoluble once the convoy system was torpedoed. Hence the problem for the Japanese tanker fleet had been a baffler since the summer of 1944. A few tanker convoys had squeezed through. Not enough to satisfy the Imperial War Machine. Not nearly enough. And every mile of the voyage, a race with death for tankermen riding in potential iron coffins. So dangerous were these oil hauling runs that the Japanese Government granted tanker crews a 15 per cent bonus which was doubled when the vessel carried gasoline.

Bonus or no bonus, a Japanese tanker convoy steamed straight for the Styx when it cruised the South China Sea in December 1944. Such a convoy was heading for oblivion on the morning of December 4, as it traveled west by south along an open sea lane from Manila to Saigon, Indo-China. Daylight found the tanker group about 300 miles west of Mindoro. Coincidence that these highly volatile ships should run into a submarine named FLASHER!

FLASHER (Commander G. W. Grider) was en route to a patrol area off Camranh Bay. She was operating in a wolf-pack composed of herself, HAWKBILL and BECUNA under group command of Captain E. H. Bryant in HAWKBILL. Her meeting with the oil convoy was not entirely coincidental, for she received a report from HAWKBILL that the oilers were heading in her direction, and Grider promptly set her on the track to intercept. The submarine was then about a third of the way between Palawan and Indo-China. The convoy was not far distant. Evidently the convoy's navigators counted on squally weather to screen its movements. If so, the thinking was overly wishful. Thirty minutes after receiving the word, FLASHER's lookouts, peering through gusts of gray rain, sighted familiar AO silhouettes. The time was 0749—zero hour for the convoy.

Tracking ahead, Grider sent the submarine under at a point 13 miles distant from the target group and waited for the convoy to come down the line. Along it came, and Grider sent FLASHER burrowing in on the approach. When she had closed the range to about 8,000 yards, a cloudburst blotted the targets from view. The submarine moved steadily forward. And suddenly a Japanese destroyer loomed up in the downpour, range 2,000 yards. Grider let the range shorten to 1,100 yards, at which point he opened fire with a four-torpedo salvo. Two hits boomed out. The destroyer stalled, smoking heavily, and assumed a drunken list.

Grider obtained a quick set-up on a large tanker beyond the destroyer, and fired four stern shots at this target. A hasty periscope sweep showed the damaged DD squatting in the water with her stern under. But as FLASHER's periscope admired this spectacle, a second destroyer rushed out through a wall of rain and bore down on the submarine. With this bone-chewing man-of-war only 700 yards away, Grider ordered the submarine deep. All of which occurred in a matter of seconds. As FLASHER coasted into deep water, two hits on the tanker target were heard. Then the depth charges came slamming down. Sixteen explosions shook the submarine; most of them were close. FLASHER evaded under a good "negative gradient."

At 1053 Grider ordered periscope depth. A brief look showed the tanker afire and settling by the stern. Five hundred yards from the tanker an ASASHIO destroyer was standing by, and a net tender and some assorted escorts were moseying around the burning ship. The submarine scrutinized this scene from a distance of 7,500 yards; then Grider rushed a reload and headed in to attack the DD and finish off the tanker. Rainsqualls blinded the periscope as FLASHER closed the range. But at 1249 a break in the downpour gave Grider a knot-hole look at the targets. Two minutes later he fired four torpedoes at the DD, and two which were set to pass beneath the destroyer and hit the wallowing tanker beyond. Four hits rumbled and roared as the submarine went deep to evade counter-attack. The counter-attack lasted half an hour, and Grider and company were perspiring when it was over. Some of the explosions were king-size and too close for polite language.

At 1410, however, the submarine was again at perioscope depth, eyeing the target group. The torpedoed destroyers were nowhere in sight. Three escorts remained in the scene as did the torpedoed tanker which was afire from stern to stem. At sundown Grider moved FLASHER in for a close-up of the flaming AO. By that time the tanker had been abandoned; all escorts had departed. The vessel was burning like a log on a grate.

But the ship was still above water—might be salvageable— so Grider decided to blow her under. He pushed the submarine to within 300 yards of the fiery hulk, lined up for a shot and readied a movie camera. At 1921, with camera trained and everything set, he fired one torpedo.

"When it hit," he reported later, "one of the great shots of the war was lost to posterity."

The shot lost was the sinking of the 10,022-ton oil tanker HAKKO MARU. It was lost because the torpedo explosion blew out the fires in the tanker's hulk, and the camera photographed nothing but darkness and a splatter of ink. But posterity was not the only loser. With the extinguishment of HAKKO MARU, the Empire had lost a valuable oil tanker and a pair of large destroyers.

FLASHER's patrol was only beginning. On the evening of December 20, the submarine was off Hon Doi Island, north of Van Fong Bay, not far from Binhdinh. This struck Grider as a good spot for the interception of traffic northbound from Camranh. At 0925 the following morning—contact!

This was a small patrol boat excursioning up the coast. Grider maneuvered his submarine to seaward to let the busybody pass at 3,000 yards. Thirty minutes later the sound of many screws came through the water from the south. Presently FLASHER's periscope was focused on a bustling CHIDORI. Behind this guard, a troop of large oil tankers steamed into view. Grider moved the submarine farther out to sea. The convoy passed within 2,000 yards of FLASHER, but high waves made torpedo performance doubtful and Grider held his fire, watching the convoy as it went by.

At noon the tanker group was well on its way up the Indo-China coastline, and Grider had his submarine 20 miles offshore to begin a long end-around. The seas continued to pile up, and Grider was compelled to order three-engine speed— as fast as he dared drive FLASHER over the hills of water. By midnight the prospects of an overhaul had apparently gone glimmering. The seas had quieted somewhat, but the convoy seemed to have evaporated. Radar picked up what appeared to be a small island off the Indo-China coast, but could find nothing else in FLASHER's vicinity.

"We had decided to reverse course at 0100," Grider recalled, "when the navigator noticed that Tortue Island was underway!"

This phenomenon soon resolved itself into five large tankers, three escorts and a destroyer traveling through the night at 11 knots. The ships were not zigzagging, but following a circuitous course which traced the shoreline, the tankers inshore and the escorts to seaward. While Grider maneuvered to gain an ahead position, the Jap DD consistently intervened, and as the tanker formation was unusually tight, with the ships traveling in column and some 500 yards apart, an attack from the seaward side was prevented. So FLASHER'S skipper decided to try for an attack from the land side.

The tankers were about 12 miles off the beach and about 15 miles south of the pass between Cape Batangan and Kulao Rai Island. FLASHER was 10,000 yards, 30° on the port bow of the leading ship. As the submarine moved into this position, the DD briefly intervened, then dropped back on the convoy's starboard. One escort now remained on the port bow of the leading ship. The others were on the convoy's starboard flank. Grider drove FLASHER in on the attack. Here is his patrol report description of the battle:

As we started in, a light flashed on the beach abeam, and another one shone from Cape Batangan. These apparently were navigational lights turned on by request.

Started in at 0415. Sighted targets at a range of 6,000 yards. At 0446 began firing three bow tubes at leading tanker. Then shifted to second tanker and fired three at him. Then swung right to bring stern tubes to bear on third tanker. While swinging observed two hits on each of first two tankers.

Just prior to firing the stern tubes, the second tanker blew up and illuminated the area like a night football game.

At 0448 fired four stern shots at the third tanker. He exploded immediately when hit and made the visibility even better. The flames from the second and third targets flowed together like a river on fire.

Swung to course 180 degrees and went ahead flank plus. This put the convoy abeam, but we didn't want to get any nearer the shallow water. Took a fathometer reading: fifty-six fathoms.

As we fired, the destroyer had dropped back to the starboard quarter of the last ship. When we headed south, we sighted him two points forward of our port beam at a range of 4,000 yards. He made one circle to the left and fell into position on FLASHER'S port beam, range 3,200 yards. Sent the lookouts below. We could see in full detail with the unaided eye. This weird formation cruised south for about two miles before the destroyer slowed down and dropped aft. Apparently he never saw us. We breathed a prayer of thanks to the camouflage artists and slowed to flank speed.

Shortly after the destroyer dropped back, the first target blew up and added his light to the flames. The entire sea aft was covered with billowing red fire which burned for about forty minutes. All hands came up, two at a time, and had a look. It was something to see. When we passed to leeward of the mess, there was a strong odor of naphtha. The explosions suggested gasoline, but the fire gave off great clouds of heavy black smoke that resembled oil.

All three tankers disintegrated with the explosions; were swallowed in the flames and were not seen again. The destroyer went back to the formation for a moment, then proceeded southward along the coast in the direction which he had come. No depth charges were dropped. No guns were fired. Apparently they had struck a minefield!

FLASHER opened out to the southeast, sent a message reporting results, then dived for a rest at 0630. Surfaced at 1631, and headed for the barn.

So Grider and company concluded the top-scoring anti-tanker patrol of the Pacific War. There in the coastal waters of Indo-China, at a point about midway between Binhdinh and Hué, they had buried three Japanese oil haulers for a total of 28,646 tons. Then there was the AO sunk on December 4—a 10,022 tonner. By downing these four tankers in a row, FLASHER subtracted from the Empire's tanker fleet a staggering 38,668 tons. Plus two DD's, as shown by the table below, FLASHER'S December score added up to 42,868 tons of enemy shipping.

Thus FLASHER downed more tanker tonnage than any other U.S. submarine. And shot into second place when it came to merchant tonnage downed in a single patrol. Only RASHER and ARCHERFISH sank greater tonnages (merchant plus naval) during one patrol. Even so, when final tonnage scores (all categories, all patrols) were totaled at war's end, FLASHER surfaced to the top. Her December run with Commander Grider on the bridge put her in the lead of the tonnage-sunk race for the duration.

1944 Summary

New Year's Eve—and American submarines are celebrating the conclusion of a whale of a year. Such a year as old-timers "Freddie" Warder, "Pilly" Lent, Creed Burlingame, "Barney" Sieglaff, "Bull" Wright, "Hal" Bruton, "Jumping Joe" Grenfell and other pioneer veterans of the pressure hulls had never dreamed would exist. At SubPac Headquarters, Operations Officer "Dick" Voge is congratulated by Admiral Lockwood for the winning Patrol Plan. In turn, "the Boss" receives congratulations for the triumphant torpedo and the sweeping SubPac offensive. Down south there are festivities at Fremantle and Brisbane. For all the submarines in the Pacific, what a sweep! During this historic 1944 the U.S. subs have swept away approximately 2½ million tons of enemy merchant shipping, and have abolished some 700,000 tons of the Imperial Japanese Navy. Success is the Master of Ceremonies on this New Year's Eve. But—Lest Auld Acquaintance Be Forgot—19 submarines have been lost in this war year.

But the big sweep has carried through, and at year's end 156 fleet-type submarines are operating with SubPac and SubSoWesPac—an over-the-year increase of 33. Five new submarine tenders have reported for duty during 1944—HOWARD W. GILMORE, PROTEUS, AEGIR, ANTHEDON and APOLLO. They bring up the tender total to 14—three of these normally operating with SubSoWesPac.

Gone are the days when force commanders could not muster the necessary submarines for sufficient area coverage; when such maintenance officers as flinty Captain J. M. Will had to comb kangaroo country for spare parts and forge submarine material out of oaths and sweat and baling wire and any other tangible or intangible that came to hand. At the close of 1944 there are enough submarines to rub elbows in vital Pacific areas; enough spares and repair facilities to warm the heart of the most exacting maintenance officer.

Gone, too, is most of the Japanese Navy. Gone is most of the Japanese merchant marine. From the Malay Barrier to the Mikado's bathing beach, and from there to Matsuwa Island, the ocean bottom is a junk yard strewn with the wreckage of torpedoed Japanese shipping.

The Mitsui Brothers and their kin are no longer in the import-export business; they run ferryboats down the River Styx to extinction. The Imperial Navy is committing suicide. The Japanese oil importation problem has but one solution—unconditional surrender. Mythical to begin with, the Greater East Asia Co-Prosperity Sphere is now little more than a remembered scheme haunting those who sit in General Koiso's Supreme War Direction Council in Tokyo.

Japan's economy is wrecked as decisively as the Imperial fleet which lies on history's trash heap. The algebra of disaster is easily figured in declining import percentages and tonnages of shipping afloat. Two statistical items serve to indicate the economic debacle. In 1942 Japan imported 50,000 metric tons of scrap iron and 2,629,200 metric tons of rice. In 1944, scrap iron imports fall to 21,000 metric tons and rice imports are down to 783,200 metric tons.

At the war's beginning, the Japanese experts had estimated that 3,000,000 tons of merchant shipping were necessary for civilian needs—or, as Admiral Nomura put it, "just for civilian living in Japan." The merchant tonnage afloat at the end of December 1944 totals 2,786,407 tons, and some

700,000 tons of this total must be allocated to the Imperial Army and Navy. So-called "civilian living" in Japan is becoming precarious existence indeed.

The bankrupt home Empire is doomed and its capital is doomed. For some weeks, Japanese shipyards have been out of essential building materials, the Imperial Navy almost out of oil, the Japanese Air Force short of gas.

On December 28, USS DACE torpedoes the last Japanese merchantman to be sunk by a submarine in 1944. This is the collier NOZAKI, estimated at 1,000 tons. Down she goes in the waters off Saigon. Another Japanese furnace is out of coal.

PART FIVE

Japanese Sunset

(1945)

☆　☆　☆

Full fathom five thy father lies;
Of his bones are coral made;
Those are pearls that were his eyes:
Nothing of him that doth fade
But doth suffer a sea-change
Into something rich and strange.
SHAKESPEARE

Chapter 28

Tokyo Approach

☆ ☆ ☆

Sarawak Maru Runs the Gantlet

Perhaps the luckiest merchant ship in the Pacific War, and possibly one of the luckiest in creation, was the 5,135-ton SARAWAK MARU. It might stretch the hawser a bit to call her as lucky as the SANTA MARIA. She probably had a better navigator than did the most fortunate of caravels. But SANTA MARIA was not a high-priority target. SARAWAK MARU was an oil tanker.

On the last day of 1944, SARWAK MARU sailed from Japan with a convoy bound for Singapore. The convoy consisted of seven or eight tankers, five dry-cargo carriers and eight escorts. In Formosa Strait on January 8 this *maru* herd was ambushed by a submarine wolf-pack. The tanker HIKOSHIMA MARU was torpedoed and sunk. Tanker SANYO MARU suffered a fatal explosion which was probably caused by a submarine torpedo. Freighter SHINYO MARU and the large passenger-cargoman ANYO MARU were blown under by torpedo fire. Lucky SARAWAK MARU legged it into the Formosan port of Takao with the remainder of the convoy.

At Takao the *marus* came under the fire of attacking United States carrier planes. Bombs thrashed the harbor on January 9, and tankers KAIHO MARU and NANSHIN MARU No. 4 were obliterated, along with two more freighters. SARAWAK MARU escaped injury.

As soon as the crews could pull themselves together, the convoy hauled out of Takao and continued its southward voyage. Off Hainan Island the escorts received warning of an impending air attack.

So the convoy reversed course and ran for shelter into the

harbor of Hong Kong. This, it appeared, was a futile defense measure. The day after the convoy reached Hong Kong, American carrier planes reached the same harbor. The Navy tanker KAMOI was disabled. Two freighters were sunk. And tankers HARIMA MARU, SANKO MARU, MATSUSHIMA MARU and TENEI MARU were pounded to the bottom. The destroyer HATSUHARU and 10 coast defense and escort vessels were mangled in the massacre. And SARAWAK MARU? Somehow she came out of the shambles unharmed.

The reduced convoy now consisted of one freighter, one oil tanker and four escorts. The freighter dropped out of the group and stayed in Hong Kong. That left SARAWAK MARU and the four escorts. She must have felt a trifle conspicuous as she set out to resume the journey down the South China Sea. As conspicuous, say, as the tenth little Indian in the nursery rhyme.

The abbreviated convoy crept down the Indo-China coast and scurried across the Gulf of Siam. Off the coast of Malaya it was attacked by a submarine. One of the escorts, damaged, was forced to drop out. On January 27, SARAWAK MARU, the sole surviving merchantman of the original baker's dozen, arrived at Singapore.

Luckier than the SANTA MARIA? Thus far. Columbus' flagship crossed the Atlantic safely, but then the admiral rammed her on the rocks of Haiti. SARAWAK MARU did not ram any rocks. But on March 19, in the Singapore roadstead, this last survivor of a once-formidable convoy rammed an American mine. And so—to quote "Ten Little Injuns"—then there were none.

But SARAWAK MARU was a lucky vessel. The submarines that just missed her in the East China Sea just north of Formosa Strait were "Loughlin's Loopers." Any vessel which managed to elude this champion wolf-pack was singularly fortunate. Lucky, indeed, was the *maru* that escaped the torpedoes of "Lucky" Fluckey.

Barb's Great Patrol (Commander Eugene B. Fluckey)

To conduct its second patrol as a coordinated attack group, Loughlin's wolf-pack left Guam on December 29, 1944, and headed for the southern end of the East China Sea.

New Year's Eve the three submarines were well on their way. As in the autumn, the pack was composed of QUEENFISH (Commander C. E. Loughlin), PICUDA (Commander E. T. Shepard) and BARB (Commander E. B. Fluckey). As Fate spun the wheel of fortune, the play consistently fell to Fluckey's submarine. So this is BARB's story.

On January 8 the wolf-pack was roaming the northern reaches of Formosa Strait. About an hour after noon the submarines picked up a large convoy which was evidently headed for Takao. This was the convoy containing lucky SARAWAK MARU. The wolf-pack containing "Lucky" Fluckey tracked for five hours. BARB, as will be noted, held back to give her team-mates time to enter the battle. Fluckey continues the story:

It would be a snap to get in the center of this outfit. However, it is imperative that we bend them to port, and prevent them from heading towards the shallow China coast. Holding off on the starboard bow. Plan to smack the four goal-poster with the four escorts in the port echelon since she is probably the most important ship, then use the other three bow tubes on the leading engines-aft job in the starboard echelon, following through with a stern tube attack on the second ship.

Finally at 1724 the skipper sent BARB boring in on a day-periscope attack. His account goes on:

Coming in nicely. Made ready all tubes. Fired six torpedoes.

Left full rudder. All ahead standard. Swinging for stern shot.

Four torpedoes hit close together, the third of which was a tremendous explosion. At the time, being intent on coming stern shot, I idly remarked, "Now that's what I call a good solid hit." I heard someone mutter, "Golly, I'd hate to be around when he hears a loud explosion!"

This, accompanied by the tinkle of glass from a shattered light bulb in the conning tower, and the expressions on the faces of the fire control party, snapped me out of my fixation and the full force of the explosion dawned upon me. BARB had been forced sideways and down, personnel grabbed the nearest support to keep from being thrown off their feet, cases of canned goods had burst open in the forward torpedo room. Later we found a section of deck grating ripped out of the superstructure aft. QUEENFISH later told us that this last ship hit blew up and was obviously an ammunition ship.

At periscope depth. A smoke cloud where the torpedoed ship had been. The stern of the transport sticking up at a 30 degree angle with two escorts close aboard. Her bow is evidently resting in the mud. Depth of water, 30 fathoms. One ship is on fire amidships, just above the water line.

The whole formation has turned away and appears to be stopped. All escorts have scampered over to the unattacked side of the formation. The destroyer has reversed course.

While the convoy floundered in consternation and the escorts dashed in the wrong direction, Fluckey rushed preparations for another attack.

Can feel aggressiveness surging through my veins, since the escorts are more scared than we are. Commenced reload forward. Heading towards convoy, with another ship in our sights. Destroyer suddenly turned towards us! Nice spot for 'down the throat' shot, but no torpedoes forward. Aggressiveness evaporated. Assumed deep submergence of 140 feet. Mud below that.

QUEENFISH and PICUDA attacking convoy.

BARB makes second and third attack.

Three hits observed, followed by a stupendous earth shaking eruption. This far surpassed Hollywood, and was one of the biggest explosions of the war. Personnel in the control room said they felt as if they were sucked up the hatch. Personnel in the conning tower who were wearing shortened shirts not tucked in at the belt, and their shirts pulled up over their heads. On the bridge, as the air was wrenched from my lungs, somehow it formed the words, "All ahead flank." The target now resembled a gigantic phosphorous bomb. In the first flash as the torpedoes hit, all we could ascertain was that the target had a long superstructure and a funnel amidships. The volcanic spectacle was awe inspring. Shrapnel flew all around us, splashing in the water in a splattering pattern as far as 4,000 yards ahead of us. Topside, we alternately ducked and gawked. The horizon was lighted as bright as day. A quick binocular sweep showed only the one ship ahead remaining and a few scattered escorts. No escorts close to the munition ship could be seen. These were probably blown up.

At this point of the game I was ready to haul ashes. However, the Engineering Officer, who had never seen a shot fired or a ship sunk in five runs, from his diving station, really had his guns out. Frantically, he pleaded that we couldn't let the last ship go; besides he loved to hear the thump, thump, thump of the torpedoes and to see millions of bucks go sky high.

Good sales talk.

Commenced the approach for a stern tube attack on the ship ahead. Then QUEENFISH said she wanted to attack. PICUDA said she would follow QUEENFISH. We had our share, so we gave them the green light. Passed our target (what a temptation) and headed down towards the pass between Formosa and a minefield to make sure nothing escaped.

The explosions described by Fluckey's pen highlight the fortunes of such a vessel as SARAWAK MARU. They also serve to highlight the fortunes of Commander Fluckey, nicknamed "Lucky." But "luck is where you find it." And, as someone once remarked, "To find it, you have to look for it." Fluckey was not the officer to loll on Easy Beach waiting for his ship to come in. He looked for the ship. For the next week and a half, BARB dodged Japanese patrol planes, ducked around fleets of Chinese junks and sighted nothing bigger than a good-sized canal barge. Fluckey took time out to analyze the enemy's traffic:

While our forces are hammering Formosa, no shipping is moving around Keelung. All traffic is now running that inshore route along the China coast. No lights have been observed burning along the coast. Consequently, the Japs are running only in the day time, when it is impossible for a submarine to attack along the new, close coast route. Anchorages being used are probably Shanghai, Wenchow. Foochow, and Lam Yit, all of which are well mined and a day's run apart. In conclusion, our prospectus appears poor, unless we can find a suitable opportunity at night to resort to torpedo boat practice.

Basing the remainder of our patrol on the latter assumption, made a complete study of the China coast from Wenchow south to Lam Yit. Recent unknown mining has taken place north of Wenchow. If our assumptions are correct, the present convoy, for which we are searching, is anchored at Foochow tonight (January 21) and will be en route Wenchow tomorrow. To substantiate our conclusions, plan to mingle with the Junk Fleet north of Seven Stars tomorrow afternoon at a point ten miles inside of the 20 fathom curve and 15 miles from the coast where we can observe the passage of our convoy.

The following day two ships were sighted traveling inside the 10-fathom curve in 8-fathom water. The sky was heavily overcast, and Fluckey decided to tackle the targets that night if the overcast blindfolded the moon. BARB tracked the vessels throughout the day, only to lose contact that night. Fluckey deduced that the ships had anchored, and he determined to search the coast—a hazardous venture as the absence of junks offshore hinted at the presence of a mine-field. But again luck is where one finds it, and Fluckey was a persistent hunter.

January 23, at 0030 started an inshore surface search for convoy anchorage. Maneuvering constantly to avoid collision with junks. Present entourage consists of several hundred darkened junks. At 0300 rounded Incog Island and contacted a very large group of anchored ships in the lower reaches of Namkwan Harbor! Slowed to take stock of the situation.

Instead of turning up one ship, BARB's skipper had found an entire convoy! It may now be observed that Dame Fortune makes a final demand of those who court her guerdons. To locate the grab-bag is not enough—one must reach in to get the prizes. The manner in which Commander Fluckey reached into the Namkwan grab bag is described below by the practitioner. As a demonstration of astuteness, capability and drive—balancing the odds and then accurately shooting the works—it remains a classic of submarine warfare.

Fully realize our critical position and the potential dangers involved. Estimate the situation as follows:

One escort appears to be patrolling several thousand yards northeast and a second escort to the east of the anchored ships covering the most logical position for entry and attack. A third escort is working close to Incog Light, apparently more concerned with keeping himself off the rocks. Visibility is very poor.

Assumed the closely anchored columns would be heading about 050 degrees true, heading into the wind and seas with a current of one knot. Plotted the navigational position from which we would attack, making our approach from the southeast.

Elected to retire through an area marked "unexplored" on our large scale chart which contained sufficient "rocks awash" and "rocks, position doubtful," to make any over-ambitious escorts think twice before risking a chase.

Countermeasures expected will be searchlights, gunfire, and hot pursuit. Against this we will have a stern tube salvo, 40mm's and automatic weapons. We will require an hour's run before being forced down. Consequently, our attack must be sufficient to completely throw the enemy off balance. We have four torpedoes forward and eight aft.

No time will be available for reload; for a speedy darting knife thrust attack will increase the probability of success.

Figure the odds are ten to one in our favor.

Man battle stations, torpedoes.

The men are more tense than I've ever seen them. Save for an occasional sounding ". . . six fathoms . . ." the control room is so quiet that the proverbial pin would have sounded like a depth charge.

Do not consider it advisable in our present precarious position to send a contact report to the PICUDA. She could not possibly attack before dawn and get out. Will send one after the attack, when our presence is known.

Range 6,000 yards. Made ready all tubes.

Ships are anchored in three columns about 500 yards apart with a few scattered ships farther inshore. This, frankly, must be the most beautiful target of the war. Ships are banked three deep. Even an erratic torpedo can't miss. Estimate at least 30 ships present. Our biggest job will be to prevent too many torpedoes from hitting one ship!

Chose one of the large ships to the left of center of the near column as target.

Fired one. Fired two. Fired three. Fired four.

Right full rudder, all ahead standard. Sounding, five fathoms. Shifted target to right for ships ahead in near column.

Fired seven. Fired eight. Fired nine. Fired ten.

All ahead flank! Commanding Officer manned bridge.

Large AK in first column was hit by torpedoes two and three. Target observed to settle and undoubtedly sink.

Unidentified ship in second column was hit by torpedo after turn to right. Damaged.

Large AK, in third column, hit by number four torpedo, shortly thereafter caught on fire. Fire later flared up five or six times then went out in a manner similar to a sinking ship. Ship probably sank.

Torpedo number six hit in the first column. Believed to have hit in ship struck by number two and three torpedoes. Observation not sufficiently accurate to claim additional damage.

Large AK hit by torpedo number eight. Ship belched forth a huge cloud of smoke. Damage.

Unidentified ship in second column hit by torpedo five. The whole side of this ship blew out in our direction in a manner similar to an ammunition ship or the magazine of a large warship. Ship sank.

Large ammunition ship in third column hit by number

seven torpedo. Ship blew up with a tremendous explosion. Ship sank.

Tracers of all descriptions flew out from the two ships which exploded. Smoke from the ships hit, on fire and exploding, completely obscured all ships and prevented any further observation of other damage.

The BARB is now high-balling it for the 20 fathom curve at 21.6 knots, broken field running through the Junk Fleet, wildly maneuvering when some of the junks are inside the sea return. Expect to see a junk piled up on the bow at any second.

Gunfire from well astern. Some poor junks are getting it. Sent contact report to PICUDA.

One hour and nineteen minutes after the first torpedo was fired, the Galloping Ghost of the China Coast crossed the 20 fathom curve with a sigh. Never realized how much water that was before. Life begins at forty fathoms!

Thirty-eight minutes later, it was dawn. Assume the Japs will expect us to submerge, so will stay on the surface!

That evening BARB headed for Midway. She reached that base on February 10th. The Japanese left no record of the ships which were sunk in the Namkwan smash-up, and it has since been impossible to estimate the tonnage downed during that raid. But SubPac Headquarters estimated that BARB's performance would merit a Presidential Unit Citation.

Commander Eugene B. Fluckey, for his performance, was awarded the Medal of Honor.

Sinking of USS Extractor

On the evening of January 23, 1945, GUARDFISH (Commander D. T. Hammond) was returning from patrol in a Joint Zone—an area in which both surface ships and submarines are permitted to operate and in which neither can attack the other unless positive of enemy character. GUARDFISH was heading for Guam. At 2038 she made a radar contact at 11,000 yards on a vessel which tracked on course 270 at 11 knots. There were no friendly radar indications, and nothing could be sighted from the bridge. Lacking detail regarding friendly forces in the area, GUARDFISH, while continuing to track, sent in a contact report and requested information. This message was cleared at 2310.

At 0113, morning of the 24th, GUARDFISH received a message from ComSubPac informing her that there were no known friendly submarines in the vicinity of the reported contact, but advising that, as the contact was made in a Joint Zone, the unidentified vessel, if a surface ship, was probably friendly. At 0130 a dispatch was received from ComTask-Group 17.7—GUARDFISH was to continue tracking. At 0338 another message from ComTaskGroup 17.7 informed GUARDFISH that no known friendly forces were in the vicinity of contact. The message reminded GUARDFISH that she was in a Joint Zone, however.

Hammond held GUARDFISH on the trail as instructed, and at 0542 he ordered the submarine submerged 13,600 yards ahead of the target and 2,000 yards off the track. This put GUARDFISH in a position where she might identify the target at dawn and be within striking distance if the vessel were an enemy submarine. At 0605 the target was identified as a Japanese submarine of the I-165 class, the commanding officer and executive officer viewing it through the scope and using the silhouette book for a studied comparison. Hammond opened fire, estimated range 1,200 yards. Four Mark 18 torpedoes were fired. Two struck the target. As the vessel sank, the stern tilted against the sky, and it was evident that the target was not a submarine.

Hammond sent GUARDFISH to the surface and made for the wreckage. Seventy-three survivors were picked up, all apparently in good condition, a few with minor bruises and lacerations. Six men of the crew were missing and could not be found. GUARDFISH's victim was an American ship—the USS EXTRACTOR!

This tragedy resulted from a concatenation of mistakes. Investigators learned that GUARDFISH had not attempted to identify the target with special identification equipment which was in operating condition and which would probably have disclosed the target's friendly character, since EXTRACTOR's corresponding gear was in use. The submariners had not used this identification equipment because they had no evidence of its employment by the target and because the enemy was known to have used similar gear for deception.

GUARDFISH's commanding officer had relied upon visual identification, and had made six periscope observations, sighting the target at various angles on the bow (between 15° and 50°) at a time when visibility was not the best. Had he waited for an angle on the bow nearer to 90°, the EXTRACTOR would probably not have been taken for a submarine.

Higher authority did not know EXTRACTOR's position in the Joint Zone because orders addressed to her the previous afternoon were received by the ship in a garbled form which made them unintelligible. Her captain did not break radio silence to request a retransmission of the unreadable message. Therefore, officers responsible for knowing EXTRACTOR'S whereabouts stated they knew of no friendly surface ship in the position reported by GUARDFISH.

The EXTRACTOR sinking was seen as resulting from the submarine captain's failure to properly identify the target, and the failure of the operations officer at Headquarters, Commander Forward Area, to check EXTRACTOR'S whereabouts at the time the submarine reported contact.

To the uninitiated who have never glimpsed a target through a periscope, the mistaking of a ship's silhouette for that of a submarine may seem incomprehensible. Ship silhouettes at sea may assume all manner of shapes and assume all manner of angles as do shadows moving along a wall. The changing light of daybreak (or clouds at noon, or sundown, or moonshine) and the movements of the sea are factors which enter the problem. Artists know the illusions created by light and shadow, the tricks of perspective.

GUARDFISH'S skipper did not fire in haste, nor was he astigmatic at the periscope. Certainly a communications failure was involved in the EXTRACTOR case. Nevertheless, the burden of positive target identification rests on a submarine attacking in a Joint Zone, and for this reason a Court of Inquiry voted a reprimand for the commanding officer of the submarine.

Loss of Swordfish

SWORDFISH (Commander K. E. Montross) left Pearl Harbor on December 22, 1944, to conduct her thirteenth war patrol in an area off the Nansei Shotos. In addition, she was to carry out a photo reconnaissance mission at Okinawa. Plans for "Operation Iceberg"—the campaign to capture this stronghold—were already incubating, and good photographs of defense installations and beaches would be invaluable.

On January 2, 1945, she was ordered to keep clear of the Nansei Shotos until a series of carrier-air strikes had been conducted. In the meantime, she was to patrol the shipping lanes off Yaku Island below Kyushu. The submarine acknowledged these instructions on January 3rd. Six days later, she was directed to proceed to the Nansei Shoto Archipelago and perform her special mission. Then she was to go to Saipan.

SWORDFISH failed to appear at Saipan on the date scheduled for her arrival. After unbroken silence was the only answer to repeated attempts to contact her by radio, SubPac Headquarters knew she must be lost.

SWORDFISH may have been lost on the morning of January 12th. On that day the submarine KETE, in the Okinawa area, reported possible contact with a near-by submersible. KETE heard prolonged depth-charging. The Japanese failed to record the A/S attack heard by KETE. But it sounded like a heavy barrage, and it could have been aimed at SWORD-FISH. Her grave would remain unmarked. Like so many of her companions in the "Silent Service," she went down silently with all hands, leaving in her wake a valiant record as her "marker."

Loss of Barbel

On January 5, 1945, BARBEL, captained by Lieutenant Commander C. L. Raguet, left Fremantle to patrol an area in the South China Sea.

Late in January she was ordered to form a wolf-pack with PERCH and GABILAN and patrol the western approaches to Balabac Strait and the southern entrance to Palawan Passage. On February 3, BARBEL sent a message to TUNA, BLACK-FIN and GABILAN—her area was buzzing with Japanese aircraft, and three times enemy planes had attacked her, dropping depth charges. Raguet stated his submarine would transmit further information the following night.

The expected transmission from BARBEL was not received. On February 6, TUNA reported that she had been unable to contact BARBEL for 48 hours and had ordered her to a rendezvous point on February 7th. BARBEL did not appear at the rendezvous. Evidently she never received the message from TUNA.

Japanese aviators reported an attack on a submarine discovered off southwest Palawan on February 4th. Two bombs were dropped, and one landed on the submarine near the bridge. The submarine plunged under a cloud of fire and spray. Unquestionably this was BARBEL, going down in battle, with all hands.

"Mac's Mops," "Latta's Lances" and "Operation Detachment"

Although the "Hotfoot" carrier-air strike on Honshu was canceled because of the Third Fleet's prolonged activities in the Philippines, plans for such a strike were not abandoned. Early in the new year "Operation Detachment" was devised for the capture of Iwo Jima, and a carrier-air strike on Honshu was included in the plan. And, as in the abortive "Hotfoot" operation, a submarine sweep to clear the carrier route of picket boats was projected.

In planning the "Detachment" sweep, ComSubPac could base the project on the experience of "Burt's Brooms." A double sweep was designed—one group of sweepers to clear the path for the aircraft carriers, and a second and smaller group to create a diversion by sweeping an "off the trail" path. The main sweep was to be conducted by a wolf-pack designated as "Mac's Mops." The diversionary sweep was assigned to "Latta's Lances" under Commander F. D. Latta.

The sweepers participating in this operation were better equipped than "Burt's Brooms." Mounted fore and aft on each submarine were 5-inch and 40-mm. guns. A special high-speed torpedo for attacks on A/S vessels had come into service, and these were distributed to the "Mops." With this lively torpedo, a submarine making an undetected submerged attack could demolish a picket boat before the picket had time to dispatch a warning.

"Latta's Lances"—the diversionary sweepers—were instructed to attack the pickets with gunfire, but not to sink them until they had time to send out a radio alarm. By this stratagem, Latta's wolf-pack would decoy the enemy to the area it was sweeping—divert him from the scene of the main sweep.

Latta's wolf-pack began its diversionary sweep on the morning of February 11. Striking the picket line in broad daylight, the "Lances" rattled against the pickets and created a fine uproar. In the process they sank two picket boats. The diversion was a complete success.

Steaming along the path traveled by the sweepers, Mitscher's carriers did not see a single picket. And vice versa. The carrier planes reached Tokyo undetected!

Iwo Jima Campaign

Civilian living in Tokyo was becoming unpleasant in January 1945. Against United States carrier aircraft from the sea and B-29's from the Marianas, the city's AA defenses were about as protective as paper parasols. However, to reach the Japanese capital, the American bombers had to break through the air screens over the Bonins and Volcanoes. Offensive plans called for the capture of a major base within shorter distance of Tokyo. Okinawa, middle link in the Nansei Shoto chain, was the objective. Only 400 miles from Japan, this stronghold would make a springboard for a final leap at the Japanese homeland.

But before Okinawa could be seized, it was necessary to obtain a fighter-plane base to support the Mariana-based B-29's. Iwo Jima in the Volcano Group was the selection.

The capture of Iwo Jima and subsequent invasion of Okinawa were operations assigned to Admiral Spruance's Fifth Fleet. D-Day for the Iwo Jima campaign was set as February 19. The Okinawa campaign, designated "Operation Iceberg," was to hit the beachheads of that island on April 1st.

Submarines played a part in both of these campaigns. From November 28 to December 2, 1944, SPEARFISH (Commander C. C. Cole) was on photo reconnaissance mission in the waters off Iwo Jima and Minami Jima.

During the Iwo Jima landings, submarines were tactically disposed as lifeguards. Several furnished the Fifth Fleet with weather information.

Iwo Jima is the Marine Corps' story. But the submarines were there. And "Dunker's Derby" had been cutting the convoy routes to the Bonins since April 1944. When the Fifth Fleet struck in February 1945, the target islands were already showing signs of a familiar blight.

Hunting the Japanese Submarine (Batfish Breaks a Record)

"The best defense against submarines is other submarines."

So wrote an author whose opinions, in the 1920's, could stir up more controversy than a bear with his paw in a beehive. The writer, of course, was forthright General William "Billy" Mitchell, whose imagination was as far ahead of his time as radar. Taken literally, many of his statements were and are open to argument. But so are many of the statements of arbitrary literalists who strain at gnats while swallowing camels.

As for the statement quoted above, submarines may not have been the *best* defense against other submarines during World War II. But U.S. submarines were never employed solely for anti-submarine duty (that is, as normal A/S units were employed) and their licks at enemy submersibles were generally side-swipes taken in passing. Japanese submarines were not high on the target priority list in 1942, 1943 and 1944. Even so, in those 36 months of warfare U.S. submarines downed a significant percentage of their opponents in the undersea field.

Although the sinkings of Jap submarines were incidental to the tremendous anti-shipping war and the offensive against the Imperial Navy's surface forces, they were incidents that blasted sizable holes in the enemy's submarine effort. And when U.S. submarines were given the opportunity to concentrate on A/S warfare, that hole was immediately and decisively enlarged. The opportunity developed in the first quarter of 1945, coincident with the shortage of surface targets that followed the gigantic harvest reaped in 1944.

After the sinking of Liscome Bay in the Gilberts, the Imperial Navy's submarines had given a most indifferent account of themselves. Partly responsible was the strategy of the Japanese High Command which shifted the submarines yon and hither, frequently under the operational control of the Imperial Army. The Japanese Submarine Force seemed to lack a primary mission, a clearly defined program.

In the Indian Ocean, Japanese submarines waged unrestricted warfare on Allied convoys, but results were militarily inconsequential as the High Command maintained but a small squadron of some 10 submarines for that campaign. The Nazis contributed a few of their 1,200-ton U-boats to this activity. On November 10, 1944, Flounder (Commander J. E. Stevens) caught one of these Germans poking a nose into the Java Sea. Down went U-537.

Over one-third of the available I-boats and RO-boats were engaged, during 1943 and 1944, in transporting supplies to last-ditch garrisons of isolated Pacific bases. The Japanese submariners did a lot of hazardous blockade-running and performed numerous tasks on the order of their evacuation work at Kiska—a remarkable exploit. But that was not fighting an offensive war.

Now, in February 1945, with Okinawa an obvious United States objective, the Japanese Submarine Force was out to defend the approaches to the Nansei Shotos. The resolve came too late. American submarines were on the lookout for their Imperial Navy rivals and those few specimens donated by Doenitz to the Pacific War. Primed for battle, they hit the enemy submarine forces a series of stunning blows in the opening months of 1945.

As of January 1, 1945, the Japanese had lost a total of 102 submarines. Some 96 or 97 replacements had been rushed from the construction yards. The Imperial Navy exerted a considerable effort to maintain its submarine strength. But, dimpled and bedraggled from long patrols, the I-boats and RO-boats were often unable to obtain repairs and spares. Strive and contrive as it would, the Japanese Submarine Force had in commission or available for duty on March 1, 1945, only 41 submarines.

Thus a total of 25 enemy submarines (23 Japanese and two German) were sunk by American submarines in the Pacific War. Although at first disposed to belittle the American submarine effort, the Japanese submariners were among the first members of the Imperial Navy to express a revised opinion in this regard.

The Japanese lost a total of some 130 submarines during World War II. Of these, five or six were operational casualties; five were downed by causes unknown. In sinking 23 of the 120 which were downed in action, U.S. submarines were responsible for approximately 20% of the losses.

Flounder and Hoe (Traffic Accident)

Circulating in Singapore in 1944 was a saying that one could walk from there to Japan on the tops of U.S. submarine periscopes—or so declared a prisoner of war rescued from the Japanese.

The reporter may have exaggerated the rumor, and the hyperbole itself is subject to punctuation with a grain of salt. However, by 1945 there were areas where American submarines were concentrated with a "density" that left little latitude for figure-skating maneuvers.

Consider the experience of FLOUNDER and HOE, patrolling adjacent areas off the coast of Indo-China. The episode occurred in the last week of February.

On the afternoon of February 23, FLOUNDER (Commander J. E. Stevens) was cruising along submerged in the vicinity of Pulo Kambir. HOE (Commander M. P. Refo, III) was running submerged in an area just to the north of FLOUNDER'S. A 4-knot current had been registered in HOE'S area, and believing his submarine on the southern boundary of the area, Refo had set course north in mid-morning. But at 1700, while running at 60 feet, speed 1.8 knots, position 13-30.9 N., 190-29.1 E., HOE came a cropper with a crash.

Refo thought his submarine had struck an undersea rock. The shock seemed to be forward on the starboard side, and the submarine took a 4° up-angle and broached. The commanding officer ordered battle stations and blew all main ballast tanks. Rushing topside, the bridge personnel found all clear—with the exception of an unidentified ship, hull down on the horizon to the northeast. Reports from below were reassuring. No underwater damage; soundheads and pitometer log were operating normally and could be housed easily. So Refo called for four-engine speed to open the range before his submarine was sighted by the vessel over the horizon. A "cut" checked HOE'S position; she had under her 65 fathoms of water. At 1711 a Japanese float plane forced her to dive, and Refo took the opportunity to begin an approach on the unidentified vessel. No torpedoes were fired, for the vessel was soon identified as a hospital ship.

Leave HOE as she stalks this disappointing target, and turn back the clock to 1700—at which moment things happened to USS FLOUNDER. Stevens' submarine had been running at 65 feet on course 090 T. on that afternoon of February 23rd. All clear by sound and periscope. Then at 1700 FLOUNDER suddenly was shaken as though seized by a paroxysm—a violent stem-to-stern shudder. FLOUNDER started to go deep. Thirty seconds later, she suffered another spasmodic jolting, and water spurted in through a slashed cable. The shear valve was closed and the leak stopped. Sound excitedly reported a tremendous rush of air and the whish-wish-whish of high-speed screws starting and stopping on the starboard bow.

Stevens needed no little bird to tell him that his submarine had been run over by another submersible. The screw noises faded out. Eleven minutes after the collision, FLOUNDER was again at periscope depth, her scope above water for a look. All was clear at that moment. For HOE was diving to elude aircraft contact just as FLOUNDER's periscope broke water. With nothing in view in FLOUNDER's vicinity, Stevens and crew entertained the hope that they had sideswiped a submerged Japanese submarine and sunk same.

About two hours later FLOUNDER heard a noise of blowing air on the starboard bow, and shortly thereafter she sighted a surfaced submarine some 3,000 yards away. The submarine was retiring eastward at high speed. Stevens tentatively identified the retiring stranger as American, and he learned she was HOE that night when dispatches established the fact that the two submarines had met in a submerged collision.

The damage was fairly extensive. HOE had run over FLOUNDER from starboard to port, just forward of the victim's periscope shears. In passing, HOE's keel sliced a 25-foot gash in FLOUNDER's superstructure directly aft of the 4-inch gun, damaging the vent line to No. 2 normal fuel-oil tank and the 10-pound blow line, and grooving a deep dent in the tank. Stanchions and deck of the forward 20-mm. gun platform were damaged, and SJ mast was bent askew and an antenna was broken. HOE herself got off with a much lighter crash bill—perhaps a couple of dollars for paint.

This was the first and only submerged submarine collision on record. But it leads to the conclusion that if World War II had lasted much longer, U.S. submarine concentrations might have necessitated special instruction in the art of patrolling subjacent as well as adjacent areas.

Last Run to Singapore (End of the Oil Line)

Somehow a few Japanese tankers won the race with death

in February and carried about 300,000 barrels of oil to Japan. In March the last tankers to reach Japan from the south brought in about 150,000 barrels. By the end of March 1945 that artery was completely severed—the flow from the south ceased. With it ceased all possibility of sustaining for more than a few months the Japanese war effort.

The severance of the Japanese oil artery had its physical expression in the closure of the Japan-to-Singapore convoy run. The termination of this line in March 1945 was as fatal to the Empire's economy as the simultaneous stoppage of the oil flow from the south was fatal to the Japanese war effort.

So the conquered southern Empire was literally if not formally surrendered. The mountains, mines, forests, plantations, oil fields, could no longer be exploited by Japan. The vast network of transportation lines which had webbed these conquered territories to the home islands had distintegrated like a chart thrown into a bonfire.

The War Machine almost out of fuel, the Empire facing bankruptcy and inevitable defeat, Emperor Hirohito had held audience with a number of senior statesmen in February. Consensus was that Japan should immediately seek peace. Now in March, Prince Higashikuni advocated peace moves through the mediation of China. But Japan's Army generals bickered, bogging down in windy debate over "national polity," public opinion and morale, discipline and personal safety. While these War Lords tried to screen their failures behind large but indefinable words—one eye hunting for a convenient exit, the while—the war went on.

Loss of Kete

Captained by Lieutenant Commander Edward Ackerman, KETE left Guam on March 1 to conduct her second patrol. Area assigned was in the Nansei Shotos. KETE was to submit weather reports and serve as lifeguard during air strikes on Okinawa. She was also to hunt.

On the night of March 9-10, KETE ambushed a convoy, and Ackerman did some crack torpedo-shooting. Down went three cargomen in a row. KETE reported these torpedoings. And on the night of March 14 she reported the firing of four torpedoes at a cable-laying vessel.

KETE acknowledged orders on March 19th. The next day she transmitted a weather report. This was the last transmission ever received from Ackerman's submarine.

She should have made Midway by March 31st. After a futile attempt to locate her by radio—two weeks of deepening silence—she was reported as presumed lost. Apparently there were no Japanese A/S attacks on submarines in the waters east of the Nansei Shotos where KETE headed after making her weather report. There were more than the usual number of Japanese submarines operating in the waters through which KETE had to pass, and she may have been lost in deep-sea battle with one of these. Somewhere en route from the Okinawa area to Midway, she went down with all hands.

Loss of Trigger

TRIGGER, scourge of the Japanese merchant marine, was on the hunt. Captained by Commander D. R. Connole, she had left Guam on March 11 to raid the sea lanes off the Nansei Shoto Archipelago. This was her twelfth war patrol.

As was the case with SWORDFISH and KETE, TRIGGER was to perform a special mission in the Okinawa area in addition to her normal patrol duty. She was also to serve as lifeguard during a scheduled carrier-air strike on Okinawa.

On March 18 TRIGGER reported that she had made a seven-hour end-around on a convoy and sunk a freighter. This vessel, later identified as the 1,012-ton TSUKUSHI MARU No. 3, went down at lat. 28-05 N., long. 126-44 E. The remainder of the convoy fled westward. TRIGGER was ordered to trail the fleeing convoy and locate, if possible, the enemy's "safety lane" through the mined area west of the Nansei Shotos.

TRIGGER replied on March 20, stating that she had been held under by A/S vessels for three hours following the convoy attack and had been unable to regain contact after surfacing. Then on March 26, she was ordered to form a wolf-pack at a designated rendezvous point with SEA DOG and THREADFIN.

The wolf-pack message required acknowledgment. On the day it was sent, TRIGGER transmitted a weather report. But she did not acknowledge ComSubPac's dispatch. The weather report was the last message ever received from TRIGGER.

It seems probable that she was sunk by Japanese A/S vessels and aircraft on the afternoon of March 28th.

On that date, SILVERSIDES, HACKLEBACK, SEA DOG and THREADFIN sharing a common area in Nansei Shoto waters, heard a thunderous depth-charge barrage. THREADFIN tracked down and torpedoed a destroyer escort that day, and was treated to 18 depth charges by way of reprisal. An hour after this onslaught, THREADFIN reported, ". . . . *many distant strings of depth charges and several heavy explosions from what was believed to be eastward. It sounded as though someone was getting quite a drubbing.*"

Undoubtedly TRIGGER was the target for the blasting heard by THREADFIN. Fighting her last battle, she went down with all hands.

Close Call for Spot

After joining some 200 Superforts in a raid which burned out a square mile of Tokyo on February 25, planes of Task Force Fifty-eight loaded up for a strike which blasted Okinawa on March 1st. Battleships of Task Force Fifty-eight, led by Vice Admiral W. A. Lee, steamed to Okinawa on March 24 and proceeded to bombard the island's southeast coast in support of minesweeping activities. These air and sea operations roused a turmoil that made the Okinawa storm center a dangerous area for submarining. The enemy was resisting fiercely, and all hell was on hand to break loose.

Some of it broke loose on SPOT (Commander W. S. Post, Jr.). Having concluded a run in Formosan waters, she headed eastward on orders to patrol an area on the Pacific side of the Nansei Shotos. Moving east, she sank two enemy trawlers, skirted around the Okinawa maelstrom, and entered her assigned area. There SPOT was put "on the spot."

The experience was unexpected, for she was operating in a Submarine Patrol Zone. This gave her skipper every reason to believe that surface vessels encountered would be enemy, and if they were not enemy, they would, *ipso facto*, be friends. Thus when radar contact was made at 1845 on the evening of March 31, range 14,400 yards, SPOT was alerted for action. But there was always some possibility that the vessel might be friendly, and when radar interference was detected, SPOT's captain assumed the contact was another U.S. submarine, probably POGY.

Post maneuvered cautiously. At about 9,000 yards the stranger's silhouette could be visually identified as a friendly destroyer or DE. Post thereupon altered course in order to remain close enough to exchange identification signals and yet show enough angle on the bow so that SPOT, in turn, could be identified.

At 1857 the range was less than 7,500 yards. As the destroyer made no attempt to challenge by light, Post turned his submarine away. According to SPOT the closest range was 4,200 yards. According to the destroyer, the range had closed to 3,000 yards. The destroyer was the USS CASE. Her version of the episode: She made visual challenge for major war vessels five times with Aldis lamp, at ranges between 3,000 and 4,000 yards. SPOT never saw these challenges, and the reason probably lay in the fact that an Aldis lamp must be turned directly on the bearing of a ship to be seen.

The destroyermen stated that a final challenge was made with a 12-inch searchlight, and then CASE opened fire. Only one small flash of red light was observed by SPOT's bridge personnel a moment before this first salvo, and the red glimmer, as seen from the submarine's position, bore no resemblance whatever to a recognition signal. The next thing the submariners saw was a flash that bore every resemblance to the flame-jet of a destroyer's guns.

As this first salvo passed overhead, the submarines fired a red "Buck Rogers" pyrotechnic signal. This was seen by those on board CASE, and the destroyermen ceased fire with the third salvo in the air. The second salvo had smashed into the sea and the third was just hitting the water at 1908 as Post "pulled the plug" and SPOT went under.

No more red stars were fired, but the air in SPOT's conning tower was red, white and blue, and some of the sparkling conversation may have sent a pyrotechnic glow to the ocean's surface. At 1920 sonar recognition signals were exchanged. The destroyermen stated that CASE had been getting off sonar recognition signals every two minutes during her sweep and that her IFF gear had been on the entire time. Both ships claimed that after exchanging recognition signals neither would exchange visual calls. However, both said they tried to do so.

Fortunately, the night's blind darkness had necessitated full radar gun control, and the salvos fired by the destroyer had missed. A little more light and they might have been right on. But then, a little more light and the submarine would probably have been recognized. Theoretical considerations which failed to soothe the ruffled feelings of Post and company.

To begin with, CASE made the attack in a Submarine Patrol Zone where normally she had no right to be. She had been on lifeguard station in position 28 N., 137 E., and upon receiving an aircraft contact report of two unidentified surface targets some 86 miles distant, she set off on an excursion to locate them. Her course took her inside the Submarine Patrol Zone, and although she endeavored to so notify her squadron commander, she had no assurance the message would be delivered. As a matter of fact, the dispatch never got through. Somebody always fails to get the word.

When the shooting was over, CASE, too, was on the spot.

The Sinking of Awa Maru

Not 24 hours after the erroneous attack on SPOT, an American submarine operating in an area west of the Nansei Shotos became involved in a torpedoing that induced most tragic results. Ironically enough, the episode occurred on April 1—a day that has implications of its own on the American calendar. This day was also D-Day at Okinawa. By a singular coincidence, the submarine's patrol area was the one which had been patrolled by SPOT before that submarine was shifted eastward.

The victim of this April 1 tragedy was the 11,600-ton passenger-cargoman AWA MARU, one of the last of Japan's large, fast, passenger liners. Normally the sinking of such a prize would constitute a feather in any submarine's cap. Not so in this instance. For on this particular voyage the United States Government had guaranteed AWA MARU safe conduct for the purpose of transporting Red Cross relief supplies to Japanese prisoner-of-war camps in Malaya and the Dutch East Indies.

AWA MARU had departed Moji, Japan, on February 17, to visit Singapore and various Indonesian ports. On return trip, she was scheduled to arrive in Miture, Japan, on April 4. Safe conduct had been granted for both the outward and homeward passage. Her immunity from attack was dependent upon visual markings—" . . . *White Cross on each side of funnel . . . Crosses to be illuminated at night . . . Two White Crosses on each side of ship . . . All navigation lights to be lighted . . .*" No procedure was prescribed for her identification in the event of fog or low visibility. On such occasions her immunity depended upon a rigid adherence to a specified schedule and track which would be promulgated to all United States and Allied air, surface and submarine forces in the areas concerned.

During the second week in February, a dispatch in plain language giving the schedule, route, description and identifying markings of AWA MARU was broadcast to all SubPac submarines. As was common with important messages to submarines, the broadcast was emphatically repeated—three times on three successive nights—nine times in all. Early in March the Japanese altered the route of AWA MARU'S return voyage, and a message conveying this information was sent out in the same manner, same number of transmissions.

The major lap of the hospital ship's voyage was through South China Sea waters patrolled by SubSoWesPac. But the last few days of the return trip were through areas patrolled by SubPac submarines. Two days before AWA MARU was scheduled to re-enter the SubPac areas, ComSubPac sent a reminder to his commanding officers. In a coded dispatch he stated in effect, ". . . *Let pass safely* AWA MARU *carrying prisoner of war supplies. . . . She will be passing through your areas between March thirtieth and April fourth. . . . She is lighted at night and plastered with White Crosses . . ."*

QUEENFISH (Commander Charles E. Loughlin) was the submarine patrolling the area recently vacated by SPOT—the waters just inside the Formosa Strait bottleneck at the southern end of the East China Sea. At 2200 on the night of April 1, Loughlin's submarine made radar contact with a single ship, range 17,000 yards. Loughlin sent the crew to battle stations, and the fire control party started tracking the target. A dense fog surged over the water. Visibility was no more than 200 yards. The target was presumed to be a destroyer or destroyer escort because of the smallness of the radar pip, the relatively low range of radar contact, and the ship's high speed. In the blind fog the ship was doing about 17 knots and was not zigzagging.

QUEENFISH paced the target at a distance of 1,000 yards off the track until the range closed to 3,600 yards. Then Loughlin turned her away and slowed to 4 knots. At 2300, the commanding officer and the bridge watch having unsuccessfully strained to get a glimpse of the target, Loughlin fired four torpedoes from the stern tubes. Radar bearings were employed in the fire control, and all four torpedoes hit. The flash of the explosions lit the fog, but the target remained unseen. Rapid disappearance of the radar pip told the submariners they had scored a fast sinking. Loughlin reversed the submarine's course and sent her back to look for survivors. Some 15 or 20 Japanese were sighted clinging to mats of wreckage, but only one could be prevailed upon to come on board. This survivor stated that the ship was the liner AWA MARU.

When word of the sinking reached ComSubPac's Headquarters at Guam, QUEENFISH was immeediately ordered to search the scene of the disaster for any remaining survivors and to obtain evidence of the character of the ship's cargo. SEAFOX, operating in the vicinity, was directed to assist in the search. No other survivors could be found, but several thousand bales of crude rubber and numerous tins of an unidentified black granular substance were seen floating on the water. Samples of this residue were picked up by both QUEENFISH and SEAFOX.

The sinking of AWA MARU placed the United States Government in a most embarrassing position, and the reaction from Washington was immediate and peremptory.

. . . ORDER QUEENFISH INTO PORT . . . DETACH LOUGHLIN FROM COMMAND AND HAVE HIM TRIED BY GENERAL COURT MARTIAL

The court, consisting of two vice admirals, two rear admirals and two captains, met at the Headquarters of Vice Admiral John H. Hoover, on Guam. Three serious charges were brought against Loughlin:

"Culpable inefficiency in the performance of duty."

"Disobeying the lawful order of his superior officer."

"Negligence in obeying orders."

Loughlin's defense was based on the theory that AWA MARU, because of the cargo and passengers she carried, had sacrificed her right to safe conduct. Intelligence had learned that on the outward passage the ship had unloaded 500 tons of ammunition, about 2,000 bombs and 20 crated planes at Saigon. On her return voyage, according to the lone survivor, she was carrying a cargo of rubber, lead, tin and sugar, and about 1,700 passengers—a few government officials, but for the most part merchant seamen who had been stranded when their ships had been sunk in Malayan and Indonesian water. The court ruled this testimony immaterial in view of the fact that the safe conduct agreement had placed no restrictions on the cargo to be carried in addition to the relief supplies, and the commanding officer of QUEENFISH, at the time of the attack, had no knowledge of the character of AWA MARU's cargo.

Defense then introduced evidence to show lack of intent. The 3-foot depth-setting used on the torpedoes, and the manner in which they were spread ($4\frac{1}{2}$°—approximately 300 feet at target track) proved beyond all reasonable doubt that Loughlin believed he was firing at a short, shallow-draft vessel rather than an 11,000-ton passenger liner.

The true cause underlying the disaster was never brought out in the court martial. Early in the trail, defense counsel admitted that all messages concerning AWA MARU had been received on board QUEENFISH. But no one at the trial thought to inquire whether or not Loughlin had seen them. And that was the key to the whole disastrous episode. Although Loughlin had seen the coded dispatch of March 28 concerning AWA MARU, none of the messages specifying her route and schedule had been delivered to him. The communicators had paid scant attention to these plain-language broadcasts which were received two weeks in advance of the time AWA MARU was to pass through QUEENFISH's area. Through the dereliction of his communications personnel, Loughlin had "failed to get the word."

Here was a tragedy of carelessness that took a heavy toll of human life, seriously impugned the word of the United States Government and put a smudge on the record of one

of the finest officers in the Submarine Service. Acquitted of
the first two charges brought against him, Commander Loughlin was found guilty of the third—negligence in obeying orders. He was sentenced to receive a letter of admonition from
the Secretary of the Navy.

March-April Attrition

While SubPac submarines in March and April were largely
devoted to the preliminaries of "Operation Iceberg" and activities which supported the Okinawa offensive, routine patrolling continued in areas far removed from the storm center.

The biggest merchant ship sent to the bottom by a submarine in March 1945 was the 10,413-ton transport HAKOZAKI
MARU sunk on the 19th by BALAO (Commander R. K. Worth-
ington) in the Yellow Sea. A notable sinking in that it was
the last large Japanese merchantman (with the exception of
AWA MARU) to go down from the torpedo fire of U.S. submarines.

In spite of target scarcity, in March and April 1945, U.S.
submarines sank approximately 130,000 tons of Japanese
merchant shipping.

They also sank one of the last Japanese warships afloat in
the Southwest Pacific.

Gabilan and Charr vs. Isuzu

ISUZU was the last of the light cruisers to fall victim to a
submarine torpedo. She was among the relics which were
dispatched to the East Indies to pick up Jap Army units marooned on beaches a thousand miles from the war.

In early April 1945, ISUZA was steaming on one of the
transport runs. Also in early April a wolf-pack consisting of
BESUGO (Commander H. E. Miller), GABILAN (Commander
W. B. Parham) and CHARR (Commander F. D. Boyle) was
patrolling off the Paternoster and Postiljon Islands in the
waters below Celebes. The group was under the leadership of
Commander Boyle.

On April 4, the pack made a mid-morning contact with
the cruiser and her four escorts. None of the three submarines was able to get in an immediate attack.

On April 6, CHARR saw the elusive cruiser enter Bima Bay.
CHARR passed the news to GABILAN, ordering Parham's submarine to guard the eastern half of the entrance to Bima Bay.
The following morning at 0255 CHARR made radar contact
with the quarry. At 0325 GABILAN reported making contact.

At 0443 Boyle ordered a message sent to GABILAN advising her that CHARR was diving to attack. Before CHARR's radio could transmit this message, word came from GABILAN—she was attacking.

CHARR soon discerned that the enemy formation was rambling and confused. The cruiser was moving slowly and wandering in circles. At 0650, the target was identified as a NATORI-class CL, and a periscope glimpse showed her listing slightly and down by the bow. GABILAN had torpedoed her.

Boyle decided it was time to put her out of her misery. Maneuvering CHARR into attack position, he opened fire at 0724. Six torpedoes. Three observed hits. End of light cruiser ISUZU.

So Jap Army units in the East Indies continued to comb the beach.

Loss of Snook

On March 27, SNOOK (Commander J. F. Walling) put in at Guam for emergency repairs. The following day she headed westward on a weather-reporting mission. On April 1, SNOOK was ordered to join an attack group—"Hiram's Hecklers"—under Commander Hiram Cassedy in TIGRONE.

TIGRONE was in contact with SNOOK on April 8 and the latter's position at that time was 18-40 N., 111-39 E. On April 9 TIGRONE attempted to communicate with SNOOK, but received no answer. It was assumed Walling's submarine had moved eastward toward Luzon Strait. On April 12 she was ordered to serve as a lifeguard during a British carrier-air strike. For this duty she was to take station in the vicinity of Sakeshima Gunto, about 200 miles east of northern Formoso. On April 20 the commander of a British carrier task force reported a plane downed in SNOOK's area. The British force commander was unable to contact SNOOK by radio. BANG was then sent to rendezvous with SNOOK. BANG arrived on the scene in time to rescue three British aviators, but she saw no sign of Walling's submarine. SNOOK was lost.

The Japanese reported no A/S attacks which could account for the loss of SNOOK. The Sakeshima Gunto area was mined, but SNOOK was fully informed on the location of the minefields. Japanese submarines were contacted in the area at the time. This suggests the possibility that SNOOK was sunk by an enemy submarine which was, in turn, destroyed at a later date.

Going down with all hands, SNOOK left behind her a superior record.

Tirante vs. Yellow Sea Transportation (Lt. Comdr. George L. Street, III)

Out of Portsmouth Navy Yard in the autumn of 1944 came the USS TIRANTE, on her bridge Lieutenant Commander George L. Street. If she arrived at Pearl Harbor late in the war, she set out to make up for lost time. And she more than made up for it on her first patrol which took her westward to beat the backwaters of the Yellow Sea.

She slid away from Pearl Harbor on March 3, 1945, and she did not return to base until April 25th. During the intervening 52 days, she attacked 12 enemy vessels, downed half of this number, shot up the rest and raised a Yellow Sea storm that snarled up the Japanese transportation lines to Seoul, Dairen, Tientsin and Tsingtao. Altogether a masterful performance for a maiden patroller.

TIRANTE downed her first ship on March 25—a small tanker off Kagoshimo. Three days later she sank a freighter southwest of Nagasaki. From there she headed into the Yellow Sea, looking for bear.

After careful analysis, Street concluded that the *marus* were following evasive routes through shallow coastal waters, heretofore unexplored by submarines. To those shallow waters he took TIRANTE.

As a result, Street's submarine slammed headlong into action on April 9, and on April 14 fought a battle that brought her a Presidential Unit Citation and the highest honors for Lieutenant Commander Street. The saga is told, Navy style, in the following excerpt from the citation with which the Submarine Board of Awards recommended Lieutenant Commander Street for the Medal of Honor.

WITH EXTREME AGGRESSIVENESS, BRILLIANT PLANNING AND DARING, THE COMMANDING OFFICER TOOK HIS SUBMARINE DEEP INTO THE ENEMY'S INNER DEFENSES IN A METICULOUS SEARCH FOR ENEMY SHIPPING. WITH SAGACITY AND CONSUMMATE SKILL, HE PENETRATED STRONG ESCORT SCREENS IN THE SHALLOW WATER AND LAUNCHED FOUR DEVASTATING TORPEDO ATTACKS. . . . AFTER THE ATTACK UPON THE TRANSPORT, TIRANTE WAS SUBJECTED TO A SEVERE DEPTH-CHARGING WHICH BOUNCED HER OFF THE BOTTOM. FIGHTING FOR HER LIFE, WITH EXPLOSIONS ROCKING HER FROM SIDE TO SIDE, THIS GALLANT SUBMARINE CAME BACK

WITH A VENGEANCE. . . . ALTHOUGH TIRANTE HAD ALREADY SUNK A VERY CREDITABLE AMOUNT OF ENEMY SHIPPING, THE COMMANDING OFFICER REFUSED TO LEAVE THIS DANGEROUS AREA UNTIL THE MAXIMUM AMOUNT OF DAMAGE HAD BEEN INFLICTED UPON THE ENEMY. . . . IT WAS DETERMINED THAT THE ENEMY SHIPS WERE USING A CONFINED HARBOR ON THE NORTH SHORE OF QUELPART FOR AN ANCHORAGE, IN ORDER TO REACH THIS ANCHORAGE, HE WOULD HAVE TO TAKE HIS SUBMARINE THROUGH MANY MILES OF SHALLOW WATER IN WHICH HIS SHIP WOULD NOT BE ABLE TO DIVE. . . . REALIZING THE MOUNTAINOUS DANGERS INVOLVED, THE COMMANDING OFFICER MADE HIS DECISION—"BATTLE STATIONS. TORPEDO."—A DECISION TO ATTEMPT AN ACT FAR ABOVE AND BEYOND THE CALL OF DUTY.

DISREGARDING THE POSSIBILITY OF MINEFIELDS AND THE FIVE SHORE-BASED RADARS IN THE IMMEDIATE VICINITY, TIRANTE CLOSED THE SHORELINE AND PROGRESSED INTO THE HARBOR THROUGH NUMEROUS ANTI-SUBMARINE VESSELS. THE GUN CREWS WERE AT THEIR STATIONS, AS TIRANTE WOULD HAVE TO FIGHT HER WAY OUT ON THE SURFACE IF ATTACKED. ONCE IN THE INNER HARBOR, THE CURRENT WAS CHECKED AND A RAPID SET-UP WAS MADE ON A NEARBY 10,000-TON TANKER. TWO TORPEDOES WERE SKILLFULLY FIRED AT THIS TARGET AND A GREAT MUSHROOM OF WHITE BLINDING FLAME SHOT 2,000 FEET INTO THE AIR AND A THUNDEROUS ROAR NEARLY FLATTENED THE CREW OF TIRANTE. IN THE LIGHT OF THE BURNING TANKER, TWO NEW MIKURA-CLASS FRIGATES SPOTTED TIRANTE AND STARTED IN FOR THE KILL. QUICKLY BRINGING HIS SUBMARINE TO BEAR ON THE LEADING FRIGATE, THE COMMANDING OFFICER TENACIOUSLY FIRED TWO "DO OR DIE" TORPEDOES AT THIS VESSEL. . . . AND THEN SWUNG HIS SHIP AND FIRED HIS LAST TORPEDO AT THE OTHER FRIGATE.

WITH ALL TORPEDOES EXPENDED, THE COMMANDING OFFICER HEADED HIS SHIP OUT OF

*THE CONFINED HARBOR. . . . WITH EMERGENCY
FULL SPEED AHEAD, THE COMMANDING OFFICER
SLIPPED RIGHT OUT OF THE ENEMY'S HANDS. . . .*

On October 5, 1945, President Truman presented the
Medal of Honor to Commander Street in Washington.

Chapter 29

Submarine Lifeguarding

✪　✪　✪

Lockwood Says "Wilco"

It all began at the time plans were afoot for the Gilbert Islands campaign. While conferring with ComSubPac on the problem of Joint Zone operations, Admiral Pownall suggested the possibility of using submarines in target areas to rescue aviators who were downed at sea.

"Just the knowledge that it was there would boost the morale of the aviators," he said. "Do you think a submarine—?"

But Admiral Lockwood already had the picture. The picture was a Navy carrier plane crash-landing in mid-ocean, desperate pilots adrift in rubber boats or clinging to wreckage, eyes staring hopelessly across a vacant desert of sea— and then a submarine silhouetted in the surface haze—advancing to come alongside—cheers! Admiral Lockwood's response was emphatically immediate and affirmative. Operations Officer Commander R. G. Voge was directed to arrange the necessary details. A program was soon devised. Endorsing the plan for lifeguard submarines, Admiral Lockwood put his stamp of approval on a project that eventually surfaced into second place on the priority list of submarine missions. Lifeguarding was second in importance only to sinking of enemy ships.

At SubPac Headquarters time was of the essence. When the preliminary Gilbert air strikes were planned, the submarine lifeguard program had to be launched in a matter of days. The planning, subject to the admiral's approval, was left up to Commander Voge, who had acquired a reputation for getting things done the best way in the shortest time.

Parenthetically, it can be noted that Lockwood was an

410

admiral who knew how to delegate authority. Better than that, he always saw to it that credit for an idea or a plan went to the officer who originated it—a measure of Lockwood's size as a leader.

So SubPac Headquarters shed its necktie, so to speak, and got on this lifeguarding job. And, as has been related, SNOOK, STEELHEAD and SKATE performed lifeguard duties at Marcus, Tarawa and Wake, respectively, and SKATE rescued six downed airmen.

Plunger at Mili

The next successful lifeguard mission was performed by PLUNGER (Lieutenant Commander R. H. Bass) during "Operation Galvanic"—the invasion of the Gilberts. Stationed off Mili, PLUNGER rescued one aviator. This fighter pilot had been downed near Knox Island, a small atoll not far from Mili. PLUNGER raced to the spot at four-engine speed. The aviator was clinging to a yellow rubber lifeboat. As the submarine drew near, a Jap Zero plummeted out of the clouds and skimmed the conning tower with guns blazing.

The rescue party was not yet on deck, but there were about a dozen men on the bridge, including the skipper, the exec, the gunnery officer, the quartermaster, an electrician and four lookouts. Six were wounded when a 20-mm. shell hit the superstructure and exploded, spraying the bridge with shrapnel.

The wounded were rushed below, the bridge was cleared, and Bass ordered a quick dive. PLUNGER went deep, then planed up to periscope depth. The Zero had disappeared; the American aviator was 50 yards away. Sighting the periscope, he waved cheerfully and dug in with the oars, rowing toward the submarine. So PLUNGER rose to the occasion to take aboard Lieutenant (jg) F. G. Schwartz, USNR. Bass then set a course for Makin, where the wounded were transferred to the transport LEONARD WOOD. Fortunately all of the injured recovered. With seven rescues to its credit, the lifeguard program was a going concern by the time of the Marshall Islands campaign.

The "Reference Point" Method

The lifeguard instructions issued for the Marshall Islands operation introduced the use of the "reference point" method of reporting the positions of downed aviators. This method proved so successful it was adopted as standard procedure. A pilot in a damaged plane about to ditch had neither time nor opportunity to encode or encrypt a message giving his position. To send this information in plain language was to invite strafing attacks upon himself and upon the lifeguard submarine by enemy aircraft. The solution of this problem was to report position in plain language by giving the bearing and distance from a reference point unknown to the enemy. Such a reference point was specified for the target of each air strike, and the lifeguard submarine assigned that station was given a voice call. The names of comic strip characters were chosen for the voice calls.

The unique voice call served three purposes. It summoned the lifeguards. (The method was instituted for surface ships and rescue planes as well as submarines.) It designated the objective, or geographical reference point. And when preceded by "distance" and followed by "bearing," it described the exact location of the crash. For example USS FIGHTERFISH has been assigned lifeguard station southwest of Oahu and is given the call "Skeezix." The name "Skeezix" is also given the reference point—say, Barber's Point. The pilot ditching off Barber's Point, or observing a brother aviator's crash in that area, would send, "12 Skeezix 195," which means, "Calling USS FIGHTERFISH . . . Plane crash 12 miles bearing 195 degrees from Barber's Point."

So the air waves over the Central Pacific were presently jocular with calls for Donald Duck, Moon Mullins, Dick Tracy, Lace and other celebrities from the best-read pages of American newspapers. Unfortunately, the Japanese soon learned of the "reference point" strategem. Whereupon they threatened to throw a wrench in the machinery by sending out false distress messages, which served to send the lifeguard submarines off on wild-goose chases, or lured them into range of enemy shore batteries.

The problem was solved by changing voice calls daily, prohibiting use of the calls for anything but actual emergency, and choosing call-words which featured the "L"—a baffler to the Jap who has more trouble with "L" than a Cockney with an "Aitch." This linguistic device opened new avenues for the exercise of imagination and ingenuity. And the enemy was soon tongue-tied by such unpronounceables as "Lonesome Luke," "Little Lulu," "Soul Mate," "Pollywog," "Lillian Russell," "Languid Love," and "Lollipop." In short, he got "ell."

Following the Marshalls campaign, carrier-air strikes smote the enemy's bases in the Marianas and Carolines. The raids on Truk, Guam, Saipan and the islands in the western Carolines have been briefly discussed in previous chapters. Submarine lifeguards participated in all these strikes, and in every case aviators were rescued. Many of the rescues were accomplished under fire, and in all instances the submarine, operating on the surface, risked attack. Danger was their business, and as practitioners of that business they were experts. The one bad mishap which occurred during the period in question was the bombing of TUNNY (Lieutenant Commander J. A. Scott) while she was on lifeguard station at Palau. Mistaking her for an enemy destroyer, American carrier planes let fly with a one-ton bomb that missed TUNNY'S stern by a scant 10 yards. The explosion caused internal injuries which forced the submarine to abandon her lifeguard duties and do some fast work to save her own skin.

Harder at Woleai

On April 1, 1944, HARDER was off Woleai in the western Carolines—a small island, but important as a "feeder base" for enemy aircraft en route from the home islands to the New Guinea front. At 0840 HARDER was some two miles offshore when Mitscher's planes came roaring in. One of the planes spoke HARDER, reporting a pilot downed off a small island west of Woleai. Dealey sent HARDER racing to the rescue. Excerpts from his patrol report tell the story.

We made full speed on four engines. From here on the picture in the skies looked like a gigantic Cleveland Air Show. With dozens of fighters forming a comfortable umbrella above us, we watched a show that made the Hollywood "Colossals" seem tame. We rounded the southeast coast of Woleai, one to two miles off the beach, and had the perfect "ringside seat." The plastering that the airmen gave this Jap base was terrific! The bombers hit Woleai from the south, waited for the smoke to clear, re-formed, and then gave it the works from the east-west course! Fighters seemed to hit the place from all directions, peeling off from high above and diving straight into the AA fire that still persisted. Many looked as if they would go right on thru the blanket of smoke and crash on the islands, but all managed to pull out just above the trees. Fires blazed intermittently on Woleai and most of its adjacent islands, and gradually on Woleai and most of its adjacent sporadic bursts.

Fighters now zoomed the HARDER, one mile off the northeast corner of Woleai, and guided us toward the downed pilot.

1145: The pilot was finally sighted on the northwest tip of the second island to the west of Woleai. Battle surface stations were manned, the ships flooded down, and maneuvered into a spot about 1,500 yards off the beach. White water was breaking over the shoals only twenty yards in front of the ship, and the fathometer had ceased to record. Planes now advised us that if rescue looked too difficult from here (and it did!) that a better approach might be made from another direction.

Backed off to make approach from another angle. The aviator had been standing on the beach and was now observed to fall and lie there stretched on the sand. His collapse was undoubtedly due mainly to physical exhaustion, but also to the disappointment in seeing his chances of rescue apparently fade away. . . .

Moved in again until the forward torpedo room reported ". . . bottom scraping forward" (soundings at zero fathom) and worked both screws to keep the bow against the reef while preventing the ship from getting broadside to the waves.

1200: Three volunteers dove over the side and commenced pushing and towing their rubber boat toward the beach, about 1,200 yards away. A line was payed out from the sub to the rubber raft in order to pull it back from the beach. Meanwhile one of the planes had dropped another rubber boat to the stranded aviator who got in and commenced feebly paddling it to sea against the tide.

After about half an hour, Logan and Ryan, alternately swimming and wading, reached the aviator whose raft had meanwhile drifted farther away. By this time he was thoroughly exhausted. They put him in the raft and by alternately pushing and swimming headed back toward their rubber boat from which a line led to the submarine about 500 yards away.

Meanwhile, a float plane, also attempting the rescue, taxied over the line to the raft, and it parted! The entire rescue party was now stranded.

Thomason. . . . managed to swim back to the sub after a hard battle against the tide. Another volunteer swimmer, Freeman Paquet, Jr., GM1c, then dove over the side and finally managed to swim a line to the three men standing just short of the heavy breakers. This line was made fast to the raft, and little by little, the four men were pulled through the breakers and brought back to the ship.

Through the entire rescue, the cooperation of the aviators was superb. They kept up a continuous pounding of the islands by bombs and flew in low to strafe the Japs and divert their attention from the rescue. In spite of this,

Jap snipers, concealed in trees along the beach, commenced shooting at the ship and rescue party, and bullets whined over the bridge, uncomfortably close. . . .

The rescued aviator, Ensign John R. Galvin, though physically exhausted, showed a character that refused to admit defeat. It is a privilege to serve with men such as these.

With pilot and rescue party aboard, HARDER was backed clear of the reef and headed seaward. Dealey and his good company would long be remembered for this rescue.

Tang at Truk

When O'Kane's submarine was assigned lifeguard duty for the late April carrier strike at Truk, ComSubPac anticipated a successful performance by TANG. But no one expected the record-breaking show which O'Kane and company staged in the turbulent waters off that Caroline stronghold. At 0400 on April 30, 1944, TANG was in her assigned position off Truk Atoll—a station well within the range of the Japanese shore batteries.

On the surface, TANG watched the bombers swarming over Truk. At 1025 the first report of a downed plane came in. O'Kane headed his submarine for the reported position, which was about two miles off Fourup Island. Fighter planes came up to guide TANG to the three survivors who were riding a raft about four miles west of the originally reported position. This trio had bailed out of a Grumman Avenger after the plane had been struck by Japanese shells. Now they were only too happy to have TANG bail them out of the unfriendly sea off Truk.

TANG, with her first three passengers aboard, was hardly under way when another call came in—plane down, two miles east of Ollan Island. To reach this position, TANG had to run within range of the shore batteries on Ollan. O'Kane decided to make the run on the surface and limber up the gun crew in passing. So TANG's gunners pumped 20 rounds in the enemy gun emplacements as the submarine went by. Returning this fire, the Japanese artillerymen opened with a salvo that sent TANG burrowing under. "We didn't spot the second salvo," O'Kane said afterward. "We remained submerged for forty minutes, and then proceeded toward the east side of Truk at emergency speed."

From this position, O'Kane sent TANG in a zigzag search of the area, firing green Very stars at 15-minute intervals, hoping for a return signal from the aviators. One of the men picked up later said he saw the submarine's signal but was afraid to answer it. Hours of futile search ended in a contact with a Japanese submarine. O'Kane sent TANG under to chase; the contact evaporated. When TANG returned to the surface, the crew spread large colors across the deck to assure identification, and the Jap submarine's presence in the area was reported to the task force commander. In return, TANG received the report that a life-raft was drifting two miles southwest of Ollan Island.

"Before we reached this raft a float plane from the NORTH CAROLINA capsized in the cross chop while attempting to rescue," O'Kane recalled. "Another NORTH CAROLINA plane made a precarious landing, and, upon our arrival, was towing both raft and fellow pilot clear of the island. This action was most helpful, for we expected competition from Ollan, and near-by fighters were already strafing the gun emplacements for us."

Later in the day TANG picked up the airmen she had searched for the previous night. This trio gave her a complement of six. Then circling fighter planes directed the submarine to another life-raft. Three more airmen were hauled aboard TANG. And this third rescue was hardly completed before word of three life-rafts adrift off Kuop Island sent O'Kane and company racing for that position.

"As our track took us close by our submarine of the morning, we requested and promptly got good air coverage," O'Kane related. "Off Mesegon Island in the action between Kuop and Truk, we expected to be driven down. But our strafing escorts evidently discouraged any opposition."

Thus O'Kane observed that the enemy gunners consistently refused to fire upon the submarine when American aircraft were in the vicinity. Obviously the Japs did not want to disclose their gun positions to the bombers. O'Kane continued to request fighter cover; the cover was supplied, and the tactic worked with precision and perfection. Thirty-five airmen were shot down during this Truk strike. TANG rescued 22. Most, if not all, of the 13 lost were shot down directly over the target or inside the atoll where they could not be reached.

TANG's record of 22 rescues on a single patrol led the field for over a year. And it settled all question about the value of fighter cover. Thereafter such cover became standard practice for all carrier air strikes.

TANG's remarkably successful lifeguard mission created a wide and immediate demand for submarine lifeguard service. Requests now came in from all sides—from bomber commands in the Solomons, the Admiralty Islands, New Guinea, far-off China. As a result of these requests, from early summer 1944 until the autumn of that year one submarine lifeguard was maintained in the vicinity of Truk, and another in the Yap-Woleai area to perform services for shore-based bombers. On July 14, GUAVINA (Commander C. Tiedeman), lifeguarding near Yap, rescued four air-crewmen of a Thirteenth Air Force Liberator which had crashed the previous day. Five days later she picked up eight aviators who had bailed out from another Liberator.

Lifeguarding for Land-based Bombers (Guavina and Mingo)

In July 1944, GUAVINA (Lieutenant Commander Carl Tiedeman) rescued 17 downed aviators in the vicinity of Yap. This heroic enterprise featured submarine lifeguard service for land-based aircraft. Army flyers were as delighted as anybody to have a friendly submarine come alongside and pluck them out of the ocean. But the GUAVINA rescues were exceptional. Lifeguarding for land-based bombers in the western Carolines was a slow business. The value of the lifeguards to the bomber commands was mostly psychological. Flight crews were heartened by the knowledge that submarines were out there to give them a hand if their motors conked or the enemy shot them down.

When the China-based Twentieth Bomber Command started B-29 strikes on Kyushu in June 1944, from two to four submarines were on duty for each strike, stationed along the outgoing and return routes.

In Borneo waters a submarine of the SoWesPac Force accomplished a most hazardous and dramatic rescue of Liberator pilots. The submarine was MINGO. Skippered by Lieutenant Commander J. R. Madison, she took up a station off Balikpapan in October 1944 to stand lifeguard for a Thirteenth Air Force Liberator strike.

MINGO reached her station a day ahead of schedule. While making time, she got into a ferocious shooting match with four oil-hauling trawlers, ran aground, backed off under fire, and had a hot time generally. Cooling off the next day, she ran to the rescue of six airmen adrift in a huddle of life rafts.

On the day after that, the lookouts sighted a small fire on the eastern fringe of Balesang Bay. MINGO scouted in for a closer look. American aviators? Or a trap of some kind. The submariners broke out a rubber boat and, armed with Tommy-guns, paddled in to investigate. Thirty minutes later they returned with four aviators. A fifth paddled out by himself in a native dugout. The five airmen were installed in the submarine. So was the dugout—marked as a present for the Officers' Club in Fremantle.

One of the flyers said he believed five more crewmen were down on the beach a few miles north. Madison headed MINGO for a search in that neck of the woods. The woods of Borneo being about as primitive as was Tarzan's favorite jungle, the submariners proceeded cautiously. Because rescued airmen said they had at first mistaken MINGO for a Jap sub, Madison ordered a large flag secured to the periscope for identification.

As the submarine rounded Cape Biroe, the lookouts saw a flashing light, and noticed a parachute spread out on a clump of rocks. Madison maneuvered in toward the beach. Five more Liberator crewmen were soon aboard. Of the downed aircraft's crew only one man remained unaccounted for.

With the 16 survivors aboard and under the care of the pharmacist's mate, Madison headed his submarine south. MINGO had not gone far in that direction when she was sighted by a high-flying Liberator bomber that made a decidedly menacing scrutiny of the submarine. Madison and company tried frantically to communicate their identity to the aircraft. Twenty minutes of that, and the bomber turned away. All hands exhaled in relief. Six minutes later the bomber was back! All hands inhaled. A 100-pound bomb landed 300 feet broad on MINGO's starboard beam. For some perverse reason, only then was voice communication established between the submarine and the bomber.

Aces High

EVEN IF YOU WERE SHOT DOWN IN TOKYO HARBOR THE NAVY WOULD BE IN TO GET YOU!

So was titled an article by Ernie Pyle, featuring the rescue of Ensign Robert Buchanan by the submarine POMFRET (Lieutenant Commander J. B. Hess) on lifeguard mission off Sagami Nada. Here is the story in POMFRET's log, dated February 17, 1945.

About noon a fighter was reported down in the submarine's area. Trailing the air cover, Hess headed POMFRET into the bay. Groping through an oyster-clammy mist, she navigated entirely by radar, using a "pip" she hoped was the Suro Saki lighthouse. Finally, after approaching uncomfortably close to the shallows in the center of Sagami Nada, she picked up Ensign R. L. Buchanan of the USS CABOT. At this juncture the last of the aircraft cover departed because of low fuel.

Hess reported later, "As he faded off the SD screen there was not a friend anywhere." Five or six small Jap vessels were in sight to the northwest as POMFRET followed her retiring air cover. But the submarine's outward passage was un-opposed. This rescue, of course, did not literally take place in Tokyo Bay, but the "even if" by Ernie Pyle was no exag-eration.

On one occasion an aviator was rescued most unexpected-ly. April 2, 1945, SEALION II (Lieutenant Commander C. F. Putnam), patrolling in the South China Sea, sighted a distant object across the water. The SEALIONERS picked up Sergeant Bauduy R. Grier of the Fifth Bomber Command. Grier had been adrift in a rubber boat for 23 days!

Probably the all-astounding rescue of the war was one ac-complished on a day in June 1944 by STINGRAY (Lieutenant Commander S. C. Loomis, Jr.) within one mile of Agaña airfield, Guam. At the time, the island was still in enemy hands. About 1015 in the morning of this day, fighter planes reported a downed airman adrift near Orote Point. The sub-marine ran to the designated spot. There she found the des-perate aviator playing target for an AA shore battery which was peppering him with a vicious fire. As the submarine approached, a shell exploded 400 yards off her starboard beam. To prevent a salvo from landing squarely on STING-RAY'S conning tower, Loomis "pulled the plug." What hap-pened after that is delightfully described in the submarine skipper's patrol report. As follows:

1233: Sighted pilot dead ahead. Had to approach from lee or across wind. Velocity 10 to 12 knots.

1235: Two shell splashes ahead.

1238: Two more splashes and burst of AA fire near pilot. Can see him ducking in rubber boat.

1240: Pilot has sighted us and is waving. Holding up left hand which shows a deep cut across the palm.

1303: Approached with about ten feet of number one scope and about three feet of number two scope out of water. Pilot very close and no signs of line ready for scope. Pilot so close I have lost him in number one field. Headed directly for him. Missed.

1319: Three shell splashes on port quarter.

1347: Heard shell land close aboard.

1349: Heard another close one.

1352: Almost on top of pilot. Now, he's paddling *away* from periscope. Missed.

1418: Planes commenced bombing Agana field and shore batteries.

1423: Shell splash, about 500 yards.

1424: Heard shell splash.
Heard another close one.
Heard another close shell.
Heard two more.

1440: Heard and saw two splashes close aboard.

1453: Pilot missed the boat again. On this try, he showed the first signs of attempting to reach periscope. Maybe shell fire has made him think that a ride on a periscope might be all right after all. I am getting damned disgusted, plus a stiff neck and a blind eye.

1500: Heard another shell.

1516: Fourth try. Ran into pilot with periscope and he hung on! Towed him for one hour during which time he frantically signalled for us to let him up. His hand was cut badly and it must have been tough going hanging onto the bitter end of the line with one hand while bumping along in the whitecaps.

1611: Lowered towing scope, watching pilot's amazed expression with other periscope.

1613: Surfaced.

1618: Picked up Ensign Donald Carol Brandt, USNR, suffering from deep wound in left hand. Glad to finally get him aboard. He said that during first and third approaches he was afraid periscopes were going to hit him and he tried to get out of the way and come in astern of me. He had been briefed on a rescue like this, but guess the shock of getting hit at 14,000 feet and falling upside down in his parachute from 12,000 feet was too much. And then the shell-fire shouldn't have done him much good either. He's taken quite a running, and taken it well. We're on speaking terms now, but after the third approach, I was ready to make him captain of the head.

The date of this periscope-ride was June 13, 1944. It was a day that the submariners in STINGRAY would not soon forget, and one that the rescued aviator would in all probability remember as long as he lived.

And he, and many more like him, lived because of Submarine Lifeguarding—an enterprise which started as a little extra duty to assist the air forces and developed in the closing months of the war into one of the major tasks assigned

U.S. submarines. The success of this remarkable submarine effort can be measured by the following table.

	Submarine-days on lifeguard station	Number of rescues
1943	64	7
1944	469	117
1945 (to 14 Aug)	2739	380
Total	3272	504

Submarine Lifesavers

The Sub Force lifeguards remained in action until the war's last day. "L" words continued to baffle the Japs who mouthed helplessly, trying to cope with "Bustle Rustle," "Flabby Flanks," "Flashy Lass" and "Fleshy Flo." Pilots saved by this word game did not think it funny.

Eighty-six submarines picked up downed airmen. GATO and QUEENFISH each saved 13. SEA DEVIL and WHALE saved 15 per sub. MINGO rescued 16. GABILAN and GUAVINA 17 each. RAY saved 21. TANG rescued 22. And TIGRONE, the lifeguard champion, saved 31.

But the statistics are too laconic. Think of the 504 as American airmen. Good lads, who were saved.

Chapter 30

Mission Accomplished

☆ ☆ ☆

Bankruptcy of an Empire

By May 1945 the submarine attrition war in the Southwest Pacific was almost over. Little remained of the Imperial transportation network which had sprawled across the southern half of the Co-Prosperity Sphere like a parasitical vine. Singapore, one-time terminal of that great trunk line which had extended from Indonesia to Japan, was now nothing more than a useless stump, hardly worth the powder to blow.

No Japan-bound convoys plowed the central waters of the South China Sea. A few lines branched from Singapore to Sumatra, Java and Celebes. These lines were still in operation at war's end. Militarily they were worthless to the Japanese—vestigial roots which maintained a sort of life in the Singapore stump.

In Borneo, Java, Bali and other islands of the Netherlands East Indies, Imperial Army forces waited glumly for evacuation. No *marus* were on hand to take home these wallflower garrisons.

The Gulf of Siam was invaded by SubSoWesPac patrollers during this closing period of the war. They found little to shoot at.

And if May's crop of targets was sparse, June's was even more so. On June 8 COBIA struck a convoy on the Saigon-Singapore run and downed a small tanker and the 3,841-ton landing-craft HAKUSA. In a lively battle with a Java Sea convoy on the 23rd, HARDHEAD demolished a shuttle boat and three subchasers. Off Bali on June 27, BLUEBACK sank a subchaser. This was the sum and substance of the SubSoWesPac attrition score for June 1945. The seas below the 18°

30′ parallel were practically swept clean. Or, to tailor the phrase to suit torpedo warfare, the waters had been "fished out."

In Japan the Imperial Navy was little more than a memory. The Japanese merchant service was on the rocks. The War Machine was out of fuel. The U.S. submarine blockade gripped the home islands in a vise, and the Japanese population faced starvation.

Yet Japan's leaders in the spring of 1945 were disposed to bandy words. Although the Empire was out of business, the stockholders were bankrupt and countless thousands of lives had been squandered in the miserable war enterprise, the Imperial "Board of Directors" continued to harangue and temporize, desperately hunting for personal security and a clever "out."

Japan's Army generals spoke of continuing resistance as a means of maintaining public discipline. What would happen when the Japanese people discovered they had been hoodwinked by mendacious propaganda? Would not the populace revolt if it learned the Emperor was no more of a god than a fisherman? While this windy word-juggling went on, the United States offensive struck Okinawa. Suzuki's cabinet carried on the prolix debate. Calls for help had gone to Nazi Germany, but in March the frantic appeals had been answered by appalling word that one Axis partner was done for—on April 27 a squad of Italian partisans had executed Benito Mussolini. The Japanese War Lords could feel their hair rise. The Axis was shattered. Still the Army High Command voted to maintain the suicidal resistance and several Imperial Navy admirals, among them Toyoda, were opposed to suing for peace.

Because these militarists had their say, the Pacific War went on. Hundreds of Americans and many thousands of Japanese would lose their lives in the ensuing weeks of a conflict prolonged by a huddle of incompetents who wished only to "save face."

Loss of Lagarto

One of the last U.S. submarines to go down in World War II was LAGARTO. On April 12, Commander F. D. Latta on her bridge, she left the Philippines to patrol an area in the South China Sea. She found nothing to sweep in the South China Sea. So she was directed to patrol in the Gulf of Siam.

There, on May 2, she joined BAYA in a convoy chase. LA-GARTO and BAYA exchanged contact reports during the day, and BAYA overhauled the convoy that evening. BAYA was driven off by the unusually alert escorts. What of LAGARTO? Early in the morning of May 4 BAYA tried to contact her team-mate. LAGARTO made no reply. BAYA did not hear from her again, and Latta's submarine never returned to port.

The Japanese minelayer HATSUTAKA reported an attack on a submarine near the mouth of the Gulf of Siam at the time the LAGARTO was in that vicinity. The blasting occurred in 30-fathom water—a depth which gave the submersible little little chance for evasion. Headquarters could only assume that LAGARTO was the minelayer's victim. Perishing in battle, then, she was lost with all hands.

Minelayer HATSUTAKA did not long survive this action. Skulking southeastward down the Malay coastline, she was ambushed on May 16 by another U.S. submarine. This patroller was HAWKBILL. HAWKBILL dealt the enemy vessel a killing blow. The torpedoes struck home, and when the smoke and fire unraveled, the minelayer was gone. LAGARTO was avenged.

SubPac Vise on Japan

While the B-29's hammered Tokyo, and American invasion forces battered their way across Okinawa, Admiral Lockwood's submarines concentrated on the blockade of Japan's Pacific ports and the cutting of Japanese shipping lines to China and Manchuria.

To the Japanese merchant marine, half-paralyzed by the fuel famine, badgered by air attack, unable to scrape up escorts, repairs or replacements, continued losses to submarines in home Empire waters must have come as Ossas of diaster piled on Pelions of ruin. In April 1945 the situation was so critical that nearly all of the available shipping had been ordered to haul only foodstuffs and salt. Now the sinkings in the Yellow Sea, the Kuriles and off northeast Honshu brought the food crisis to a head.

While the submarine vise tightened on Japan, a SubPac lifeguard reported an incident which gives one a vivid periscope-glimpse of battle action perhaps typical of this period.

Atule Spots Planes

Lifeguard duty not infrequently provided American submarines with a box seat for an air show, and on a number of occasions the up-thrust periscopes watched in fascination as American aircraft shot down enemy planes. But only a few submarines were able to assist the action by vectoring the victors in. ATULE (Commander J. H. Maurer) was one of these.

On May 5, 1945, ATULE was on lifeguard station 12 miles south of Okino Shima.

For a time the morning was peacefully routine. Then the air show began. Commander Maurer's patrol report narrates the action as seen from the submariner's point of view.

1000: Sighted Jake and Rufe [Jap aircraft] coming in on starboard beam. Dumbo [a B-29 serving as air cover for the sub] was opening out on the port beam at this time. Immediately reported enemy to him, and received acknowledgment as we dived to periscope depth to watch the show. The Jake passed almost directly overhead, close enough for us to distinguish the type of tail fins on the bomb between his floats. In the meantime, the Rufe began investigating conditions in an adjacent area, leaving his team mate to tackle the monster alone. . . . The fight was short and unequal, and the panorama through the periscope was unforgettable as the scene unfolded, low over the water and less than two miles away. The C.O. at the periscope was commentator, giving a play-by-play account throughout the ship over all communication systems—mostly by direct voice.

1006: The twisting, weaving Jake received one short and devastatingly deadly barrage from the B-29 (tracers plainly visible), burst into flames aft, and crashed into the sea in a sheet of flame from the exploding bomb and gasoline.

1009: Surfaced. Dumbo thanked us for the assist and departed for home.

1020: Reached scene of crash. One survivor was calling for help, but of the remaining two, one had been completely decapitated, and the other was dead and floating face downward in the gasoline covered water. The survivor, Lt. Masayosi Kojima, a naval observer, was pulled past the grisly body and floating head of his team mate and hauled aboard. He was suffering from shock, second degree burns of the face and hands, flesh wounds in the neck and arm, and gunshot or crash wounds in his right ankle. How he escaped alive from the exploding plane is amazing in itself. . . . The numerous pockets in the clothes, uniform and life-jacket of our English and German speaking POW provided a wealth of printed matter including identi-

fication, seven packs of Jap and one of British cigarettes, calling cards, ration books, club tickets, diary,
notebook, flight record, and, of prime importance, two
magnetic detector traces and notes concerning them.
A thick wad of currency, vial of perfume and other
personal items showed he was ready for any eventuality. . . . The time schedule of this action is rather unusual since the total action, from initial sighting, including diving, the attack, surfacing and the rescue,
covered only twenty minutes.

Maurer's description of the time schedule as "rather unusual" could be applied, it would seem, to other features of
the incident. Everyone seems to have done some fast work,
including Lieutenant Kojima with his calling cards, club
tickets, currency and perfume.

V-E Day

Somebody at Pearl Harbor stared at a dispatch.
At Fremantle a radioman's fingers shook slightly.
"The Nazis have surrendered! The Allies are in Berlin!"
But the Allies had yet to enter Tokyo. Submariners had
only time to clap each other on the back. May 17, 1945, was
just another day in the Pacific War.
In SubPac Headquarters at Guam, Admiral Lockwood's
staff officers concentrated on charts and discussed the Sea
of Japan.

"Operation Barney" (Under-running Enemy Minefields)

Ever since the loss of WAHOO in those waters in the autumn of 1943, the Sea of Japan had been "out of bounds"
for SubPac patrollers. Too many mine barriers.
The Sea of Japan was not to retain its immunity to torpedo
warfare. In the autumn and winter of 1944-1945 American
scientists and technicians of the University of California Division of War Research worked overtime to develop a mine-
detecting device which would permit submarines to penetrate mined areas. By the spring of 1945 this equipment was
ready for the business at hand. The business at hand was an
invasion of the Japan Sea.
Admiral Lockwood's Operations Officer, Captain R. G.
Voge, selected one of his assistants at Guam to take charge
of the project. The officer selected was Commander W. B.
"Barney" Sieglaff. Conductor of six successful patrols as
captain of TAUTOG, Sieglaff brought to the invasion enter-

prise a veteran's knowledge of undersea warfare and a lively intellect—the right sparkplug for the energizing of such a venture.

Equipped with the new mine-detecting device, nine Sub-Pac submarines assembled at Guam to complete preliminary training. Commander Sieglaff put skippers and crews through a "third degree" course in Japan Sea navigation and mine-field penetration. Everything depended on the mine-detecting gear and the skill of the operators. The apparatus required experts. It had them. The submarines were manned by expert crews and captained by expert skippers. The project had expert direction. Thus success was assured for "Operation Barney."

"Hydeman's Hellcats"

Under group leadership of Commander E. T. Hydeman, the nine submarines that were detailed to "Operation Barney" formed a wolf-pack answering to the name of "Hydeman's Hellcats." The "Hellcats" were subdivided into three task groups.

"Hydeman's Hepcats"—SEA DOG (Commander E. T. Hydeman); CREVALLE (Commander E. H. Steinmetz); SPADE-FISH (Commander W. J. Germerhausen).

"Pierce's Polecats"—TUNNY (Commander G. E. Pierce); SKATE (Commander R. B. Lynch); BONEFISH (Commander L. L. Edge).

"Risser's Bobcats"—FLYINGFISH (Commander R. D. Risser); BOWFIN (Commander A. K. Tyree); TINOSA (Command R. C. Latham).

Leaving Guam on May 27, the nine submarines headed northwestward, their bows pointing like compass needles for Tsushima Strait. En route, "Risser's Bobcats" performed life-guard duties, and TINOSA rescued 10 men of the crew of a B-29 which had crashed about 18 miles northeast of Sofu Gan. Sideline issue compared to the venture in prospect—slipping across the northern waters of the East China Sea and stealing through the narrow passage between Korea and Tsushima Island. It was off this island centered in Tsushima Strait midway between Korea and Kyushu that the Czar's Baltic fleet in 1905 was trapped and destroyed by the Japanese. The "Hellcats" would encounter no Japanese fleet, but mines were a certainty. Would the new detection device do the trick? It had its idiosyncrasies. Sensitive as it was, the contrivance detected many submerged objects which were not mines. Contacts registered an alarm, and it took an ace specialist to distinguish the real from the semblance. As is the case with most specialists and technicians, the operators of this mine-detecting gear developed a terminology of their own. Registered by the submarine detecting device, authentic mine-warning signals were termed "Hell's Bells."

With "Hell's Bells" ringing here and there, and not a few false warnings to keep their nerves at attention, the "Hell-cats" crept through Tsushima Strait and entered the Sea of Japan on schedule. Shooting was timed to begin at sunset on June 9th.

Overconfident even at this catastrophic season, the Japanese were caught completely off guard by the invaders at their back door. Astounded by the sudden thunder of torpedo fire off the west coast of Honshu, they could not believe American submarines had entered the Sea of Japan by normal means. Radio Tokyo, always imaginative, announced that the submarines had been "smuggled in."

The "Hepcats" covered the waters off northwest Honshu, cutting the inside shipping lanes to Hakodate and Ominato. Shortly after sunset on June 9, SEA DOG attacked a freighter a few miles north of Sado Shima and downed the vessel with one shot. Before midnight her torpedoes had sunk a second freighter in the same area. Three more cargomen and a passenger-cargo carrier fell to Hydeman's submarine before her foray in the "Emperor's private ocean," was concluded. Pack-mate CREVALLE also opened fire on the 9th, picking off a cargoman. Commander "Steiny" Steinmetz and company sank another medium-sized freighter on the 10th and a third on the 11th. SPADEFISH, under Commander "Bill" Germerhausen, worked the waters northward from Wakasa Wan to Hokkaido. Five vessels were shoveled under by this old hand.

Ranging the southeastern waters of the Japan Sea, "Pierce's Polecats" had their share of fast action. Commander George Pierce's TUNNY found the action more exciting than the targets. Hunting game, the submarine steamed boldly into the harbors of Etomo Ko and Uppuri Wan, but shipping was not in evidence. Then TUNNY herself played target in a running gun battle with two Jap DD's. Meantime, SKATE found shooting around the Noto Peninsula. There, mid-morning of June 10, Commander "Ozzie" Lynch and crew encountered the Japanese submarine I-122. This I-boat's number was up when it zigged across SKATE's bow at a range of 800 yards, thereby collecting two torpedoes of a four-torpedo spread. Two days later SKATE entered Matugashita Cove to attack an anchored convoy. Three "sitting ducks" were downed during this ticklish action. And while SKATE was littering the southwest coast of Honshu with wreckage, BONEFISH, skippered by Commander "Larry" Edge, was strewing the neighboring littoral with similar scrap. To her torpedoes fell the two largest vessels downed by the invading "Hellcats"—a 6,892-ton freighter sunk on the 13th, and a 5,488-ton passenger-cargoman blasted under on the 19th.

Combing the western waters of the Japan Sea, "Risser's Bobcats" slashed at shipping off the east coast of Korea. Captained by Commander "Bob" Risser, FLYINGFISH sank a medium-sized freighter, and the following day she downed a small passenger-cargoman. Farther north, "Alec" Tyree's BOWFIN encountered creamy fog, hundreds of friendly Korean fishermen and two *marus*—a passenger-cargoman and a small freighter. The *marus* were dispatched to the bottom. In adjacent Korean waters, TINOSA likewise was enmeshed by fog and fishermen. Fishnets proved more of a nuisance than fog, but neither prevented "Dick" Latham and company from downing four Japanese freighters that steamed into range. These were the last *marus* downed by the June invaders in the Sea of Japan.

Statistics impressively summarize the handiwork of "Hydeman's Hellcats."

Accomplished in 12 days, the sinkings enumerated—27 Japanese merchantmen and an I-boat—cost Japanese shipping a total of some 57,000 tons. For good measure the "Hellcats" shot up a number of small craft. A few *marus* were damaged by torpedo fire. The tonnage sunk would not have seriously hampered the Japanese in an earlier period of the war, but in June 1945, when their merchant service was falling apart like the One Horse Shay, the blow was absolutely disastrous.

The "Hellcats" were elated. They had circumvented the dangerous minefields and given the enemy's shipping arteries in the Japan Sea a memorable clawing. In accordance with plans, Commander Hydeman assembled his pack off La Perouse Strait, and on the night of June 24, running on the surface through cotton-thick fog, the submarines began their dash for the Pacific. Colors flying, they entered Pearl Harbor on the Fourth of July.

But one tragedy marred this triumphal return. BONEFISH was not among the submarines that made home.

Loss of Bonefish

When BONEFISH entered the Japan Sea with the "Hellcats" she was making her eighth war patrol. She made the entry on the 5th without misadventure and like the other "Hellcats," she held her fire until the 9th. On the 16th she kept a rendezvous with Tunny, and her skipper, Commander Edge, reported the sinking of a ship later identified as the 6,892-ton Oshikayama Maru—the largest vessel sunk by the invading "Hellcats."

At a second rendezvous Commander Edge asked permission to conduct a submerged daylight patrol in Toyama Wan, a bay farther up the Honshu coast. Permission was granted.

The "Hellcat" plan called for the transit of La Perouse Strait on the night of June 24th. Bonefish did not appear at the assembly point on the evening of the 23rd. After running through the Strait, Tunny waited at the Pacific entrance until June 26, hoping to contact her missing pack-mate. Tunny waited in vain.

Provision had been made for the "Hellcats," in event of emergency, to proceed to Russian waters and claim a 24-hour haven. Too, they had been given liberty to leave the Japan Sea before or after June 24 if circumstances warranted. The submariners hoped that Bonefish had availed herself of one of these alternatives. But Bonefish never got out.

Japanese A/S forces reported an attack on a submarine in Toyama Wan. Savage depth-charging brought to the surface a swirling pool of oil and pieces of splintered wood. There could be little doubt that Bonefish was the victim of a severe counter-attack. Going down with all hands, she was the last SubPac submarine lost in World War II.

Tirante off Nagasaki

The submarine war did not by-pass Kyushu in June 1945. Early in that warm month Tirante (Lieutenant Commander G. L. Street) was patrolling directly off Nagasaki. About 0800 on the morning of the 11th, Street spied a ship alongside the wharf at Ha Shima. This little island is about seven miles southwest of the entrance to Nagasaki—a short run for an excursion steamer, a mere dash for a destroyer, and practically nothing flat for an artillery projectile. Japanese destroyers were not likely in this or any area at that date, but coastal batteries could be expected, and it was ticklish territory for submarining. However, 3,000-ton targets were at a premium. The ship at the dock was a novel sight after a long and fruitless hunt, and Street decided to take the bird in hand.

This meant going into the bush after it, and there was a considerable distance to go. Tirante would have to move in under a headland and pass within spitting, or at least gunshot, distance of a beach. Street and company remained undismayed. There was the target. Let's go.

The approach was made submerged. Absence of minefields could be inferred from the criss-crossing sampan traffic. Dexterous navigation took the submarine past the inside of Mitsue Se Shoals. In these shallows TIRANTE walked as though barefoot on coral. Soundings were taken every five minutes. They were not the only things that were taken. As the submarine crept forward, movies were taken through the periscope. Submarine photography had come a long way. TIRANTE took color movies of this action.

The target vessel measured 310 feet, bow to stern. On her stern, was a 4.7 gun, and the crew happened to be standing by. At 1115 TIRANTE was lined up for a shot. Street fired one torpedo, with ½-knot target speed set on T.D.C. to offset the observed current. This was intended as a ranging shot to test the accuracy of the current observation. Rigged to the periscope in time to catch the explosion, the movie camera was buzzing as the torpedo hit home 50 feet forward of the point of aim. Geyser! Smoke-pall! Then the scene cleared and Street could see a hole in the target's bow and an avalanche of coal spilling into the sea. Two sailors who had been leaning over the bow rail were no longer in the scene.

Now the Japanese Navy gunners on the vessel's quarterdeck snapped into action. They were training the gun aft and up, squinting skyward in search of aircraft.

TIRANTE began a swing to the left. Street steadied her down and fired one electric torpedo, aimed to eliminate the ship's gun and its crew. The torpedo ran true, but came to a sudden stop without exploding. Either the torpedo was a dud or it had been stopped by a mud bank or net. This was not the moment for the freighter's gun crew to sight TIRANTE'S SD radar antenna which had been used preparatory to surfacing. Shells began to smack the water around the submarine. The battle was on.

Street set another electric torpedo for shallow depth, aimed it just aft of the freighter's mid-section in order to miss any obstruction that might have stopped the previous shot, and fired. When the smoke lifted, the ship was listing 20° to starboard. The stern gun was still there, but its crew had vanished.

With the wreck 1,800 yards astern, Street surfaced TIRANTE and ordered emergency speed. The Diesels were galloping when the SD reported aircraft a mile distant. Those on the bridge could not spot the aircraft, but automatic gunfire from the beach jumped into view, and bullets began to whine around TIRANTE'S conning tower. Fortunately this fire was spasmodic and inaccurate. The SD contacts proved to be

land, and TIRANTE was safely on her way out when the submariners made an alarming discovery. While the submarine
was running at flank speed across the water, her bow planes
would not rig in. With these huge fins "catching crabs,"
TIRANTE had been bumping along like a sea cow on a gravel
beach.

Assembling all hands on the bridge behind the armored
section, Street rang up "Stop." Trouble-shooters rigged in the
recalcitrant bow planes as Japanese shore guns continued to
shoot at TIRANTE. All hands were sweating when the planes
were finally rigged. And hotter work was in the offing. To
clear the shoal spot, it was necessary to run directly toward the headland of Nomo Saki. Automatic guns on the
bluff-top along the cape opened up on the submarine at a
range of 3,000 yards as she skirted the shoals. Racing through
a storm of lead, TIRANTE cleared the headland and ran seaward, tagged by angry projectiles. Unharmed, the submarine reached safewater. It had been a Hollywood finish,
and it photographed as one of the most spectacular submarine dramas of the war. Produced by TIRANTE and company. Directed by Commander G. L. Street. Filmed in
"Technicolor!"

Barb Bombards Japan

While "Hydeman's Hellcats" were rampaging in the Sea
of Japan and patrollers such as TIRANTE were nuzzling the
home Empire's waterfronts, a SubPac raider appeared off the
port of Shari on the north coast of Hokkaido and proceeded
to blow holes in the center of the city. The submarine that
thus employed a town for a target was BARB, captained by
Commander E. B. Fluckey. On the assumption that cargo
in a warehouse was as valuable as that in the hold of a *maru*,
Fluckey opened fire on this snug seaport. BARB was not the
first American submarine to bombard a Japanese town, but
she was first to give the local citizenry a glimpse of the
American rocket's red glare. A rocket-launcher had been installed on the submarine's deck, and the attack was something novel by way of undersea warfare.

Twelve days later Fluckey's submarine was off the island
of Kaihyo at the eastern extremity of the Karafuto Peninsula.
Here a large seal fishery was operated by the Japanese Government. As BARB moved in on the surface at dawn, Fluckey
remarked the stockades of the seal rookery and noted "two
beacons, radio antenna and an observation post . . . on the
flat top of the island." Commander Fluckey decided to

pound the island's top a little flatter. Up from below came
the submarine gunners. Barracks, warehouses and buildings
were sighted, and the local islanders could be seen running
in panic. When the range closed to 1,100 yards, Fluckey
gave the order, and BARB'S gun crew opened fire. Simultaneously the shore gunners sent machine-gun bullets chat-
tering at the submarine. They failed to hit her. BARB'S gunnery was better. Her sharpshooters dropped shell after shell
into observation posts, buildings, and a huddle of anchored
sampans. As Fluckey expressed it: *"Really a wonderful sight
and ideal submarine bombardment—sampans destroyed, oil
drums tumbled and split, a field piece overturned and a
machine gun hanging loose, unattended."*

The next morning (July 3) Fluckey again trotted out the
rockets. Target this time was the town of Shikuka on the western shore of Patience Bay, Karafuto Peninsula. At 0240 the
rockets were away, range 4,000 yards from the beach. Explosions racketed and flared, but no fires were started.

Passing the Fourth of July in quiet cruising, Fluckey and
company took time out on the 5th to torpedo and sink a
2,820-ton freighter. Mere routine. The crew was more interested in the skipper's plan for sabotaging a railroad
train. A waterproof electrical hook-up had been rigged for a
55-pound demolition charge suitable for planting alongside a
railroad track. Coupled with a micro switch, the charge
would be set off when a locomotive came larruping along on
the rails. Perhaps this enterprise was suggested by the fact
that BARB was operating in the Kurile waters of the "Polar
Circuit"—an area subdivided into patrol beats titled "Day
Coach," "Diner," "Club Car," "Locomotive" and "Pullman."
BARB was operating in the "Locomotive" subdivision.

A position near Otasamu on the east coast of Karafuto was
selected. Train times were noted. The operation was scheduled for a night when clouds darkened the moon. The dark
night arrived, and a saboteur party of eight men under Lieutenant W. M. Walker, USNR, went ashore. While the submariners were busy landing their gear, one train whistled
by. As its sparks twinkled off in the distance, the saboteurs
began their nocturnal work. Then, as the party paddled
back to the submarine, another train came highballing up
the track.

The party was still paddling furiously when *"Wham!*
(quoting Fluckey). *What a thrill! The charge made a much
greater explosion than we expected. The engine's boilers
blew, wreckage flew two hundred feet in the air in a flash of
flame and smoke, cars piled up and rolled off the track in a*

writhing, twisting mass of wreckage. Cheers!" A prisoner of war captured later said the newspaper reported a bomb had hit the train and killed 150 passengers.

From train-wrecking BARB turned to ship-sinking and rocket-bombardments. Two more towns were rocketed on July 25.

Midday, July 26, some large canneries in the town of Chiri were subjected to 43 rounds from BARB'S 5-inch gun. The last and probably the most damaging bombardment of this land-strafing submarine patrol was delivered that afternoon at Shibertoro on the west coast of Kunashiri Island. Aircraft were not in evidence, and BARB cruised along the beach in bright daylight looking for targets. A lumber mill, adjacent buildings, fuel tanks and a sampan building-yard were sighted. Mill, buildings, and sampan yard were camouflaged to deceive aircraft observation. Obviously the Japanese in the area had not anticipated attack by submarine.

Fluckey sent BARB excursioning past the waterfront to draw fire. As no fire eventuated, the submarine gunners opened up on the shipyard. The yard went up like a tinderbox and the sampans were shattered to kindling. When the submariners returned that evening for a look, the town was a black yawn of charred ruins and smoking embers.

BARB'S incendiary raids were match-flares compared to the great fire-raids at that time consuming the industrial and residential sections of Tokyo. But when a lone submarine could roam at will along a nation's coastline, bombard the shore defenses with impunity, wreck a railroad train and reduce a town to ashes, it was apparent that the defenders had reached the exhaustion point.

Japan Torpedoed

In July 1853 a United States fleet under Commodore Perry opened up the Closed Empire to world commerce. In June 1945, United States fleet submarines reestablished the Empire's status as closed.

Rough statistics present a picture of Japan's plight. As of May 1945 Japanese merchant tonnage afloat approximated 2,384,000 tons. Tonnages sunk by submarines in May and June reduced this figure by some 125,000 tons. Mines laid by aircraft subtracted the lion's share of Japanese shipping during this two-month period, accounting for approximately 375,000 tons. This figure includes damage and disablement, but any vessel which suffered a material casualty at this time was to all intents and purposes "sunk." By June's end the Japanese merchant fleet was down to a skimpy 2,058,000 tons.

But the tonnage afloat which remained to the Japanese merchant fleet was not the tonnage in active service. In May and June a large percentage of the merchant fleet was immobilized by lack of fuel. The dazed Government placed all merchant shipping under a War Power Council. The Council could scrape together only 1,200,000 tons of cargo ships for service in June. Japan needed 3,000,000 tons to survive.

By the end of June the War Power Council arrived at figures which proved that Japan's water transport situation was hopeless. There could be no denying the ruthless mathematics. Japan had begun the war with approximately 6,000,000 tons of merchant shipping. Now, after three and a half years of war, the merchant tonnage added up to a scant 1,200,000 tons of ships serviceable.

Tokyo was tottering. A food famine ravaged the gaunt populace. Still the incompetents around the Emperor continued to pantomime, bluster, and delay surrender. Realities were evaded by medieval thinking, and figures were juggled to aid self-deception.

So the war dragged on through July 1945.

The Vanishing I.J.N.

Another sequel to "Operation Barney" and the successful mine-detection exploit ensued when Admiral Halsey asked Admiral Lockwood for minefield reconnaissance off Kyushu and Honshu. Accordingly, RUNNER II, REDFIN and CATFISH were dispatched to perform these perilous reconnaissance missions. Object was to determine the extent of the coastal field and locate safe channels for the Third Fleet which was preparing to close in on Japan.

With Okinawa secured, United States forces girded for "Operation Olympic"—the invasion of Japan. Carrier air strikes were scheduled, and submarines were called on for anti-picket sweeps in July.

Commander B. F. McMahon in PIPER was in charge of the sweep, the submarines in the group going by the name of "Mac's Moppers." These were PIPER, POMFRET, PLAICE and SEA POACHER. Working in conjunction with the sweepers, RUNNER II, REDFIN and CATFISH probed for minefields with their sensitive detecting gear. The mine detectors found an open path, the "Moppers" on the surface encountered no pickets. As in "Operation Detachment" the air strike was undetected.

On July 10 carrier aircraft hammered Tokyo with a pulverizing weight of bombs. In a final raid, the carrier planes flew to the Inland Sea and pounded the Imperial Navy's base at Kure. When the last carrier plane departed, Japanese sea power was defunct. What had been the third largest navy in the world was now shrunk to a couple of small cruisers, some 50 submarines, and a few destroyers.

Last of the I-boats

It speaks something for the submersible's ability to survive that, at a time when Japanese capital ships were in oblivion, the Jap cruiser force was reduced to a CL and a training cruiser, and the Jap DD's could not muster at a good dozen, the Imperial Navy possessed some 50 ocean-going submarines. Not all of these were in operating condition. But in July 1945, when the Imperial Navy's surface forces were virtually non-existent, Japanese submersibles were still in action in the Southwest Pacific and in the waters of the home Empire.

Stationed in Japan during the war, German Vice Admiral Paul H. Weneker, in charge of blockade running by submarines between Japan and Germany, did not think much of the I-boat. After the war he stated:

"The Japanese had poor types of submarines. They were too big for easy handling when under attack, and consequently were too easily destroyed. Then the asdic and sonic and radar equipment was very far behind in development."

Weneker arranged for a Japanese submarine crew to be sent to Germany for training. *"They had, I think, very good training in German boats and German attack methods. But unfortunately they got caught in the North Atlantic in early 1944 while returning to Japan."*

However, this Nazi admiral expressed great respect for the American submarine effort. German submarines, he explained, ran from Germany to Penang or Singapore with such war materials as optical goods, aircraft plans and machine tools for the Japanese. In exchange the U-boats picked up quinine, tin, rubber and other items scarce in Nazi Germany.

"But this was not so easy an arrangement because of the American submarines on the route between Japan and the South [Singapore]. *I knew much of this because of the shipping for which I was responsible. It was terrible. Sometimes the entire convoy including all my material would be lost. It seemed that nothing could get through."*

Vice Admiral Miwa, Commander-in-Chief of the Imperial Navy's Sixth (Submarine) Fleet, stated that the average number of Japanese submarines in operation during the war was somewhere between 40 and 45. The force maintained this strength throughout the war. Scores of two-man subs were built to defend the home islands from invasion; few of them got into action, and at war's end they were found rusting on Japanese waterfronts. Such dwarfs were little more than novelties.

Japanese submarines were not equipped with radar until June 1944. Attempting to defeat Allied radar, the Japanese tried coating submarine hulls with gum, and devised a cork-shaped conning tower which they hoped would deflect radar beams down into the water. Neither of these measures proved effective. Miwa stated with pride that he had fostered a plan for submarine "breather tubes" some time before the German *"Schnorkel* stack" was introduced.

At war's end the Japanese had in commission several 5,000-ton submarines, intended for use as plane-carriers. These unwieldy submersibles did not get into action. Miwa testified that he opposed the building of these big submarines as wasteful of construction material and because large superstructures were "a weak point against radar." Toward the end of the war the Imperial Army put its finger in the pie of submarine building, and Miwa felt that the soldiery were getting in over their heads.

"The Navy explained to the Army that building of submarine very difficult, and the Navy wanted to show how to build them; but military did not want to be assisted by Navy, so military themselves built the submarines. . . . I think they were of no use."

Asked who controlled the operations when Navy submarines were supplying Army troops, Miwa declared, *"It was undecided."*

When one considers the Japanese radar situation, the lag in electronics, the material shortages, the sea of confusion in which the Imperial Navy's submariners operated, the hardihood of the submersible becomes even more apparent. Japan's submarine losses were heavy. The I-boats stuck their necks out. But they were hauling supplies in the Southwest Pacific, scouting off the Nansei Shotos and patrolling off the coasts of Japan to the bitter end.

On July 29 the submarine I-58 struck the United States Third Fleet an agonizing blow by torpedoing the heavy cruiser INDIANAPOLIS as that warship neared Leyte. This was the last major loss suffered by the U.S. Navy in World War II. The American cruiser sank in 15 minutes. About half of her crew of 1,196 escaped from the sinking vessel, but through a grievous blunder nobody noticed that the cruiser was overdue at her port of destination. When the survivors were picked up four days later—and then quite by accident—only 316 remained.

Just two weeks after this anti-climactic disaster, SPIKEFISH (Commander R. R. Managhan) caught a Japanese submarine in the East China Sea. Late in the evening of August 13, SPIKEFISH made radar contact. Closing in, the American submariners identified the target as a Jap submersible. The wary enemy submerged. Managhan started SPIKEFISH on the hunt. A few minutes after midnight radar contact was regained.

While the hide-and-seek was going on, Managhan radioed a report to SubPac Headquarters, and a return dispatch advised him that no friendly submarines were in the area. Managhan held SPIKEFISH at periscope depth, and just before dawn she sighted the target. Managhan promptly fired six torpedoes.

One survivor was recovered. The prisoner identified the torpedoed submarine as I-373.

Thus the last Japanese submersible destroyed in World War II was sunk by a U.S. submarine.

Loss of Bullhead

Lombok Strait—the narrow passage between Lombok Island and Bali—was patrolled by Japanese A/S vessels throughout the war.

A few enemy planes also drifted over Lombok during the closing weeks of the war. The area remained as a small cancer spot in the Netherlands East Indies, and U.S. submarines entered the strait with caution.

On the last day of July, 1945, BULLHEAD (Lieutenant Commander E. R. Holt, Jr.) left Fremantle to begin her third war patrol. Her orders were to patrol in the Java Sea and then head for Subic Bay in the Philippines. To reach her Java Sea area she would transit Lombok Strait.

BULLHEAD reported herself through the Strait on August 6th. On the 6th, a Japanese Army plane depth-charged a submarine off the Bali coast near the northern mouth of Lombok Strait. The pilot claimed two direct hits and reported a gush of oil and air bubbles at the spot where the target went down. When friendly subs tried to contact BULLHEAD she did not answer. With all hands she went down in action—the last United States submarine lost in the war.

The Rising Sun Is Sunk

One of the last periscope attacks of the war was made in the Yellow Sea by BILLFISH (Lieutenant Commander L. C. Farley, Jr.). The day was August 5, 1945. To get a shot at anything like a *maru* at this late date, U.S. submarines were practically crawling into Japanese docks and climbing into the laps of Japanese shipyards. BILLFISH advanced to the very doormat of Dairen harbor at the Manchurian end of the Yellow Sea to find a torpedo target.

There she flushed two small freighters, a sea truck and a PC-boat. Operating in 15- to 20-fathom water, Farley closed in for a shot at one of the freighters, and three torpedoes sank the 1,091-ton KORI MARU.

On that same August day POGY sank the 2,220-ton freighter KOTHIRASAN MARU in the Sea of Japan off the west coast of Honshu. Off the Korean coast, PARGO struck on August 8 to sink the 5,454-ton transport RASHIN MARU in the Sea of Japan. JALLAO downed the 5,795-ton transport TEIHOKU MARU in the middle of the Japan Sea on the 11th.

These August sinkings were drowned out by the explosion that shook the world. For several months Hirohito and Prime Minister Suzuki had been trying to end the hopeless war. Late in June, Prince Konoye was dispatched to Moscow with secret instructions to accept any terms he could negotiate through the Russians. The Soviet leaders, refusing to deal with Konoye, had promptly informed the United States of these panicky Japanese maneuvers.

On July 26 the Allies issued the Potsdam Declaration, demanding immediate and unconditional surrender. Favoring acceptance of the ultimatum, the Emperor and his Inner Cabinet were once more balked by Japan's reactionary militarists. Struggling in the coils of gold braid and red tape, the Cabinet was unable to break the deadlock. This miserable muddle could only result in tragedy. Discussions of "national polity," the Emperor's status as a deity and the need for maintaining that illusion were interrupted on August 6 by the terrible blast at Hiroshima.

Two days later a second atomic bomb wiped out the city of Nagasaki. On that same day the Soviet Union declared war on Japan. Even then the die-hard militarists could not make up what was left of their minds. On August 13 the Emperor's Cabinet voted 13 to 3 in favor of capitulating to American terms. Admiral Toyoda remained one of the three opposed. His reasons furnish an inside view of that medieval, ritual-bound mentality which had led Japan to disaster.

"The main point . . . had to do with the Emperor's position, since it was the conviction of the Japanese people that the Emperor was a living god above whom there could be no earthly being. It was feared the Japanese people would not readily accept the wording of a reply which placed the Emperor in a subordinate position."

However, 13 of Japan's leaders and the Emperor himself were not inclined to share the viewpoint of the anachronistic admiral.

On August 14 the Emperor dispensed with evasions, fables and precedent and asked the Government to draft an Imperial rescript to stop the war.

Last Torpedo Shot

The first verifiable sinking of a Japanese ship by a U.S. submarine was scored by SWORDFISH on December 15, 1941, when she downed ATSUTASAN MARU off Hainan. On August 14, 1945, just three years and eight months later, TORSK (Commander B. E. Lewellen) scored the last killing torpedoshot of the war.

TORSK was patrolling in the Sea of Japan off the southwest coast of Honshu. The previous day she had downed KAIHO MARU, 873-ton freighter—conventional day-periscope attack. Only a few hours before the cessation of hostilities, she encountered and sank Coast Defense Vessel No. 13. Her last torpedo shot was fired at another frigate. Hapless Coast Defense Vessel No. 47 went down in history as the last Japanese vessel sunk by a U.S. submarine in World War II.

Submarines in Tokyo Bay

The "Cease fire" order was in the making as TORSK launched the war's last torpedo shot. When the greatest war in world history ended on August 15 a ring of United States submarines surrounded Japan, the United States Third Fleet stood at the entrance of Tokyo Bay, Army and Navy aircraft clouded the sky. The Imperial Navy was at sea bottom, the residual Japanese merchant marine was at the end of its rope.

"I do not believe it would be accurate to look upon the atomic bomb and the entry of Soviet Russia as direct causes of the termination of the war," stated Admiral Toyoda. *"But I think those two factors did enable us to bring the war to an end without creating utter chaos in Japan."*

Oriental casuistry—for if anything saved Japan from black chaos it was the entry of the United States Pacific Fleet into Tokyo Bay on September 2 and the signing of the surrender instrument aboard the battleship MISSOURI.

In the offing, symbolic, the submarine tender PROTEUS rode at anchor with her brood alongside. With PROTEUS was the rescue vessel GREENLET. Witness to the historic surrender were the submarines ARCHERFISH, CAVALLA, GATO, HADDO, HAKE, MUSKALLUNGE, PILOTFISH, RAZORBACK, RUNNER II, SEGUNDO, SEACAT, and TIGRONE.

Four weeks later a great fleet assembled at Pearl Harbor for the long voyage home. Entering San Francisco Bay on October 15, the warships paraded in column under Golden Gate Bridge. First in column was SOUTH DAKOTA. Then—more symbolism—came the submarines PUFFER, BAYA, KRAKEN, LOGGERHEAD, PILOTFISH and STICKLEBACK. Three destroyers, a light cruiser and three battleships trailed the submarines.

At Pearl Harbor, taking command as CinCPac in January 1942, Fleet Admiral Nimitz had raised his flag on the submarine GRAYLING. And on a submarine—the USS MENHADEN—Admiral Nimitz lowered his flag when he relinquished command of the fleet.

That, too, was symbolic.

Empire Liquidated

Having begun the war with some 6,000,000 tons of merchant shipping in action (3,000,000 tons of which were needed for "civilian living" in the home islands), Japan ended up with some 312,000 tons of steel ships manned, fueled and hauling cargo. Former mistress of the East and one of the world's three great maritime powers, Japan now possessed a merchant service about the size of the "Old Fall River Line."

Due to slipshod Japanese records, exact statistics may never be computable. But the part played by United States submarines in Japan's maritime demise is depicted with reasonable accuracy in the figures compiled after the war by the Joint Army-Navy Assessment Committee. According to this authority, United States submarines sank 1,113 Japanese merchant ships (of over 500 gross tons) for a tonnage total of 4,779,902 tons. They "probably" sank an additional 65 vessels, for an extra 225,872 tons. United States submarines also sank 201 Japanese naval vessels—a total of 540,192 naval tons. Thirteen "probables" in this category added 37,434 tons to the naval score. With the few "probables" added to the many certainties, U.S. submarines scored as below:

Number of Merchant Ships Sunk:	*1,178*
Merchant Tonnage Sunk:	*5,053,491 tons*
Number of Japanese Naval Vessels Sunk:	*214*
Japanese Naval Tonnage Sunk:	*577,626 tons*

The economic crash of Japan caused by the collapse of

the maritime nation's merchant service will keep the analysts and the adding machines busy for a generation. The final figures may never be assessed. Financial losses resulting from the decline in industrial output, the stoppage of overseas commerce, the dislocation of domestic trade, the reduction in agriculture are beyond computation.

The commentary of a more or less impartial observer adds an interesting footnote to this point. Asked what he considered the causes for Japan's loss of the war, German Vice Admiral Weneker stated that in his opinion Japanese overconfidence, underestimation of the enemy and over-extended supply lines which could not be protected were basic causes. *"After that I would say the reasons for their disaster could be classed about as follows in order of importance: First, and by far the worst, were the attacks of the highly efficient American submarines on merchant shipping. Most serious of all, here, was the sinking of tankers and hence the loss of oil from the south. The second factor in importance was the destruction of the Japanese Navy . . . the third was the air bombing attack on this country (Japan)."*

So a trained observer notes that submarines played the leading role in Japan's defeat. They wrecked Japan's merchant marine. They sank a sizable chunk of the Imperial Navy. They bankrupted Japan's home economy with a blockade which established a new adage: viz., an island is a body of land surrounded by submarines.

Here is the statistical accounting:

In 1944, U.S. submarines sank one-third of all the major enemy combat vessels destroyed in the Pacific that year. The 201 Japanese warships and 13 "probables" sunk by U.S. submarines during the war comprised 29% of the enemy war-shipping sunk by all agencies in the Pacific conflict. About 55% of all Japanese shipping (merchant and naval) downed in World War II was sunk by U.S. submarines. Perhaps the tables at the end of this book best illustrate this stupendous submarine achievement—*an achievement accomplished by a force that consisted of less than 2% of the United States Navy's personnel.*

American submarine losses must be taken into account, and the Service suffered heavy casualties. Fifty-two out of 288 American submarines were lost in the war—almost one out of five. But only 48 went down in combat operations, and of these not more than 41 were downed by enemy action. The toll of lives was severe. Personnel strength of the submarine operating forces averaged 14,750 officers and men. The fatalities totaled 3,131 men and 374 officers. The hazards of undersea warfare are indelibly recorded in American casualty lists which show that six submariners lost their lives in the line of duty for every one non-submariner who died in Naval Service (exclusive of aviation). Axis submarine losses, however, were far greater. The Japanese lost 130 submarines, the Italians 85, and the Germans the appalling total of 781.

Again statistics fail the story—for those to whom this book is dedicated, and for those who saw the final victory. The valiant efforts and incomparable achievements of United States Navy submariners cannot be summarized in statistics. Neither graphs nor percentages could measure the leadership of an Admiral Lockwood, the genius of a Captain Voge, the skill of such commanders as Morton and O'Kane, the courage of every submarine's crew. But the American submariners of World War II need no encomiums. From mess attendants to admirals, all were captains courageous. Their war record speaks for them, and the liquidation of the Japanese Empire stands in evidence.

Epilogue

If nothing else, World War II proved the prodigious power of ships (sea and air) capable of operating in the third dimension. It was in that third dimension that Japan lost the Pacific War. He who lived by the Samurai sword died by the air bomb and the submarine torpedo.

The holocaustal incandescence which consumed Hiroshima and Nagasaki could not blind observers to the fact that the maritime Empire was already destroyed. And long before the first mass air-raids smote Tokyo, many Japanese-held harbors in the Southwest Pacific were as deserted as the bays of the moon, and in many of Japan's home seaports there were vacant docks with rusting bollards where only spiders tied their lines. The atomic bomb was the funeral pyre of an enemy who had been drowned.

United States

SUBMARINES LOST

in World War II

☆ ☆ ☆

SEALION	GRENADIER	GRAYBACK	TANG
S-36	RUNNER	TROUT	ESCOLAR
S-26	R-12	TULLIBEE	ALBACORE
SHARK I	GRAYLING	GUDGEON	GROWLER
PERCH	POMPANO	HERRING	SCAMP
S-27	CISCO	GOLET	SWORDFISH
S-39	S-44	S-28	BARBEL
GRUNION	DORADO	ROBALO	KETE
ARGONAUT	WAHOO	FLIER	TRIGGER
AMBERJACK	CORVINA	HARDER	SNOOK
GRAMPUS	SCULPIN	SEAWOLF	LAGARTO
TRITON	CAPELIN	DARTER	BONEFISH
PICKEREL	SCORPION	SHARK II	BULLHEAD

☆ ☆ ☆

There is a port of no return, where ships
May ride at anchor for a little space
And then, some starless night, the cable slips,
Leaving an eddy at the mooring place . . .
Gulls, veer no longer. Sailor, rest your oar.
No tangled wreckage will be washed ashore.

LESLIE NELSON JENNINGS
"LOST HARBER"

Leading Individual
SUBMARINE SCORES
(TOP 25)

☆ ☆ ☆

NUMBER OF SHIPS SUNK		TONNAGE SUNK	
Submarine	*Ships*	*Submarine*	*Tonnage*
TAUTOG	26	FLASHER	100,231
TANG	24	RASHER	99,901
SILVERSIDES	23	BARB	96,628
FLASHER	21	TANG	93,824
SPADEFISH	21	SILVERSIDES	90,080
SEAHORSE	20	SPADEFISH	88,091
WAHOO	20	TRIGGER	86,552
GUARDFISH	19	DRUM	80,580
RASHER	18	JACK	76,687
SEAWOLF	18	SNOOK	75,473
TRIGGER	18	TAUTOG	72,606
BARB	17	SEAHORSE	72,529
SNOOK	17	GUARDFISH	72,424
THRESHER	17	SEAWOLF	71,609
BOWFIN	16	GUDGEON	71,047
HARDER	16	SEALION II	68,297
POGY	16	BOWFIN	67,882
SUNFISH	16	THRESHER	66,172
TINOSA	16	TINOSA	64,655
DRUM	15	GRAYBACK	63,835
FLYINGFISH	15	POGY	62,633
GREENLING	15	BONEFISH	61,345
JACK	15	WAHOO	60,038
GRAYBACK	14	SUNFISH	59,815
KINGFISH	14	ARCHERFISH	59,800

☆ ☆ ☆ ☆ ☆ ☆ ☆ ☆ ☆ ☆ ☆ ☆ ☆ ☆ ☆

Notes to tables on pages 447-449
Japanese Merchant Marine Ship Losses

[1] Figures in parentheses are ships damaged and put out of action for the duration (not included in sinkings).

[2] At least 12 percent of Army air sinkings listed were by Allied planes (Australian, British, Russian, etc.).

[3] At least 23 percent of carrier air sinkings in July 1945 were by British carrier planes.

[4] About 2 percent of submarine sinkings were known to have been the work of British and Dutch subs. "Half" ships listed above are cases where credit is divided between two attacking agents; tonnage is divided equally.

Japanese Merchant Marine Ship Losses

(Ships over 500 gross tons)

Year and Month	Army Air[2]		Navy Land-based Air		Carrier Air	
	No. of ships	GRT	No. of ships	GRT	No. of ships	GRT
1941-1942						
December	3	16,901	....	....	....	....
January	1	6,757	....	....	....	....
February	....	....	....	....	....	....
March	1	4,109	....	....	3	21,610
April	2	9,798	....	....	....	....
May	....	....	....	....	....	....
June	2	12,358	....	....	....	....
July	2 ½	20,775	....	....	....	....
August	½	420	1	9,309	....	....
September	1	7,190	....	....	....	....
October	1	5,863	3	25,546	....	....
November	5	24,510	11	77,607	....	....
December	3	9,590	1	548	....	....
1943						
January	9	41,269	....	....	....	....
February	3 ½	19,478	2	10,568	....	....
March	10	37,939	....	....	....	....
April	7	24,521	....	....	....	....
May	3	2,060	1	1,917	....	....
June	1	953	....	....	....	....
July	3	4,425	....	....	....	....
August	1	4,468	....	....	....	....
September	5	15,429	....	....	....	....
October	7	15,253	....	....	....	....
November	20 ½	70,458	1	5,824	....	....
December	13	36,266	5	14,397	6	26,017
1944						
January	12	22,823	15	55,184	4	6,738
February	16	40,983	4	8,207	29	186,725
March	5	13,224	1	2,655	20	86,812
April	8	21,942	1	2,230	2	1,775
May	3 ½	9,626	....	....	1	992
June	3	7,753	1	966	15	65,146
July	5	7,865	....	....	5	9,486
August	6	13,610	1	6,659	5	22,918
September	3	3,258	5	8,095	55	213,250
October	9	23,627	4	12,256	40 ½	131,308
November	11	37,350	2	8,627	26	120,373
December	13	54,996	3	4,158	2	8,217
1945						
January	7 ½ (1)	20,620 (2,830)	1	549	83 ½ (3)	283,234 (23,185)
February	3 (1)	8,593 (10,605)	2	1,677	2	1,384
March	13 (6)	30,931 (21,482)	10 ½	14,373	15 (3)	27,563 (22,874)
April	14	18,174	1 (2)	875 (1,725)	....	....
May	...... (2)	2,358 (1,760)	29 (5)	57,041 (10,438)	....	....
June	2 (8)	11,470 (23,839)	12 (4)	16,163 (4,864)	....	....
July	9 (8)	11,802 (23,709)	11 (2)	16,372 (1,743)	43 (23)	113,831 (63,450)
August	10 (14)	22,884 (50,757)	2 (1)	1,715 (880)	2 (5)	1,805 (14,442)
Total	260 (40)	774,680 (134,892)	130 ½ (14)	363,518 (19,650)	359 ½ (34)	4,329,184 (123,951)
Grand total disables	300	909,572	144 ½	383,168	393 ½	1,453,135

Japanese Merchant Marine Ship Losses

(Ships over 500 gross tons)

Year and Month	Submarines[a]		Mines		Surface Gunfire	
	No. of ships	GRT	No. of ships	GRT	No. of ships	GRT
1941–1942						
December.....	6	31,693	.....	.....	4	22,751
January......	7	28,351	1	1,548	3	10,485
February.....	5	15,975	.....	.....	3	10,485
March........	7	26,183	2	14,618	1	7,170
April.........	5	26,886	.....	.....	.....	.....
May..........	20	86,110	2	10,546	.....	.....
June.........	6	20,021	.....	.....	.....	.....
July.........	8	39,356	.....	.....	½	4,286
August.......	17 ½	76,652	.....	.....	.....	.....
September....	11	39,389	.....	.....	.....	.....
October......	25	118,920	.....	.....	1	3,331
November....	8	35,358	.....	.....	1	10,438
December....	14	48,271	.....	.....	.....	.....
1943						
January......	18	80,572	.....	.....	.....	.....
February.....	10 ½	54,276	.....	.....	1	3,121
March........	26	109,447	.....	.....	.....	.....
April.........	19	105,345	.....	.....	.....	.....
May..........	29	122,319	.....	.....	.....	.....
June.........	25	101,581	.....	.....	.....	.....
July.........	20	82,784	.....	.....	.....	.....
August.......	19	80,799	.....	.....	.....	.....
September....	38	157,002	1	2,663	.....	.....
October......	27	119,623	.....	.....	.....	.....
November....	44 ½	231,683	1	2,455	.....	.....
December....	32	121,531	.....	.....	.....	.....
1944						
January......	50	240,840	1	2,428	1	3,535
February.....	54	256,797	1	5,307	.....	.....
March........	26	106,529	.....	.....	.....	.....
April.........	23	95,242	.....	.....	1	2,722
May..........	63 ½	264,713	.....	.....	.....	.....
June.........	48	195,020	.....	.....	2	8,742
July.........	48	212,907	1	2,284	.....	.....
August.......	49	245,348	1	1,018	.....	.....
September....	47	181,363	7	13,411	.....	.....
October......	68 ½	328,843	5	5,964	.....	.....
November....	53 ½	220,476	2	2,350	.....	.....
December....	18	103,836	.....	.....	.....	.....
1945						
January......	22	93,796	6	17,322	1	584
February......	15	55,746	3 (4)	13,166 (16,293)	.....	.....
March........	23 ½	70,727	7	21,402	.....	.....
April.........	18	60,696	16 (9)	20,145 (21,396)	.....	.....
May..........	17	32,394	66 (31)	109,991 (106,302)	.....	.....
June..........	43	92,267	45 (38)	69,009 (94,176)	.....	.....
July.........	12 (1)	27,408 (803)	34 (44)	63,323 (134,372)	(2)	(8,811)
August........	4 (1)	14,559 (880)	8 (21)	18,462 (48,186)	.....	.....
Total.......	1,150 ½ (2)	4,859,634	210 (147)	397,412 (420,725)	16 ½ (2)	77,145 (8,811)
Grand total.. disabled...	1,152 ½		356	818,137	18 ½	85,956

Japanese Merchant Marine Ship Losses

(Ships over 500 gross tons)

Year and Month	Marine Casualties		Unknown		Totals	
	No. of ships	GRT	No. of ships	GRT	No. of ships	GRT
1941-1942						
December.....	3	7,466	....	....	12	56,060
January.......	4	14,388	....	....	17	73,795
February......	....	....	1	6,788	9	33,248
March........	1	4,469	....	....	15	78,159
April..........	....	....	....	....	7	36,684
May..........	....	....	....	....	22	96,656
June..........	....	....	....	....	8	32,379
July..........	1	3,111	....	....	12	67,528
August........	1	5,950	....	....	20	92,331
September.....	....	....	....	....	12	46,579
October......	2	11,187	....	....	32	164,827
November.....	2	11,079	....	....	27	158,992
December.....	3	13,377	....	....	21	71,787
1943						
January.......	....	....	1	179	28	122,590
February......	2	5,732	....	....	19	93,175
March........	2	3,187	....	....	38	150,573
April..........	....	....	1	1,916	27	131,782
May..........	2	5,144	....	....	35	131,440
June..........	2	6,581	....	....	28	109,115
July..........	2	3,298	....	....	25	90,507
August........	2	7,730	1	5,831	23	98,828
September.....	3	22,812	....	....	47	197,906
October......	4	10,178	....	....	38	145,594
November.....	1	4,370	....	....	68	314,790
December.....	4	8,374	1	544	61	207,129
1944						
January.......	3	7,214	1	889	87	339,651
February......	9	17,584	2	3,956	115	519,559
March........	9	16,546	....	....	61	225,766
April..........	1	2,913	1	3,022	37	129,846
May..........	1	1,891	....	....	69	277,222
June..........	5	7,020	1	557	75	285,204
July..........	4	9,110	....	....	63	241,652
August........	3	4,546	....	....	65	294,099
September.....	4	4,772	....	....	121	424,149
October.......	6	11,519	1	1,428	134	514,945
November.....	2	2,232	....	....	97	391,408
December.....	9	20,669	....	....	45	191,876
1945						
January.......	3	8,857	1	1	543	425,505
	(1)	(873)	....	....	(5)	(26,888)
February......	4	6,898	....	....	29	87,464
	(2)	(4,412)	....	....	(7)	(31,310)
March........	3	19,987	1	1,135	73	186,118
	(3)	(3,711)	....	....	(12)	(48,067)
April..........	2	1,812	....	....	51	101,702
	(6)	(5,611)	....	....	(17)	(28,732)
May..........	2	9,752	....	....	116	211,536
	(5)	(6,426)	....	....	(43)	(124,836)
June..........	4	3,871	2	3,400	108	196,180
	(4)	(6,511)	....	....	(54)	(129,390)
July..........	1	2.220	1	874	111	235,830
	(9)	(10,126)	....	....	(89)	(243,014)
August.......	....	....	....	....	26	59,425
	(4)	(6,664)	(2)	(1,756)	(48)	(123,565)
Total.......	116	308,386	16	31,632	2,259	8,141,591
	(34)	(44,334)	(2)	(1,756)	(275)	(775,802)
Grand total disabled...	150	352,720	18	33,388	2,534	8,897,393

This book was originally published by the U. S. Naval Institute—"The Professional Society of the U. S. Navy"—as part of its continuing program of publishing authentic histories of World War II from both the Allies' and the enemy's side. Others are:

> *The Italian Navy in World War II,* by Commander Marc' Antonio Bragadin, Italian Navy   (price, $5.75)

> *Der Seekrieg—The German Navy's Story, 1939-1945,* by Vice Admiral Friedrich Ruge, German Federal Navy   (price, $5.00)

> *The United States Coast Guard in World War II,* by Lieutenant M. F. Willoughby, USCGR (T) (price, $6.00)

> *The Sea War in Korea,* by Commanders Malcolm W. Cagle and Frank A. Manson, USN   (price, $6.00)

> *The Divine Wind,* by Captain Tadashi Nakajima and Commander Rikihei Inoguchi   (price, $4.50)

NOW IN PREPARATION
AND TO BE PUBLISHED IN 1959 ARE:

> *The French Navy in World War II,* by Admiral Paul Auphan, French Navy, and Jacques Mordal

> *The Memoirs of Admiral Erich Raeder,* former Commander in Chief of the German Navy; and other important books covering the conflict from all points of view.

The U. S. Naval Institute, publisher of professional naval and maritime texts since 1873, is a private non-profit organization of present and former members of the U. S. Navy, U. S. Marine Corps, and U. S. Coast Guard, as well as many thousands of private individuals interested in naval and maritime affairs. Members not only may obtain any Naval Institute book at a substantial discount, but also receive the Institute's monthly illustrated magazine, *U. S. Naval Institute Proceedings,* at no cost other than the annual dues of $4.00. Any loyal U. S. citizen is invited to join the U. S. Naval Institute. A sample copy of its magazine, with full information about the Naval Institute and its publications, will be sent free to any U. S. citizen writing to:

The Secretary-Treasurer
UNITED STATES NAVAL INSTITUTE
ANNAPOLIS, MARYLAND